Shojo Beat

15

Story & Art by
Rinko Ueda

Volume 15

CONTENTS

Story Thus Far...

It is the Era of the Warring States. Usagi is working as an herbalist under Tokugawa Ieyasu at Okazaki Castle. She goes to Iga with her friend Yukimaru to investigate a rumor and is reunited with her great-grandpa, grandpa, and Goemon.

Usagi decides to marry Yukimaru, but Yukimaru calls the wedding off once he realizes Usagi's true feelings. Yukimaru tells Usagi he has seen someone who looks like her old love Hanzo, so she heads over to Azuchi Castle to see for herself.

Usagi catches Oda Nobunaga's attention and ends up working for him at Azuchi Castle. She is reunited with Hanzo, but Hanzo is bent on getting revenge on Nobunaga and leaves Usagi again. Usagi tries to assassinate Nobunaga herself, but she finds herself unable to do it. After being moved by disgraced Mitsuhide's magnanimous attitude, she decides to stop Hanzo from getting his revenge, but...?!

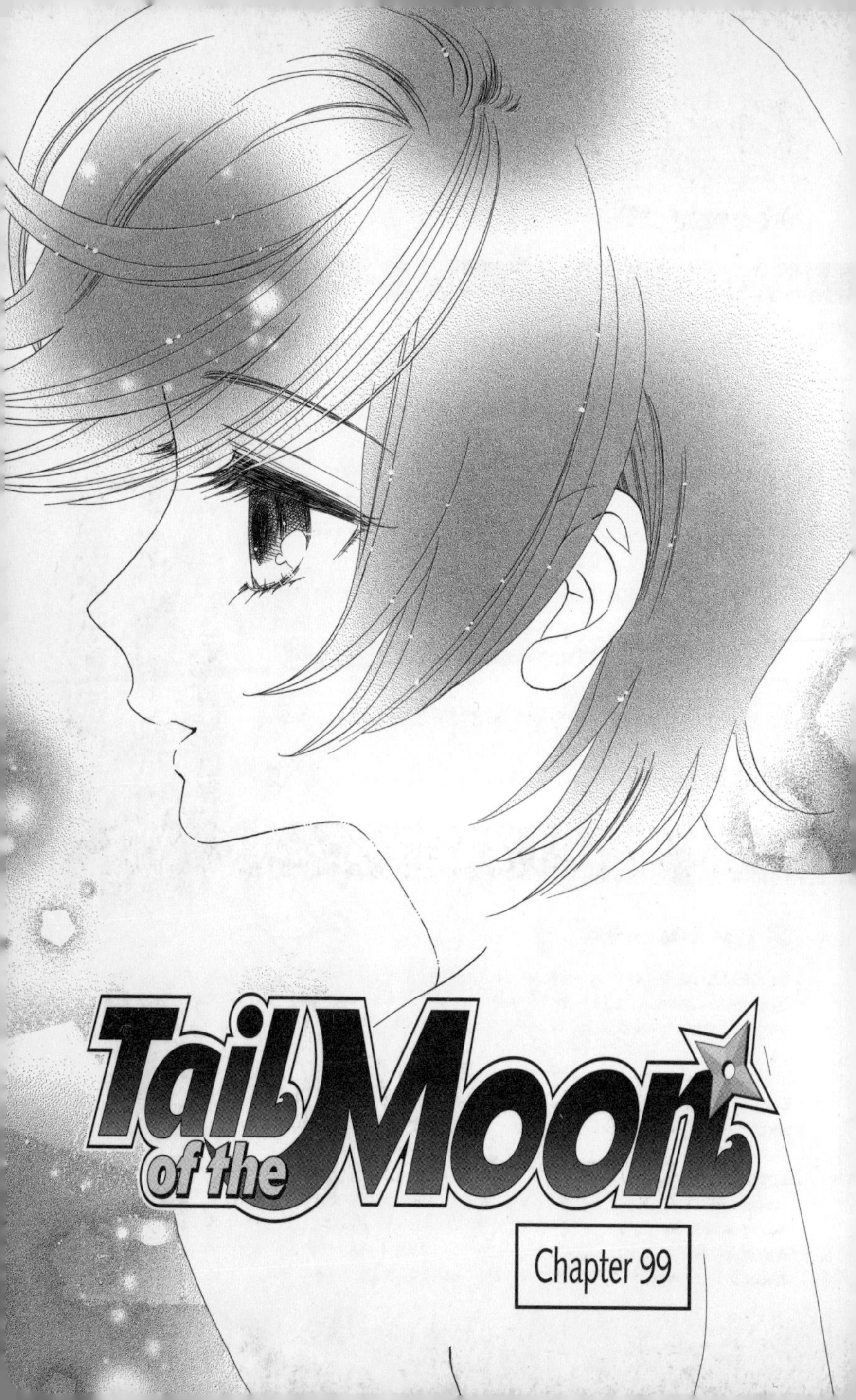
Tail of the Moon
Chapter 99

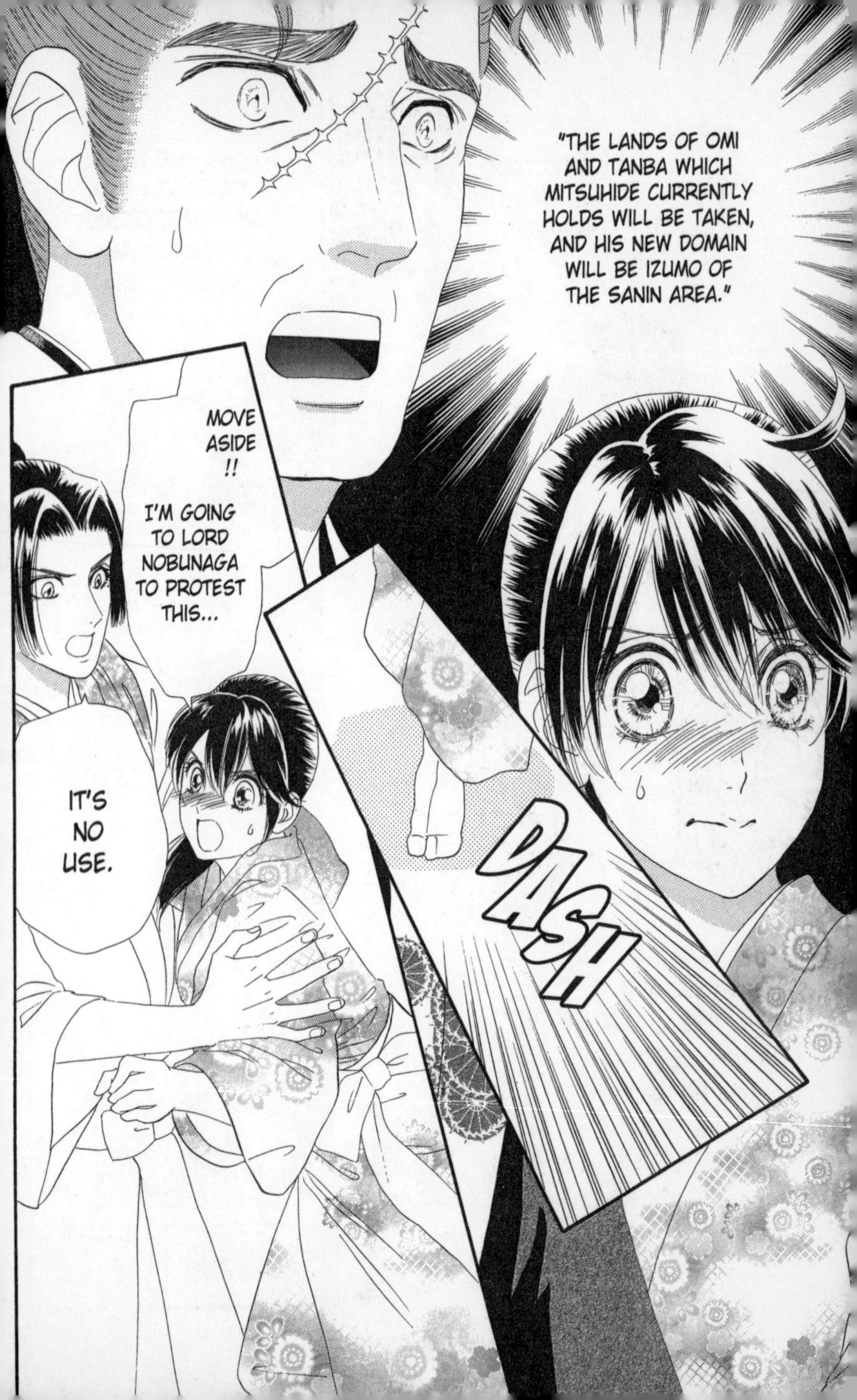
"THE LANDS OF OMI AND TANBA WHICH MITSUHIDE CURRENTLY HOLDS WILL BE TAKEN, AND HIS NEW DOMAIN WILL BE IZUMO OF THE SANIN AREA."
DASH
MOVE ASIDE !!
I'M GOING TO LORD NOBUNAGA TO PROTEST THIS...
IT'S NO USE.

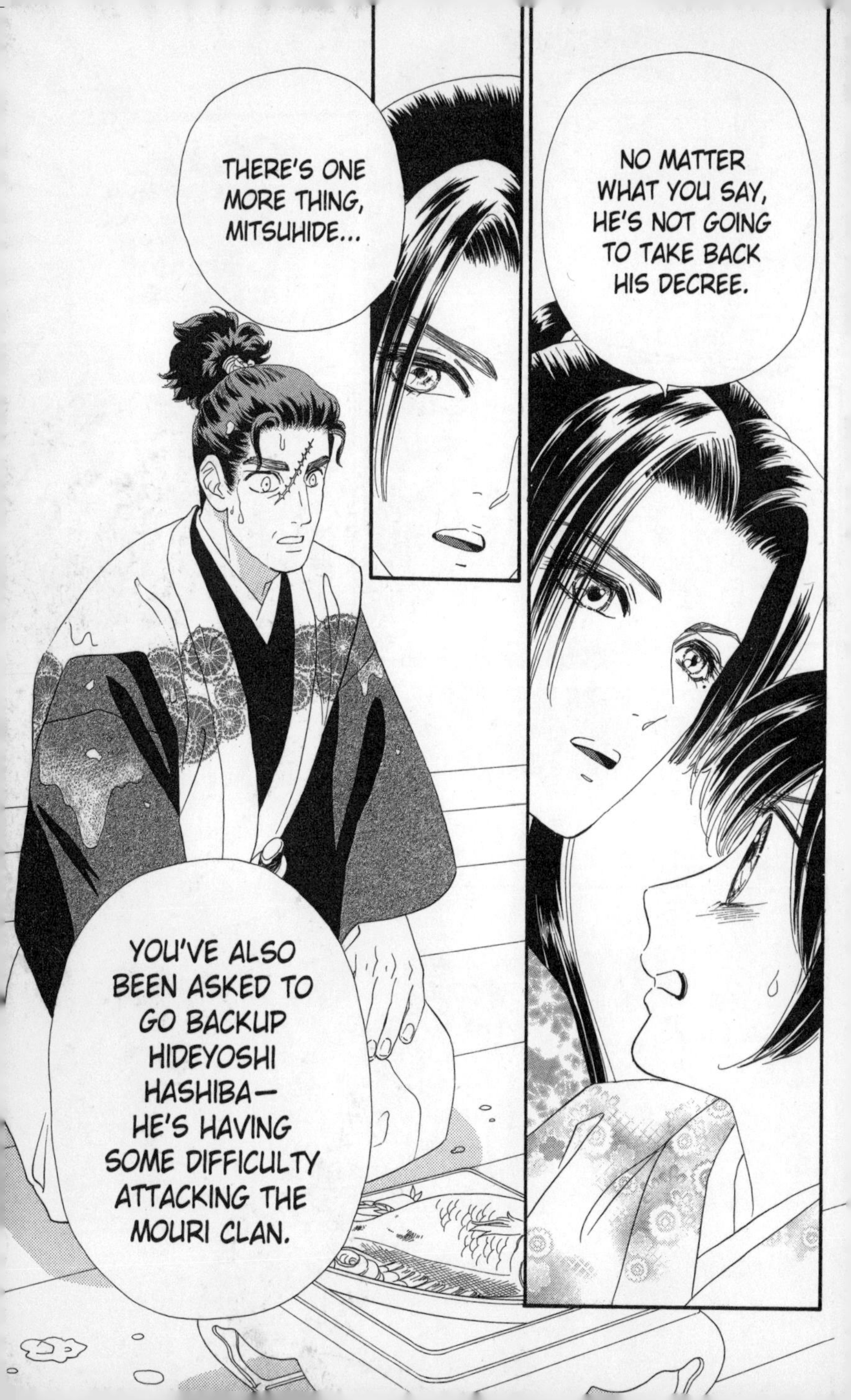
NO MATTER WHAT YOU SAY, HE'S NOT GOING TO TAKE BACK HIS DECREE.
THERE'S ONE MORE THING, MITSUHIDE...
YOU'VE ALSO BEEN ASKED TO GO BACKUP HIDEYOSHI HASHIBA— HE'S HAVING SOME DIFFICULTY ATTACKING THE MOURI CLAN.

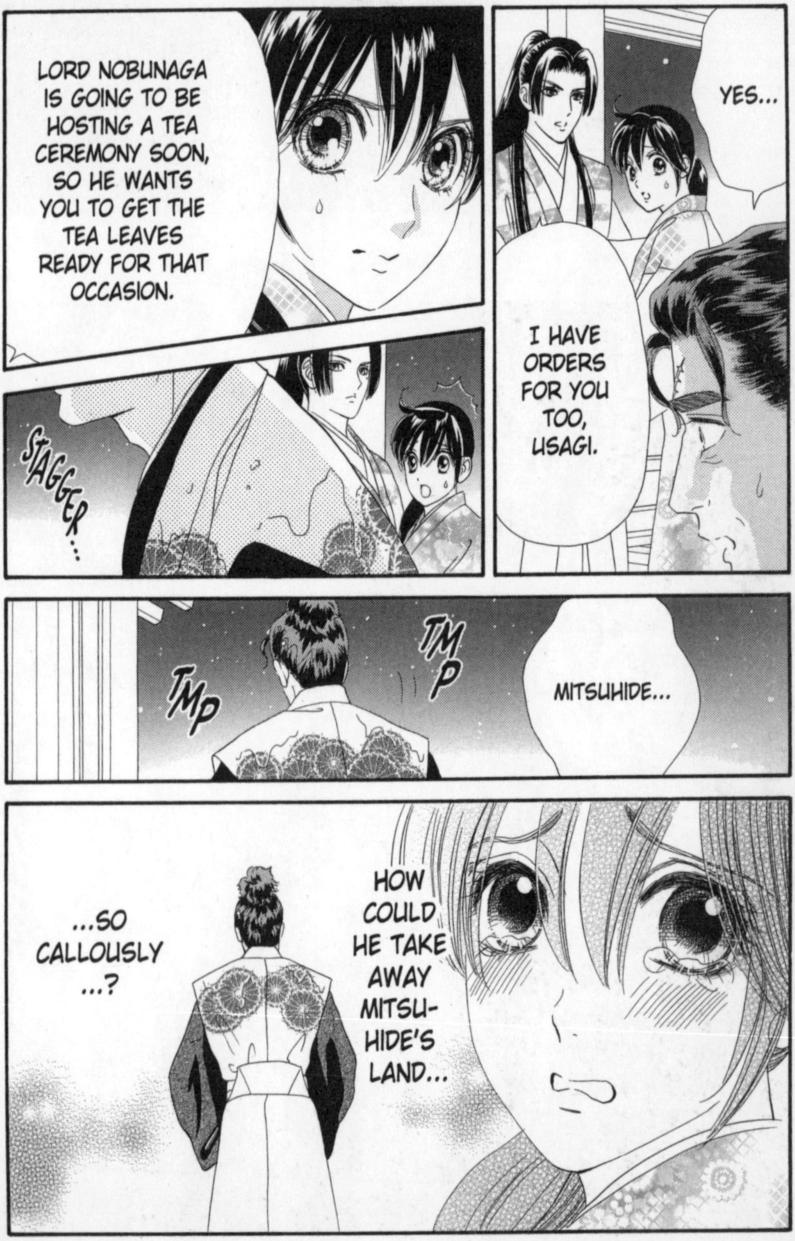
YES...
I HAVE ORDERS FOR YOU TOO, USAGI.
LORD NOBUNAGA IS GOING TO BE HOSTING A TEA CEREMONY SOON, SO HE WANTS YOU TO GET THE TEA LEAVES READY FOR THAT OCCASION.
STAGGER...
MITSUHIDE...
TMP
TMP
HOW COULD HE TAKE AWAY MITSU-HIDE'S LAND...
...SO CALLOUSLY ...?

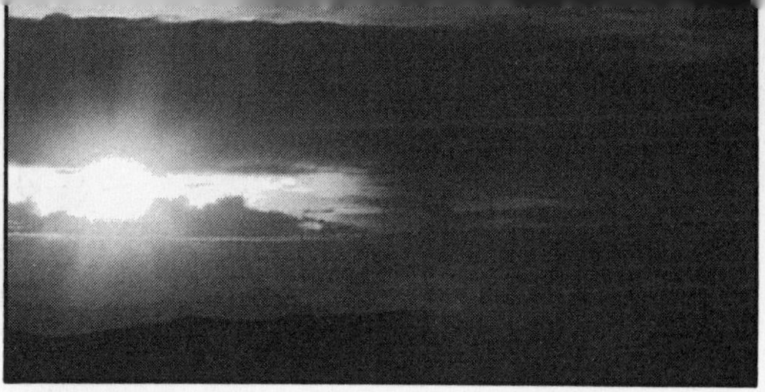

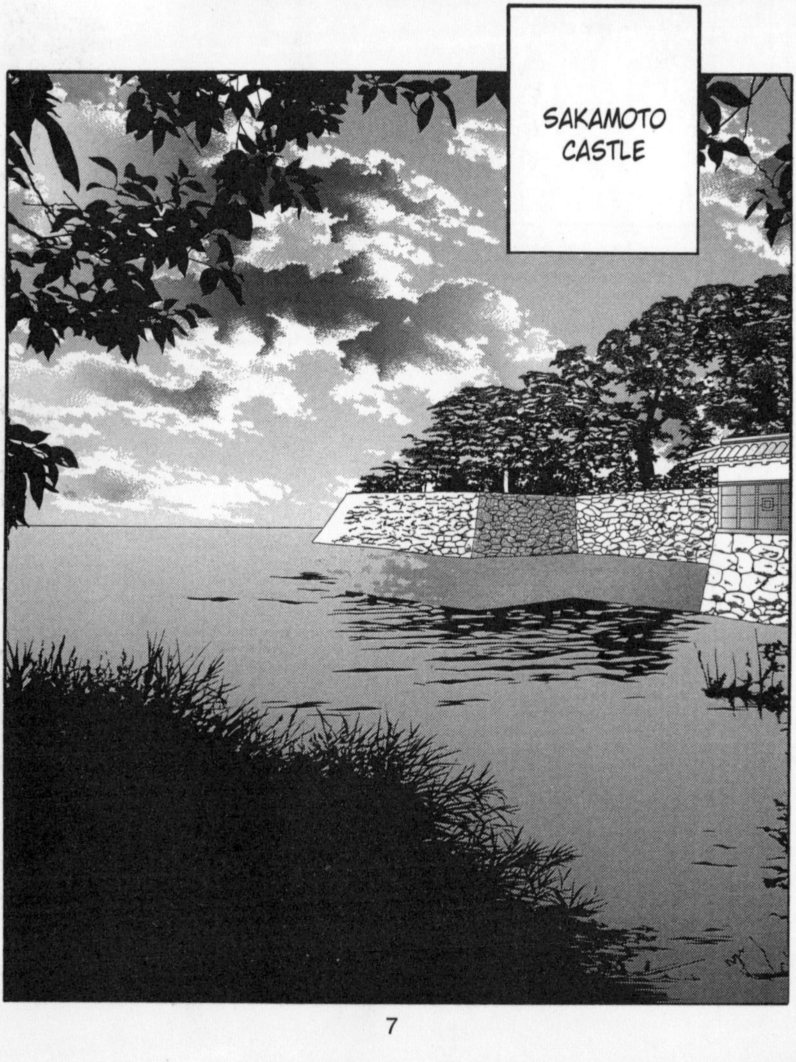
SAKAMOTO
CASTLE

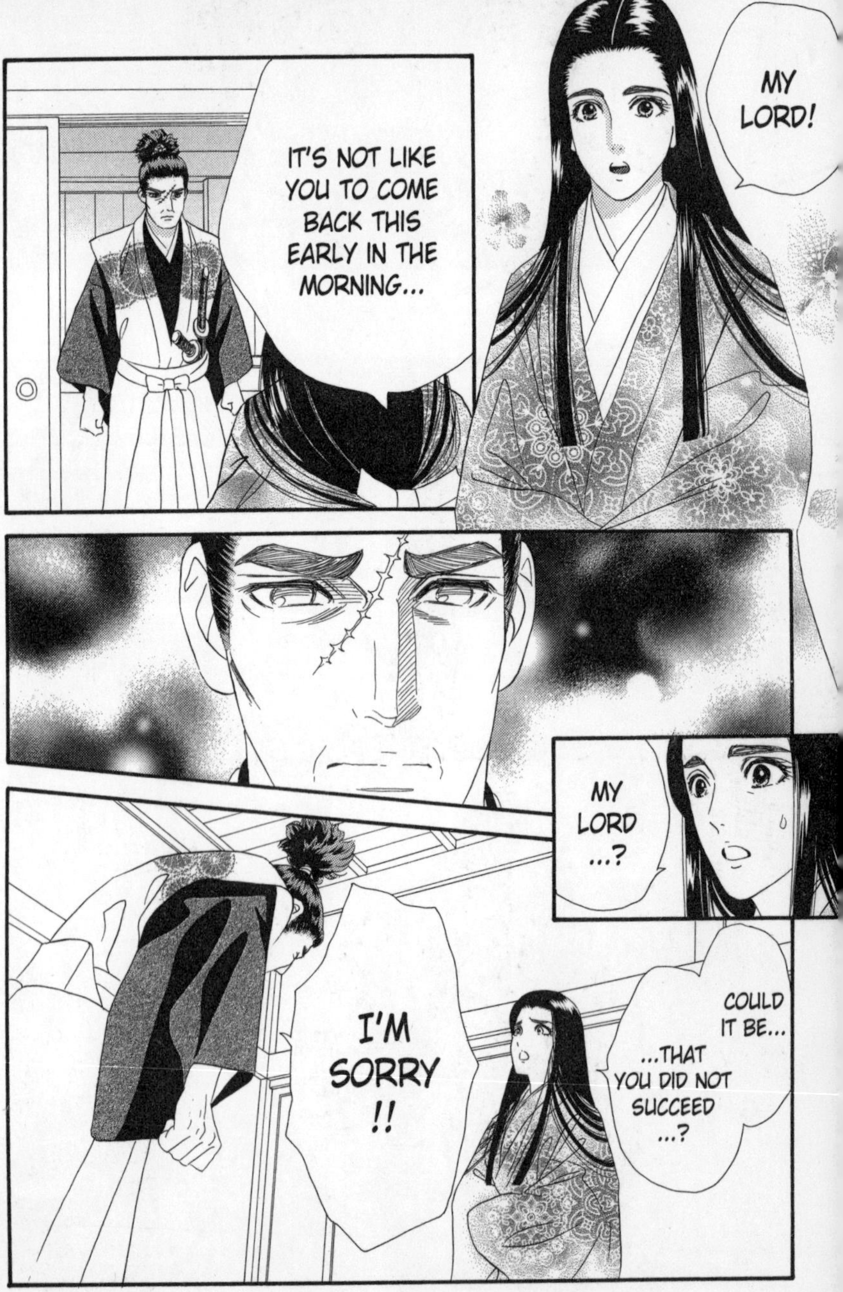
MY LORD!
IT'S NOT LIKE YOU TO COME BACK THIS EARLY IN THE MORNING...
MY LORD ...?
COULD IT BE...
...THAT YOU DID NOT SUCCEED ...?
I'M SORRY !!

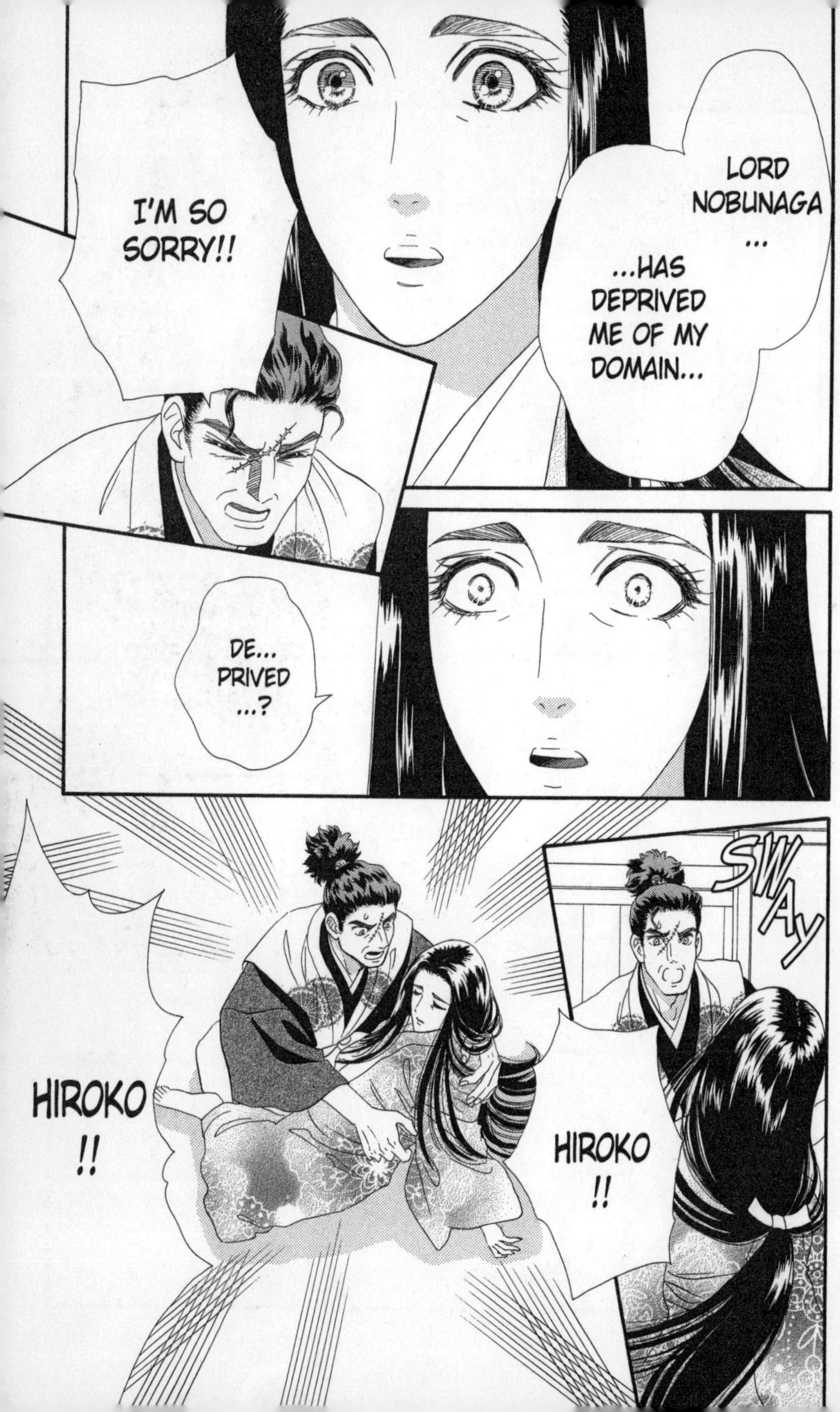
LORD NOBUNAGA ...
...HAS DEPRIVED ME OF MY DOMAIN...
I'M SO SORRY!!
DE... PRIVED ...?
SWAY
HIROKO !!
HIROKO !!

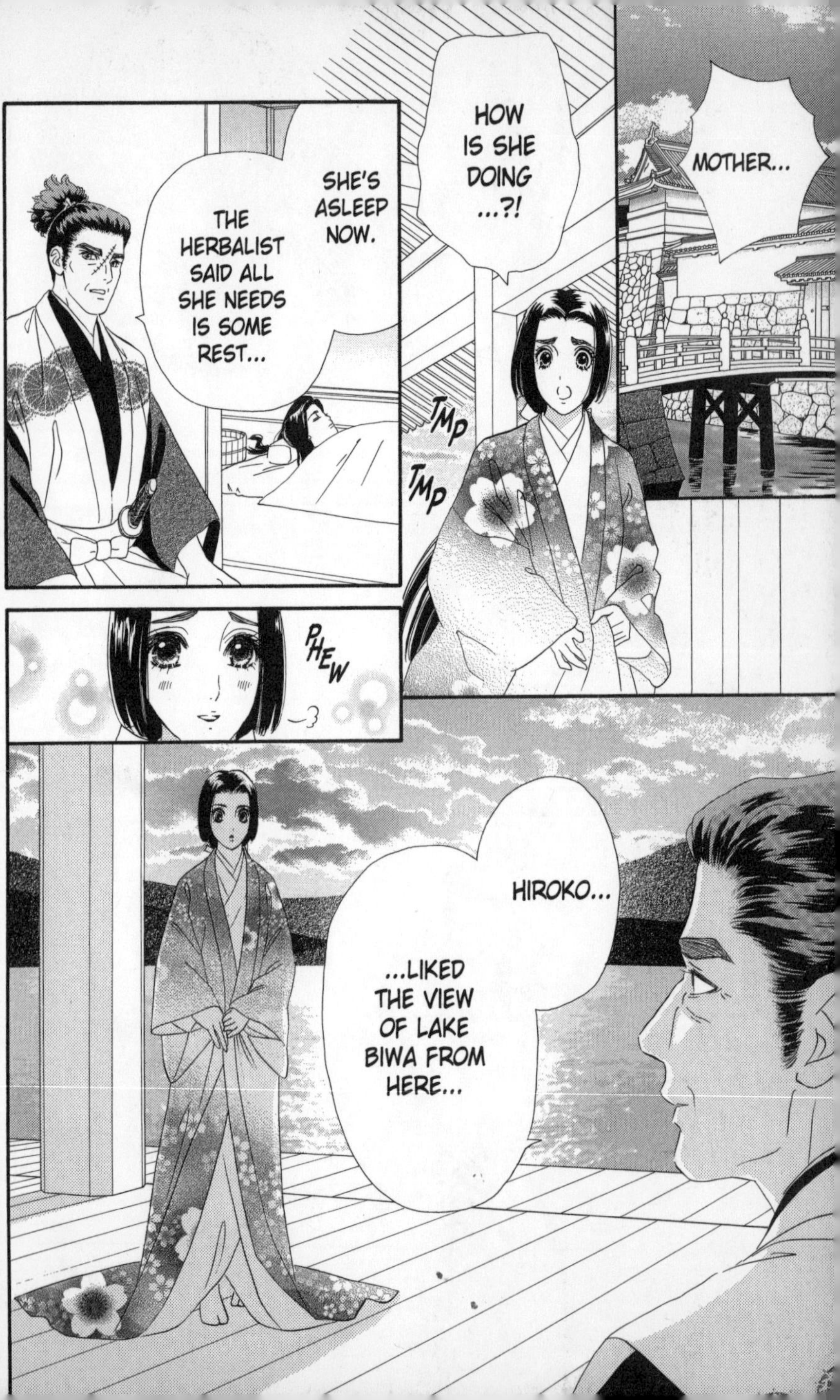
MOTHER...
HOW IS SHE DOING ...?!
TMP
TMP
SHE'S ASLEEP NOW.
THE HERBALIST SAID ALL SHE NEEDS IS SOME REST...
PHEW
HIROKO...
...LIKED THE VIEW OF LAKE BIWA FROM HERE...

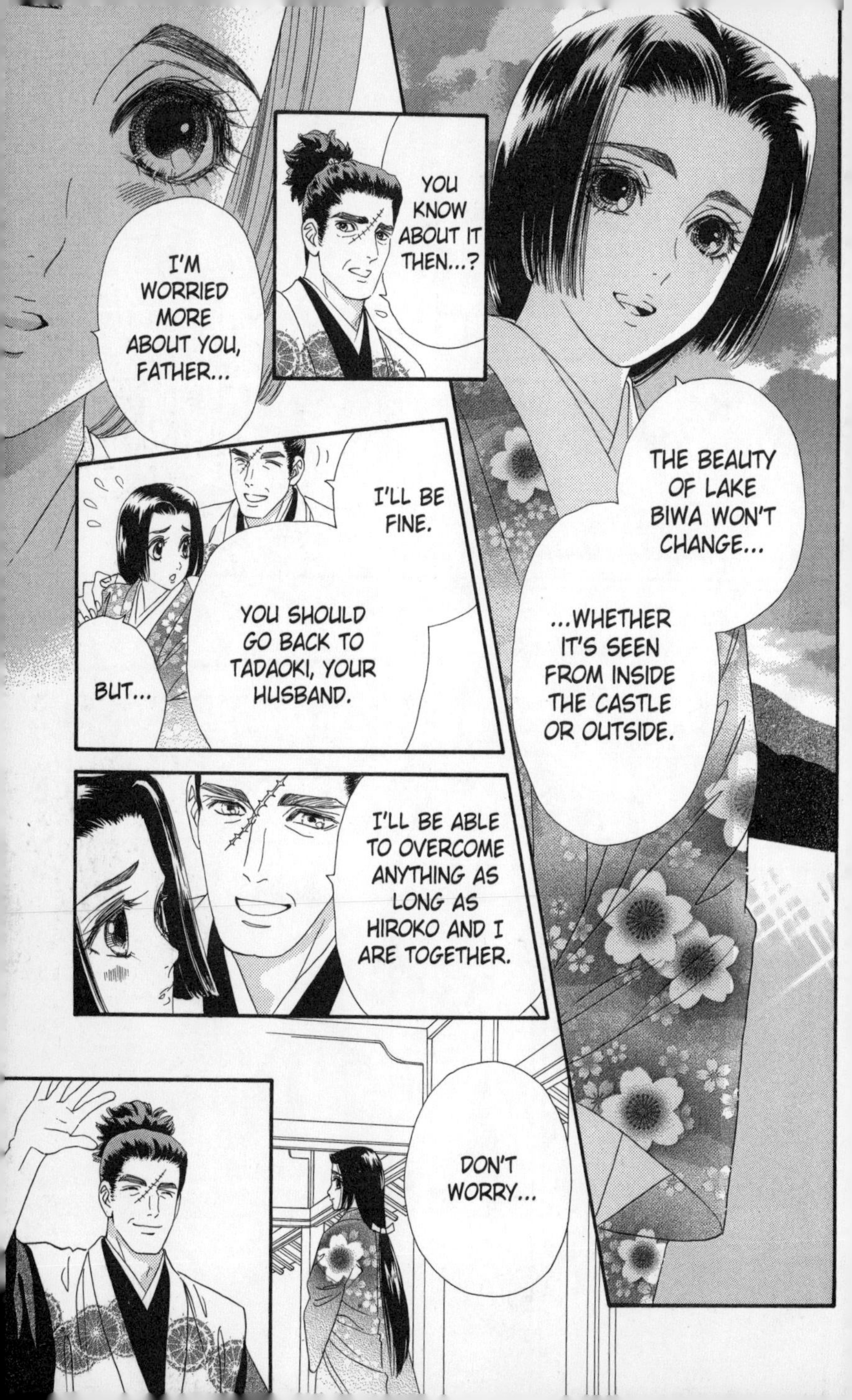
THE BEAUTY OF LAKE BIWA WON'T CHANGE...
...WHETHER IT'S SEEN FROM INSIDE THE CASTLE OR OUTSIDE.
YOU KNOW ABOUT IT THEN...?
I'M WORRIED MORE ABOUT YOU, FATHER...
I'LL BE FINE.
YOU SHOULD GO BACK TO TADAOKI, YOUR HUSBAND.
BUT...
I'LL BE ABLE TO OVERCOME ANYTHING AS LONG AS HIROKO AND I ARE TOGETHER.
DON'T WORRY...

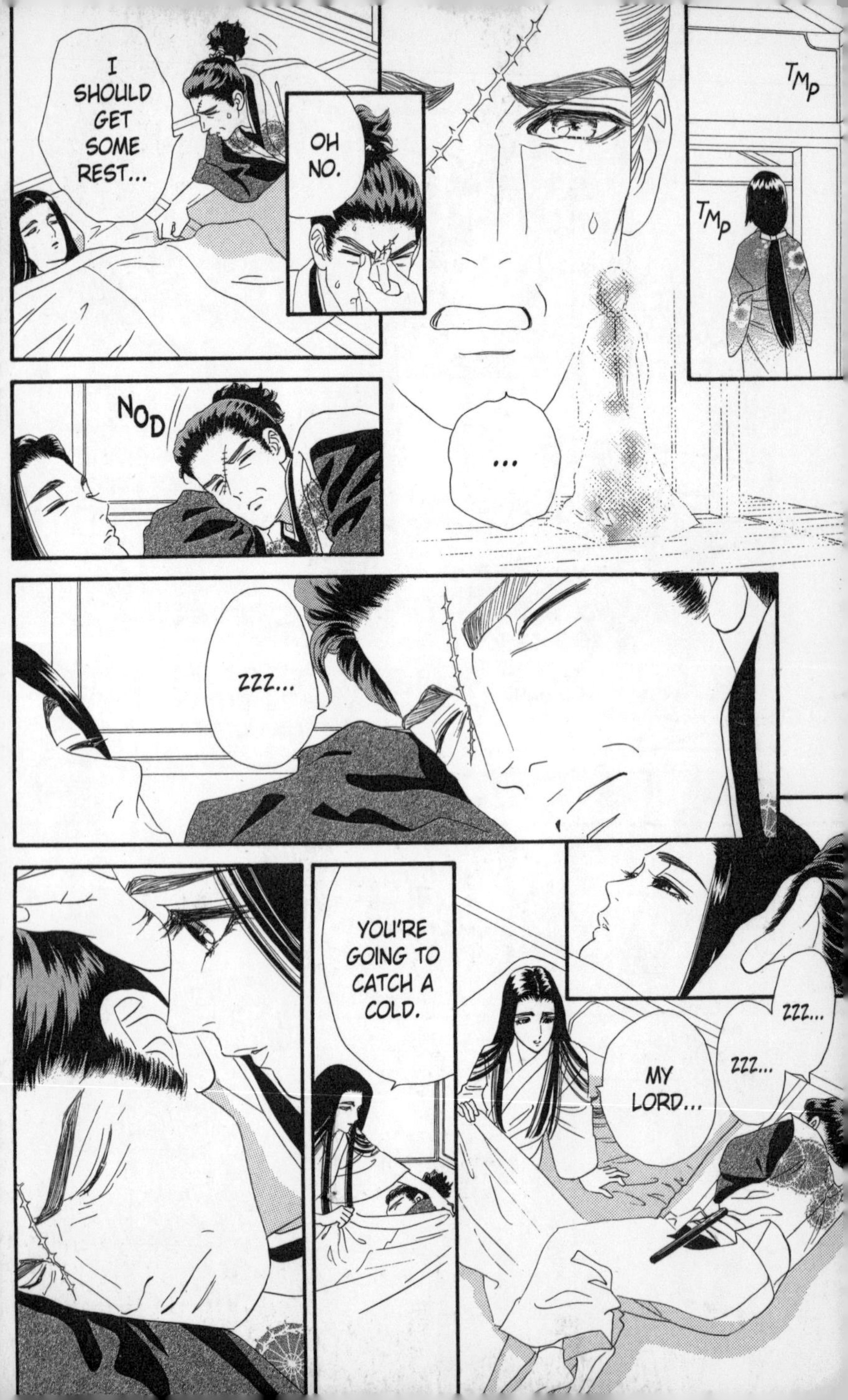
TMP
TMP
...
OH NO.
I SHOULD GET SOME REST...
NOD
ZZZ...
ZZZ...
ZZZ...
MY LORD...
YOU'RE GOING TO CATCH A COLD.

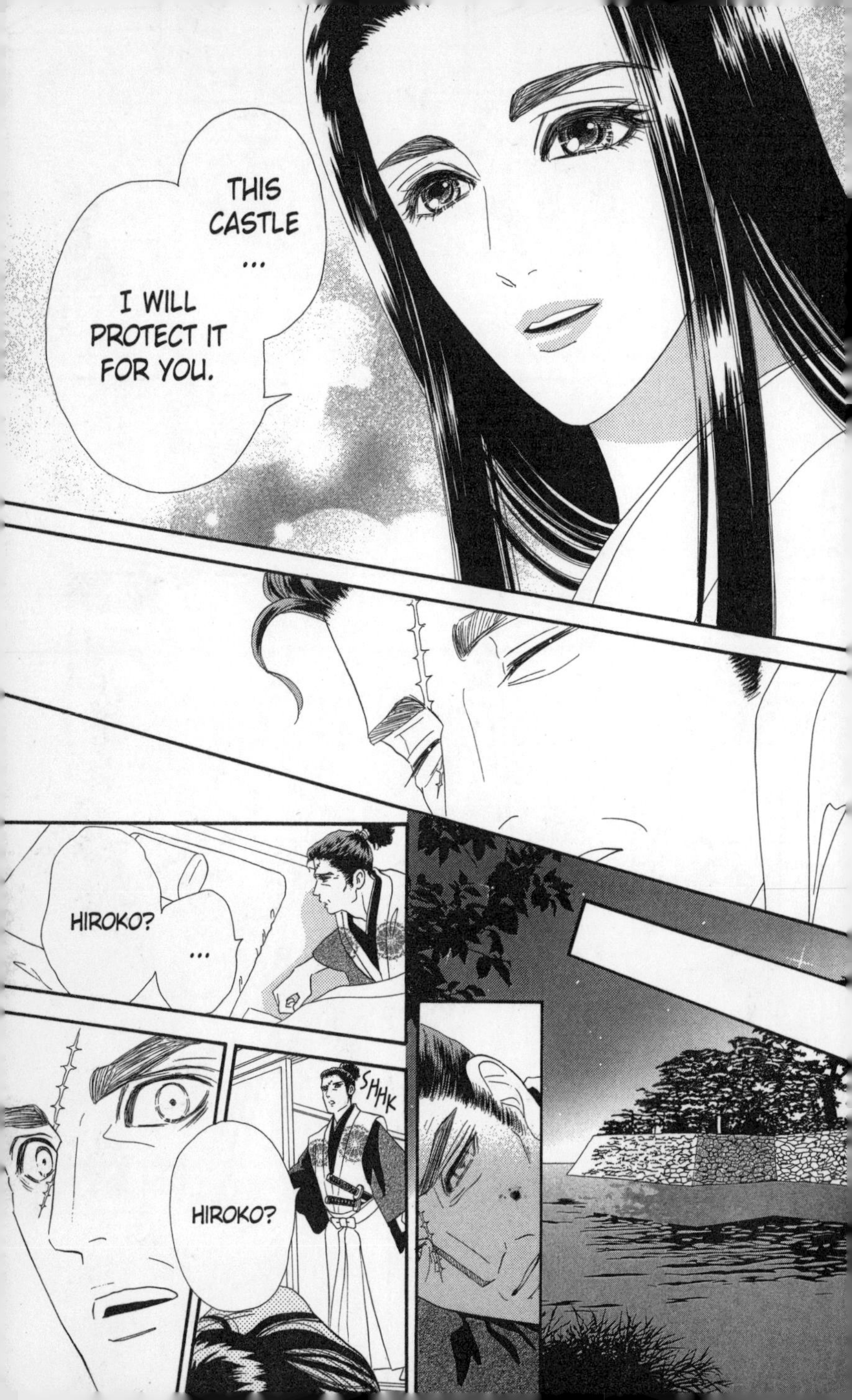
THIS CASTLE ... I WILL PROTECT IT FOR YOU.
HIROKO?
...
SHHK
HIROKO?

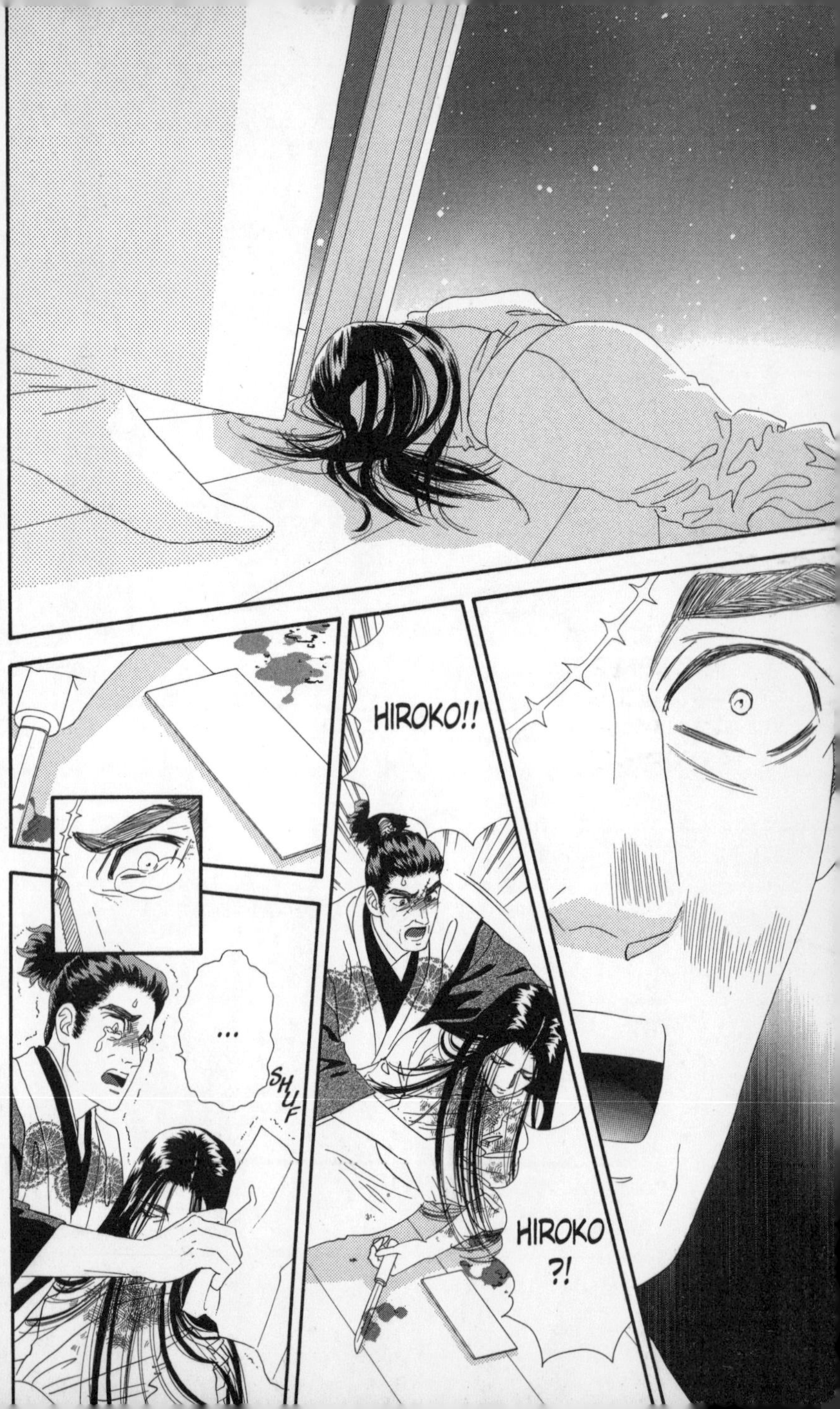
HIROKO ?!
HIROKO!!
...
SHUF

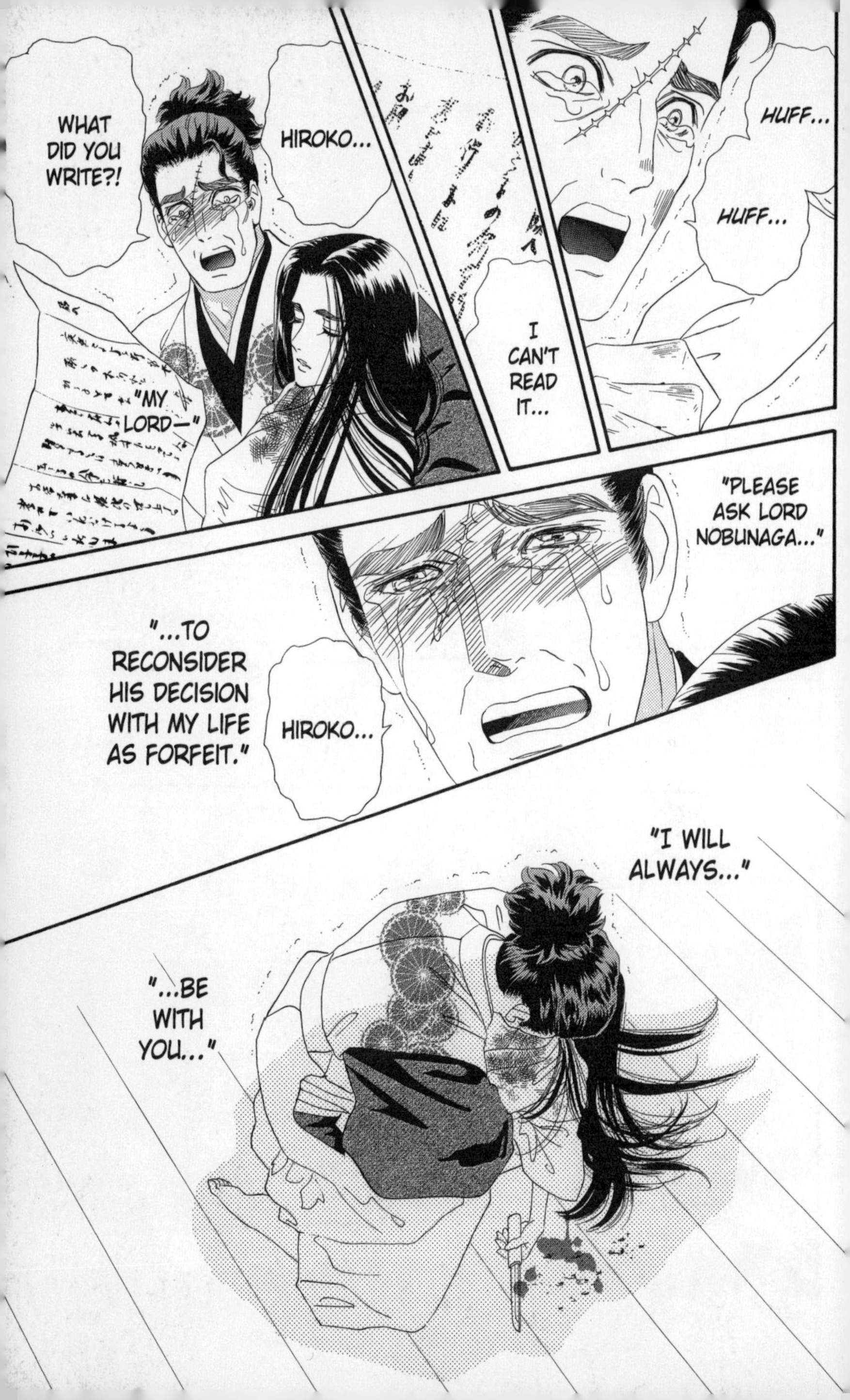
HUFF...
HUFF...
I CAN'T READ IT...
HIROKO...
WHAT DID YOU WRITE?!
"MY LORD—"
"PLEASE ASK LORD NOBUNAGA..."
"...TO RECONSIDER HIS DECISION WITH MY LIFE AS FORFEIT."
HIROKO...
"I WILL ALWAYS..."
"...BE WITH YOU..."

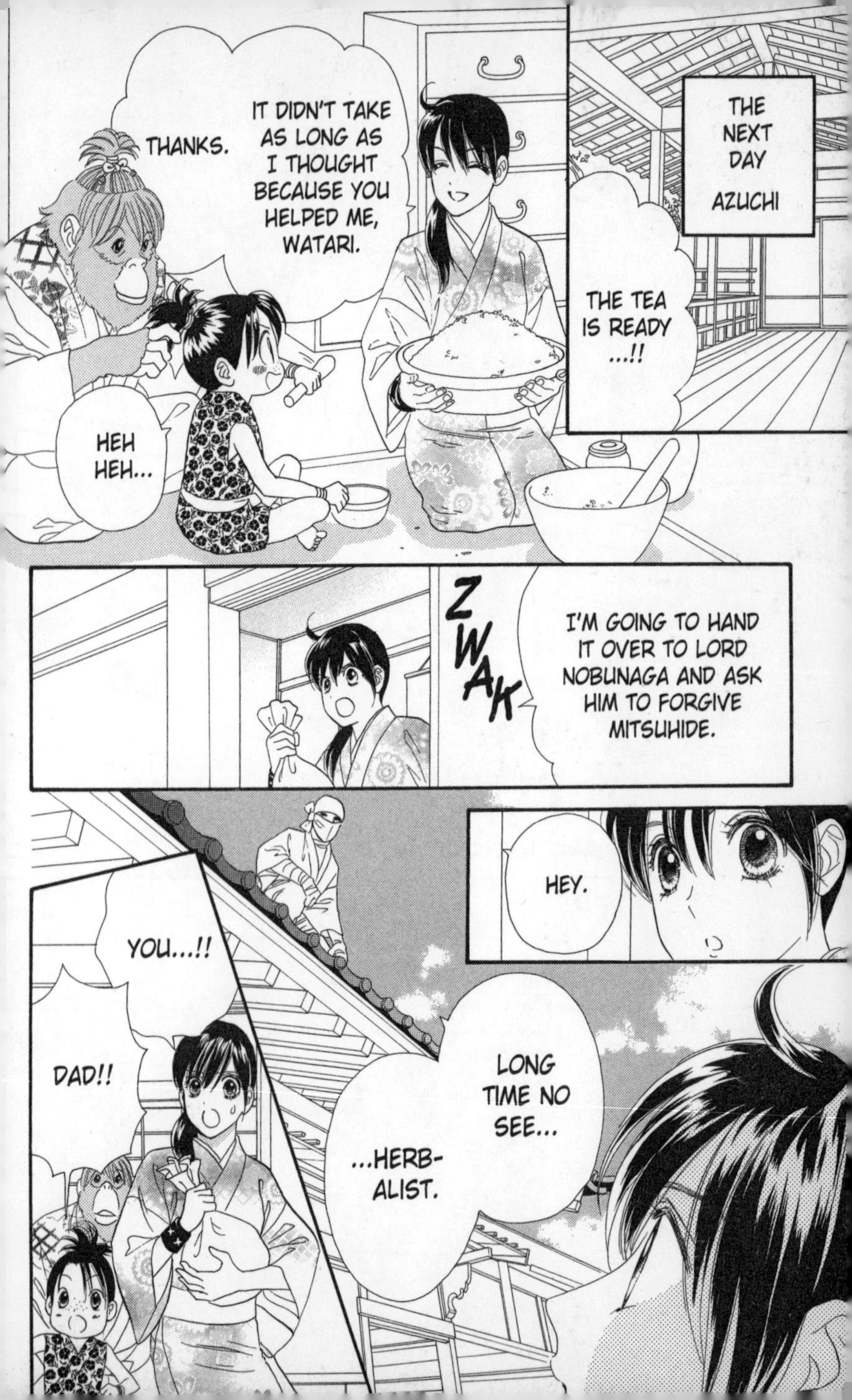
THE NEXT DAY
AZUCHI
THE TEA IS READY ...!!
IT DIDN'T TAKE AS LONG AS I THOUGHT BECAUSE YOU HELPED ME, WATARI.
THANKS.
HEH HEH...
ZWAK
I'M GOING TO HAND IT OVER TO LORD NOBUNAGA AND ASK HIM TO FORGIVE MITSUHIDE.
HEY.
LONG TIME NO SEE...
...HERB-ALIST.
YOU...!!
DAD!!

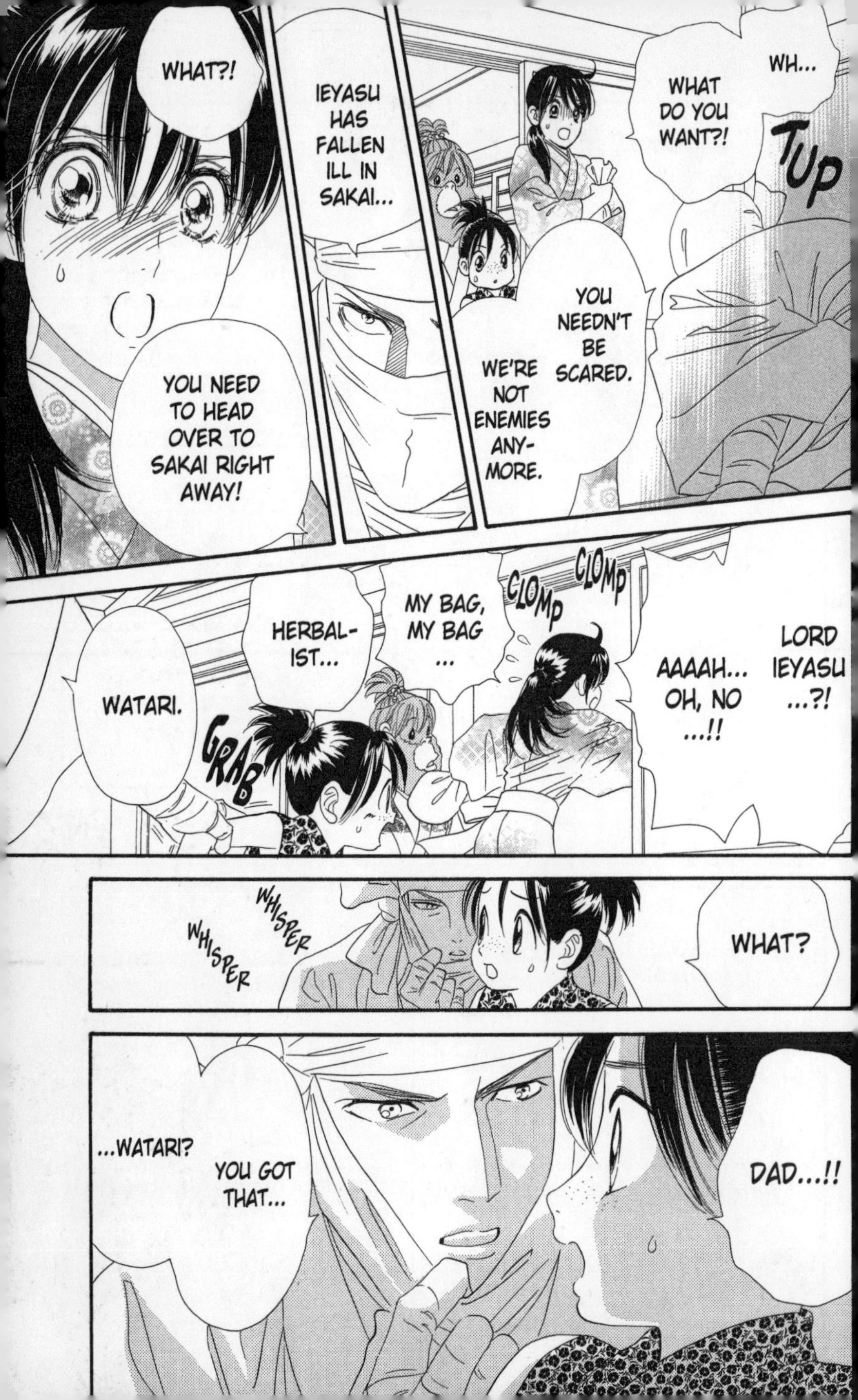
WH...
TUP
WHAT DO YOU WANT?!
YOU NEEDN'T BE SCARED.
WE'RE NOT ENEMIES ANYMORE.
IEYASU HAS FALLEN ILL IN SAKAI...
WHAT?!
YOU NEED TO HEAD OVER TO SAKAI RIGHT AWAY!
LORD IEYASU ...?!
AAAAH... OH, NO ...!!
CLOMP
CLOMP
MY BAG, MY BAG ...
HERBAL-IST...
WATARI.
GRAB
WHAT?
WHISPER
WHISPER
DAD...!!
YOU GOT THAT...
...WATARI?

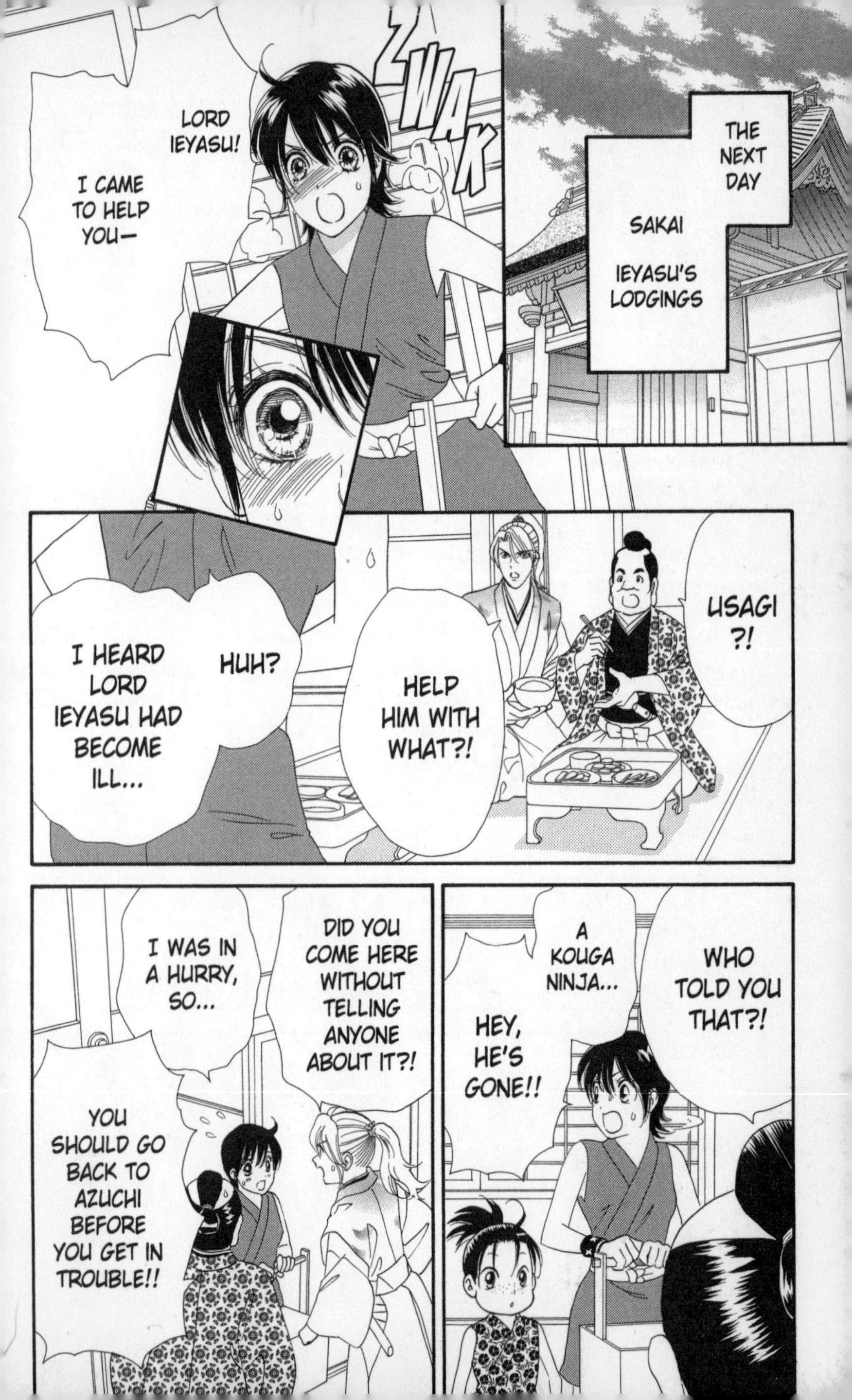
THE NEXT DAY
SAKAI
IEYASU'S LODGINGS
ZWAK
LORD IEYASU!
I CAME TO HELP YOU—
USAGI?!
HELP HIM WITH WHAT?!
HUH?
I HEARD LORD IEYASU HAD BECOME ILL...
WHO TOLD YOU THAT?!
A KOUGA NINJA...
HEY, HE'S GONE!!
DID YOU COME HERE WITHOUT TELLING ANYONE ABOUT IT?!
I WAS IN A HURRY, SO...
YOU SHOULD GO BACK TO AZUCHI BEFORE YOU GET IN TROUBLE!!

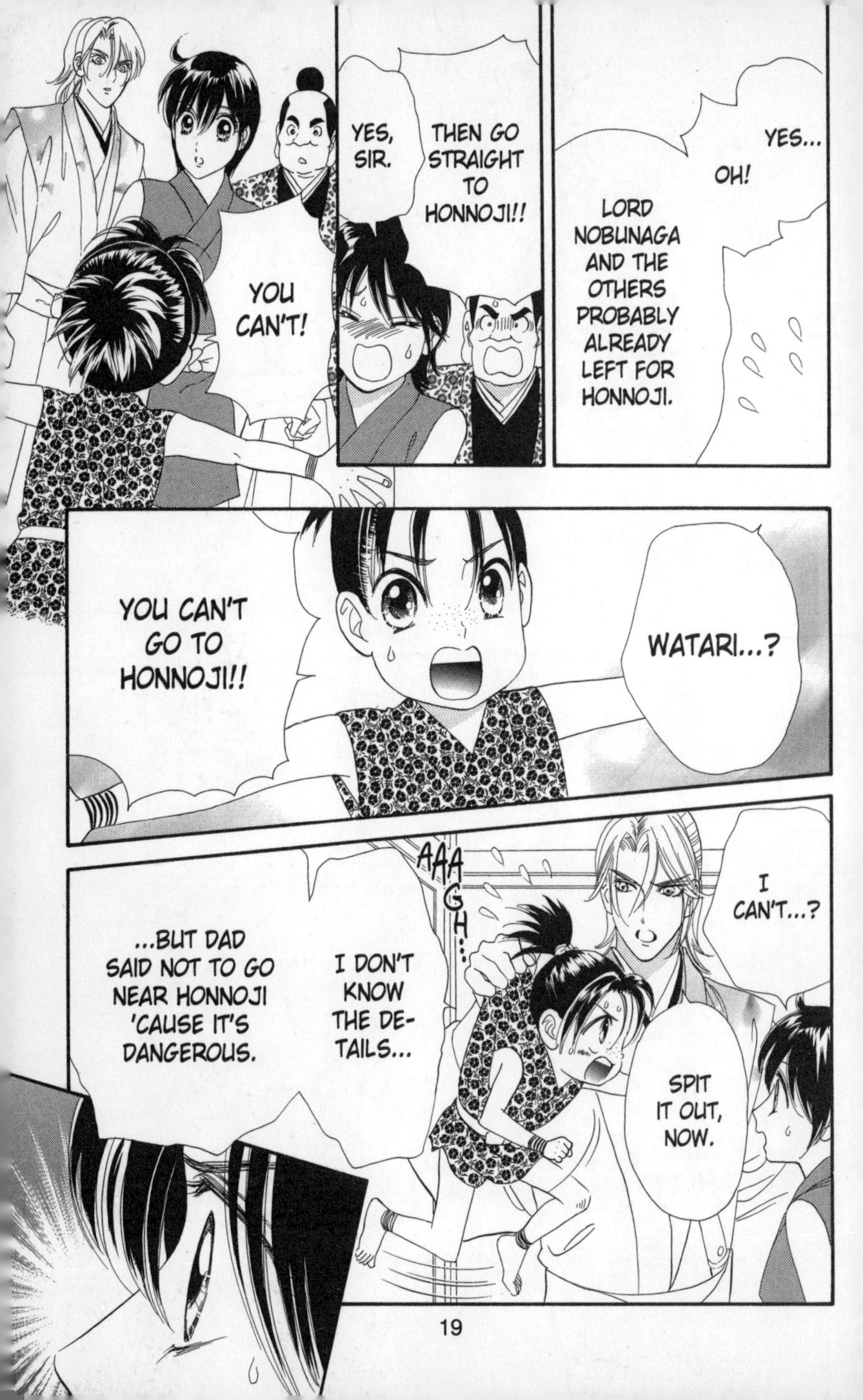
YES...
OH!
LORD NOBUNAGA AND THE OTHERS PROBABLY ALREADY LEFT FOR HONNOJI.
THEN GO STRAIGHT TO HONNOJI!!
YES, SIR.
YOU CAN'T!
WATARI...?
YOU CAN'T GO TO HONNOJI!!
I CAN'T...?
AAAGH...
SPIT IT OUT, NOW.
I DON'T KNOW THE DE-TAILS...
...BUT DAD SAID NOT TO GO NEAR HONNOJI 'CAUSE IT'S DANGEROUS.

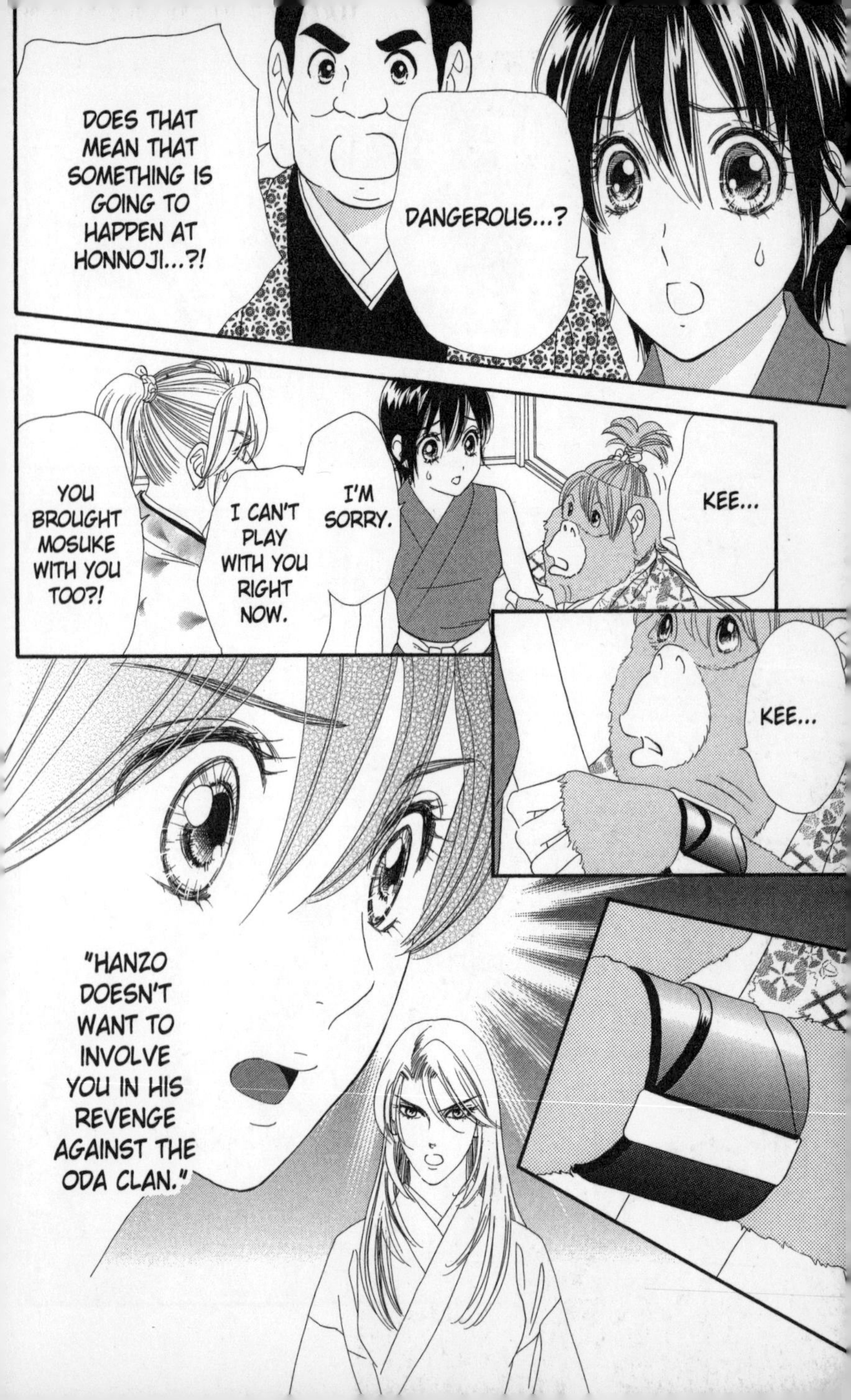
DANGEROUS...?
DOES THAT MEAN THAT SOMETHING IS GOING TO HAPPEN AT HONNOJI...?!
KEE...
I'M SORRY.
I CAN'T PLAY WITH YOU RIGHT NOW.
YOU BROUGHT MOSUKE WITH YOU TOO?!
KEE...
"HANZO DOESN'T WANT TO INVOLVE YOU IN HIS REVENGE AGAINST THE ODA CLAN."

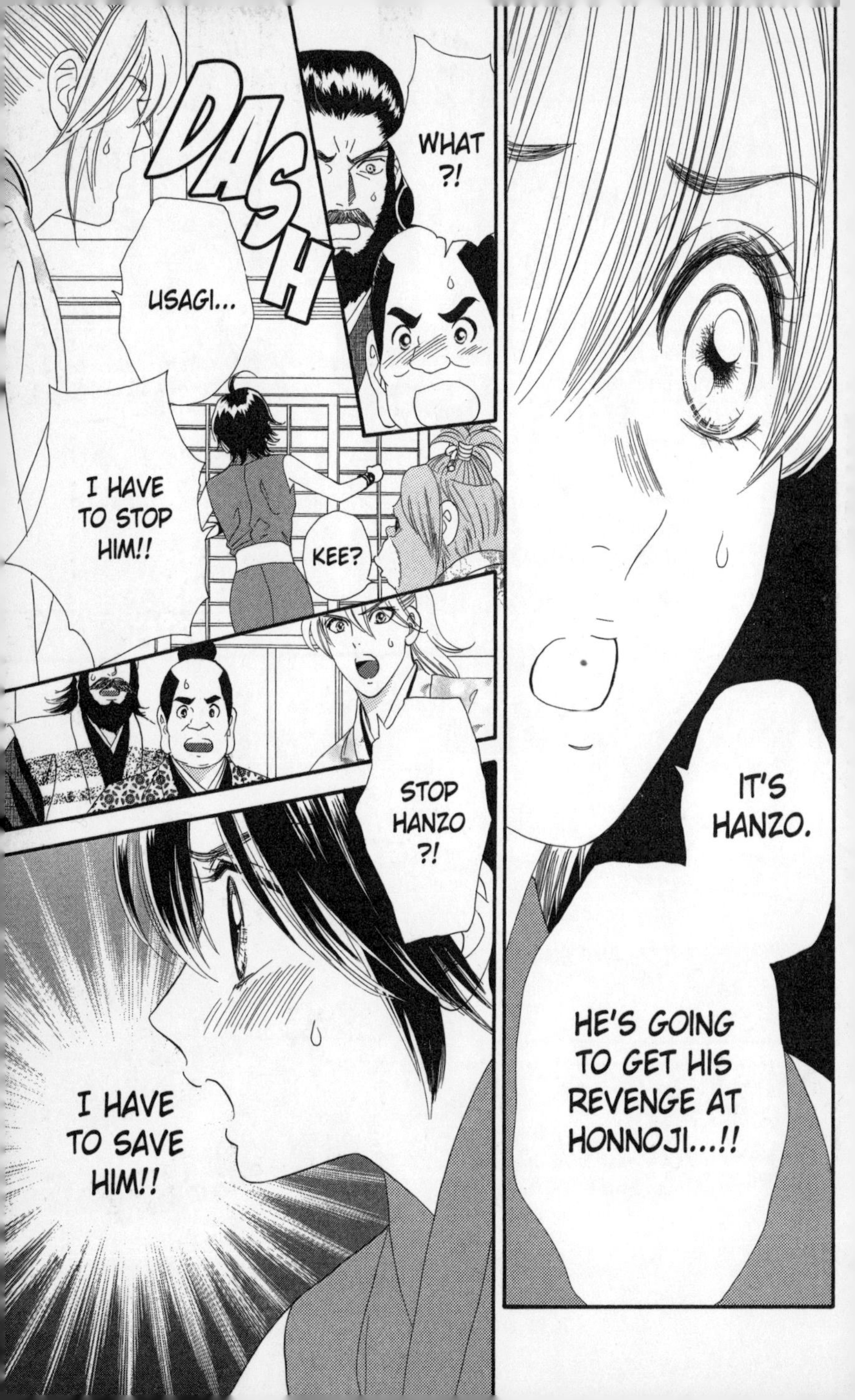
IT'S HANZO.
HE'S GOING TO GET HIS REVENGE AT HONNOJI...!!
WHAT ?!
DASH
USAGI...
KEE?
I HAVE TO STOP HIM!!
STOP HANZO ?!
I HAVE TO SAVE HIM!!

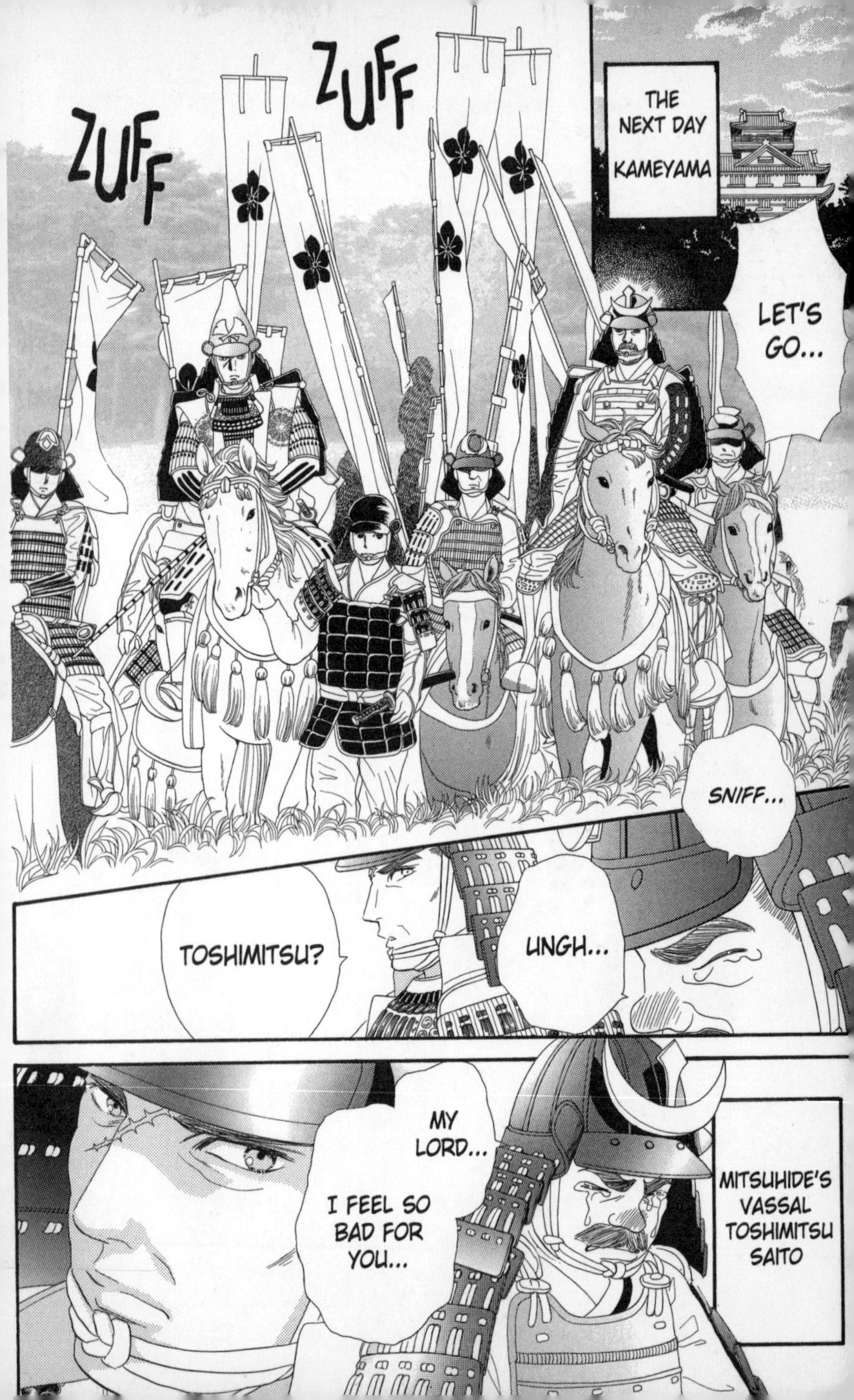
THE NEXT DAY
KAMEYAMA
LET'S GO...
ZUFF
ZUFF
SNIFF...
UNGH...
TOSHIMITSU?
MITSUHIDE'S VASSAL TOSHIMITSU SAITO
MY LORD...
I FEEL SO BAD FOR YOU...

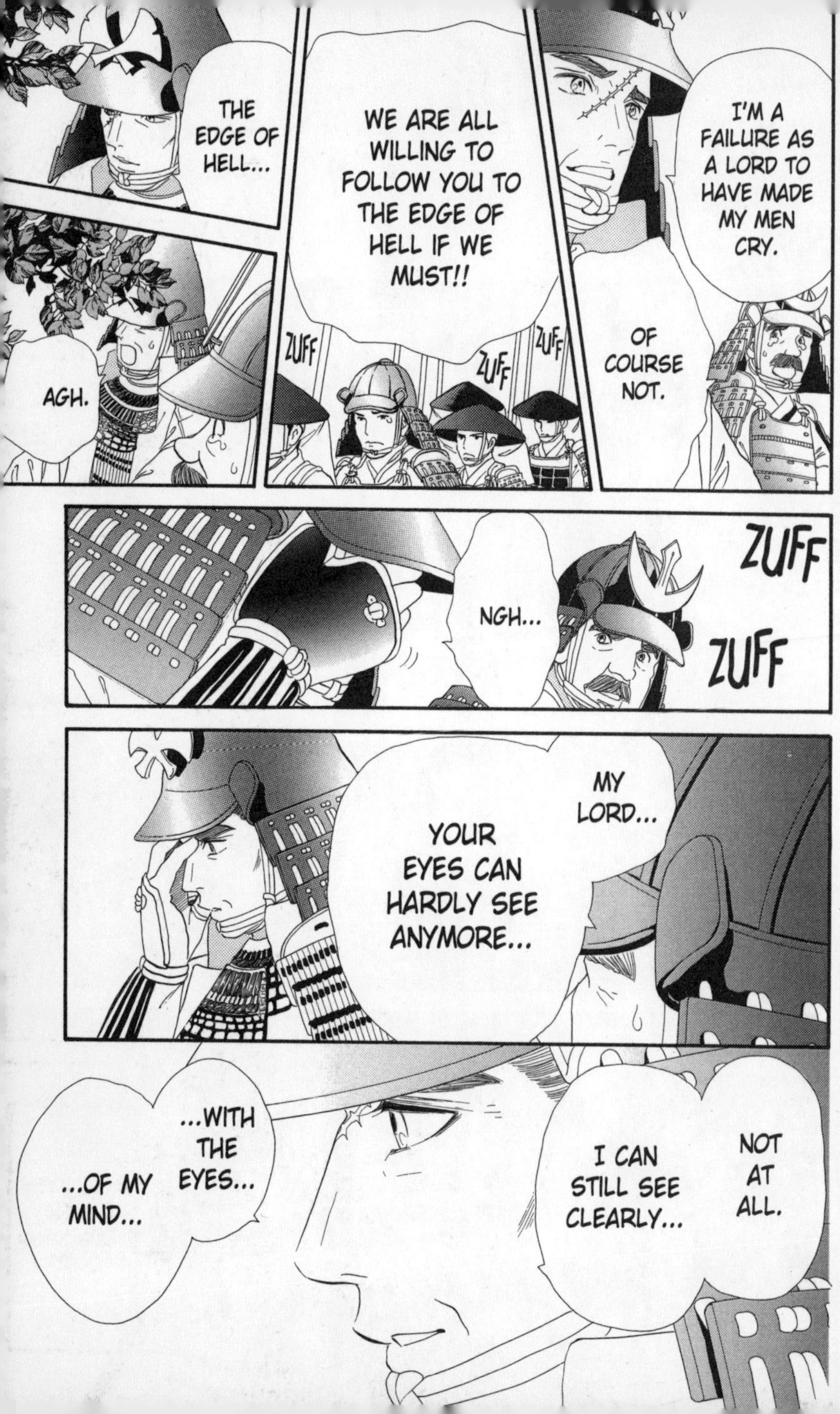
I'M A FAILURE AS A LORD TO HAVE MADE MY MEN CRY.
OF COURSE NOT.
WE ARE ALL WILLING TO FOLLOW YOU TO THE EDGE OF HELL IF WE MUST!!
ZUFF
ZUFF
ZUFF
THE EDGE OF HELL...
AGH.
ZUFF
ZUFF
NGH...
MY LORD...
YOUR EYES CAN HARDLY SEE ANYMORE...
NOT AT ALL.
I CAN STILL SEE CLEARLY...
...WITH THE EYES...
...OF MY MIND...

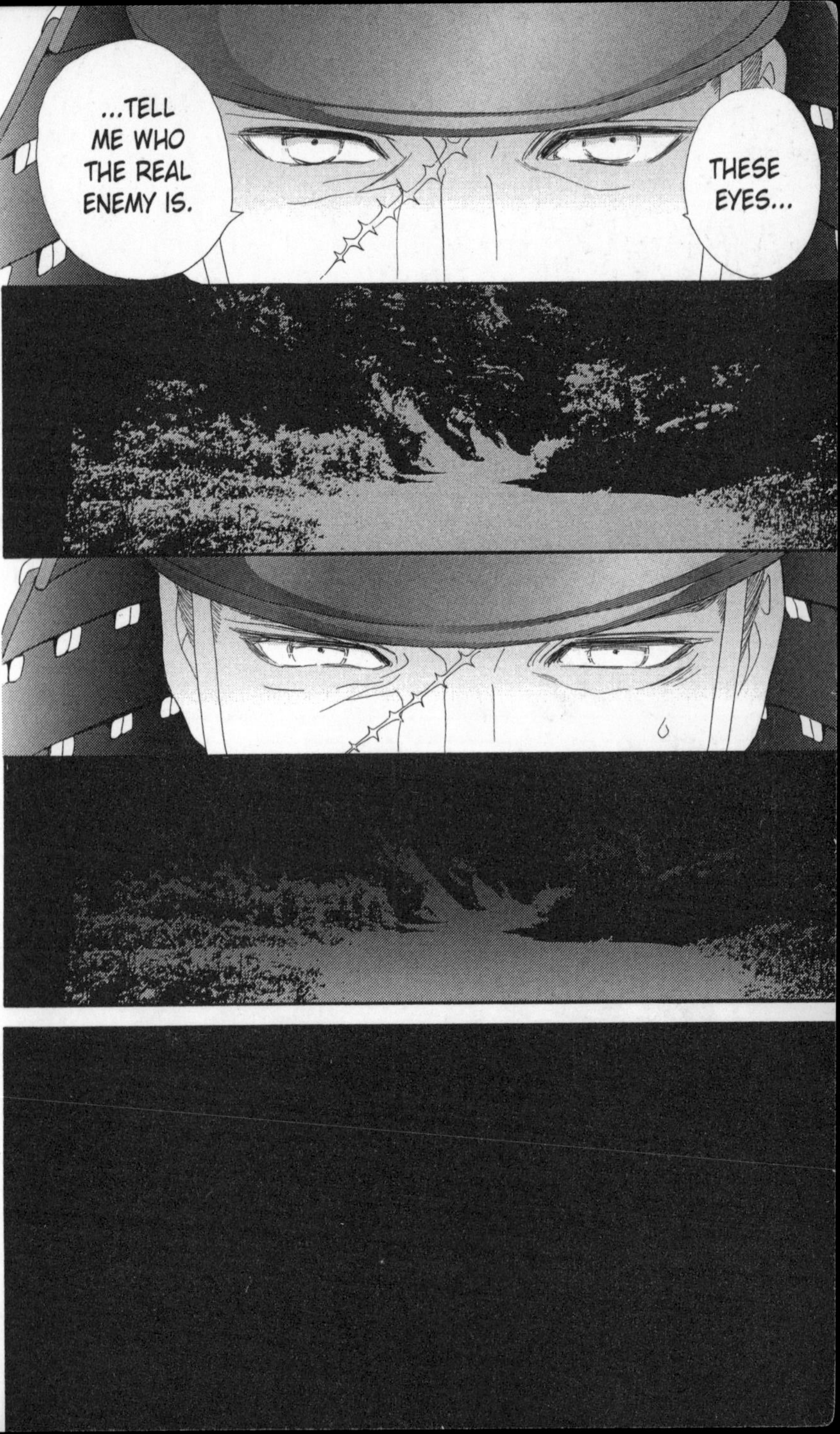
THESE EYES...
...TELL ME WHO THE REAL ENEMY IS.

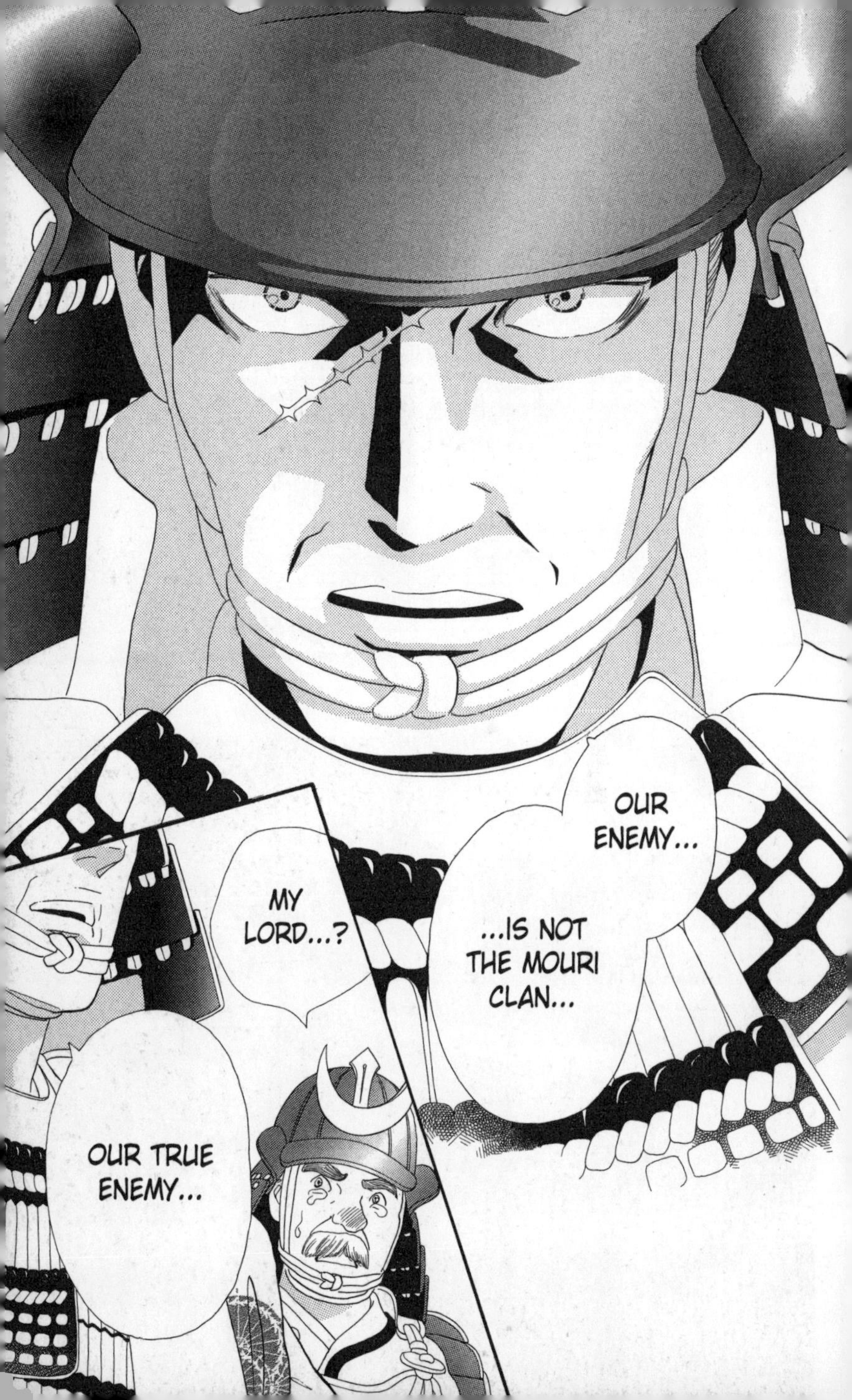
OUR ENEMY...
...IS NOT THE MOURI CLAN...
MY LORD...?
OUR TRUE ENEMY...

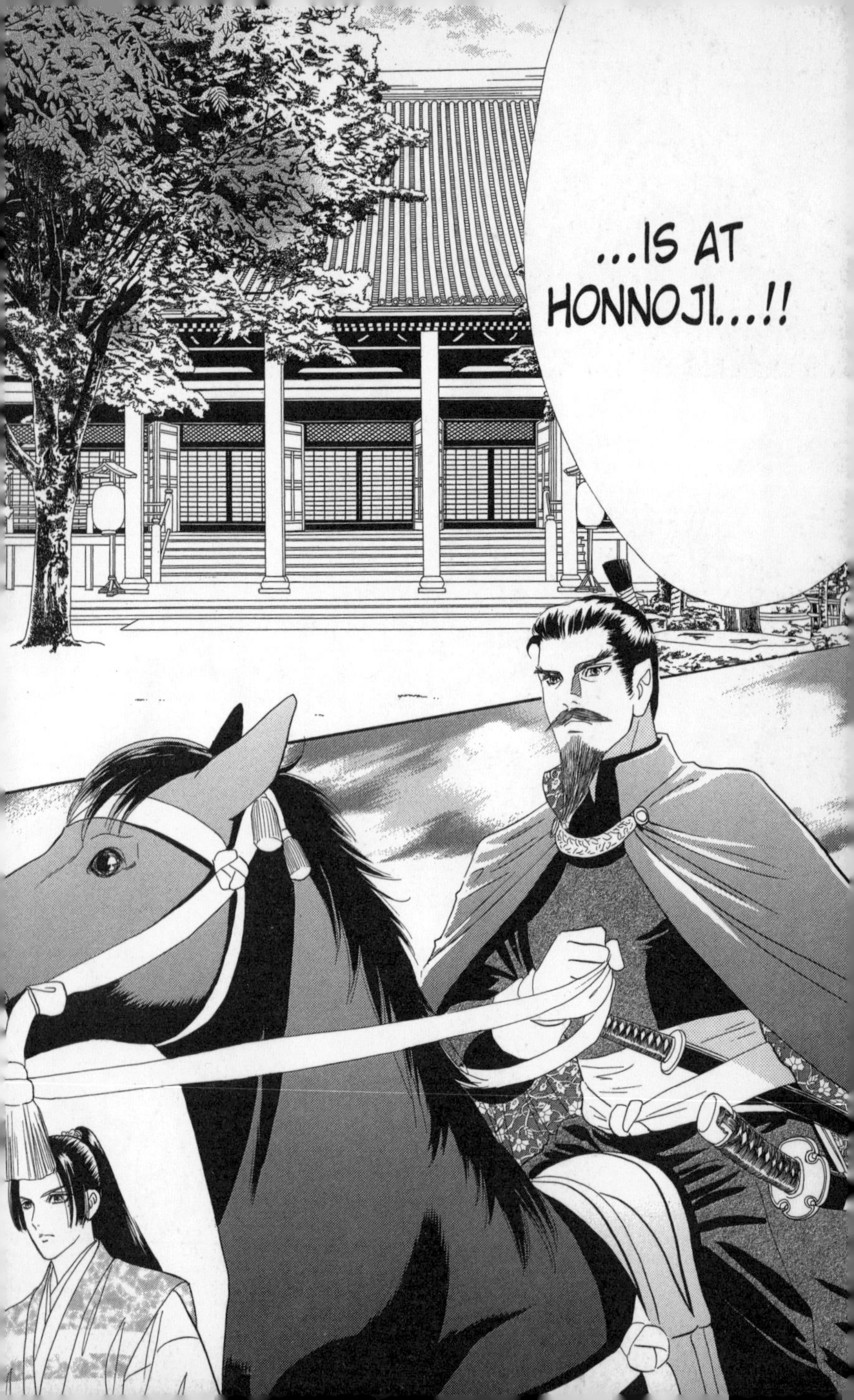
...IS AT HONNOJI...!!

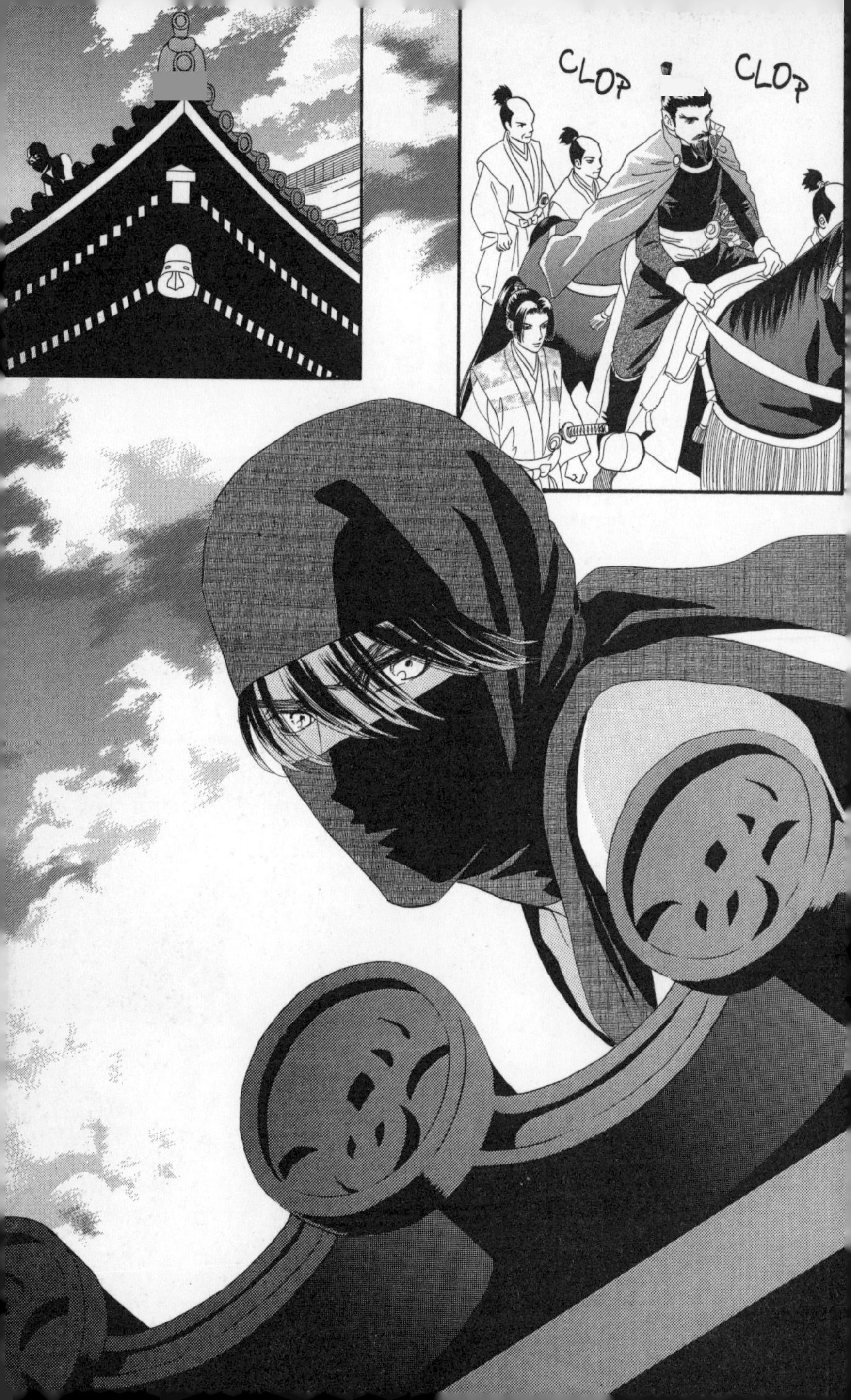
CLOP
CLOP

LET'S GO! LITTLE HANZO

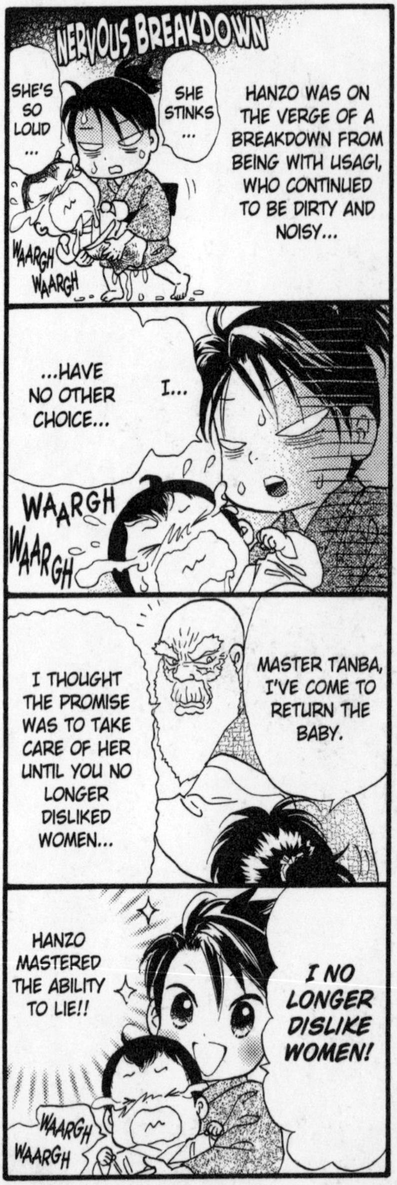
NERVOUS BREAKDOWN
HANZO WAS ON THE VERGE OF A BREAKDOWN FROM BEING WITH USAGI, WHO CONTINUED TO BE DIRTY AND NOISY...
SHE STINKS ...
SHE'S SO LOUD ...
WAARGH
WAARGH
I...
...HAVE NO OTHER CHOICE...
WAARGH
WAARGH
MASTER TANBA, I'VE COME TO RETURN THE BABY.
I THOUGHT THE PROMISE WAS TO TAKE CARE OF HER UNTIL YOU NO LONGER DISLIKED WOMEN...
I NO LONGER DISLIKE WOMEN!
HANZO MASTERED THE ABILITY TO LIE!!
WAARGH
WAARGH

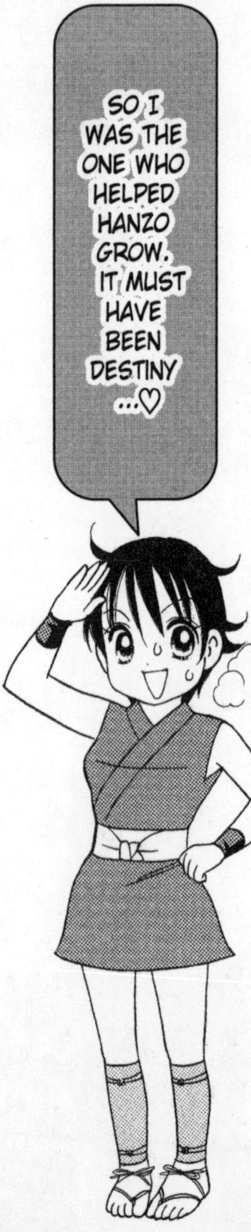
SO I WAS THE ONE WHO HELPED HANZO GROW. IT MUST HAVE BEEN DESTINY ...♡

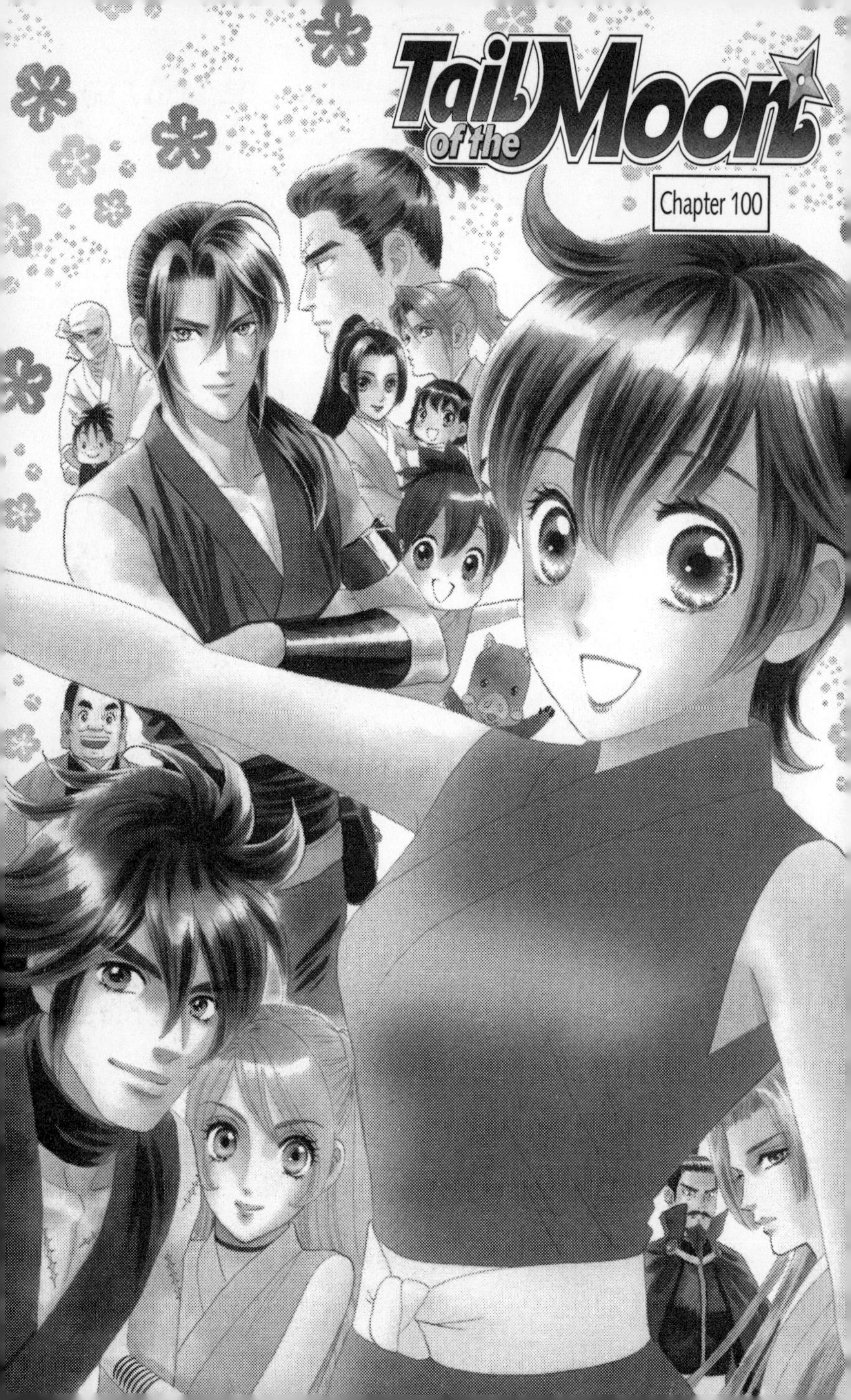
Tail of the Moon
Chapter 100

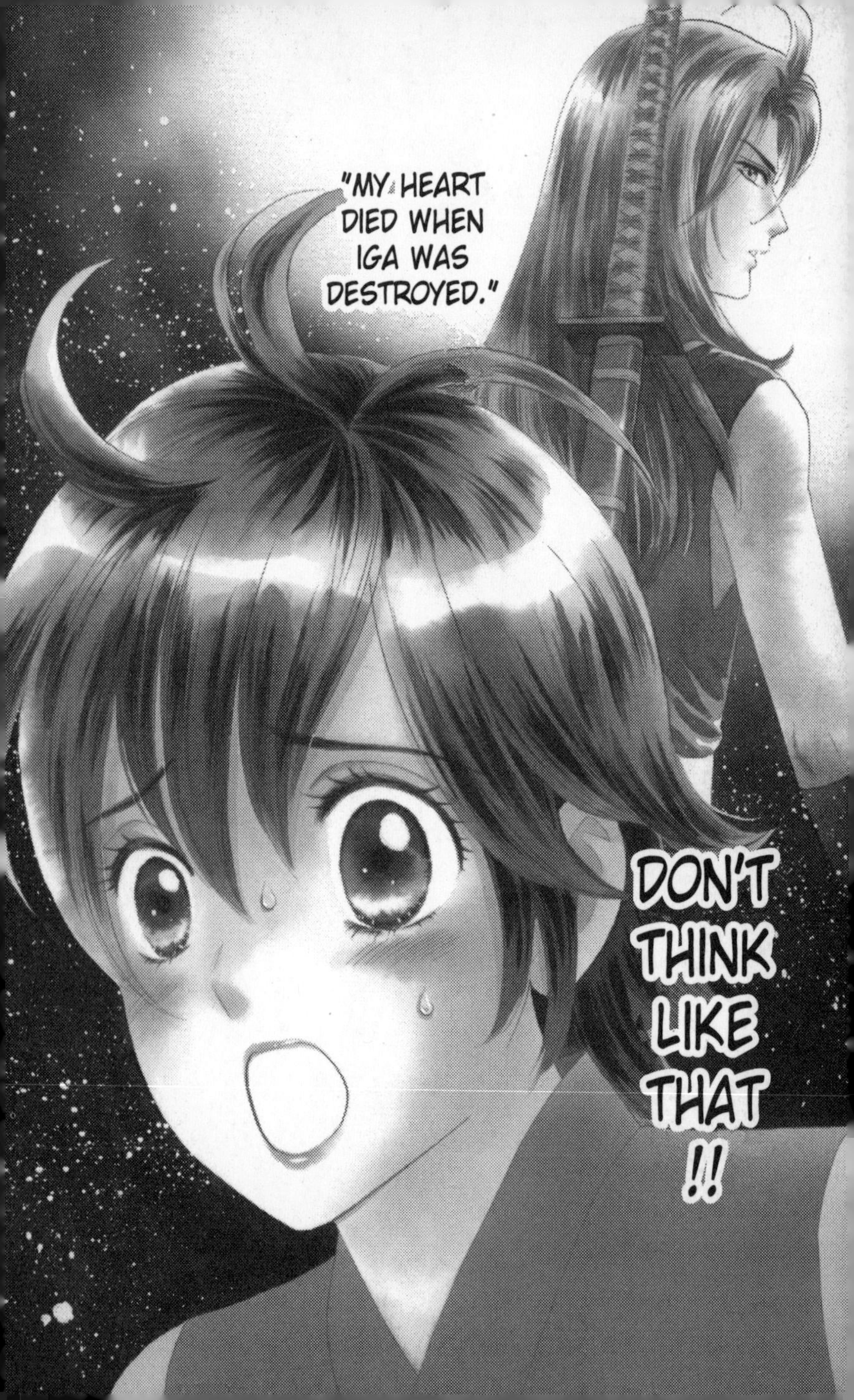
"MY HEART DIED WHEN IGA WAS DESTROYED."
DON'T THINK LIKE THAT!!

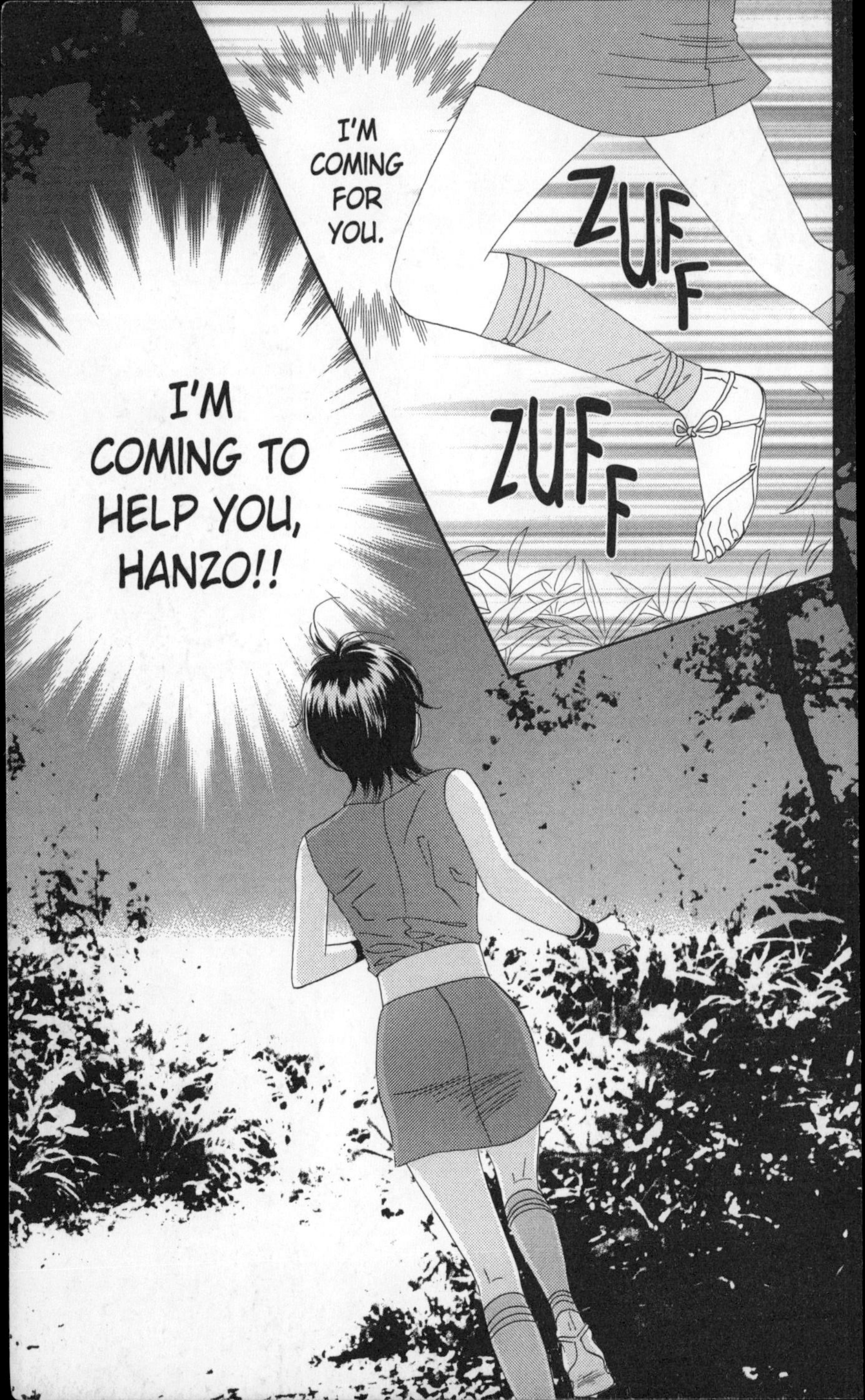
I'M COMING FOR YOU.
ZUFF
ZUFF
I'M COMING TO HELP YOU, HANZO!!

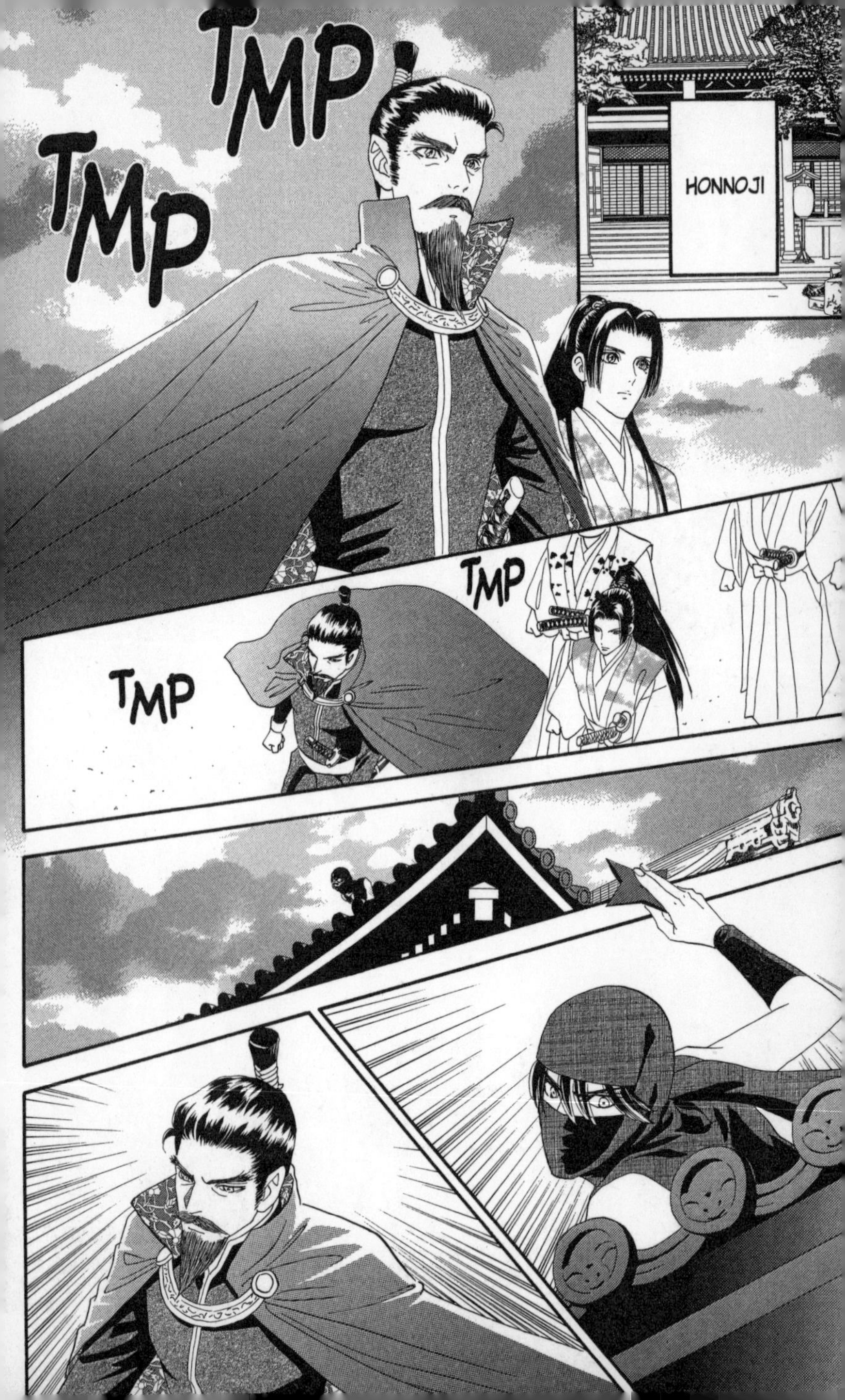
HONNOJI
TMP
TMP
TMP
TMP

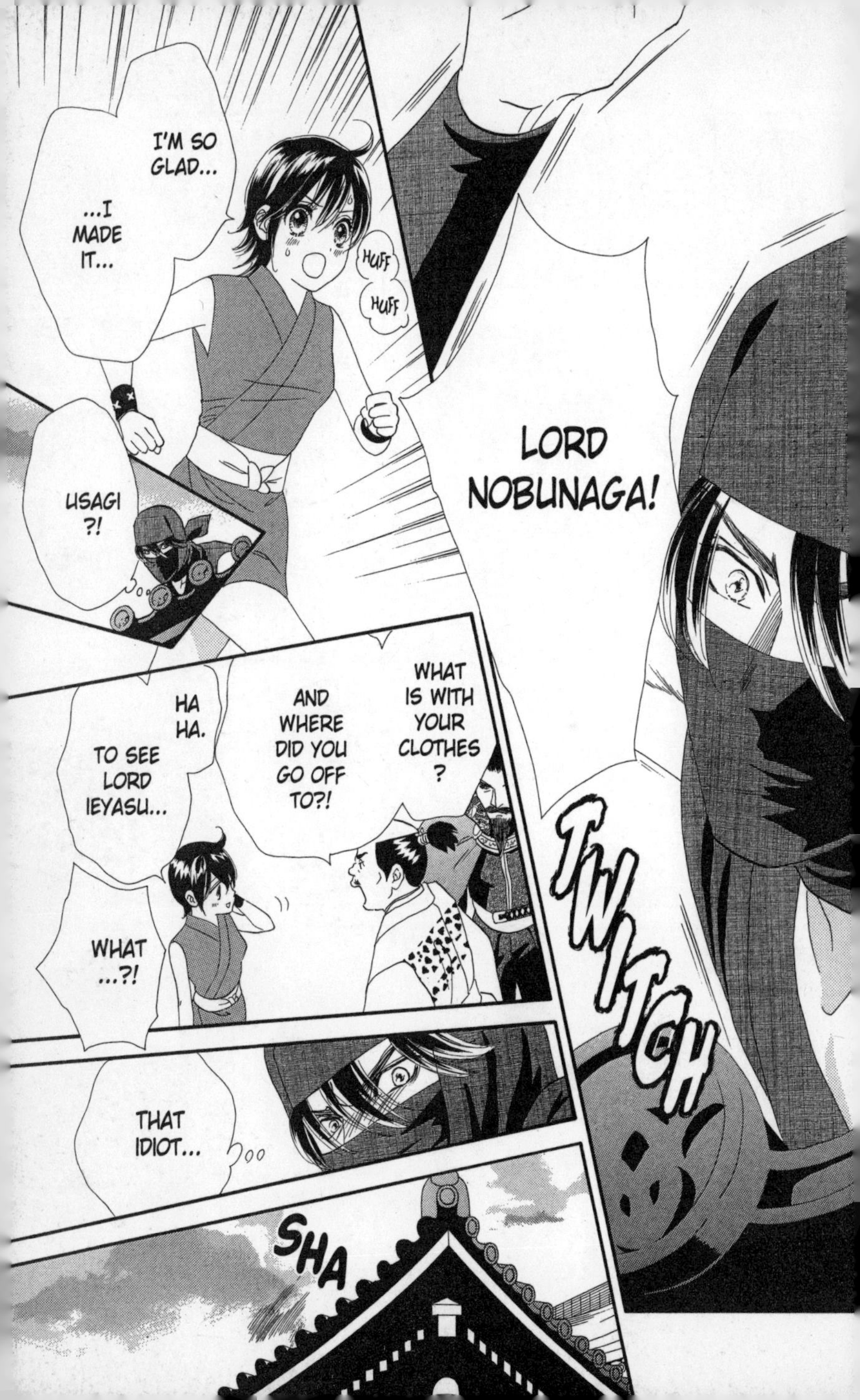
I'M SO GLAD...
...I MADE IT...
HUFF
HUFF
LORD NOBUNAGA!
USAGI ?!
TWITCH
WHAT IS WITH YOUR CLOTHES ?
AND WHERE DID YOU GO OFF TO?!
HA HA.
TO SEE LORD IEYASU...
WHAT ...?!
THAT IDIOT...
SHA

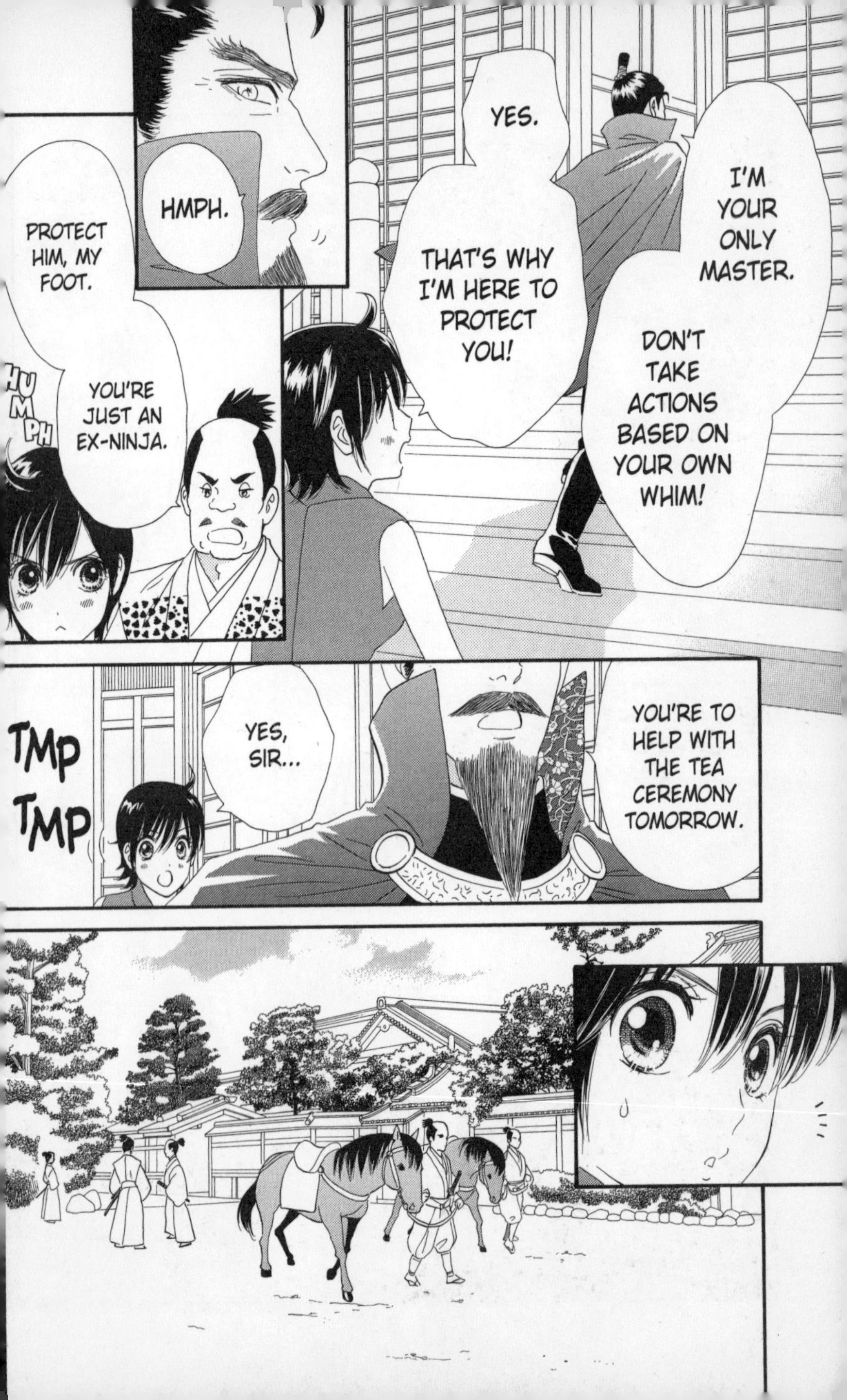
I'M YOUR ONLY MASTER.
DON'T TAKE ACTIONS BASED ON YOUR OWN WHIM!
YES.
THAT'S WHY I'M HERE TO PROTECT YOU!
HMPH.
PROTECT HIM, MY FOOT.
YOU'RE JUST AN EX-NINJA.
HUMPH
YOU'RE TO HELP WITH THE TEA CEREMONY TOMORROW.
YES, SIR...
TMP TMP

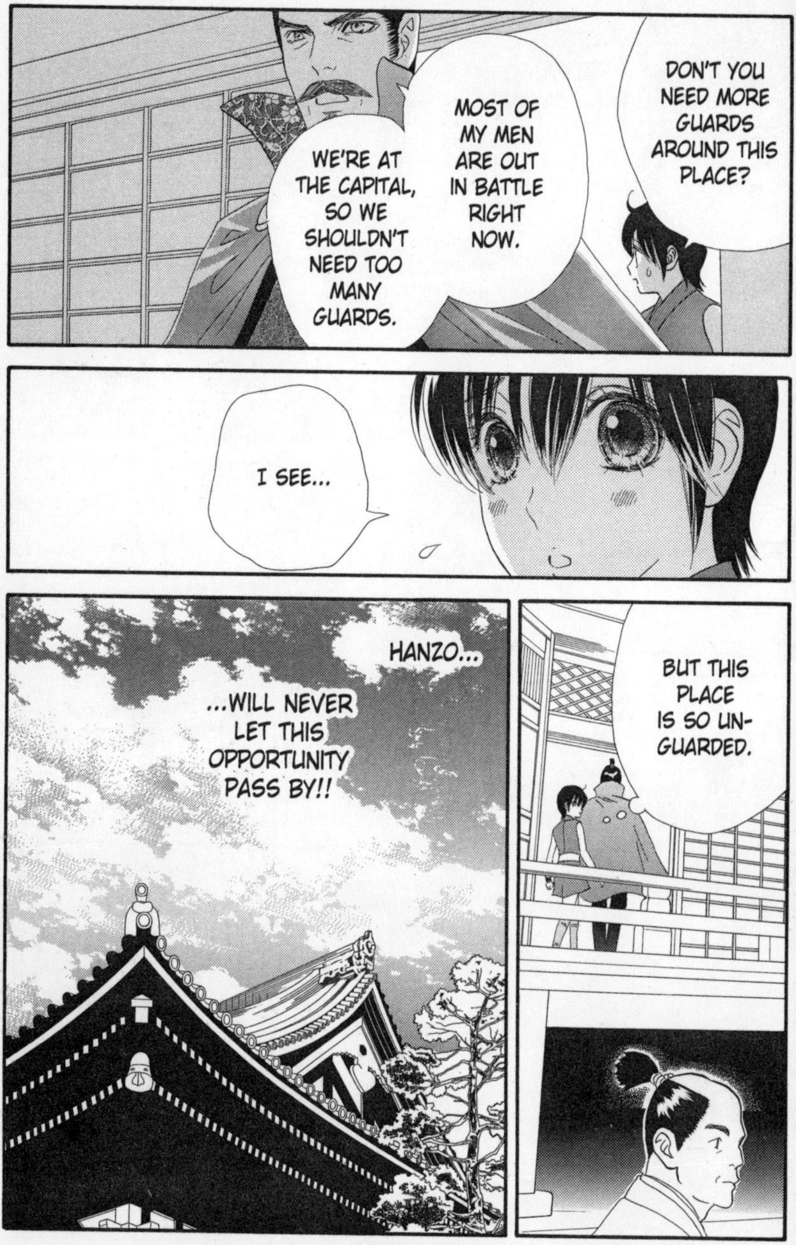
DON'T YOU NEED MORE GUARDS AROUND THIS PLACE?
MOST OF MY MEN ARE OUT IN BATTLE RIGHT NOW.
WE'RE AT THE CAPITAL, SO WE SHOULDN'T NEED TOO MANY GUARDS.
I SEE...
BUT THIS PLACE IS SO UN-GUARDED.
HANZO...
...WILL NEVER LET THIS OPPORTUNITY PASS BY!!

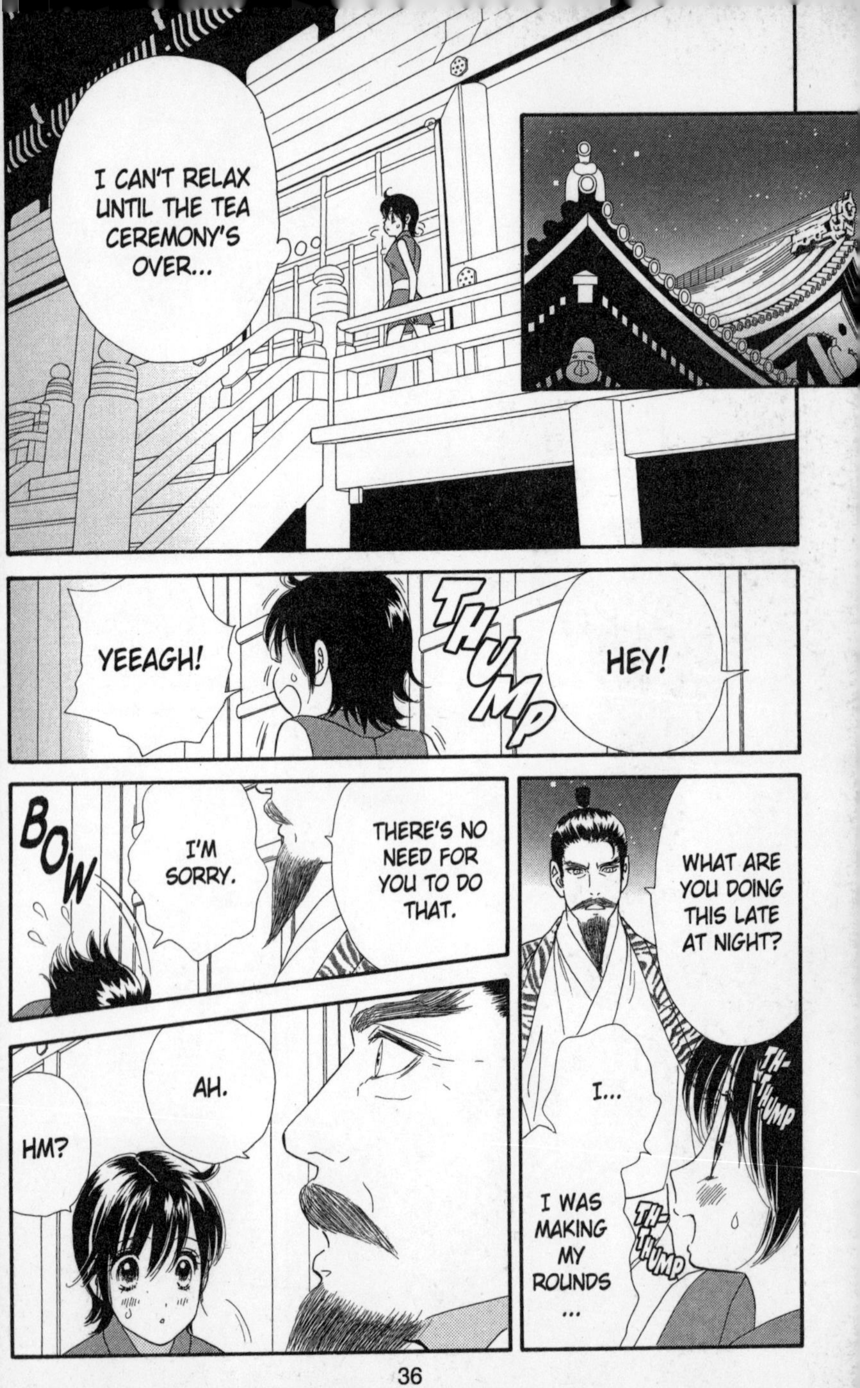
I CAN'T RELAX UNTIL THE TEA CEREMONY'S OVER...
HEY!
THUMP
YEEAGH!
WHAT ARE YOU DOING THIS LATE AT NIGHT?
TH-THUMP
I...
TH-THUMP
I WAS MAKING MY ROUNDS ...
I'M SORRY.
THERE'S NO NEED FOR YOU TO DO THAT.
BOW
AH.
HM?

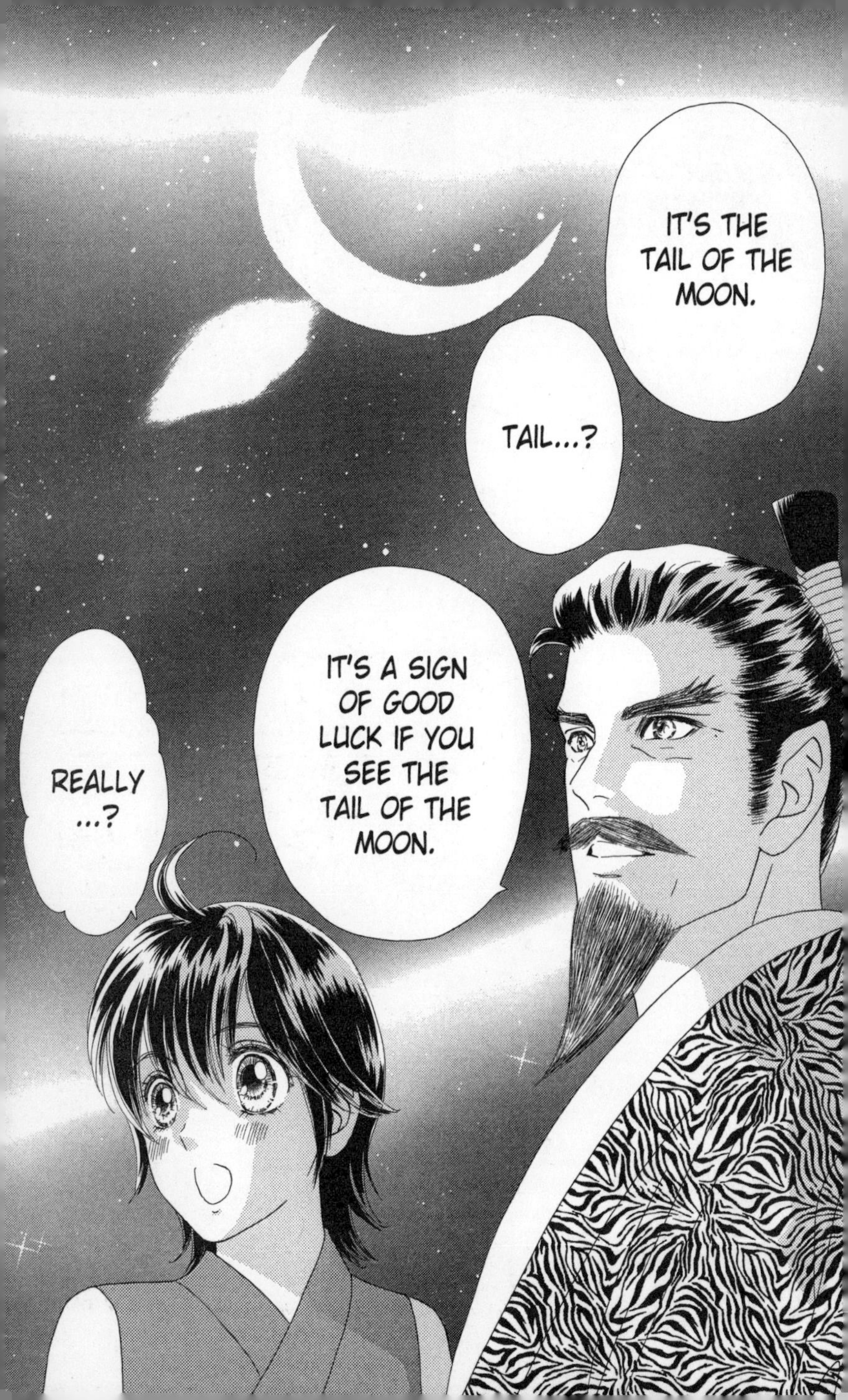
IT'S THE TAIL OF THE MOON.
TAIL...?
IT'S A SIGN OF GOOD LUCK IF YOU SEE THE TAIL OF THE MOON.
REALLY ...?

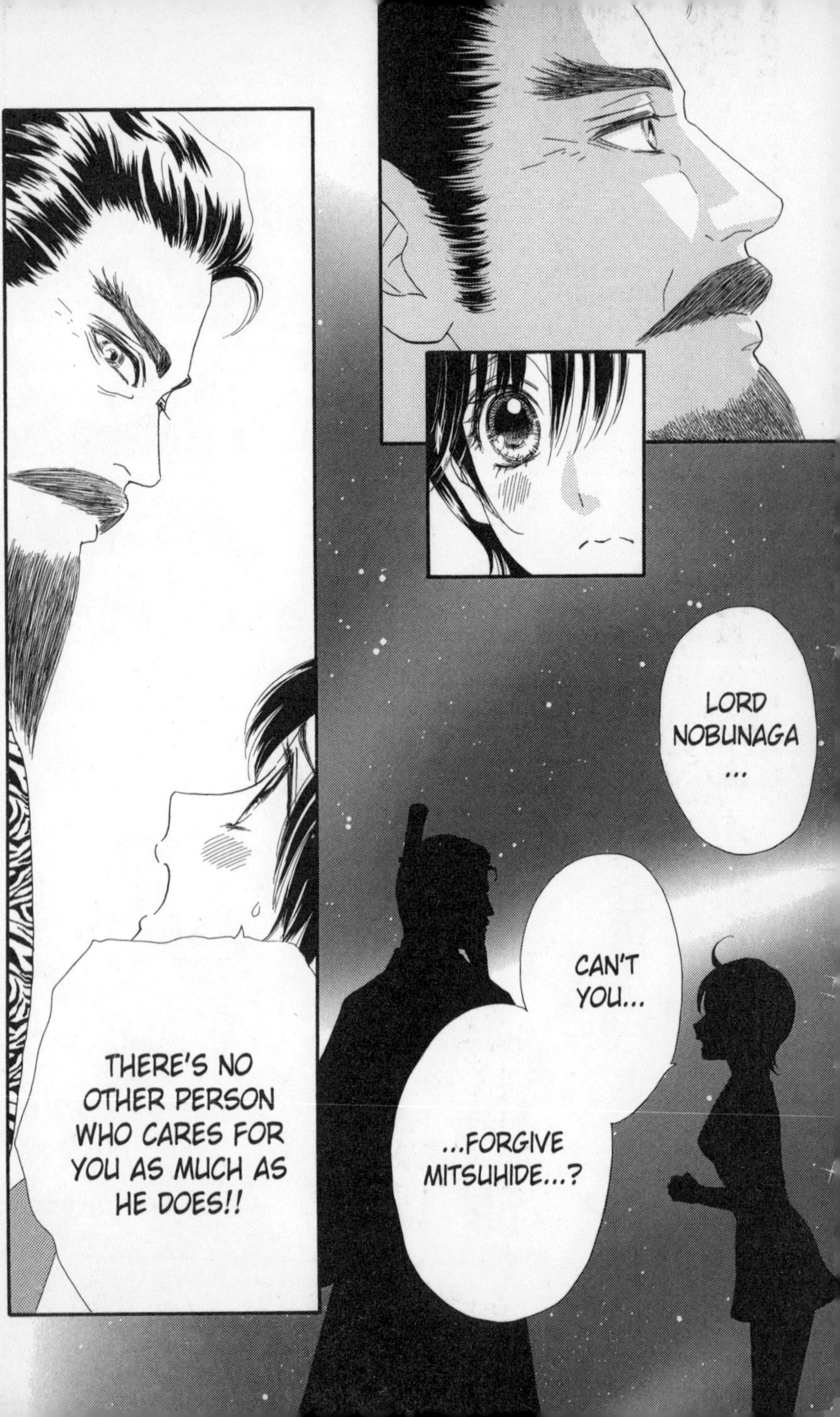
LORD NOBUNAGA ...
CAN'T YOU...
...FORGIVE MITSUHIDE...?
THERE'S NO OTHER PERSON WHO CARES FOR YOU AS MUCH AS HE DOES!!

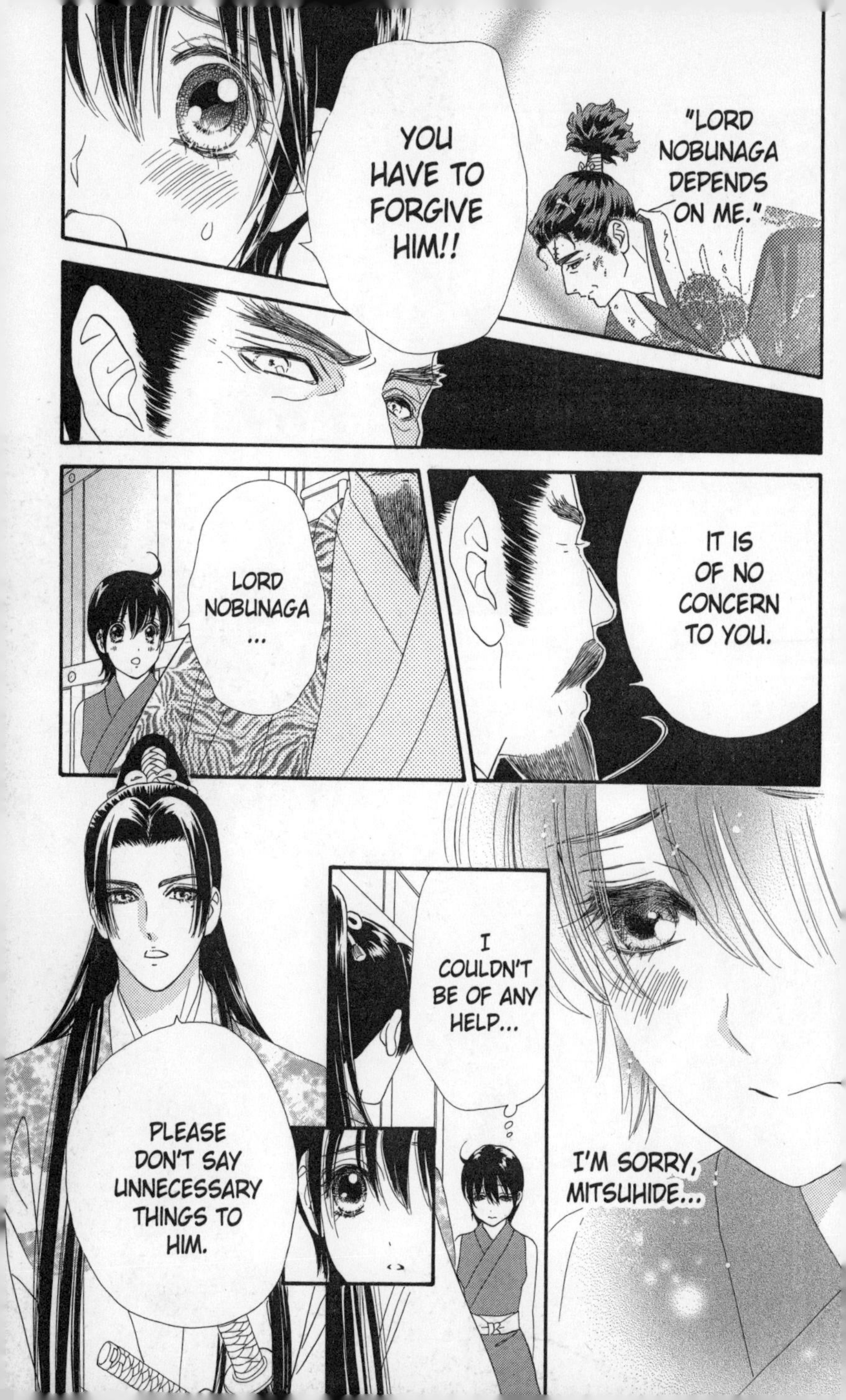
"LORD NOBUNAGA DEPENDS ON ME."
YOU HAVE TO FORGIVE HIM!!
IT IS OF NO CONCERN TO YOU.
LORD NOBUNAGA ...
I'M SORRY, MITSUHIDE...
I COULDN'T BE OF ANY HELP...
PLEASE DON'T SAY UNNECESSARY THINGS TO HIM.

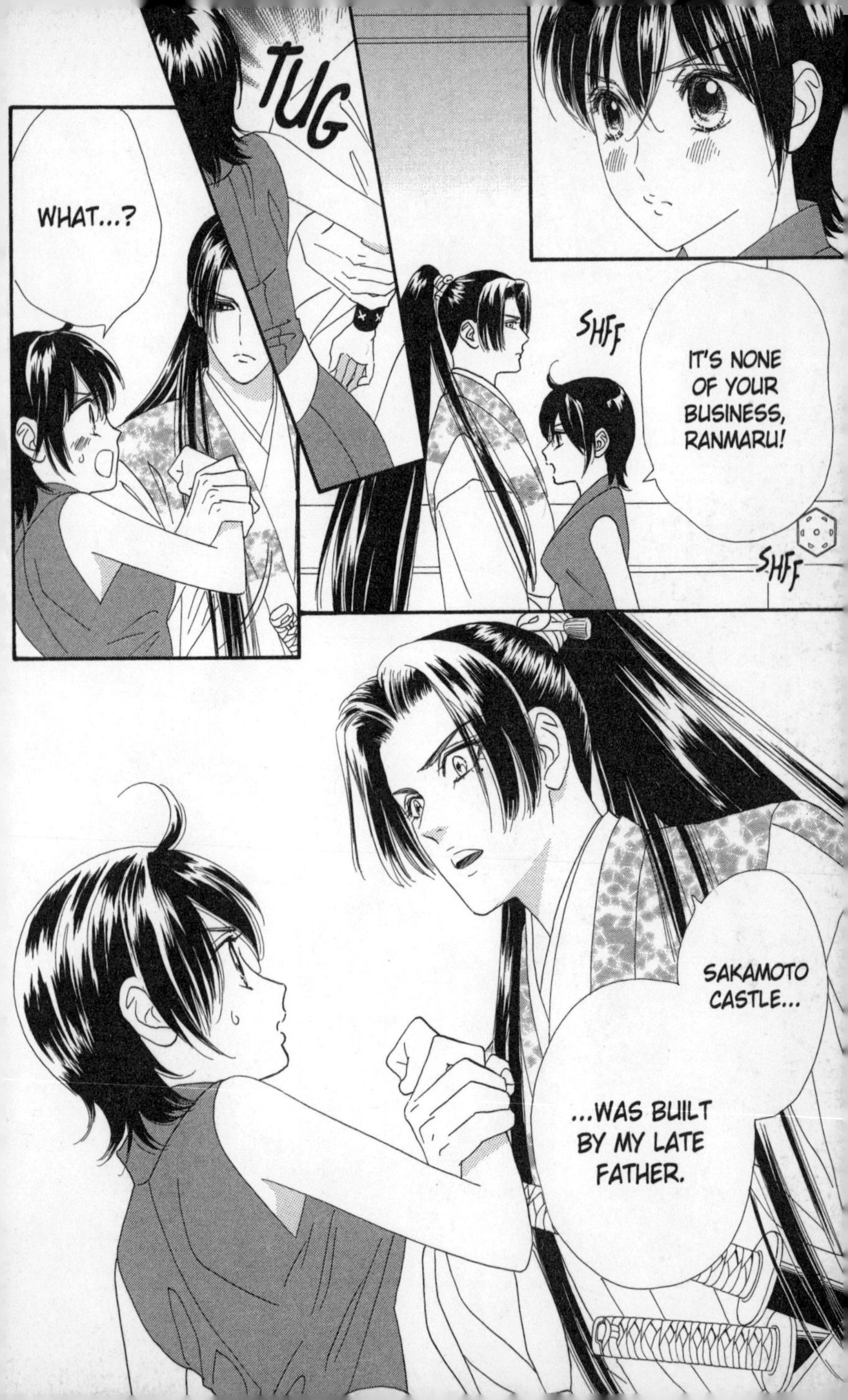

IT'S NONE OF YOUR BUSINESS, RANMARU!
SHFF
SHFF
TUG
WHAT...?
SAKAMOTO CASTLE...
...WAS BUILT BY MY LATE FATHER.

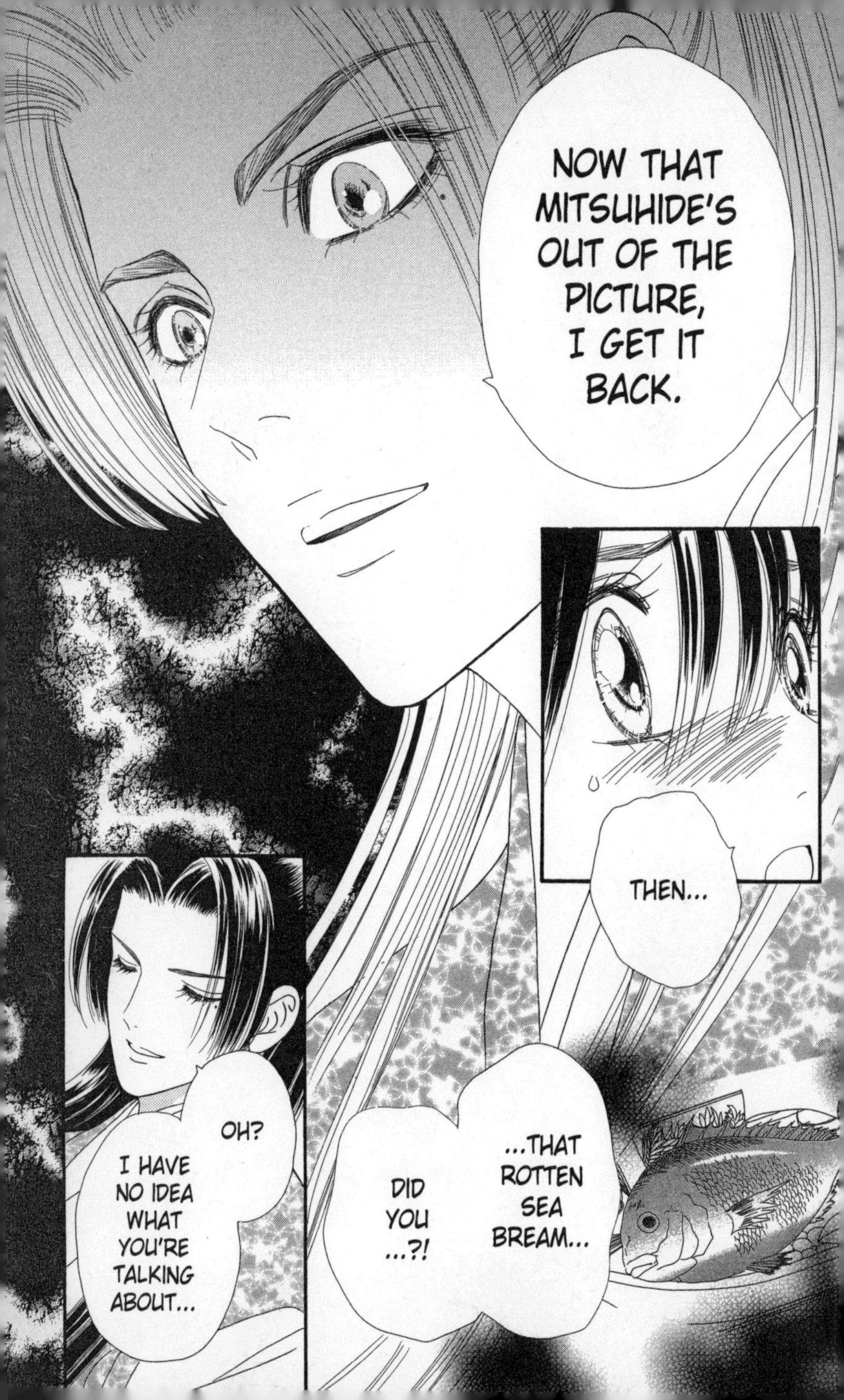
NOW THAT MITSUHIDE'S OUT OF THE PICTURE, I GET IT BACK.
THEN...
...THAT ROTTEN SEA BREAM...
DID YOU ...?!
OH?
I HAVE NO IDEA WHAT YOU'RE TALKING ABOUT...

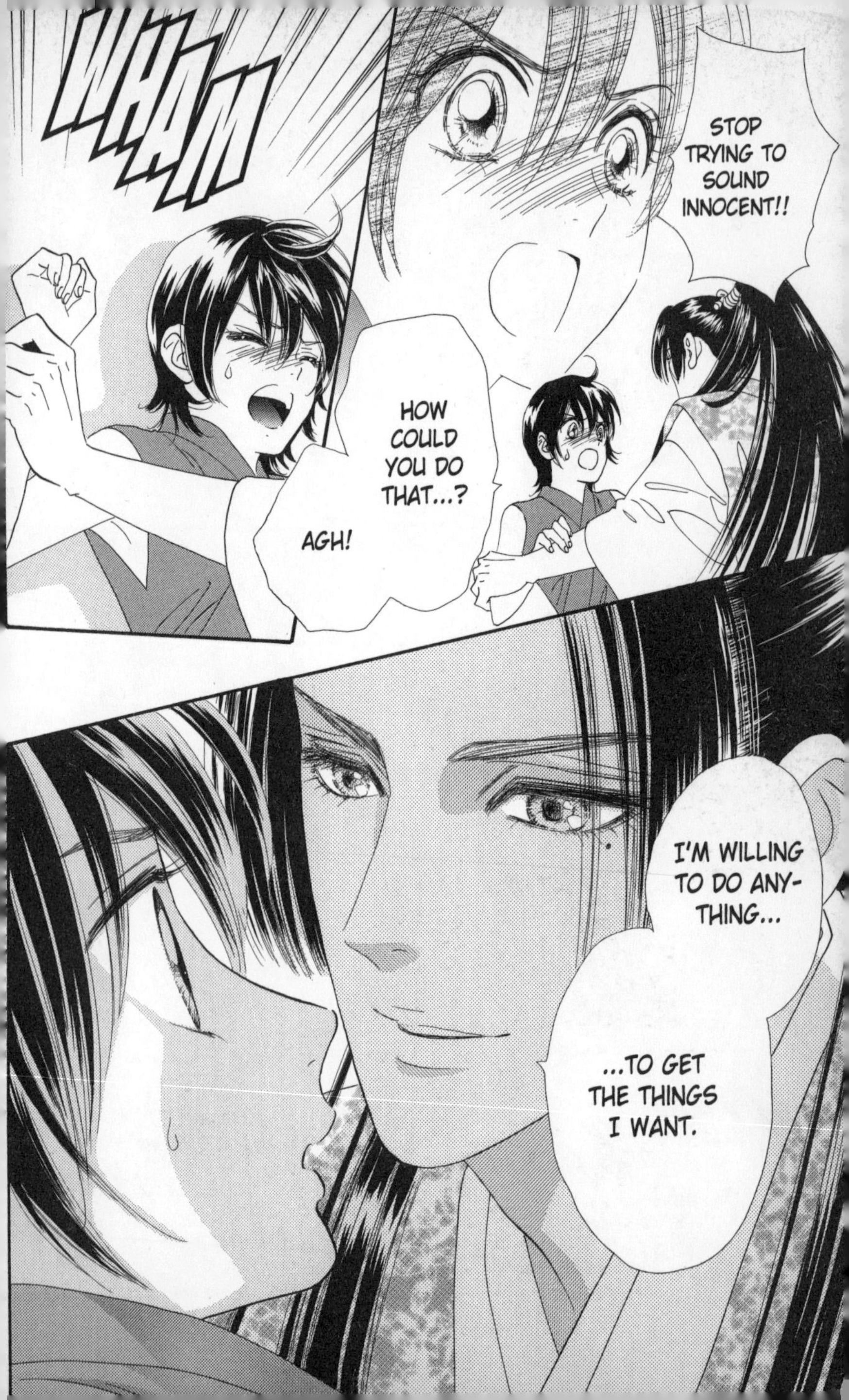
STOP TRYING TO SOUND INNOCENT!!
HOW COULD YOU DO THAT...?
WHAM
AGH!
I'M WILLING TO DO ANY-THING...
...TO GET THE THINGS I WANT.

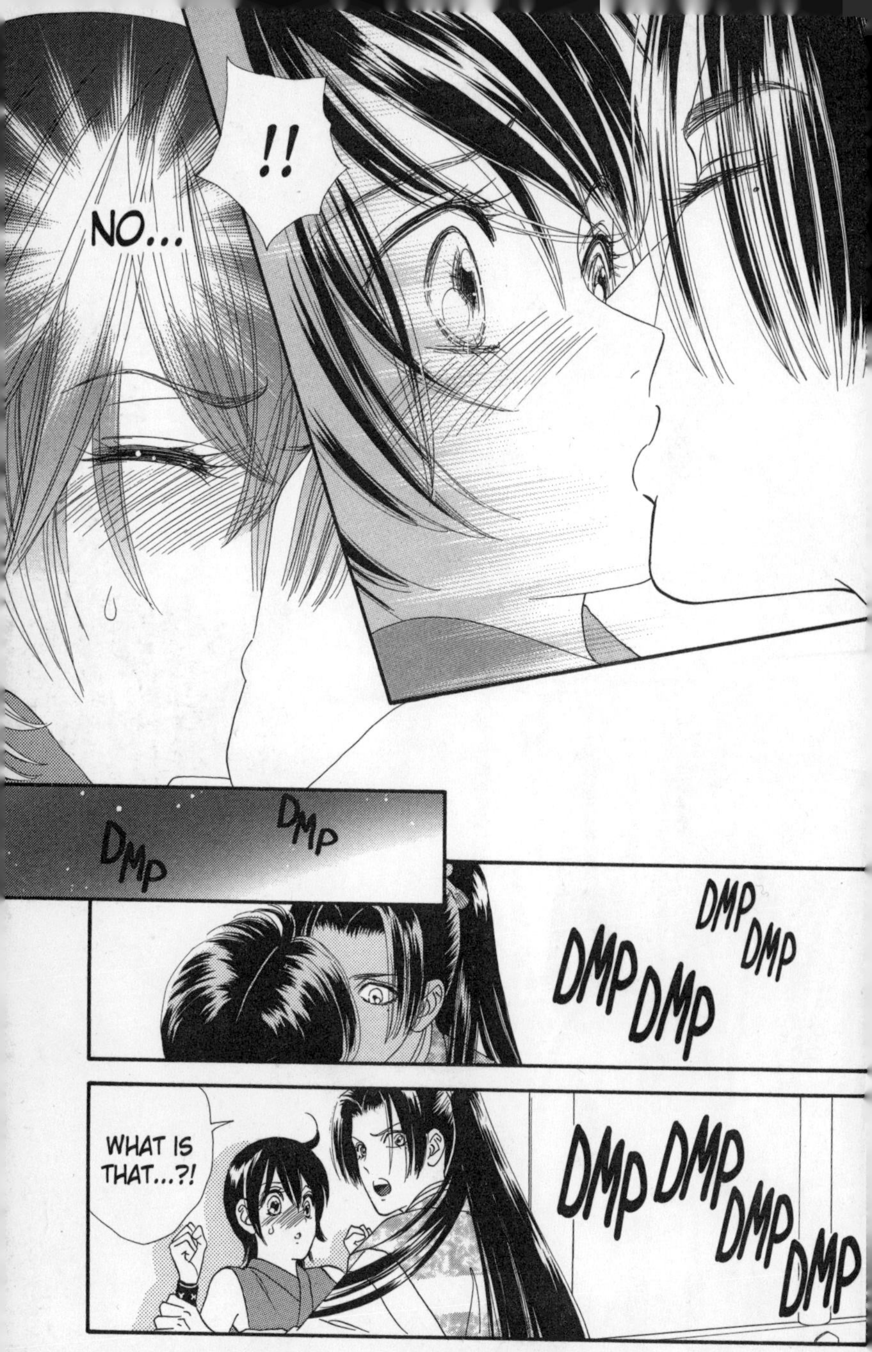
!!
NO...
DMP
DMP
DMP
DMP
DMP
DMP
DMP
DMP
DMP
DMP
WHAT IS THAT...?!

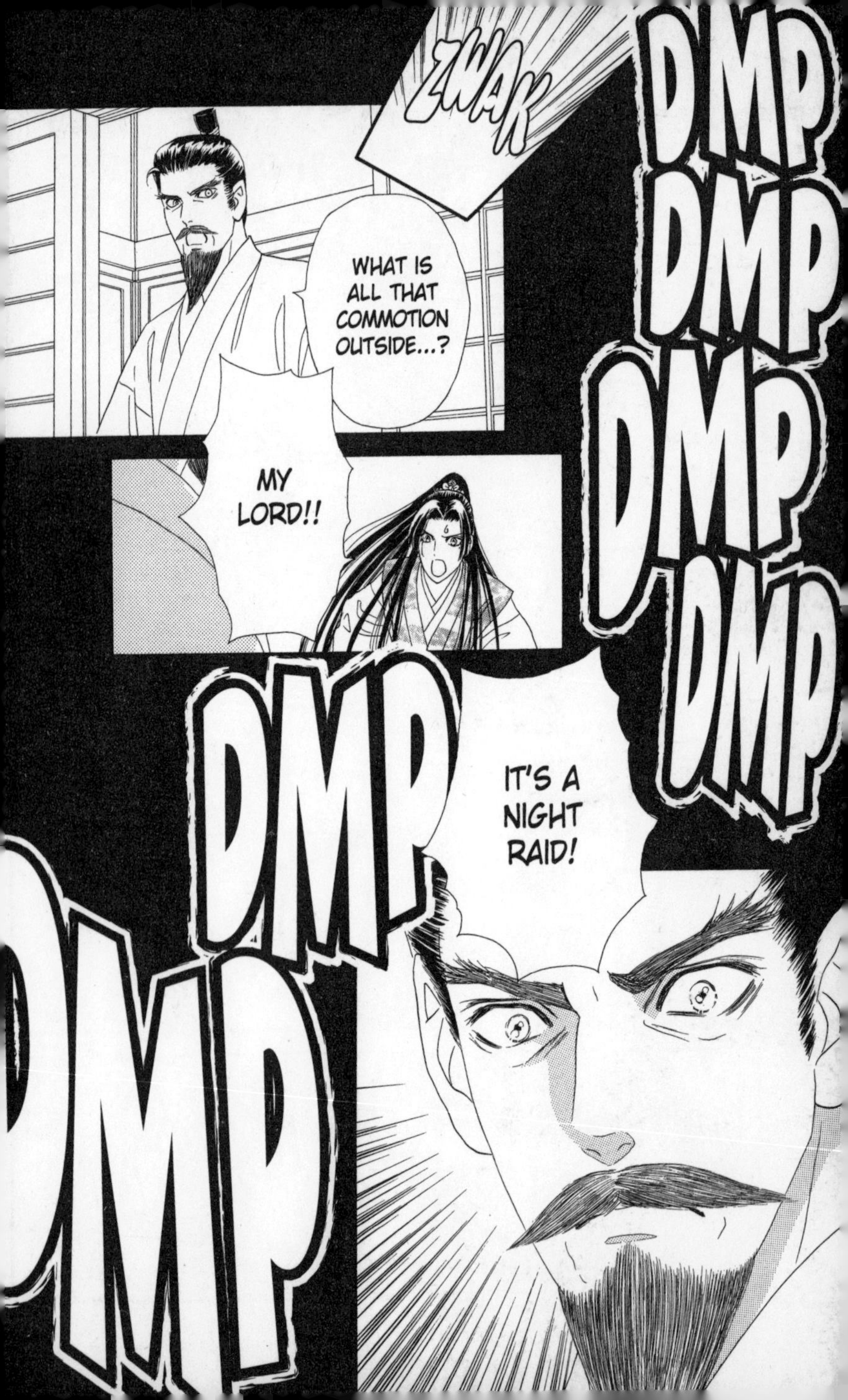
ZWAK
DMP
DMP
DMP
DMP
DMP
WHAT IS ALL THAT COMMOTION OUTSIDE...?
MY LORD!!
IT'S A NIGHT RAID!
DMP
DMP

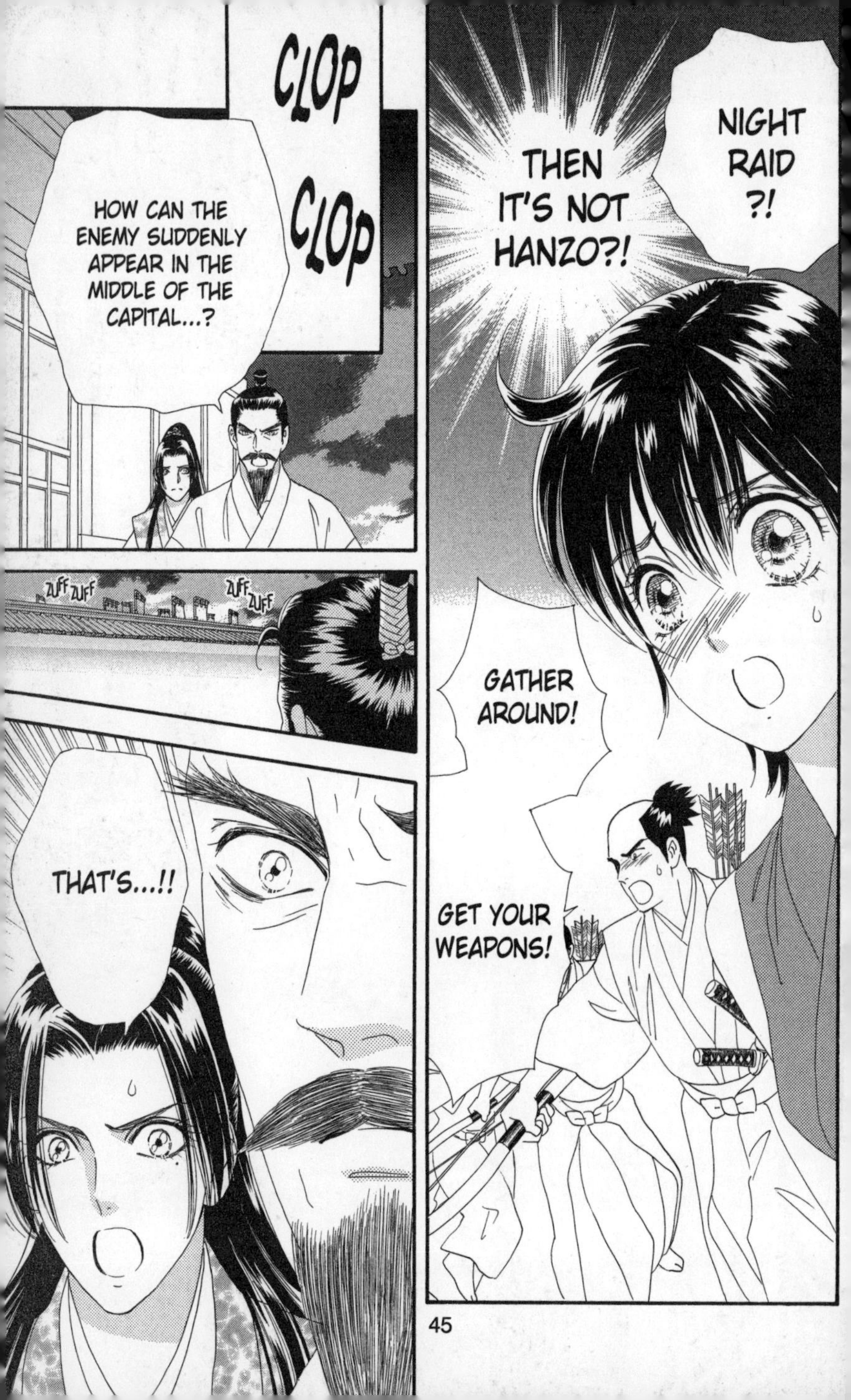
NIGHT RAID ?!
THEN IT'S NOT HANZO?!
GATHER AROUND!
GET YOUR WEAPONS!
CLOP
CLOP
HOW CAN THE ENEMY SUDDENLY APPEAR IN THE MIDDLE OF THE CAPITAL...?
ZUFF ZUFF
ZUFF ZUFF
THAT'S...!!

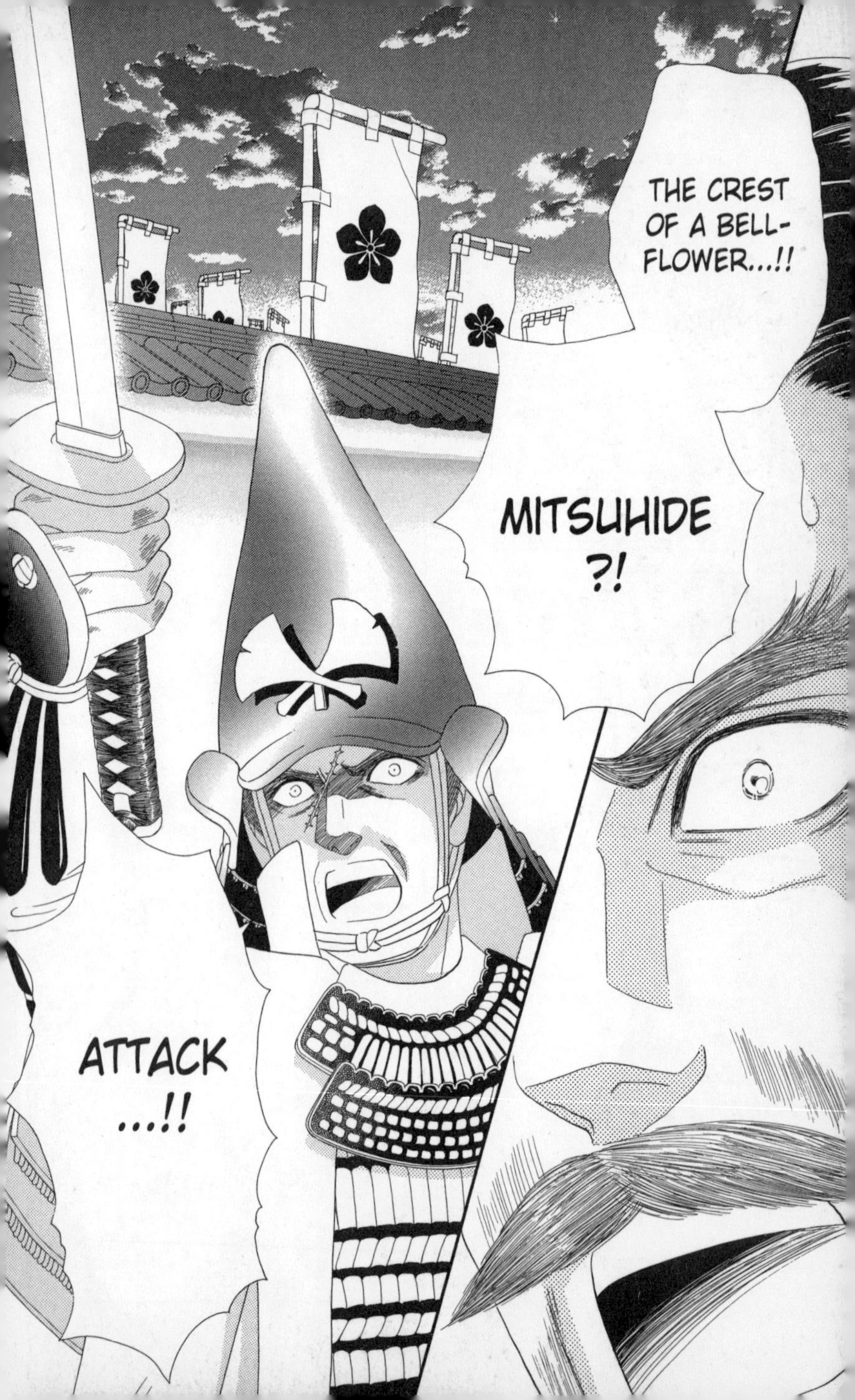
THE CREST OF A BELL-FLOWER...!!
MITSUHIDE ?!
ATTACK ...!!

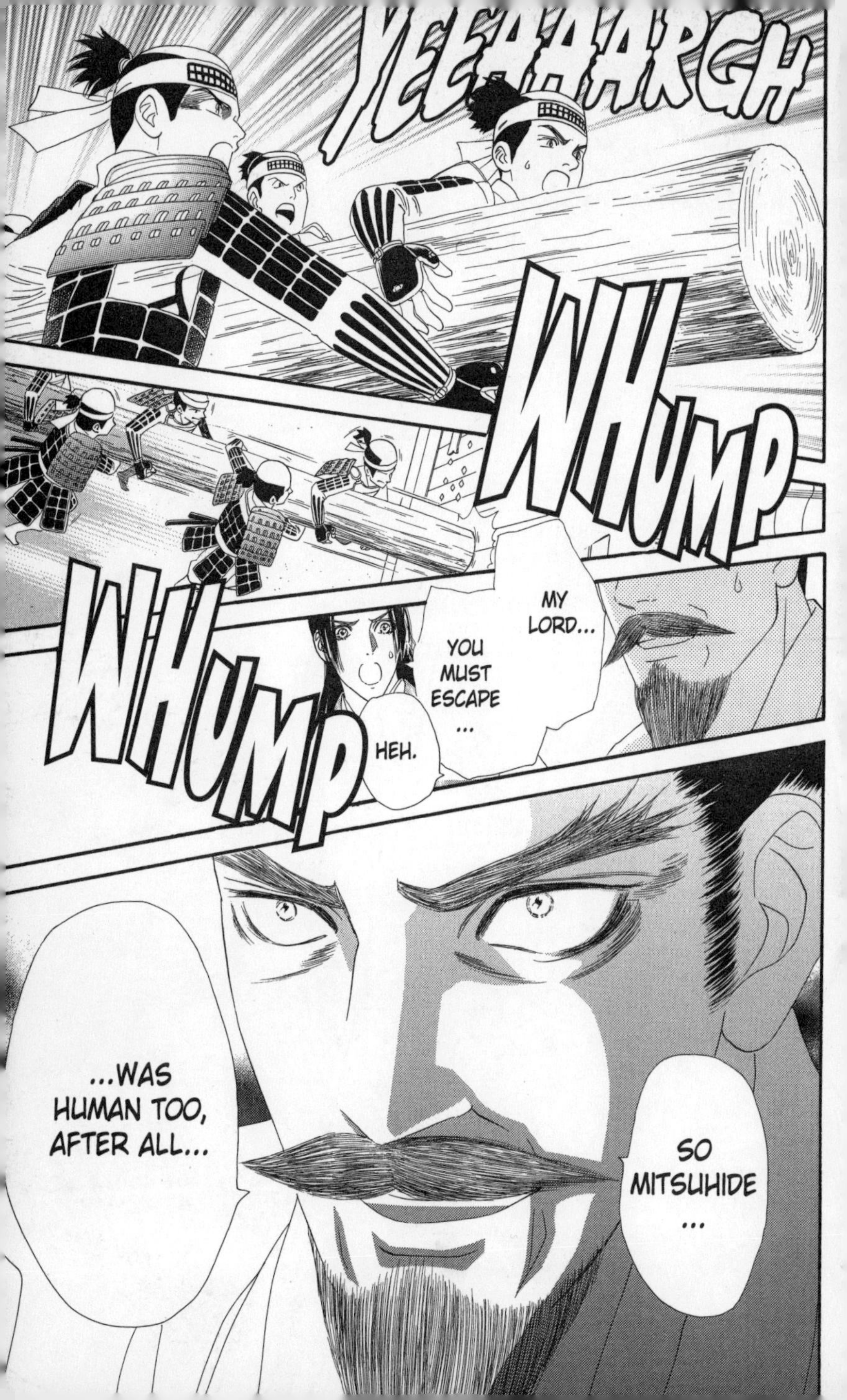
YEEAAARGH
WHUMP
WHUMP
MY LORD...
YOU MUST ESCAPE ...
HEH.
SO MITSUHIDE ...
...WAS HUMAN TOO, AFTER ALL...

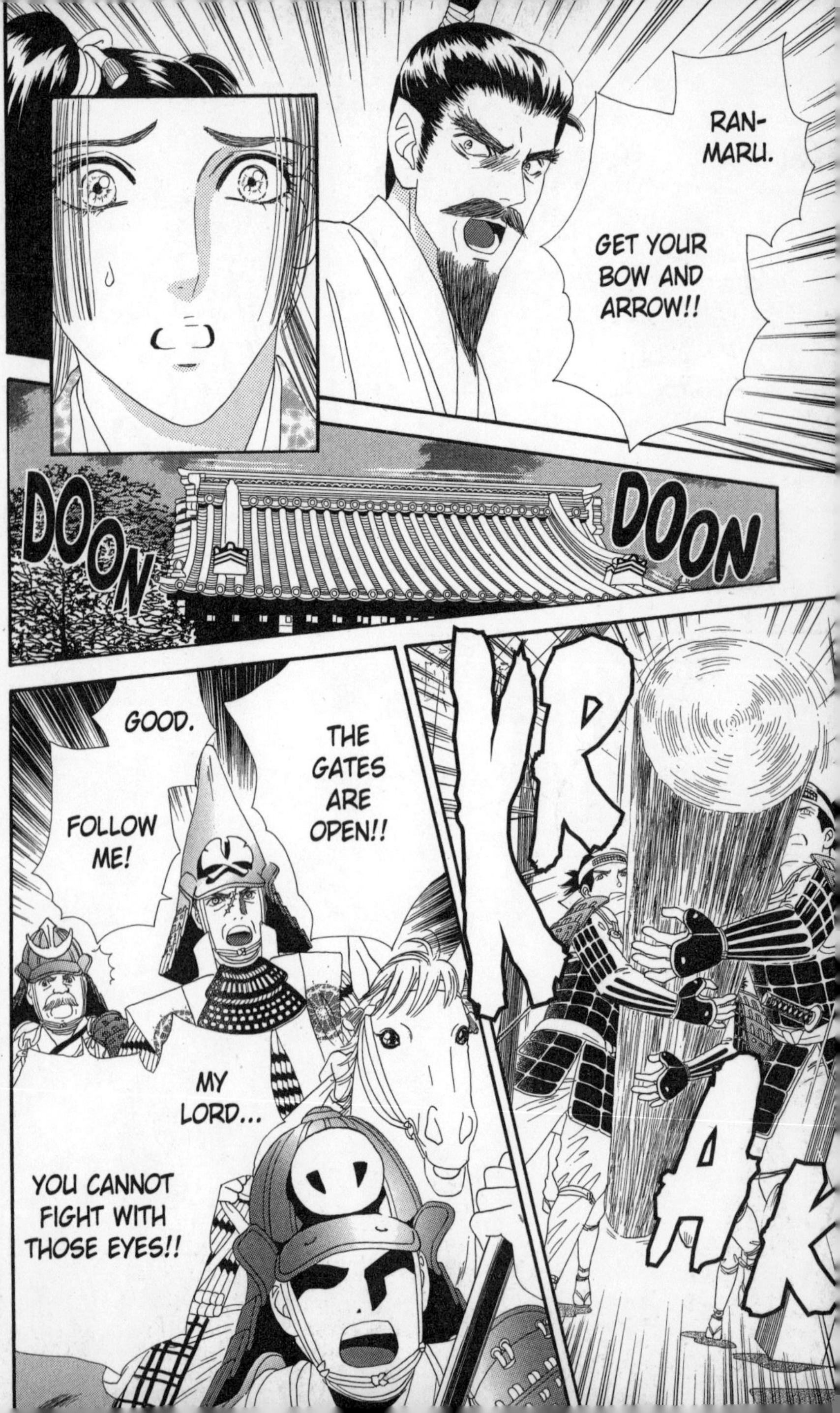
RAN-MARU.
GET YOUR BOW AND ARROW!!
DOON
DOON
KRAK
THE GATES ARE OPEN!!
GOOD.
FOLLOW ME!
MY LORD...
YOU CANNOT FIGHT WITH THOSE EYES!!

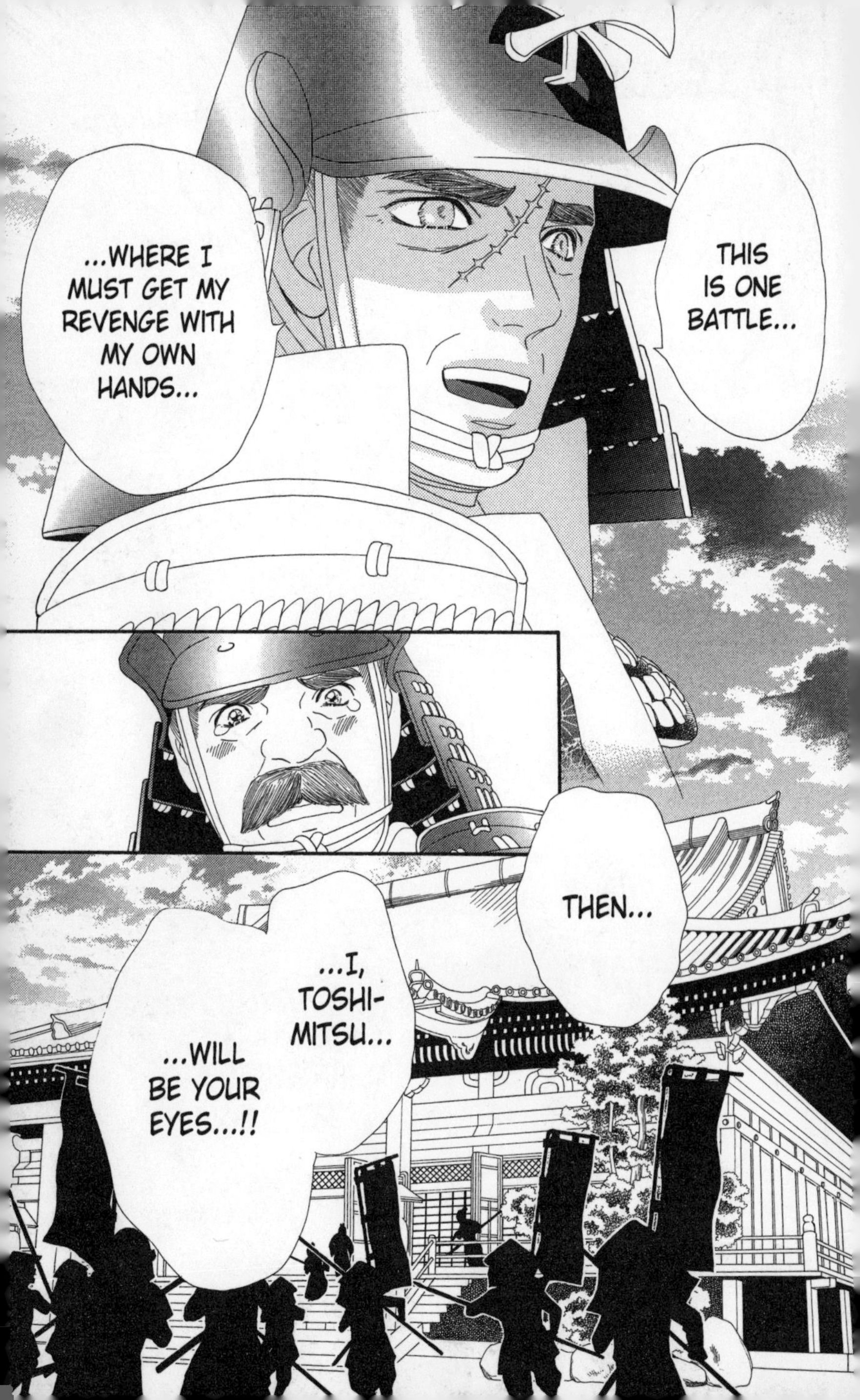
THIS IS ONE BATTLE...
...WHERE I MUST GET MY REVENGE WITH MY OWN HANDS...
THEN...
...I, TOSHI-MITSU...
...WILL BE YOUR EYES...!!

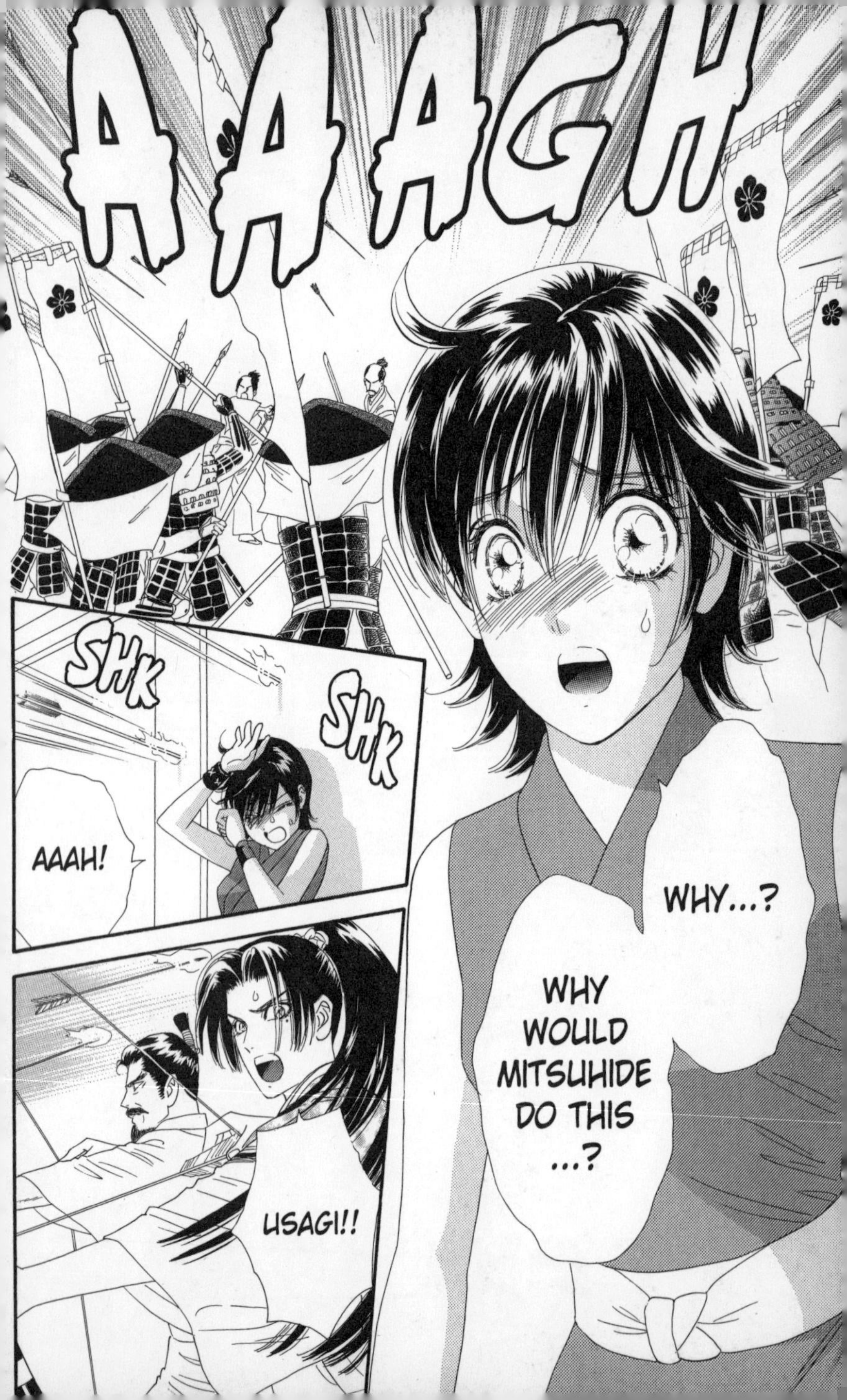
AAAGH
WHY...?
WHY WOULD MITSUHIDE DO THIS ...?
SHK
SHK
AAAH!
USAGI!!

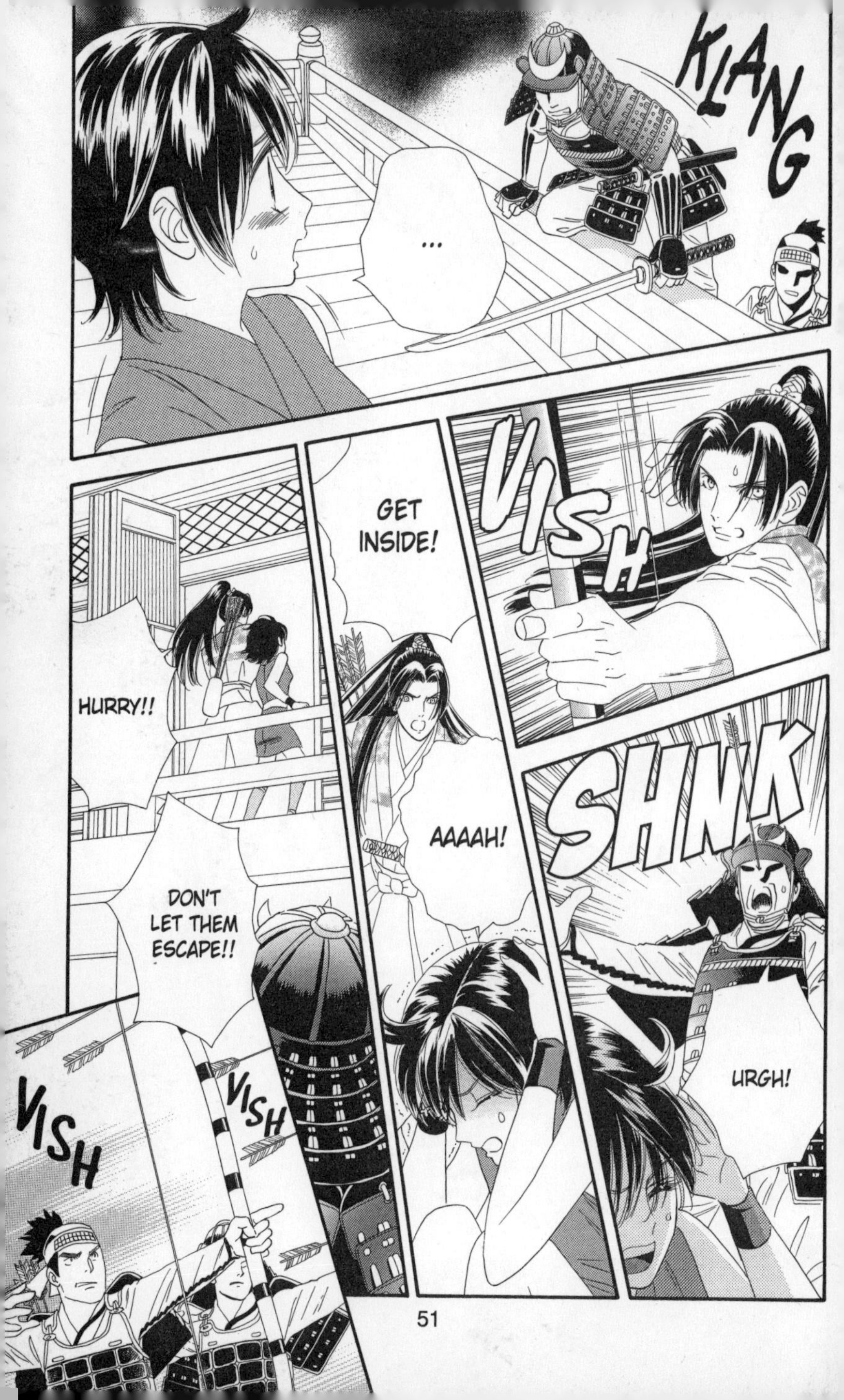
KLANG
...
VISH
GET INSIDE!
HURRY!!
SHNK
URGH!
AAAAH!
DON'T LET THEM ESCAPE!!
VISH
VISH

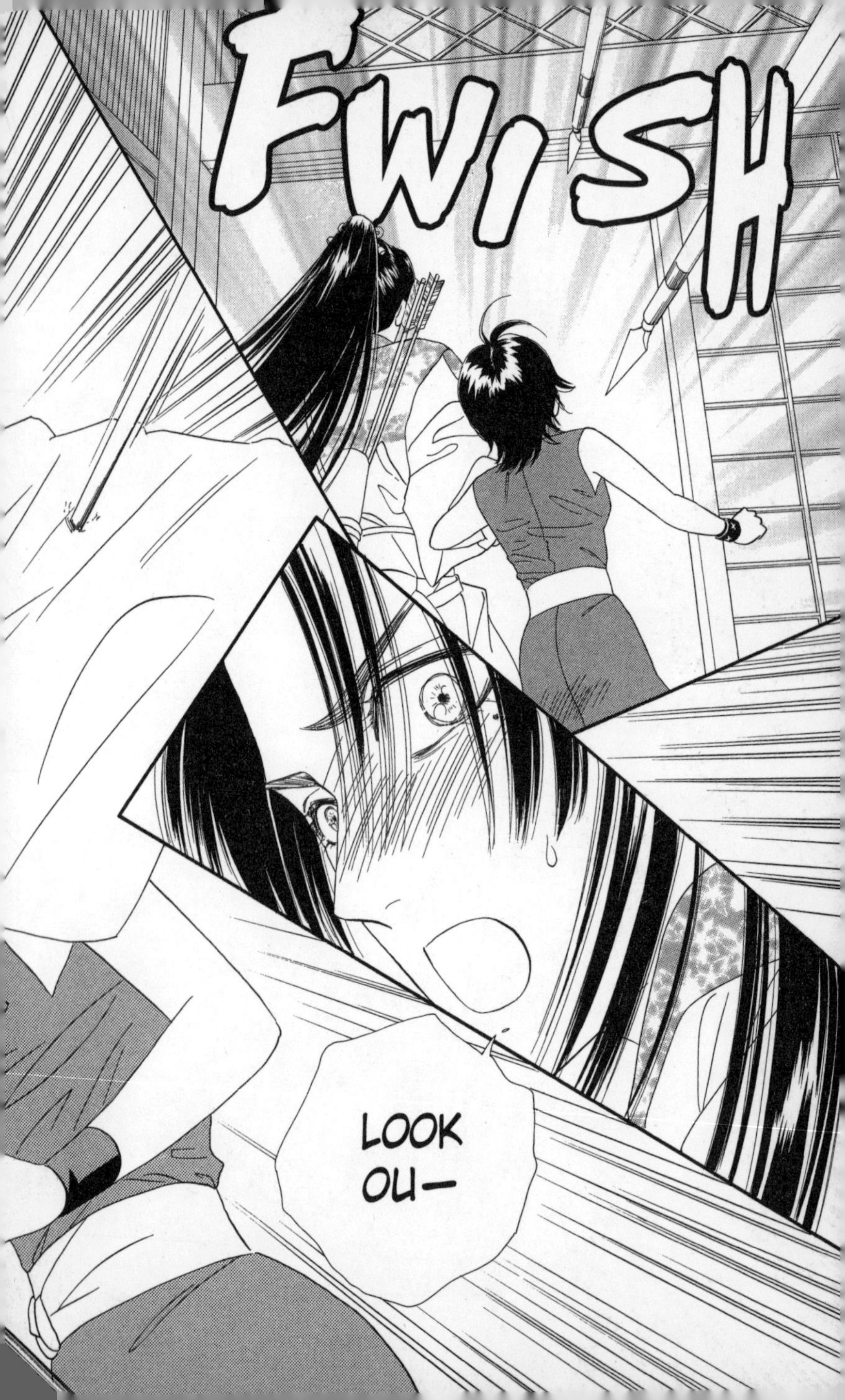
FWISH
LOOK OU—

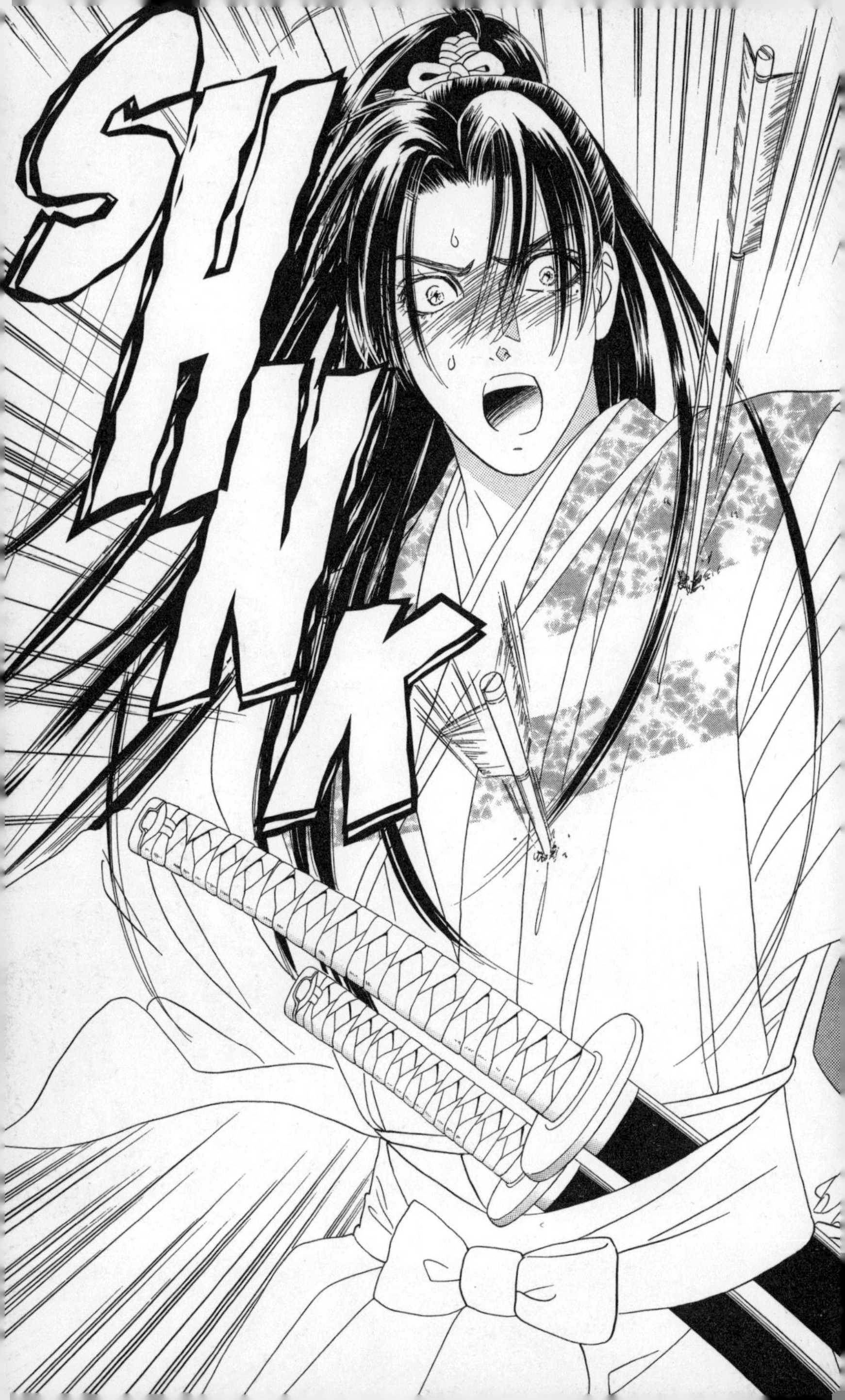
SHAK

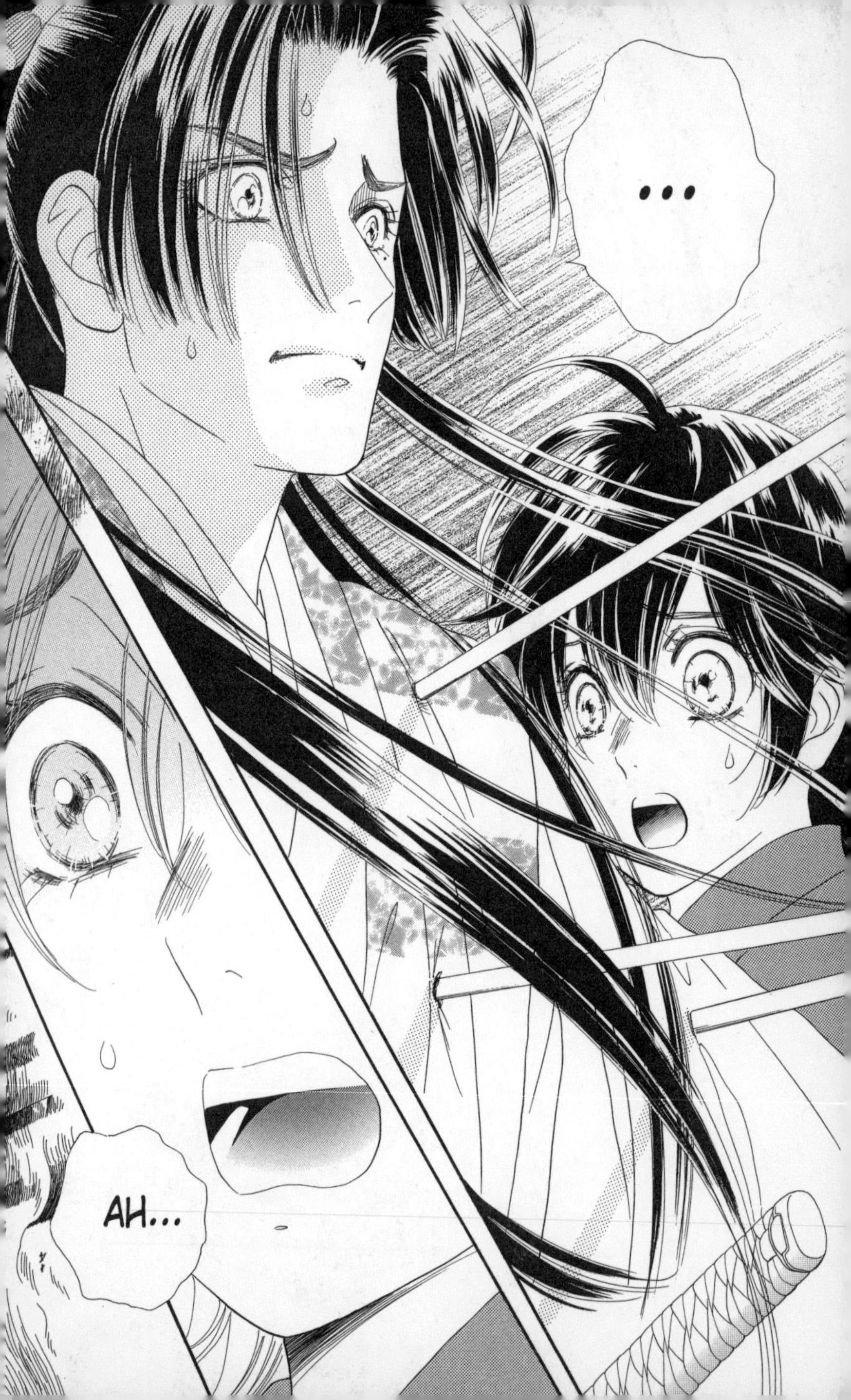
...
AH...

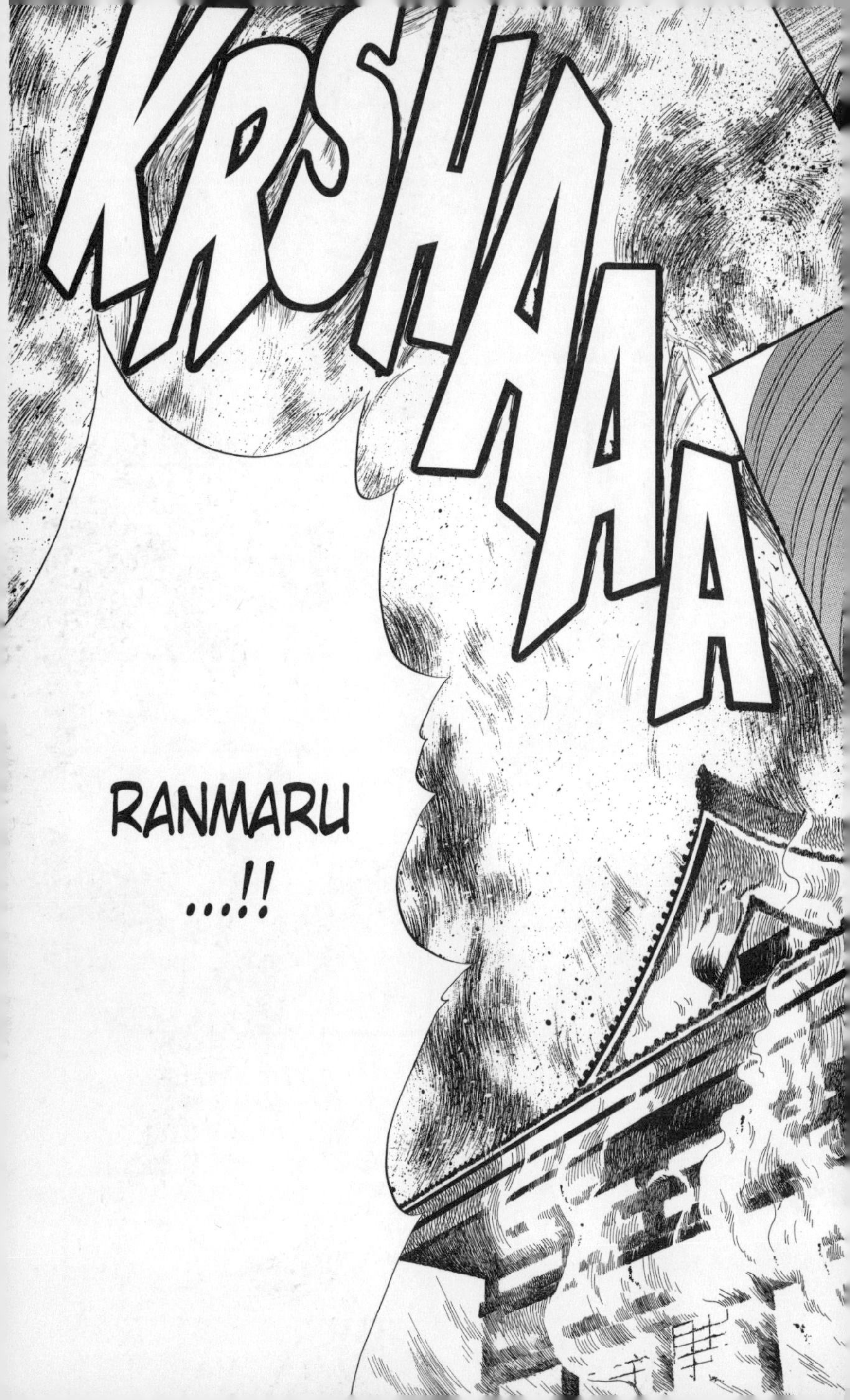
KRSHAAA
RANMARU
...!!

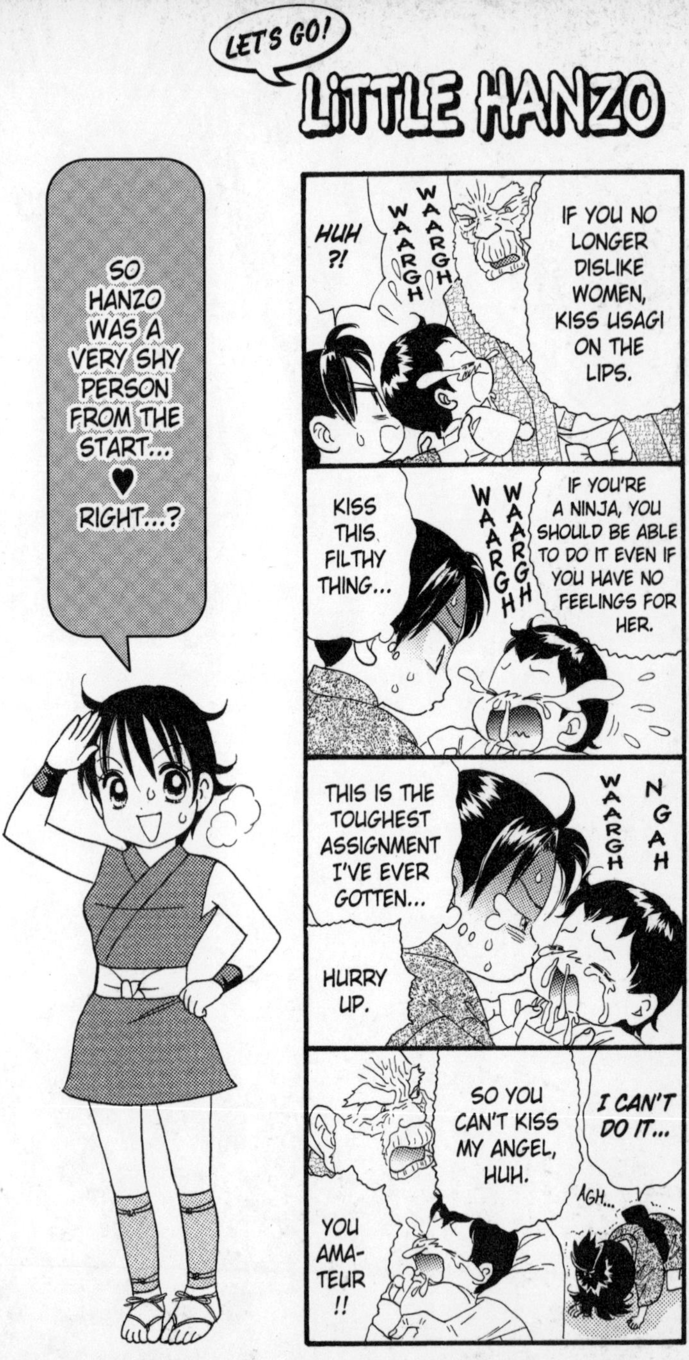
LET'S GO!
LITTLE HANZO
IF YOU NO LONGER DISLIKE WOMEN, KISS USAGI ON THE LIPS.
WAARGH
WAARGH
HUH ?!
IF YOU'RE A NINJA, YOU SHOULD BE ABLE TO DO IT EVEN IF YOU HAVE NO FEELINGS FOR HER.
WAARGH
WAARGH
KISS THIS FILTHY THING...
NGAH
WAARGH
THIS IS THE TOUGHEST ASSIGNMENT I'VE EVER GOTTEN...
HURRY UP.
I CAN'T DO IT...
SO YOU CAN'T KISS MY ANGEL, HUH.
AGH...
YOU AMA-TEUR !!
SO HANZO WAS A VERY SHY PERSON FROM THE START... ♥ RIGHT...?

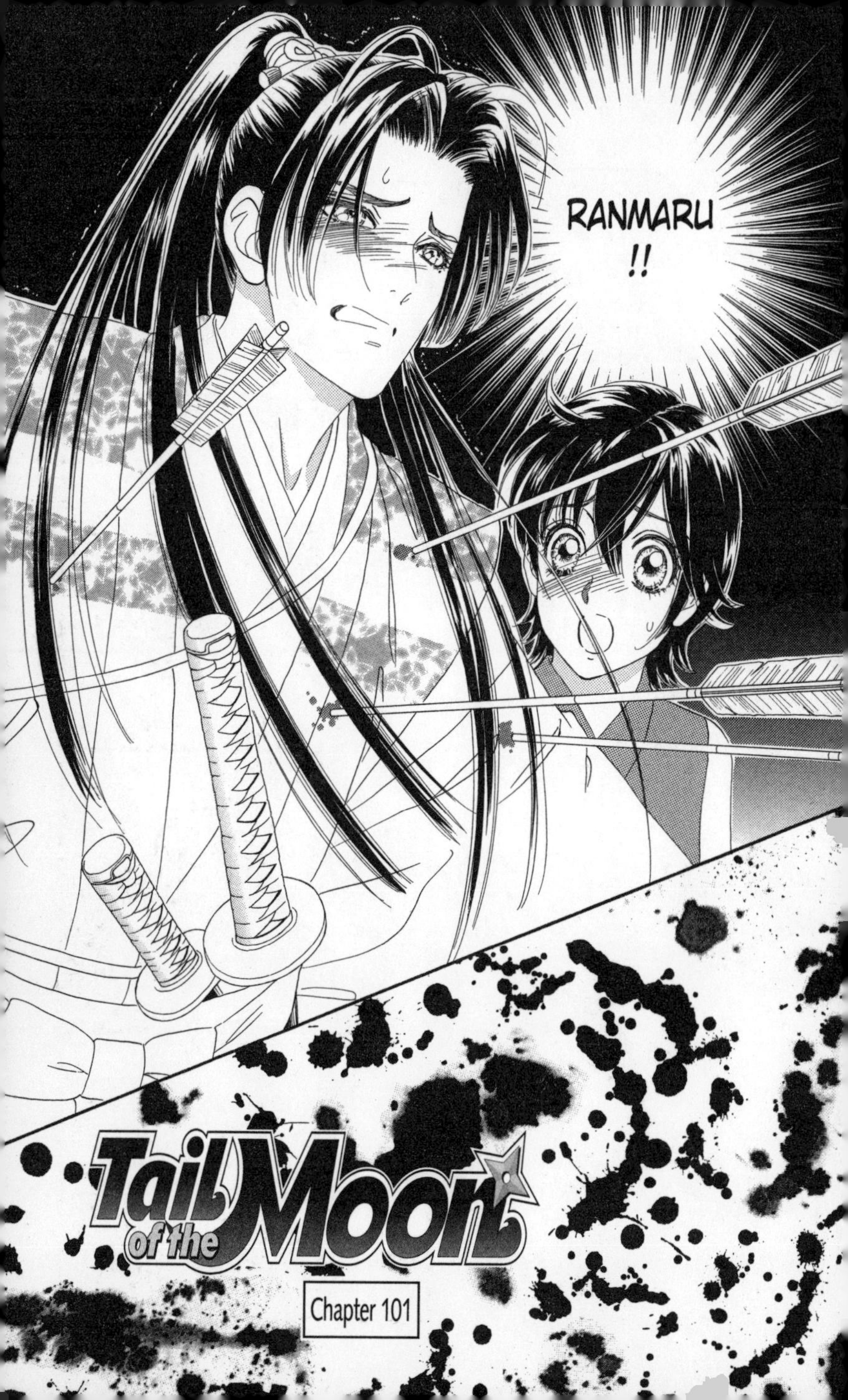
RANMARU
!!
Tail of the Moon
Chapter 101

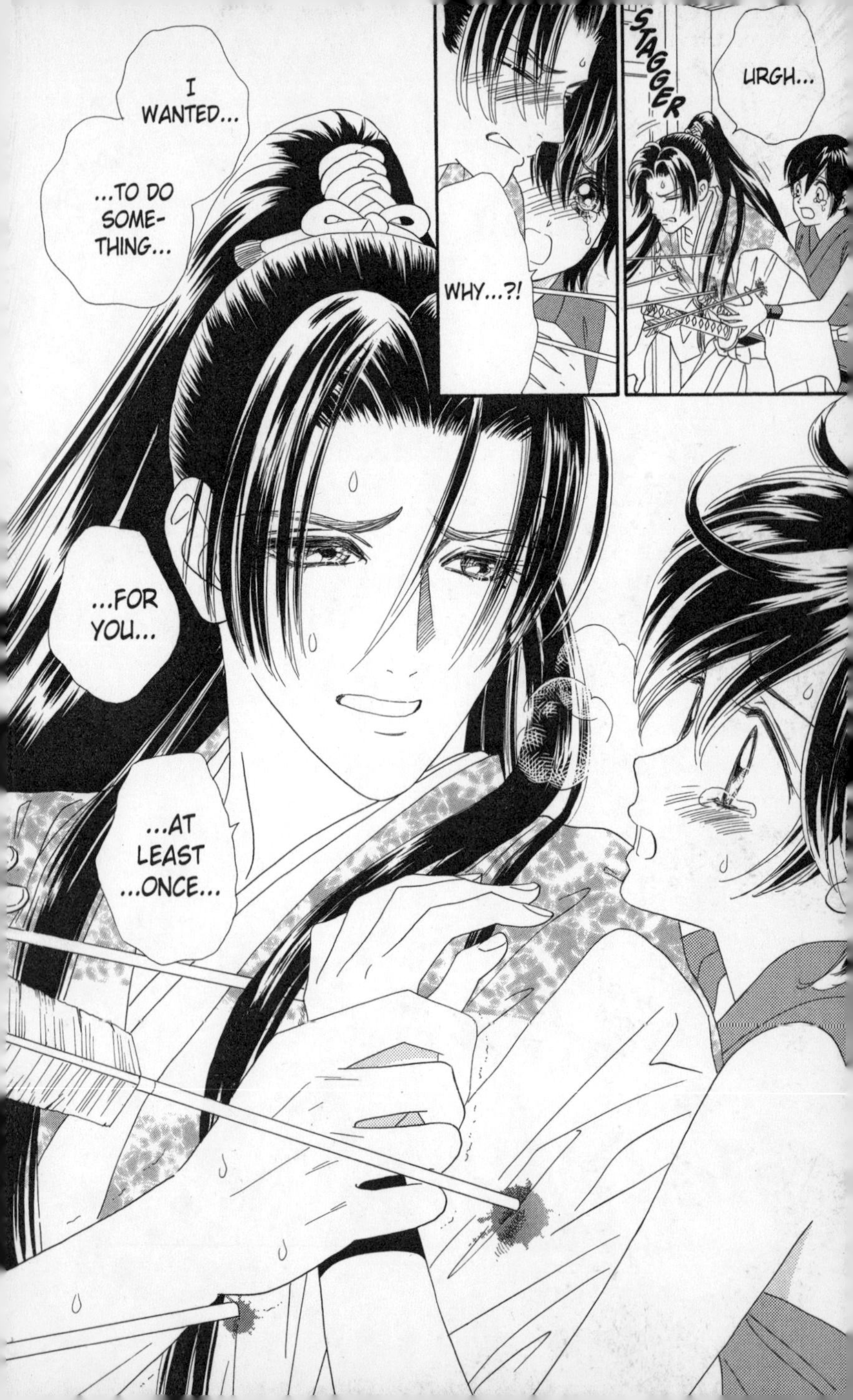
URGH...
STAGGER
WHY...?!
I WANTED...
...TO DO SOME-THING...
...FOR YOU...
...AT LEAST ...ONCE...

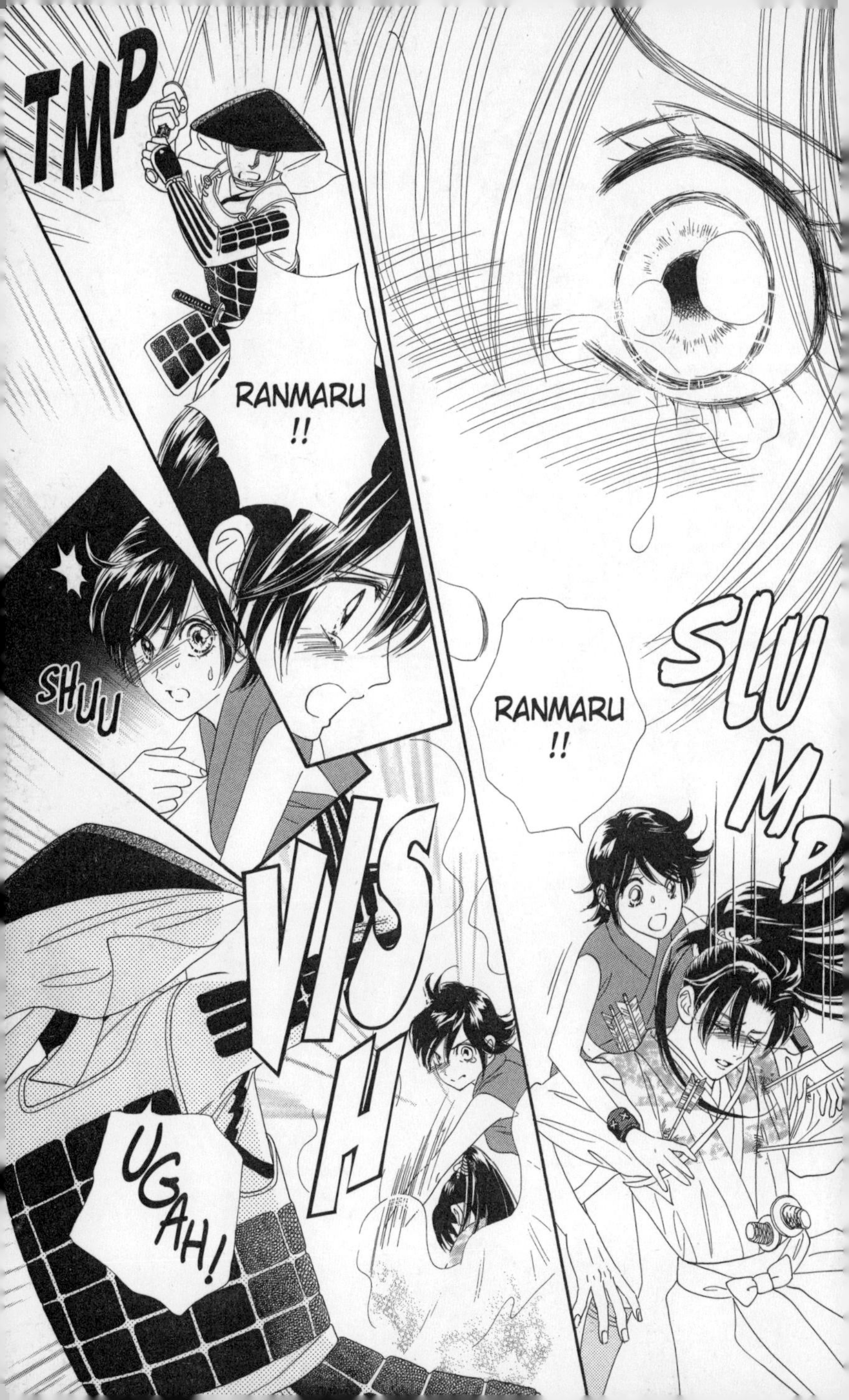
RANMARU !!
SLUMP
TMP
RANMARU !!
SHUU
VISH
UGAH!

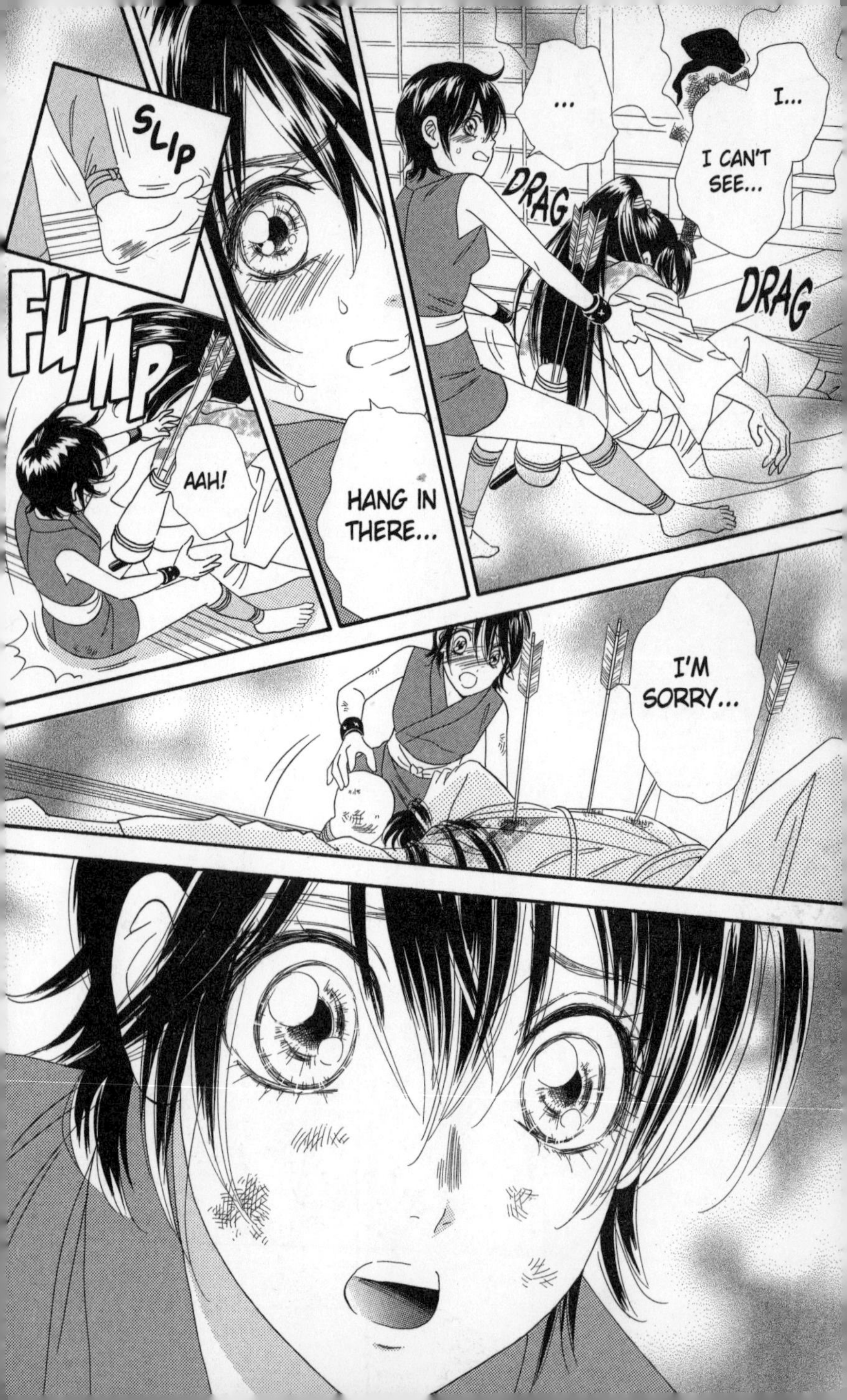

I...
I CAN'T SEE...
...
DRAG
DRAG
HANG IN THERE...
SLIP
FUMP
AAH!
I'M SORRY...

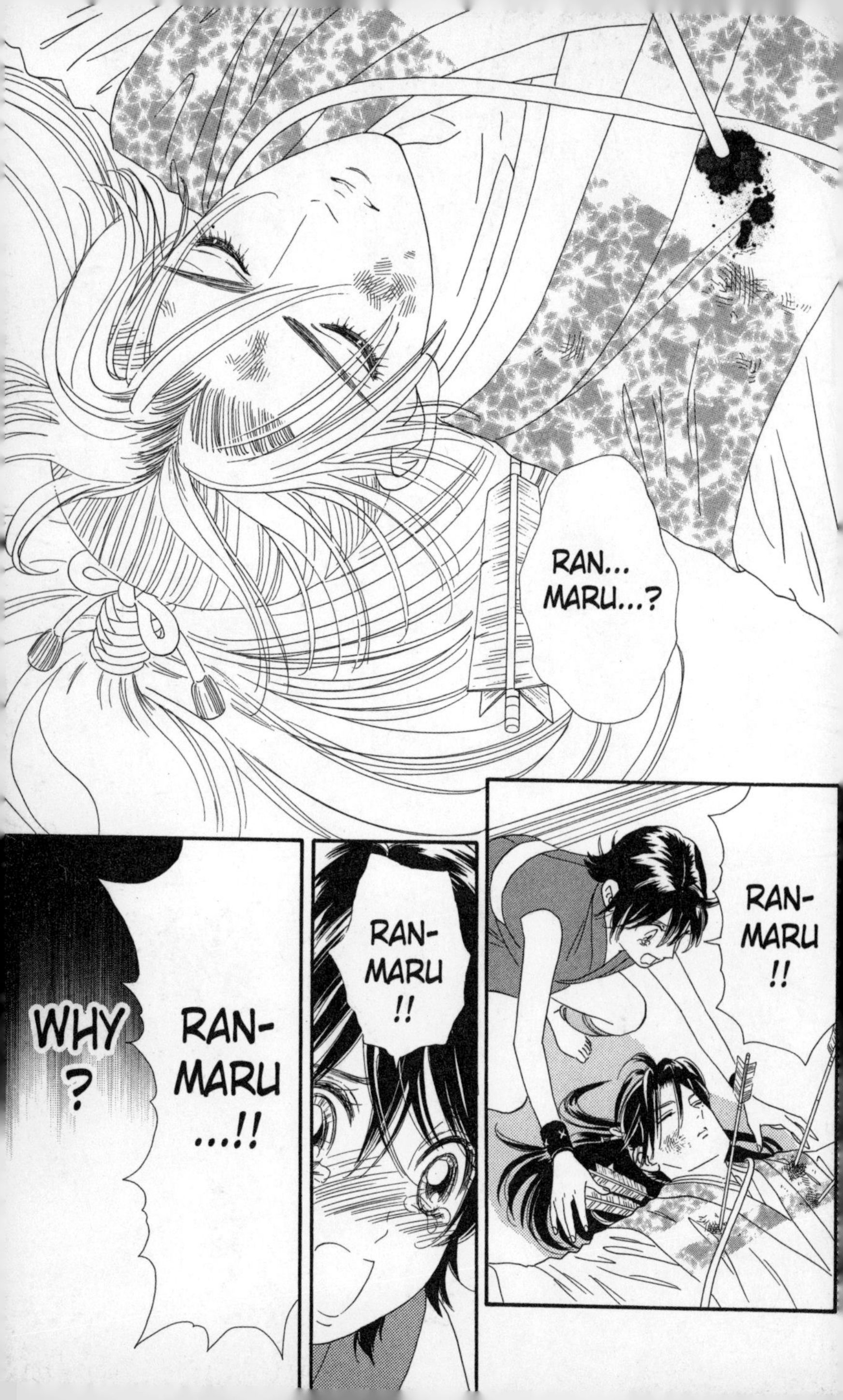
RAN... MARU...?
RAN-MARU!!
RAN-MARU!!
RAN-MARU...!!
WHY?

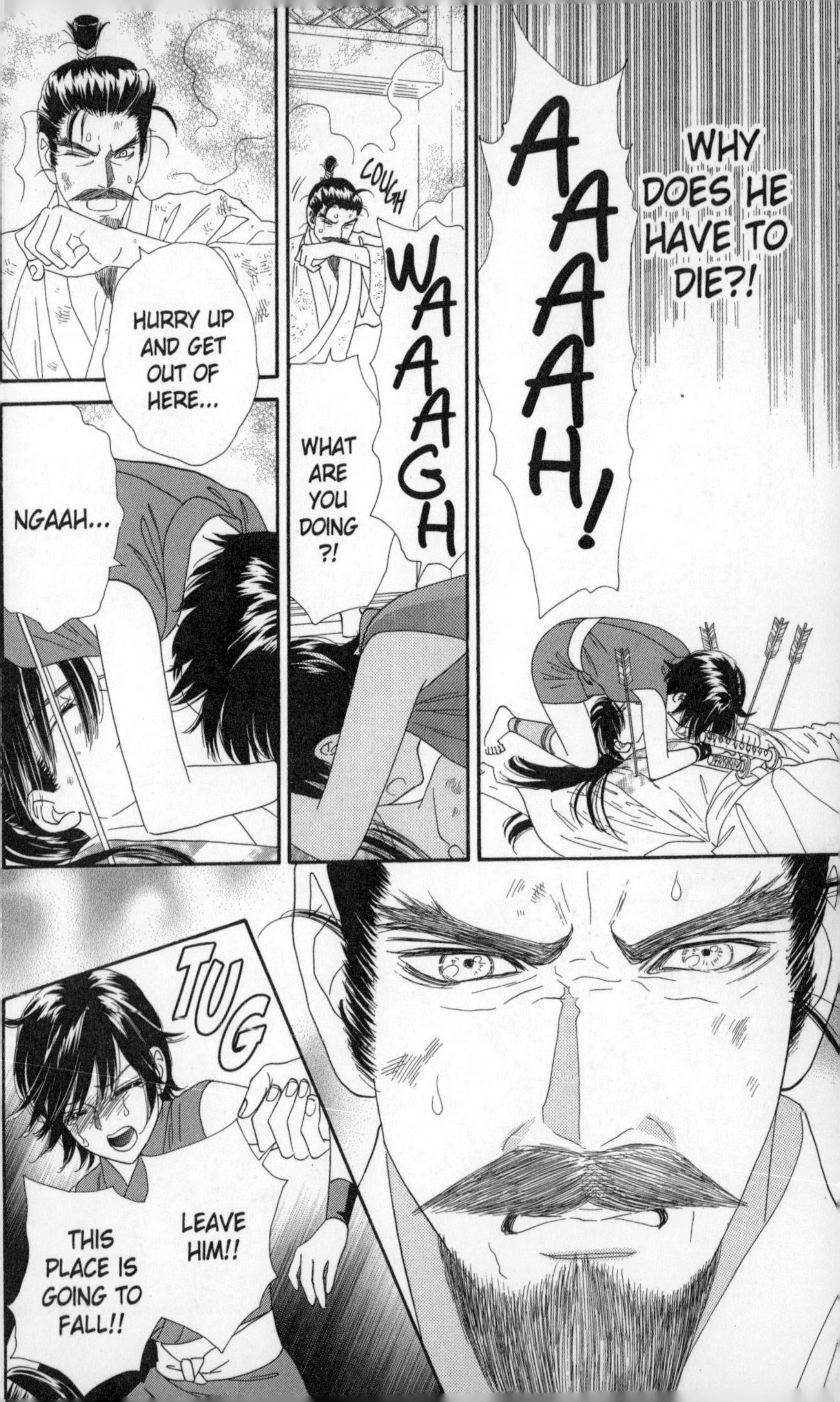

AAAAAH!
WHY DOES HE HAVE TO DIE?!
COUGH
WAAAGH
WHAT ARE YOU DOING?!
HURRY UP AND GET OUT OF HERE...
NGAAH...
TUG
LEAVE HIM!!
THIS PLACE IS GOING TO FALL!!

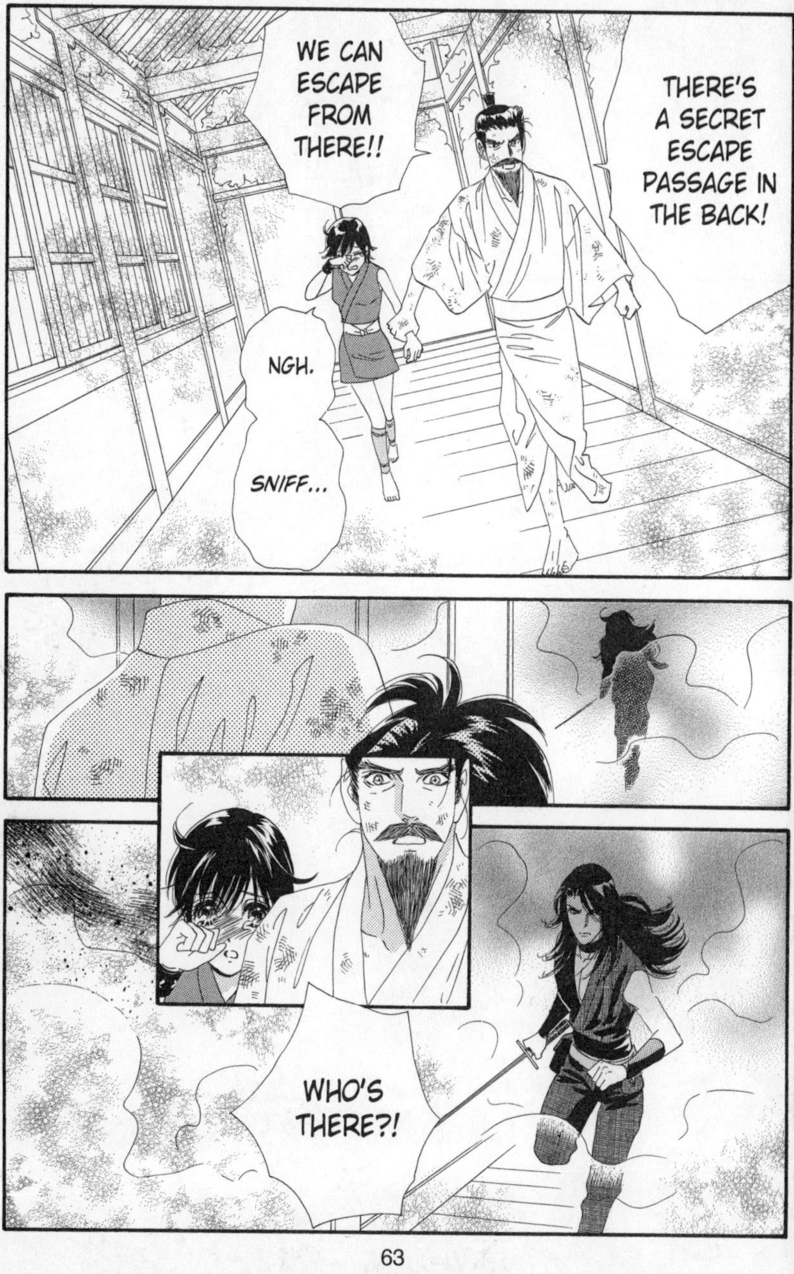
THERE'S A SECRET ESCAPE PASSAGE IN THE BACK!
WE CAN ESCAPE FROM THERE!!
NGH.
SNIFF...
WHO'S THERE?!

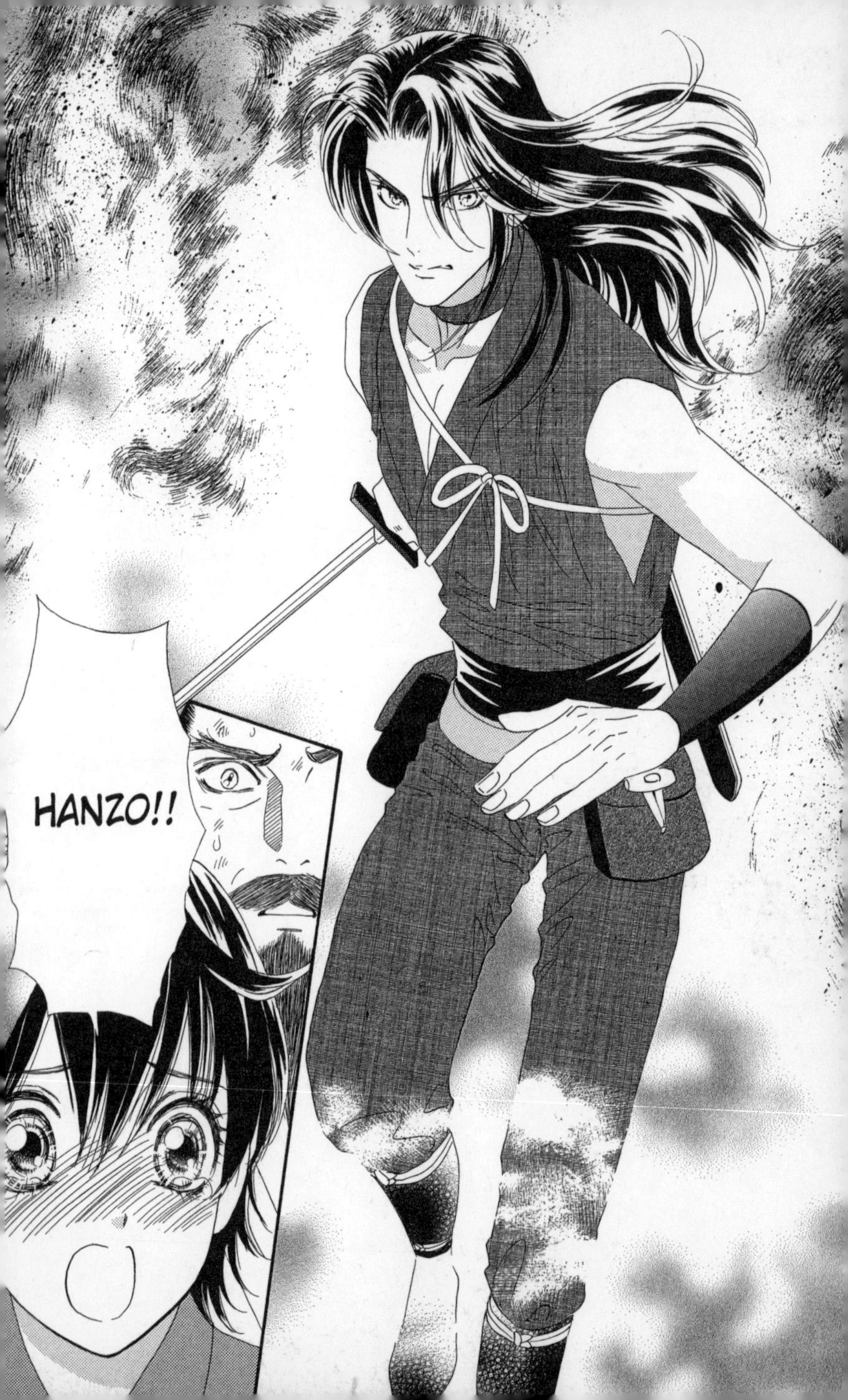
HANZO!!

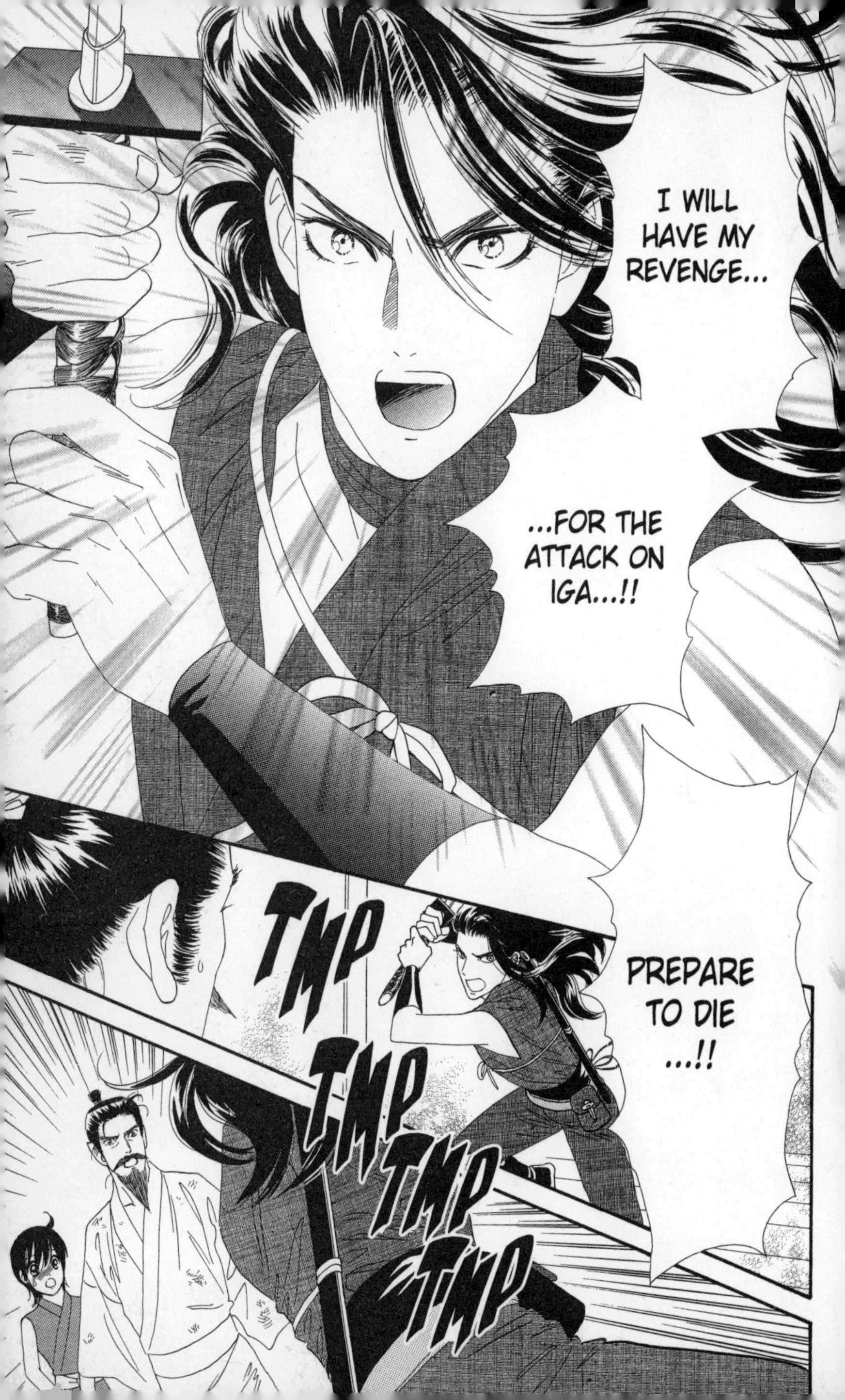
I WILL HAVE MY REVENGE...
...FOR THE ATTACK ON IGA...!!
PREPARE TO DIE ...!!
TMP
TMP
TMP
TMP

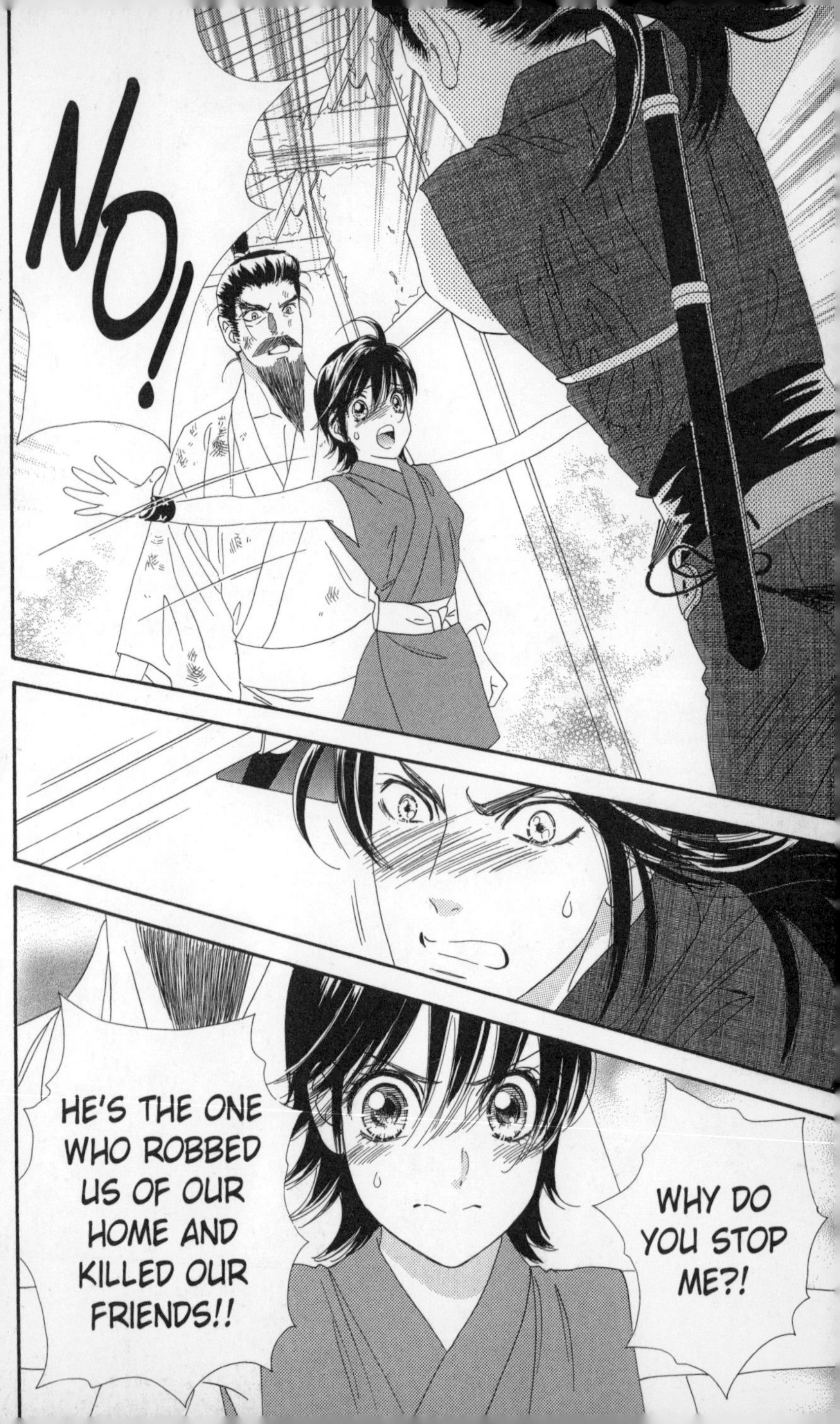
NO!
WHY DO YOU STOP ME?!
HE'S THE ONE WHO ROBBED US OF OUR HOME AND KILLED OUR FRIENDS!!

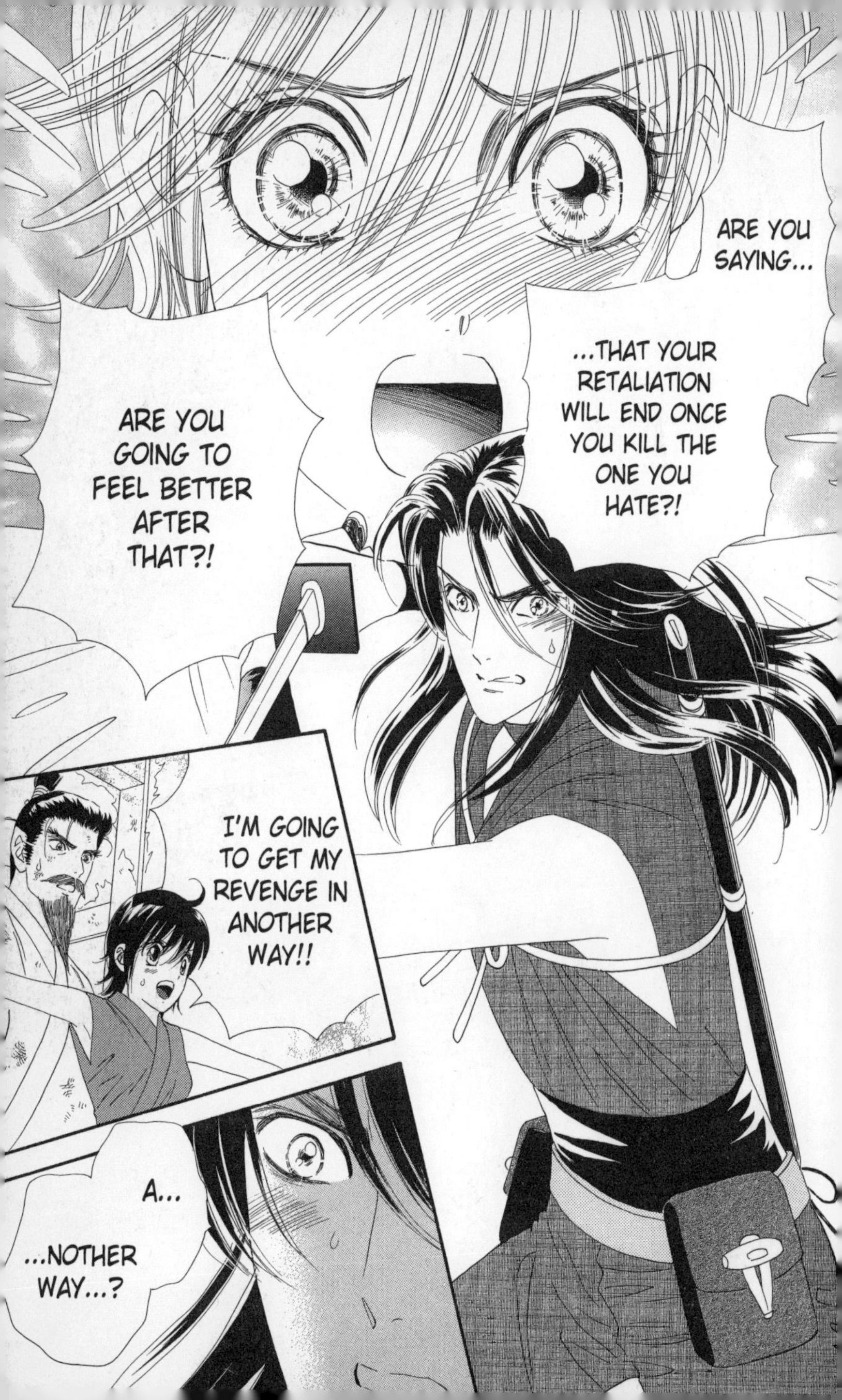
ARE YOU SAYING...
...THAT YOUR RETALIATION WILL END ONCE YOU KILL THE ONE YOU HATE?!
ARE YOU GOING TO FEEL BETTER AFTER THAT?!
I'M GOING TO GET MY REVENGE IN ANOTHER WAY!!
A...
...NOTHER WAY...?

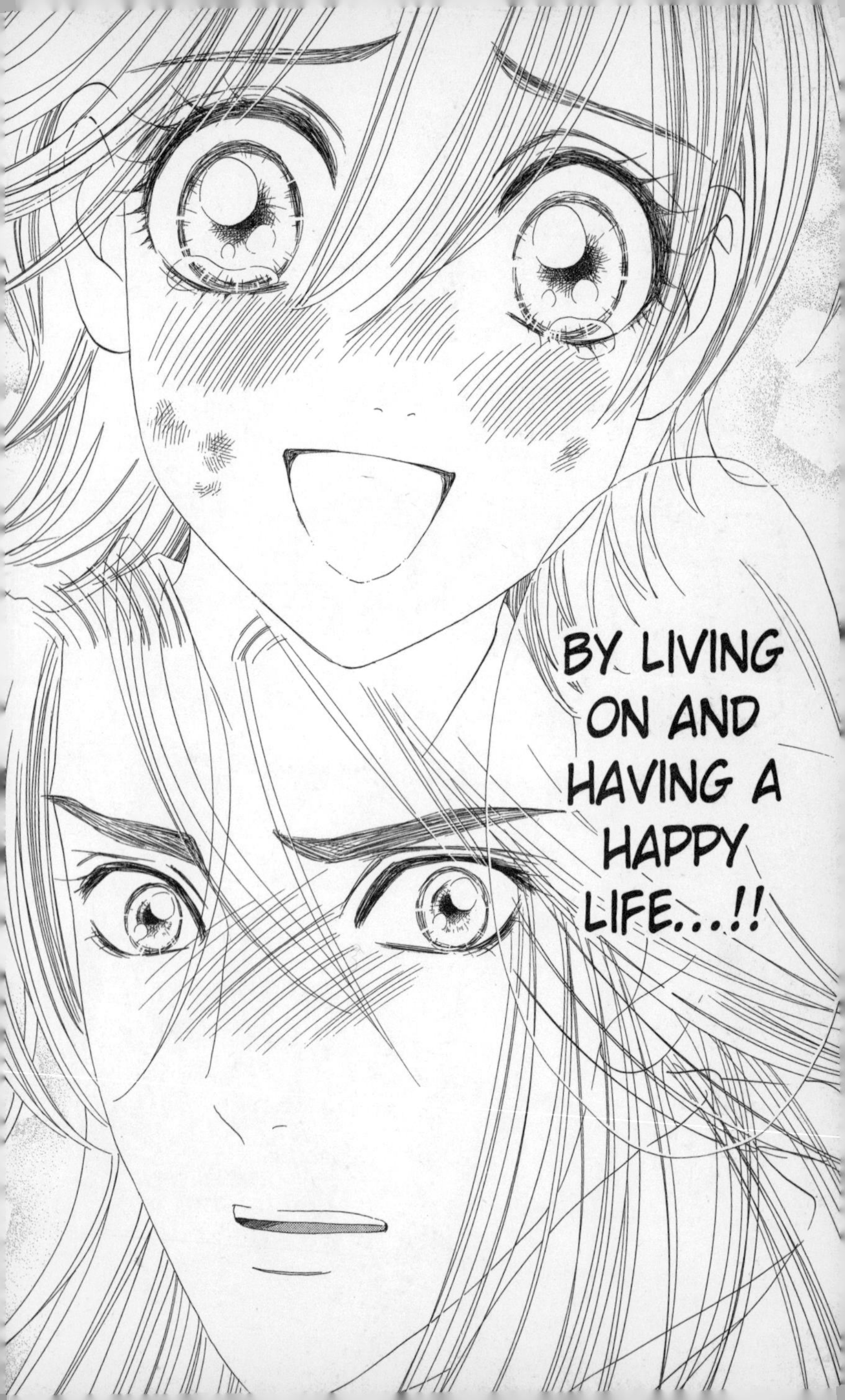
BY LIVING ON AND HAVING A HAPPY LIFE...!!

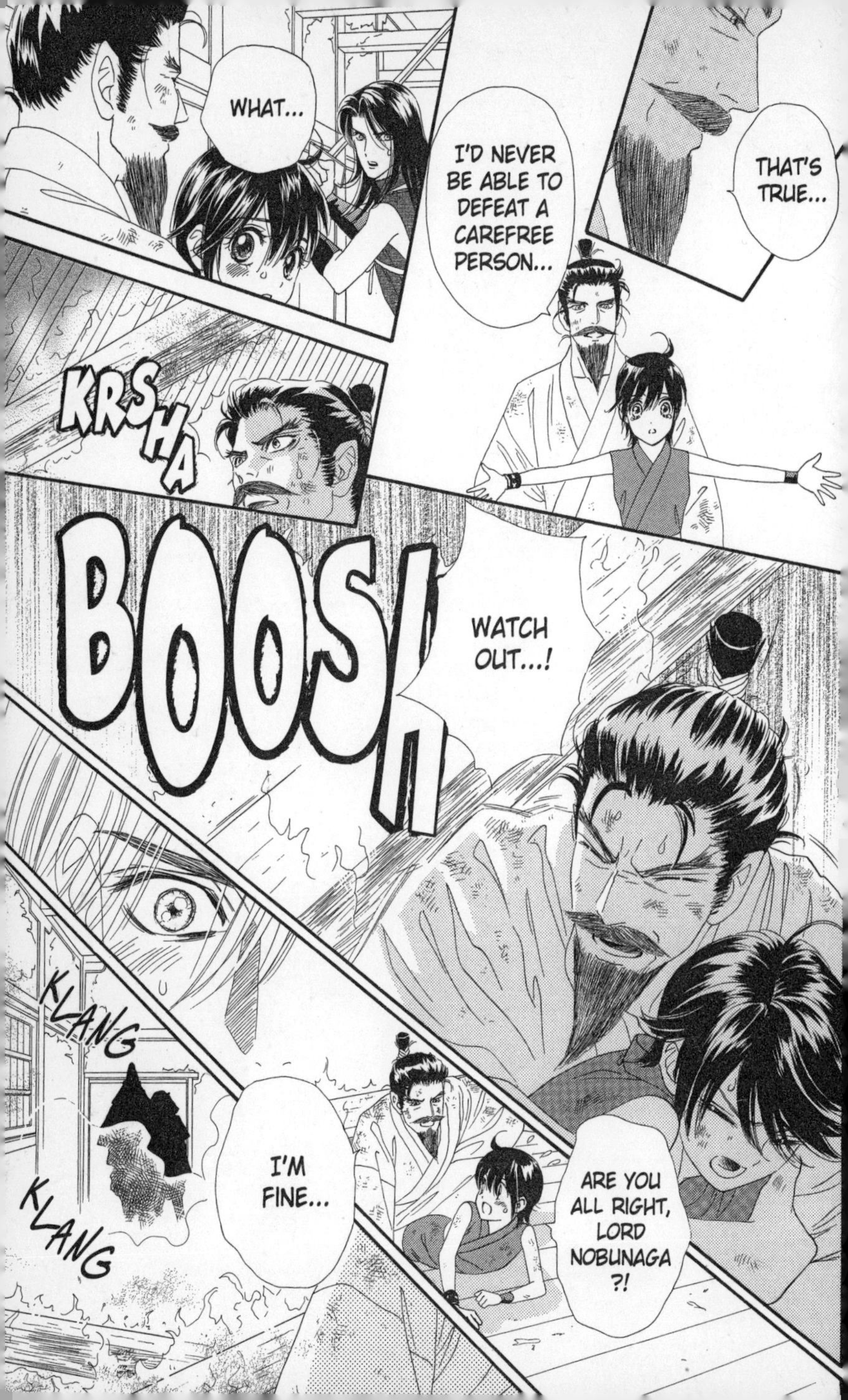
THAT'S TRUE...
I'D NEVER BE ABLE TO DEFEAT A CAREFREE PERSON...
WHAT...
KRSHA
BOOSH
WATCH OUT...!
ARE YOU ALL RIGHT, LORD NOBUNAGA ?!
I'M FINE...
KLANG
KLANG

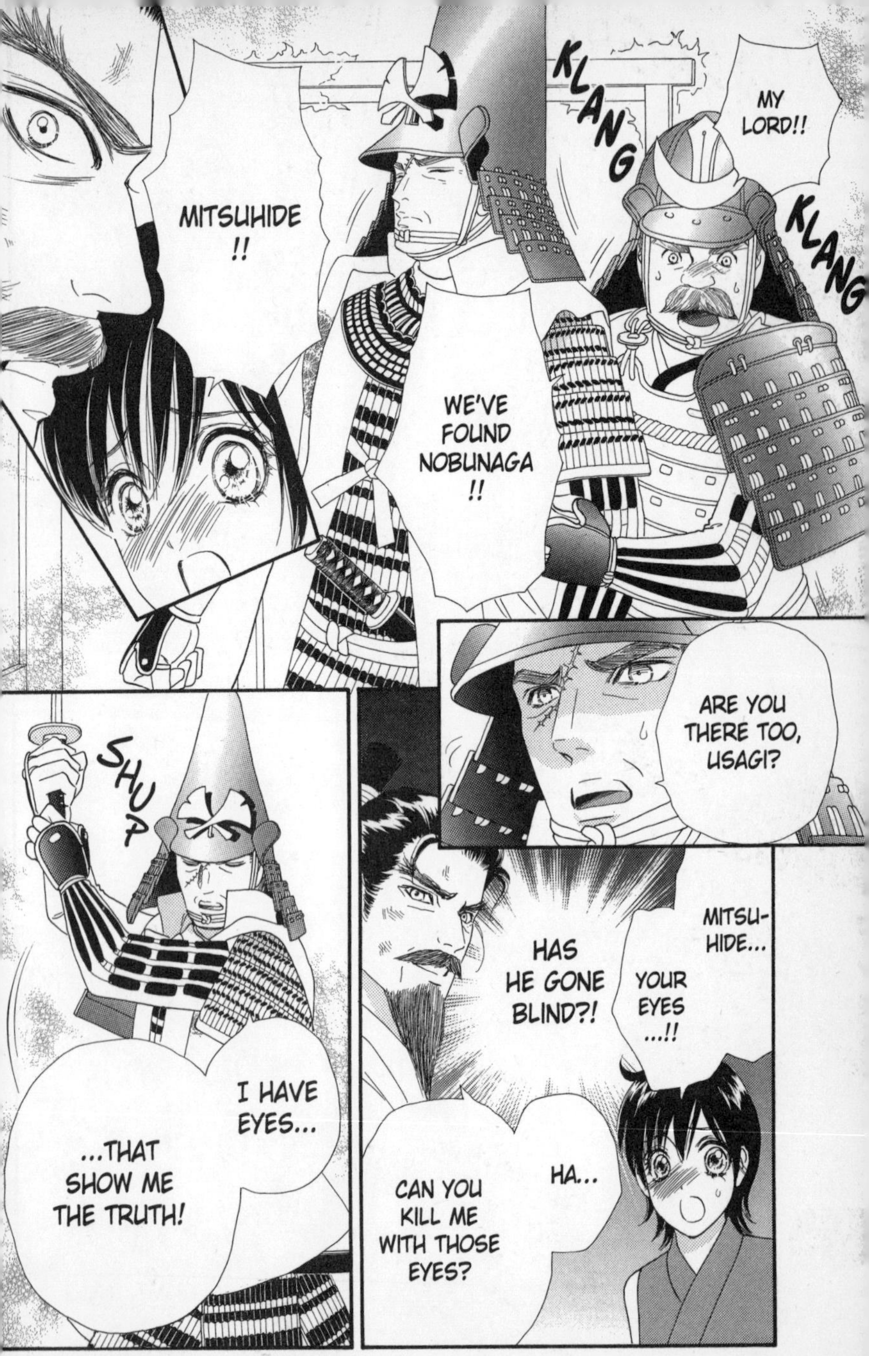
KLANG
MY LORD!!
KLANG
WE'VE FOUND NOBUNAGA!!
MITSUHIDE!!
ARE YOU THERE TOO, USAGI?
MITSU-HIDE...
YOUR EYES...!!
HAS HE GONE BLIND?!
HA...
CAN YOU KILL ME WITH THOSE EYES?
SHUP
I HAVE EYES...
...THAT SHOW ME THE TRUTH!

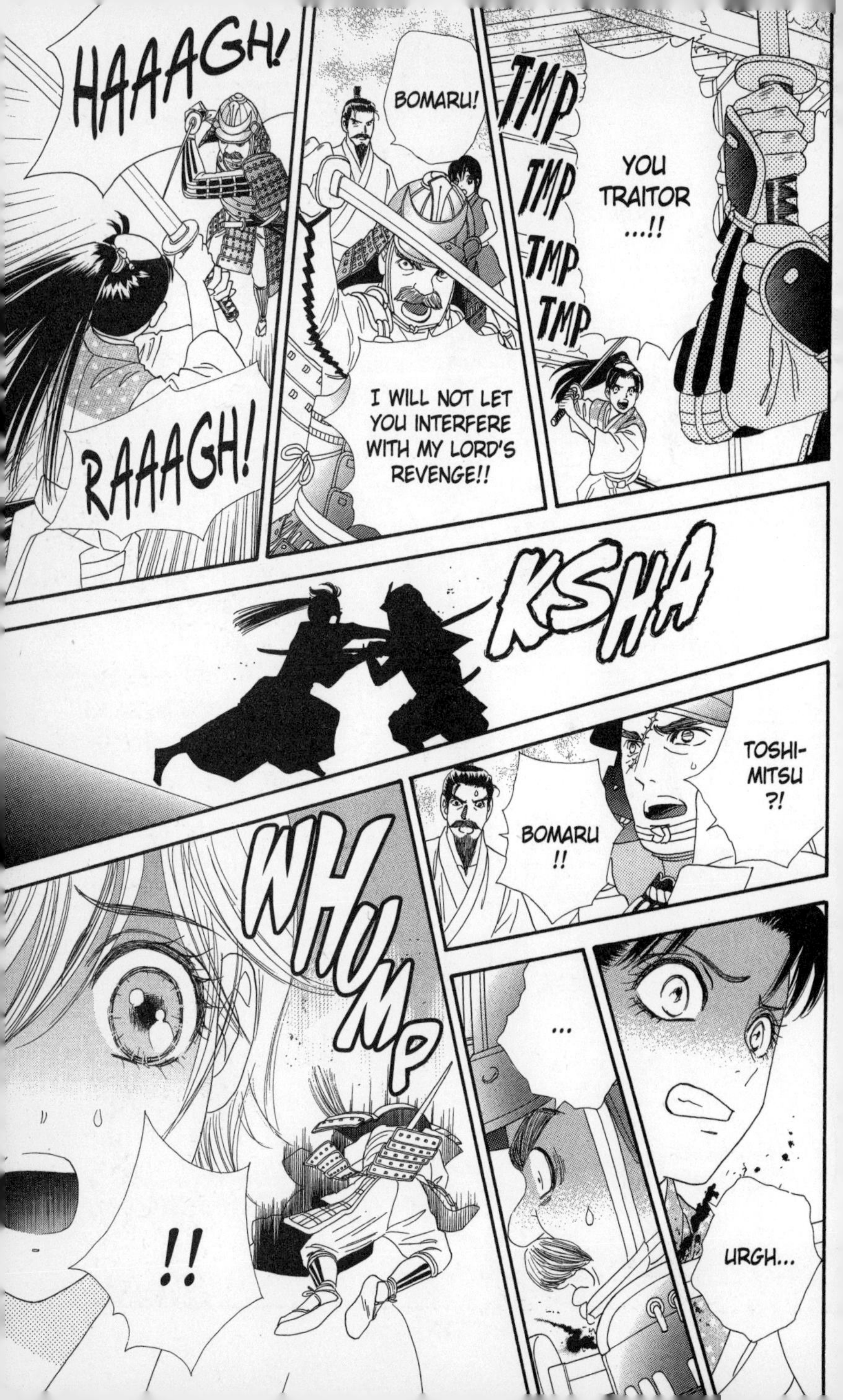
TMP
TMP
TMP
TMP
YOU TRAITOR ...!!
BOMARU!
I WILL NOT LET YOU INTERFERE WITH MY LORD'S REVENGE!!
HAAAGH!
RAAAGH!
KSHA
TOSHI-MITSU ?!
BOMARU !!
URGH...
...
WHUMP
!!

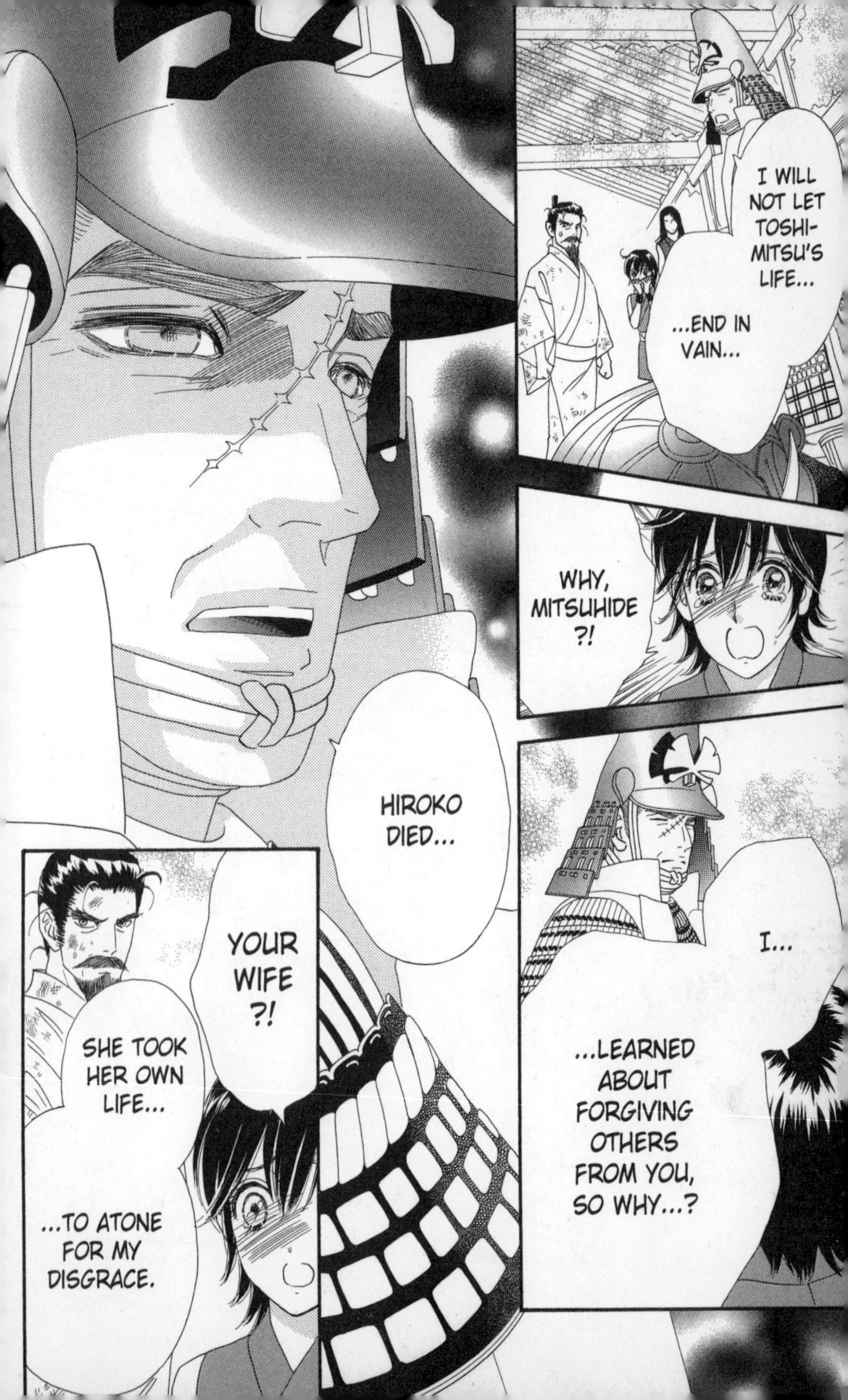

I WILL NOT LET TOSHI-MITSU'S LIFE...
...END IN VAIN...
WHY, MITSUHIDE ?!
HIROKO DIED...
I...
...LEARNED ABOUT FORGIVING OTHERS FROM YOU, SO WHY...?
YOUR WIFE ?!
SHE TOOK HER OWN LIFE...
...TO ATONE FOR MY DISGRACE.

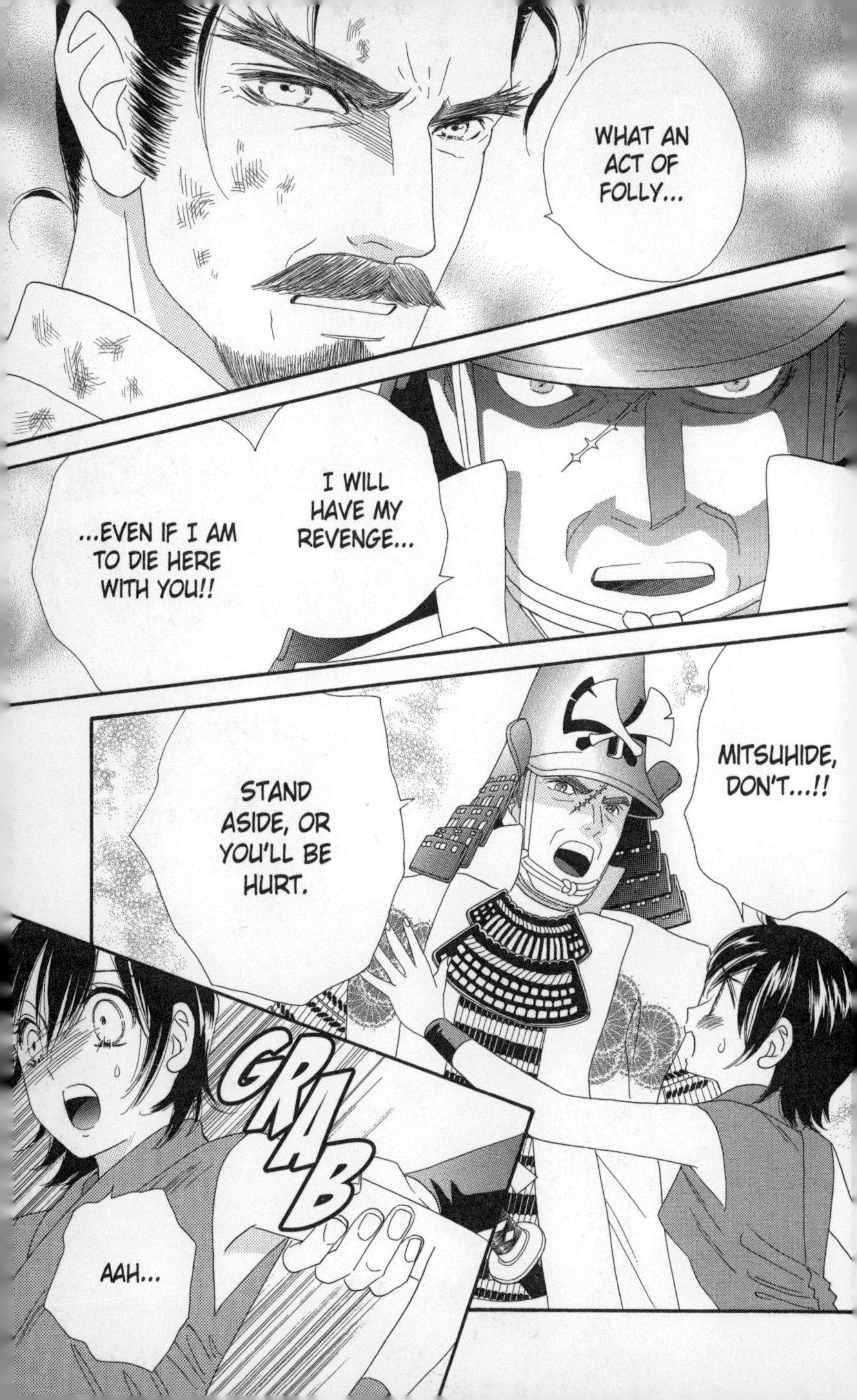
WHAT AN ACT OF FOLLY...
I WILL HAVE MY REVENGE...
...EVEN IF I AM TO DIE HERE WITH YOU!!
MITSUHIDE, DON'T...!!
STAND ASIDE, OR YOU'LL BE HURT.
GRAB
AAH...

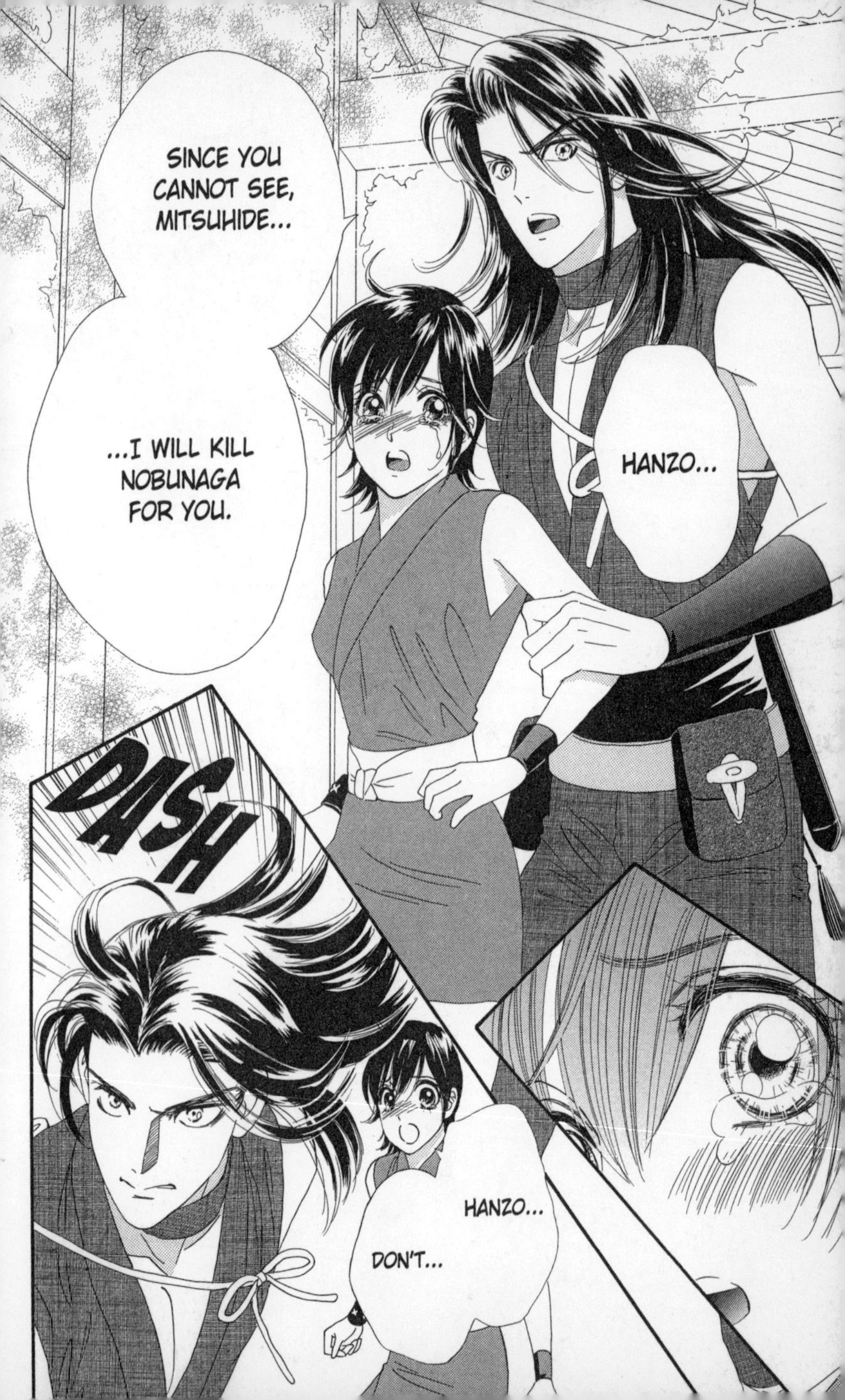
SINCE YOU CANNOT SEE, MITSUHIDE...
...I WILL KILL NOBUNAGA FOR YOU.
HANZO...
DASH
HANZO...
DON'T...

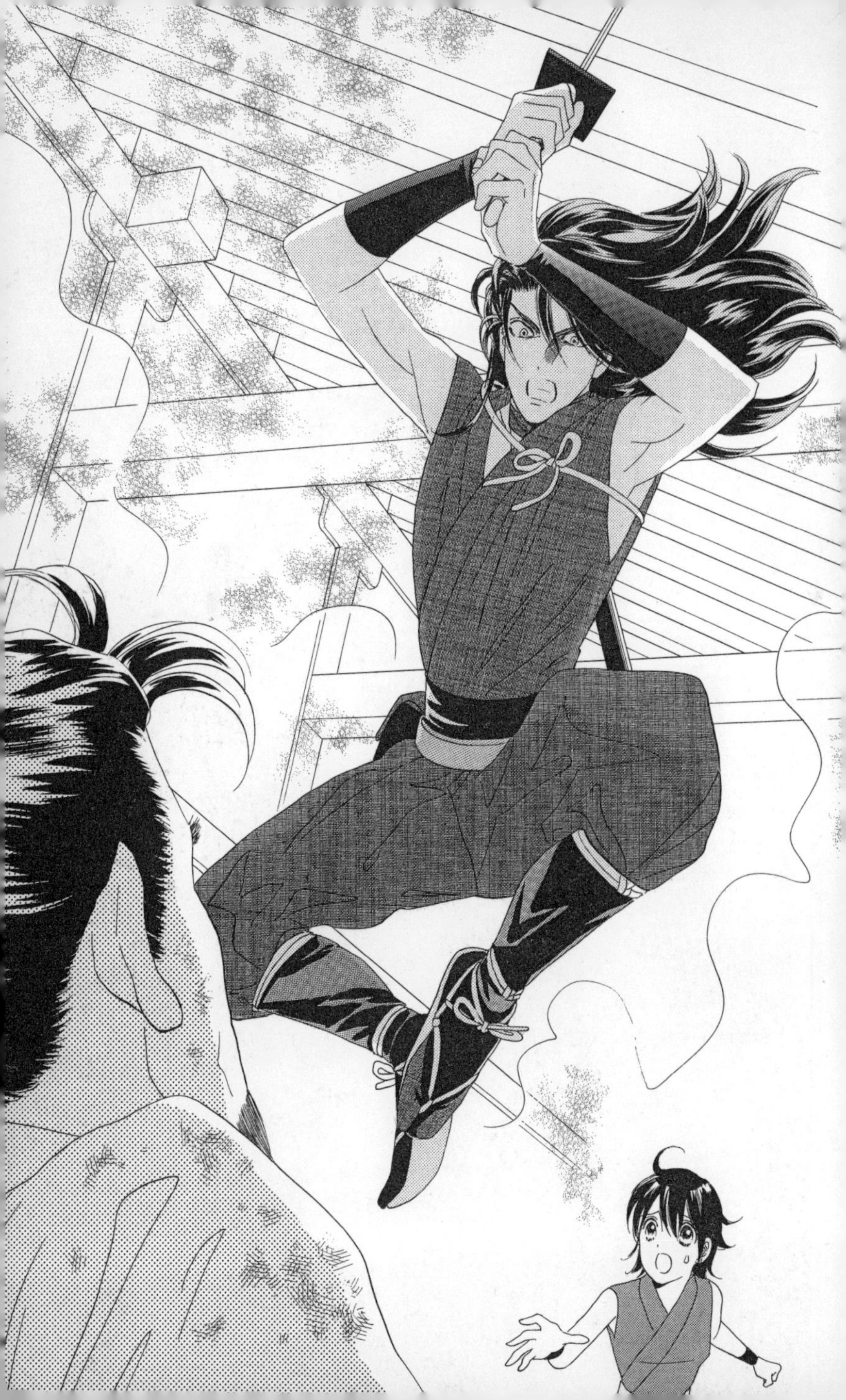

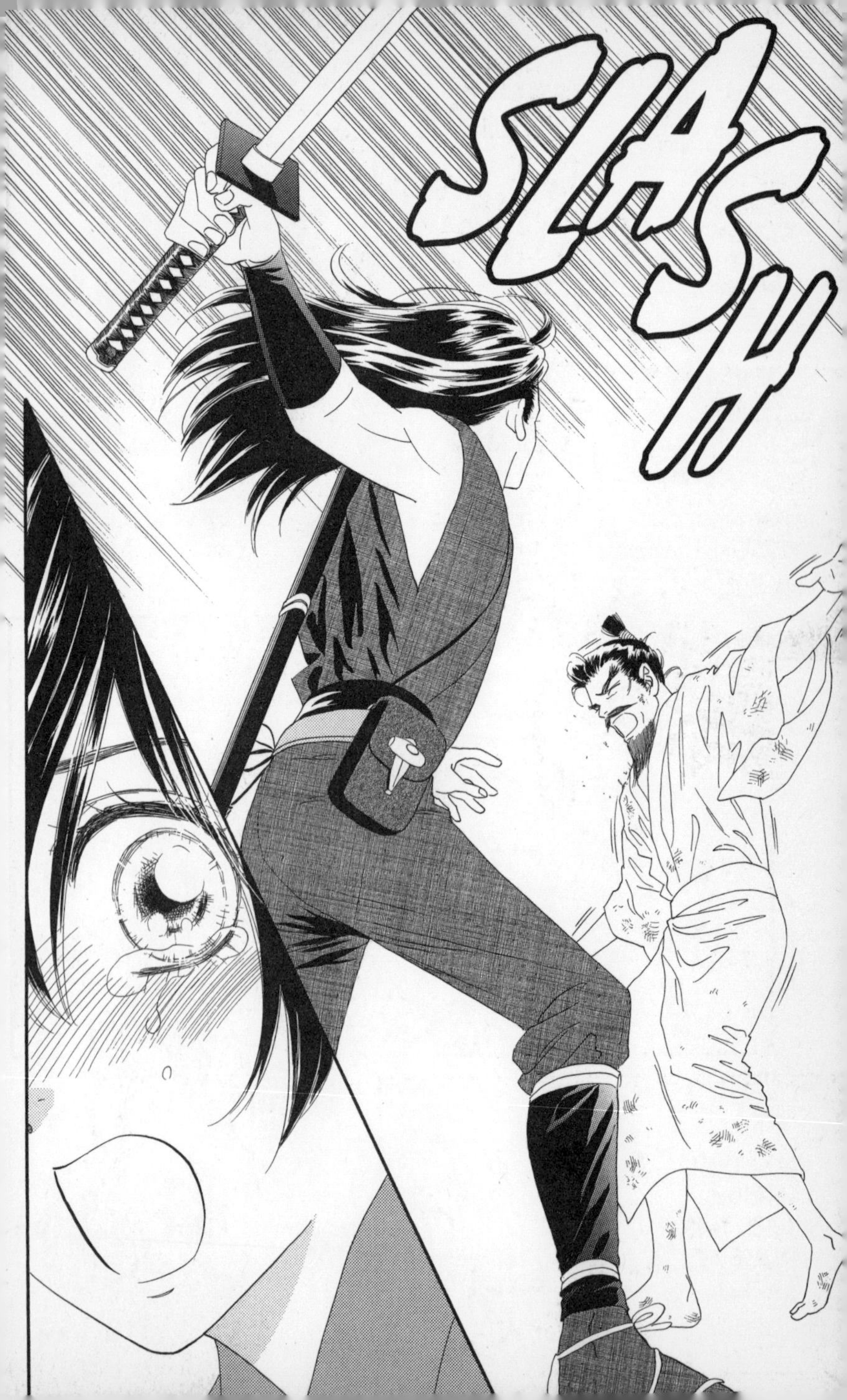
SLASH

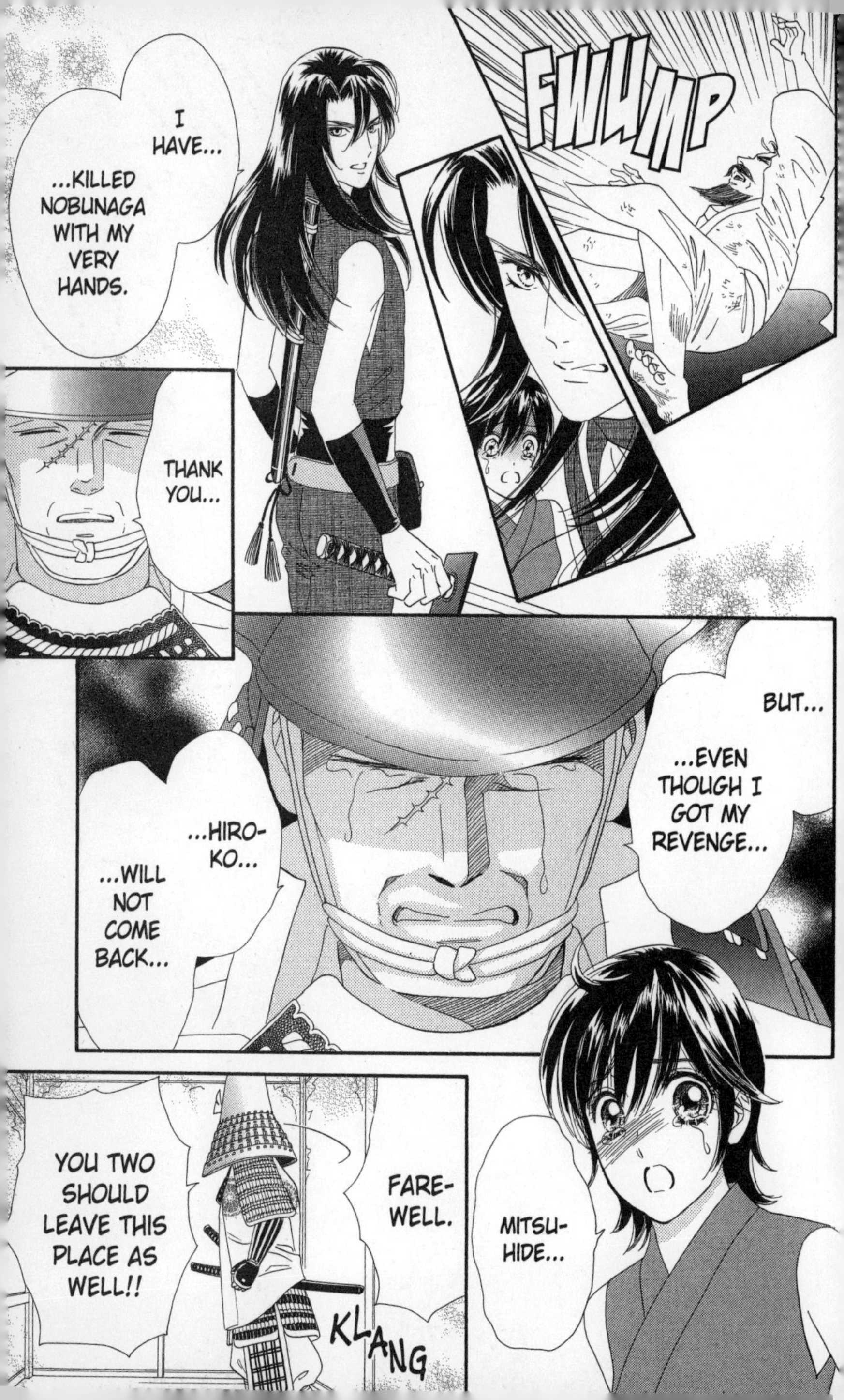
FWUMP
I HAVE...
...KILLED NOBUNAGA WITH MY VERY HANDS.
THANK YOU...
BUT...
...EVEN THOUGH I GOT MY REVENGE...
...HIRO-KO...
...WILL NOT COME BACK...
MITSU-HIDE...
FARE-WELL.
YOU TWO SHOULD LEAVE THIS PLACE AS WELL!!
KLANG

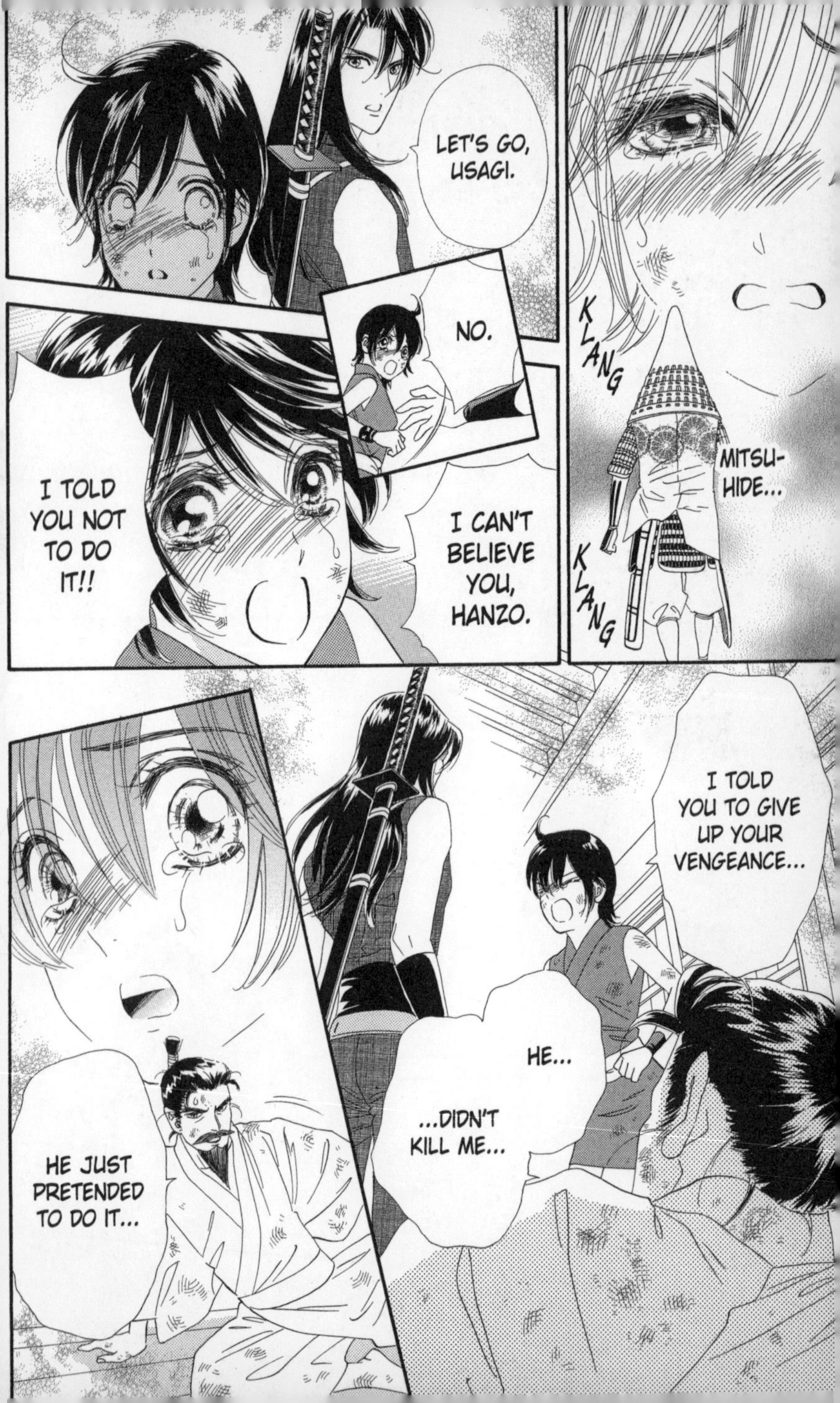
KLANG
MITSU-HIDE...
KLANG
LET'S GO, USAGI.
NO.
I CAN'T BELIEVE YOU, HANZO.
I TOLD YOU NOT TO DO IT!!
I TOLD YOU TO GIVE UP YOUR VENGEANCE...
HE...
...DIDN'T KILL ME...
HE JUST PRETENDED TO DO IT...

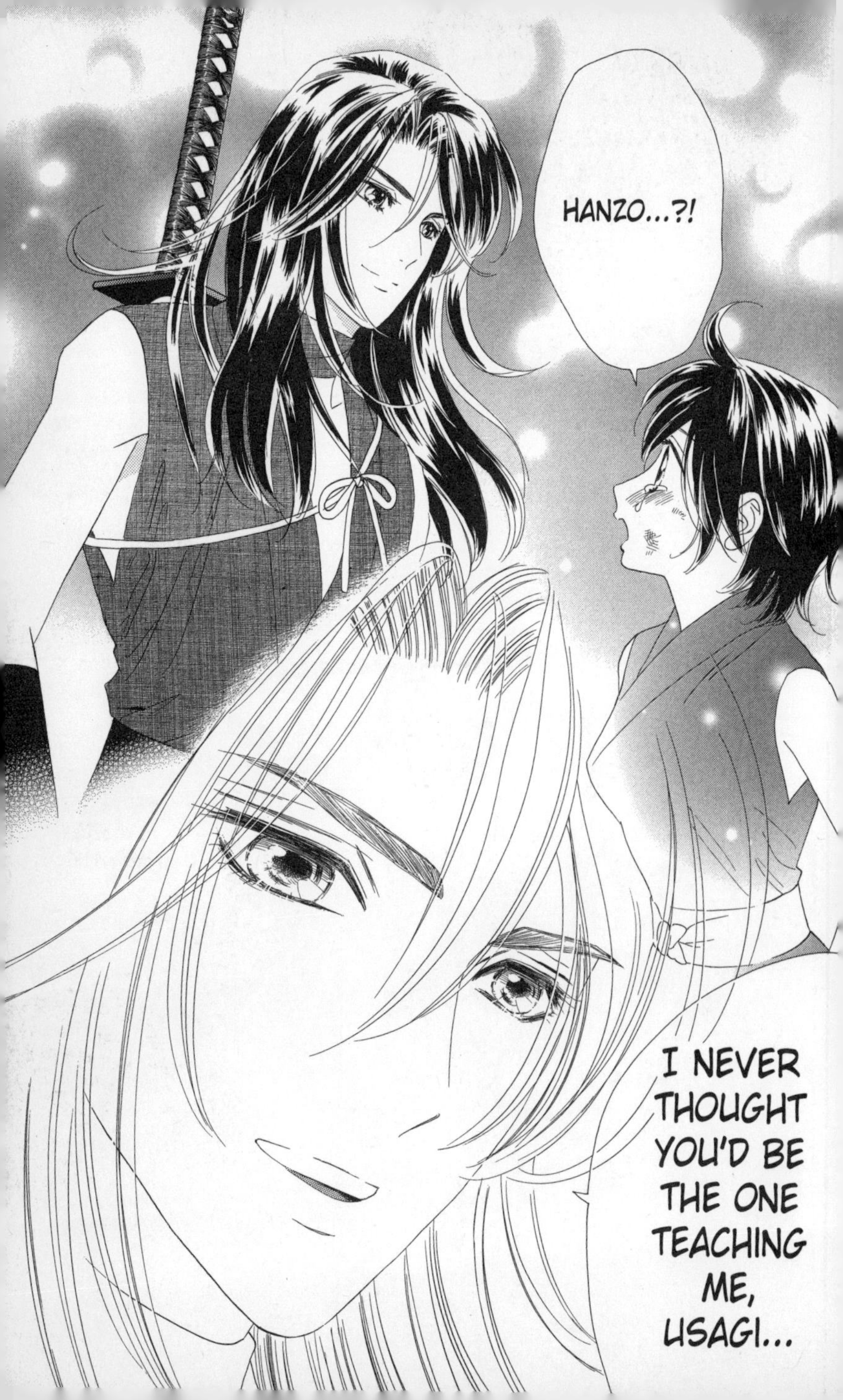
HANZO...?!
I NEVER THOUGHT YOU'D BE THE ONE TEACHING ME, USAGI...

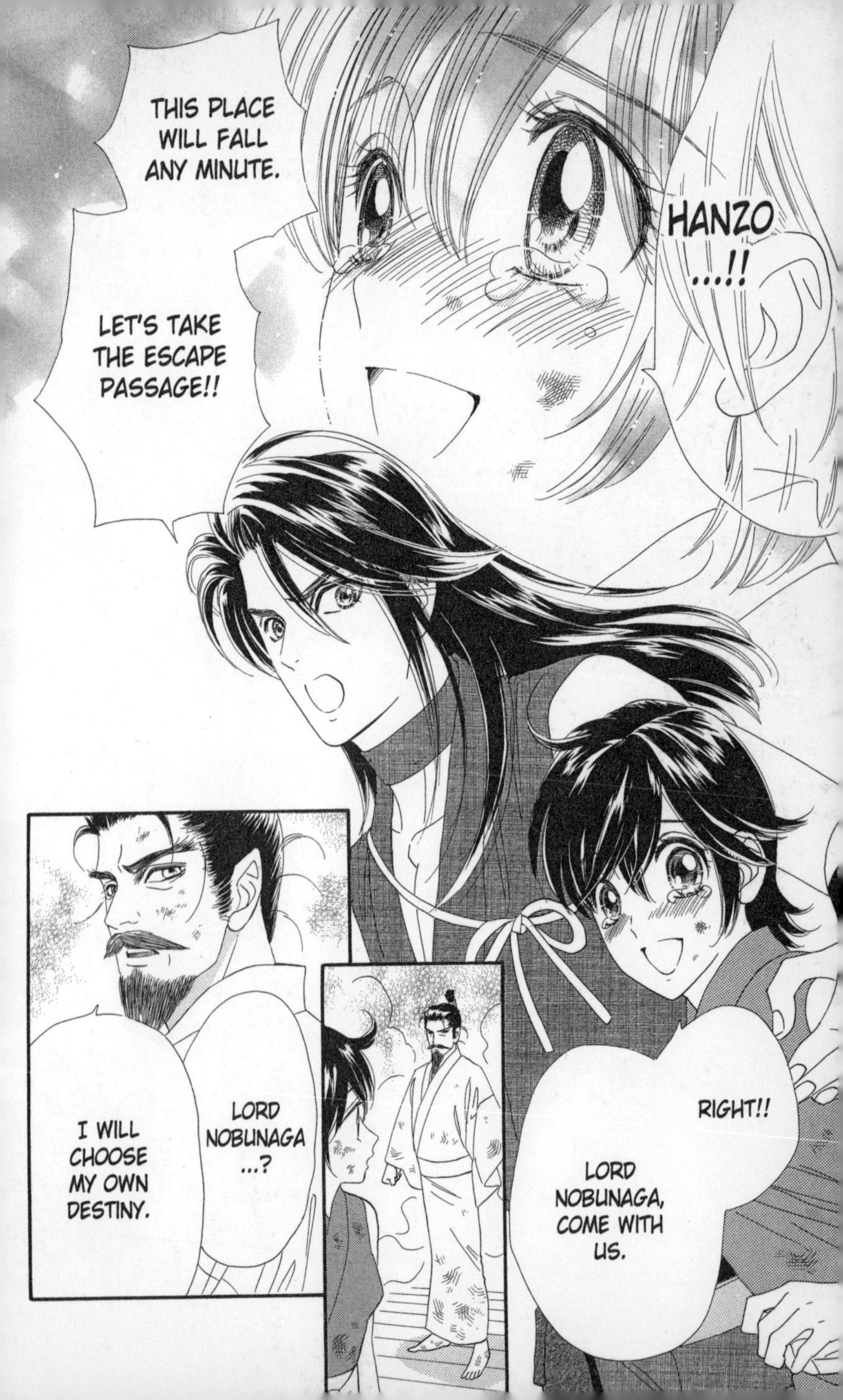
HANZO ...!!
THIS PLACE WILL FALL ANY MINUTE.
LET'S TAKE THE ESCAPE PASSAGE!!
RIGHT!!
LORD NOBUNAGA, COME WITH US.
LORD NOBUNAGA ...?
I WILL CHOOSE MY OWN DESTINY.

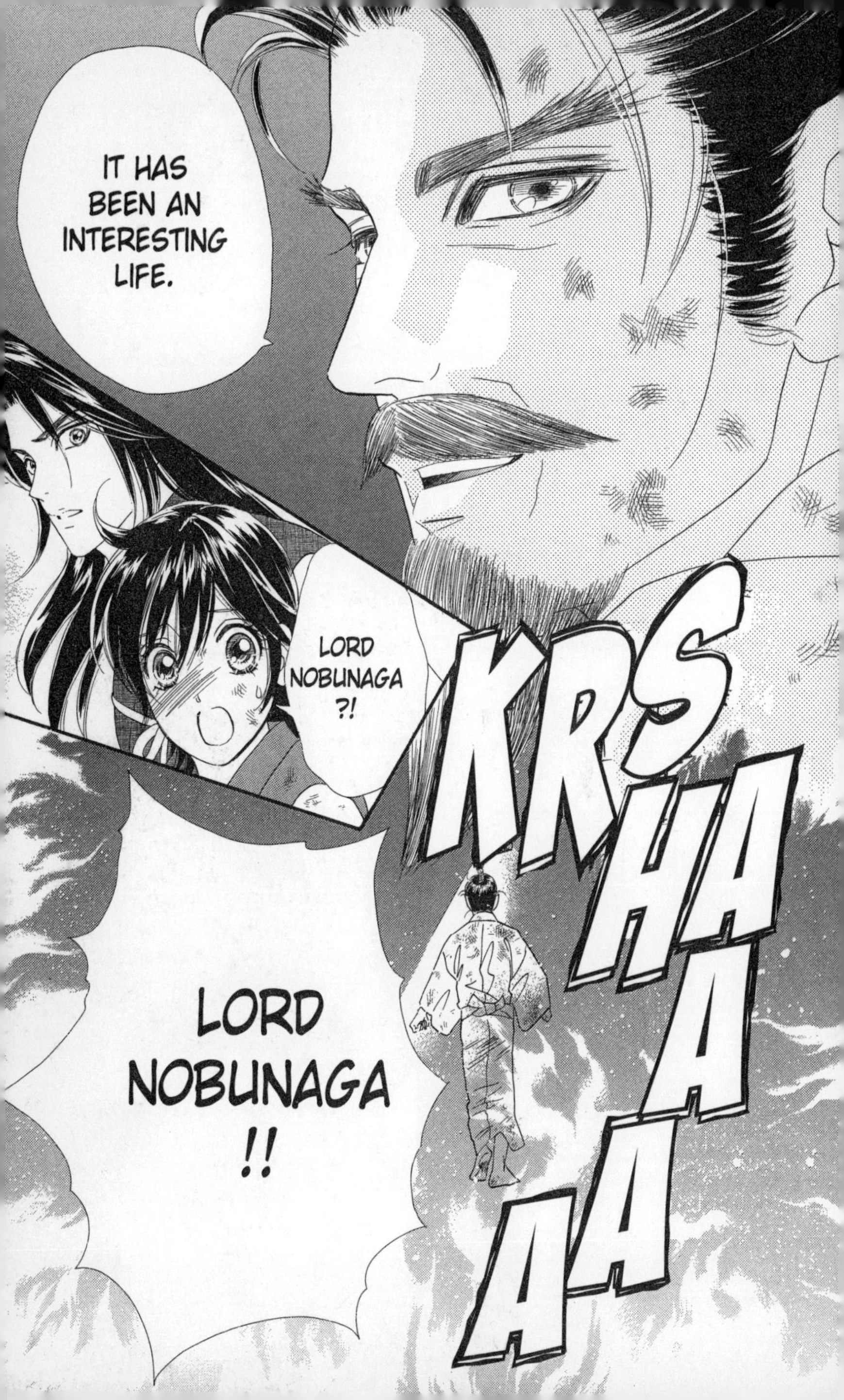
IT HAS BEEN AN INTERESTING LIFE.
LORD NOBUNAGA ?!
KRSHAAAAA
LORD NOBUNAGA !!

LET'S GO! LITTLE HANZO

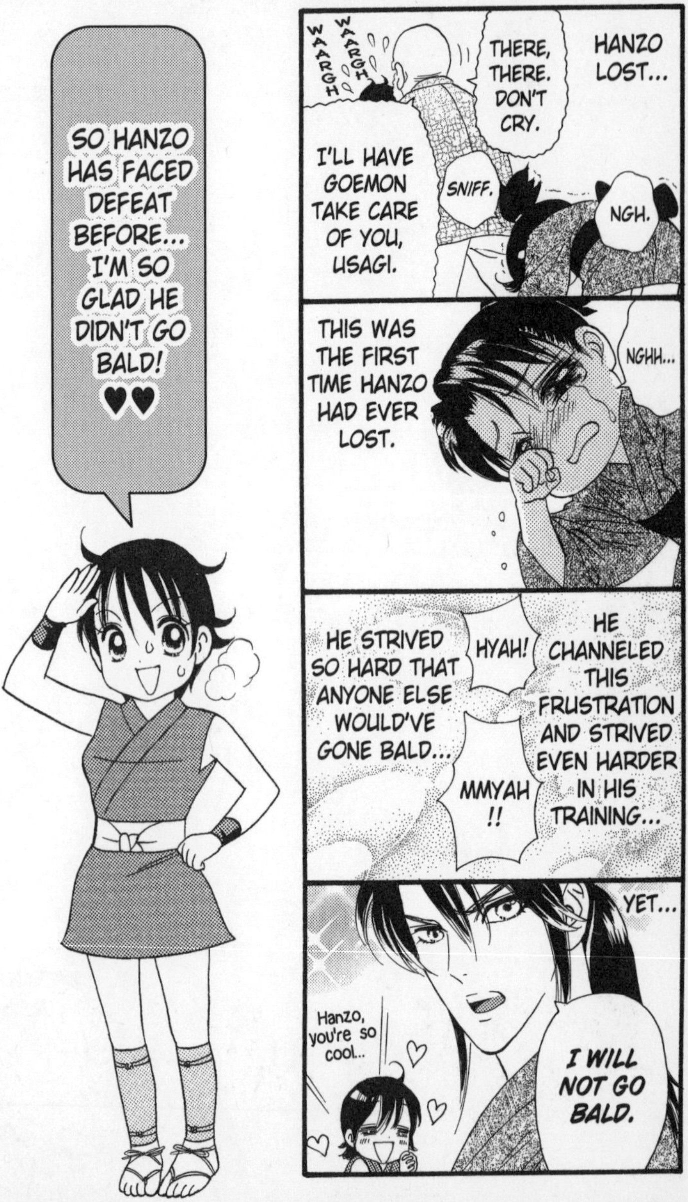
HANZO LOST...
THERE, THERE. DON'T CRY.
WAARGH WAARGH
NGH.
SNIFF.
I'LL HAVE GOEMON TAKE CARE OF YOU, USAGI.
NGHH...
THIS WAS THE FIRST TIME HANZO HAD EVER LOST.
HE CHANNELED THIS FRUSTRATION AND STRIVED EVEN HARDER IN HIS TRAINING...
HYAH!
HE STRIVED SO HARD THAT ANYONE ELSE WOULD'VE GONE BALD...
MMYAH !!
YET...
I WILL NOT GO BALD.
Hanzo, you're so cool...
SO HANZO HAS FACED DEFEAT BEFORE... I'M SO GLAD HE DIDN'T GO BALD! ♥♥

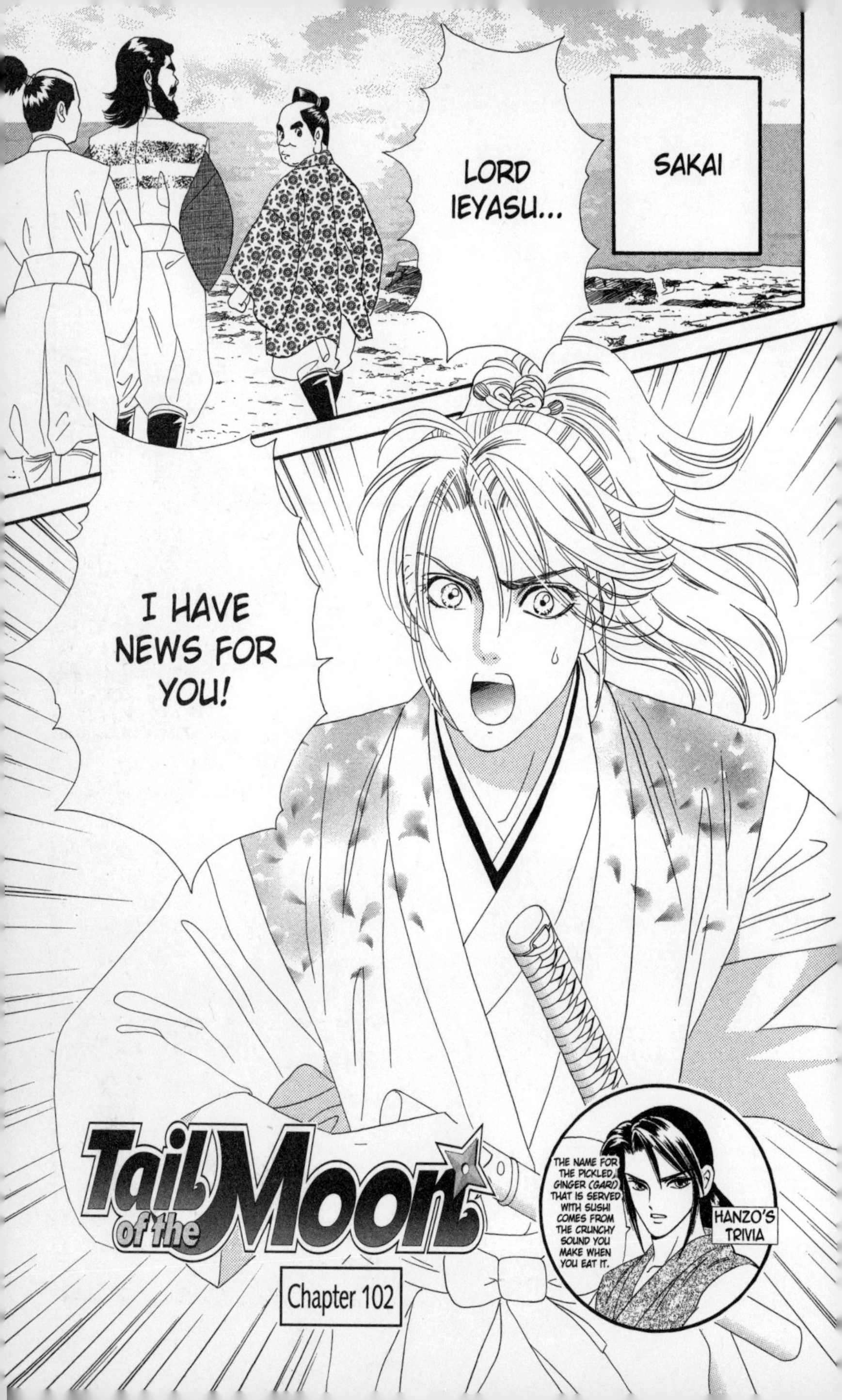
SAKAI
LORD IEYASU...
I HAVE NEWS FOR YOU!
Tail of the Moon
Chapter 102
HANZO'S TRIVIA
THE NAME FOR THE PICKLED GINGER (GARI) THAT IS SERVED WITH SUSHI COMES FROM THE CRUNCHY SOUND YOU MAKE WHEN YOU EAT IT.

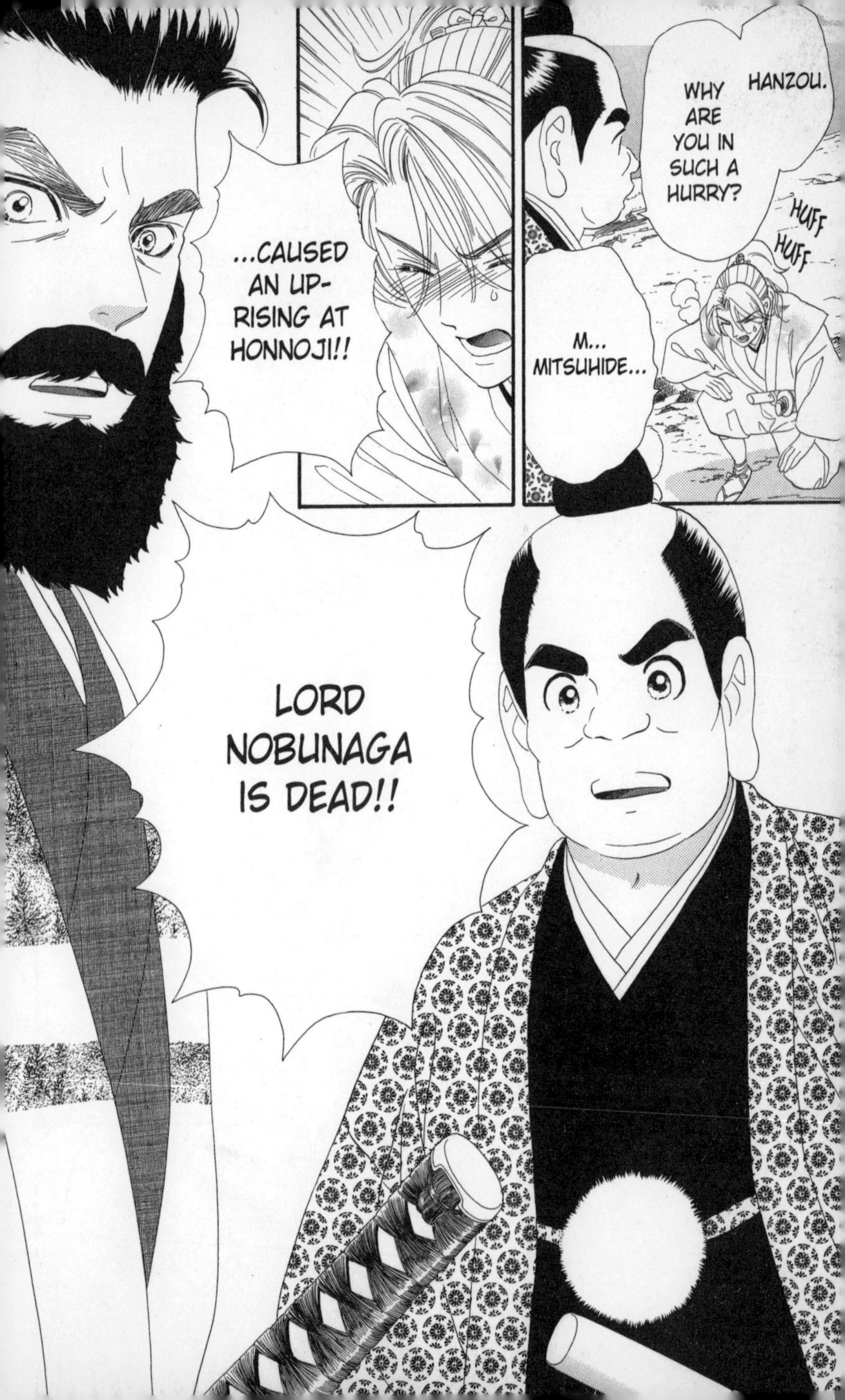
HANZOU.
WHY ARE YOU IN SUCH A HURRY?
HUFF HUFF
M... MITSUHIDE...
...CAUSED AN UP-RISING AT HONNOJI!!
LORD NOBUNAGA IS DEAD!!

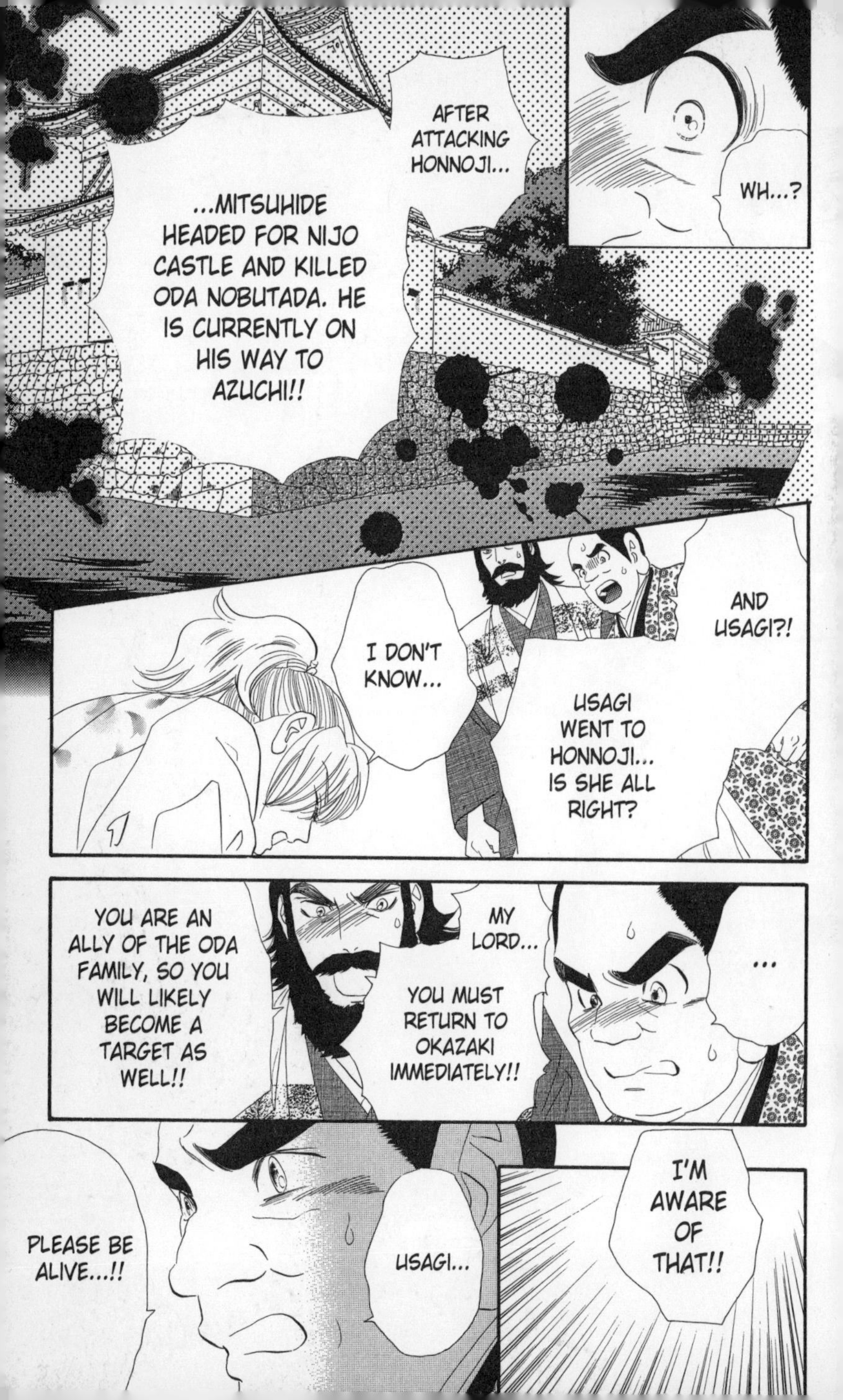
WH...?
AFTER ATTACKING HONNOJI...
...MITSUHIDE HEADED FOR NIJO CASTLE AND KILLED ODA NOBUTADA. HE IS CURRENTLY ON HIS WAY TO AZUCHI!!
AND USAGI?!
USAGI WENT TO HONNOJI... IS SHE ALL RIGHT?
I DON'T KNOW...
...
MY LORD...
YOU MUST RETURN TO OKAZAKI IMMEDIATELY!!
YOU ARE AN ALLY OF THE ODA FAMILY, SO YOU WILL LIKELY BECOME A TARGET AS WELL!!
I'M AWARE OF THAT!!
USAGI...
PLEASE BE ALIVE...!!

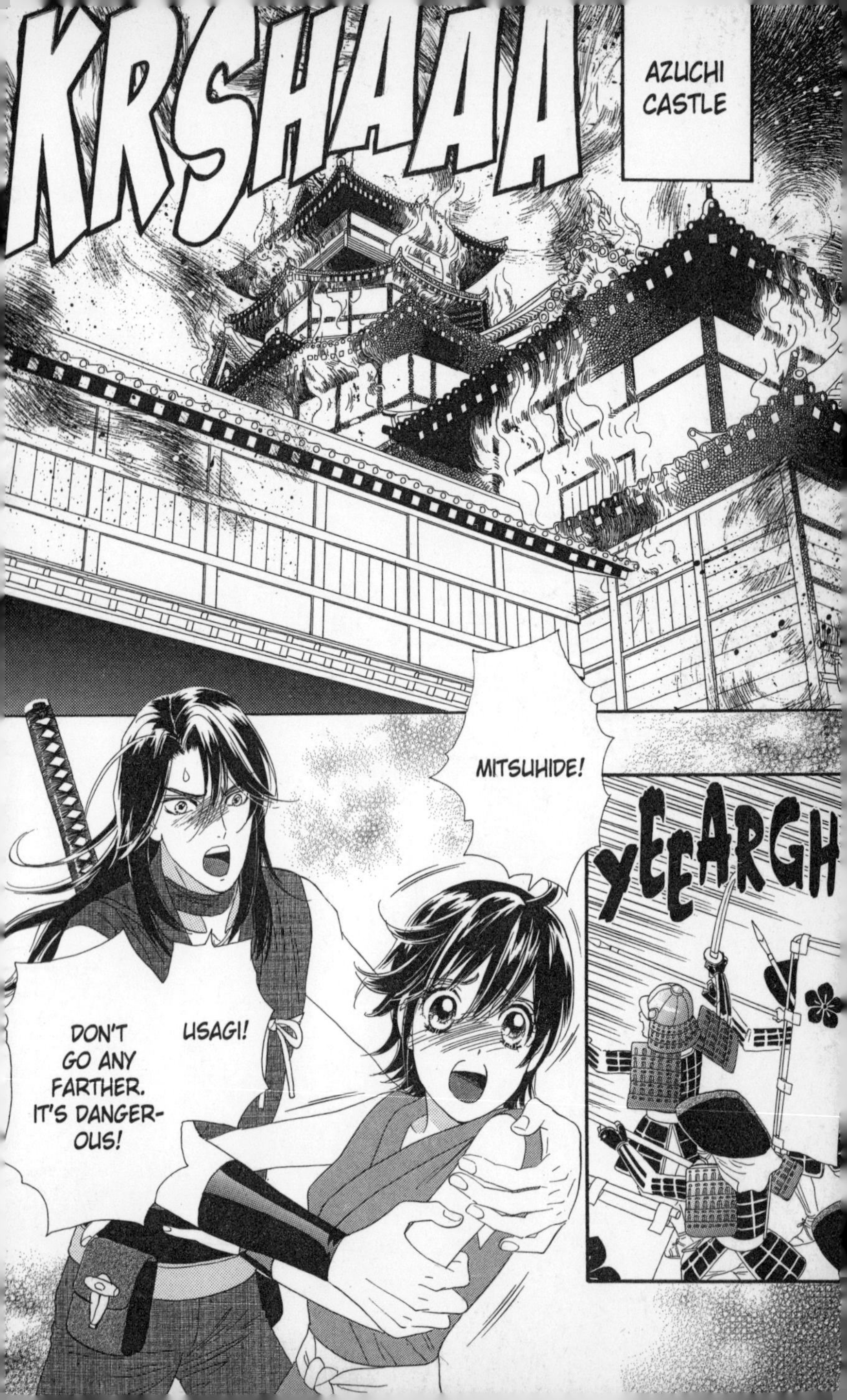
AZUCHI CASTLE
KRSHAAA
YEEARGH
MITSUHIDE!
USAGI!
DON'T GO ANY FARTHER. IT'S DANGER-OUS!

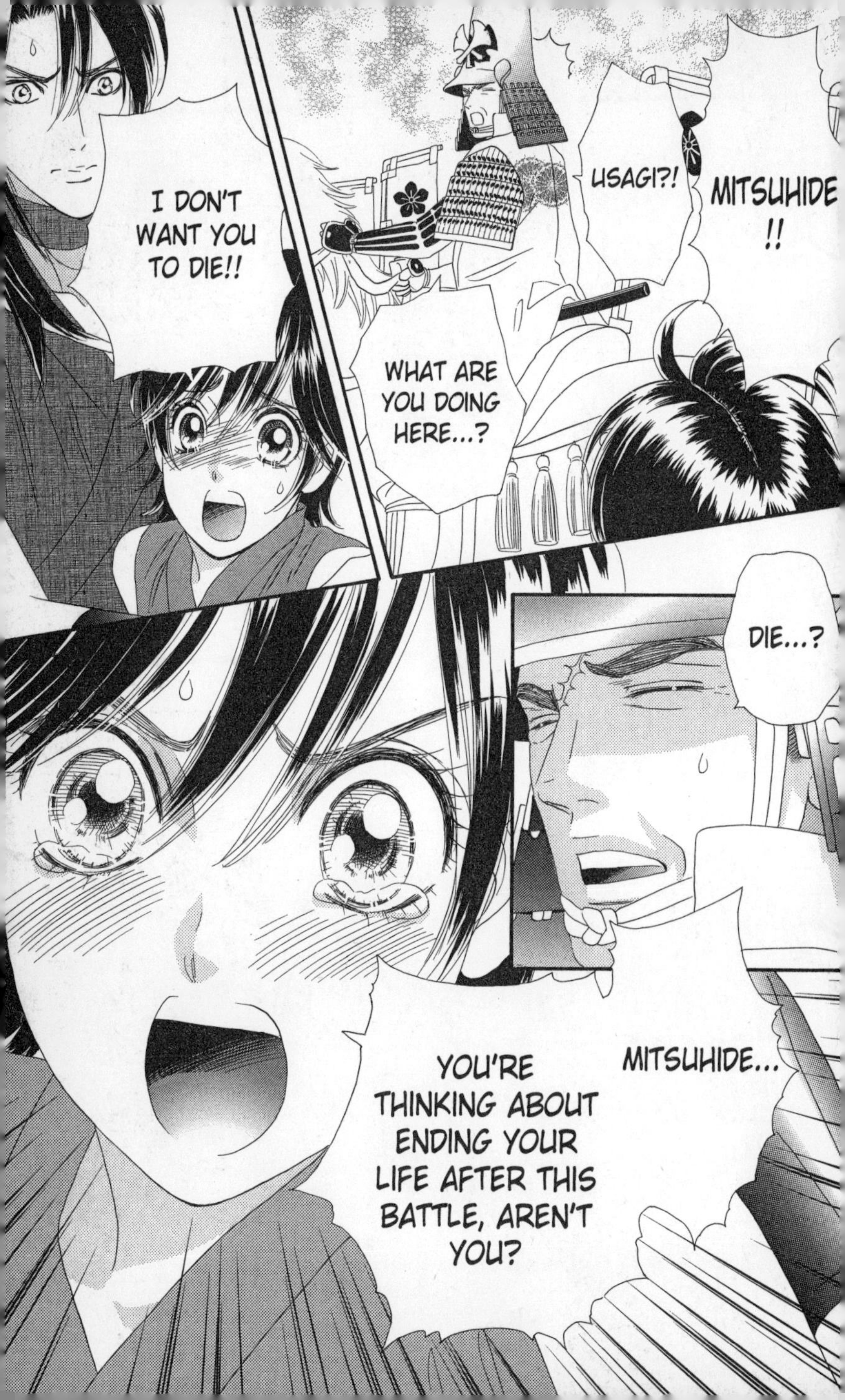
MITSUHIDE !!
USAGI?!
WHAT ARE YOU DOING HERE...?
I DON'T WANT YOU TO DIE!!
DIE...?
MITSUHIDE...
YOU'RE THINKING ABOUT ENDING YOUR LIFE AFTER THIS BATTLE, AREN'T YOU?

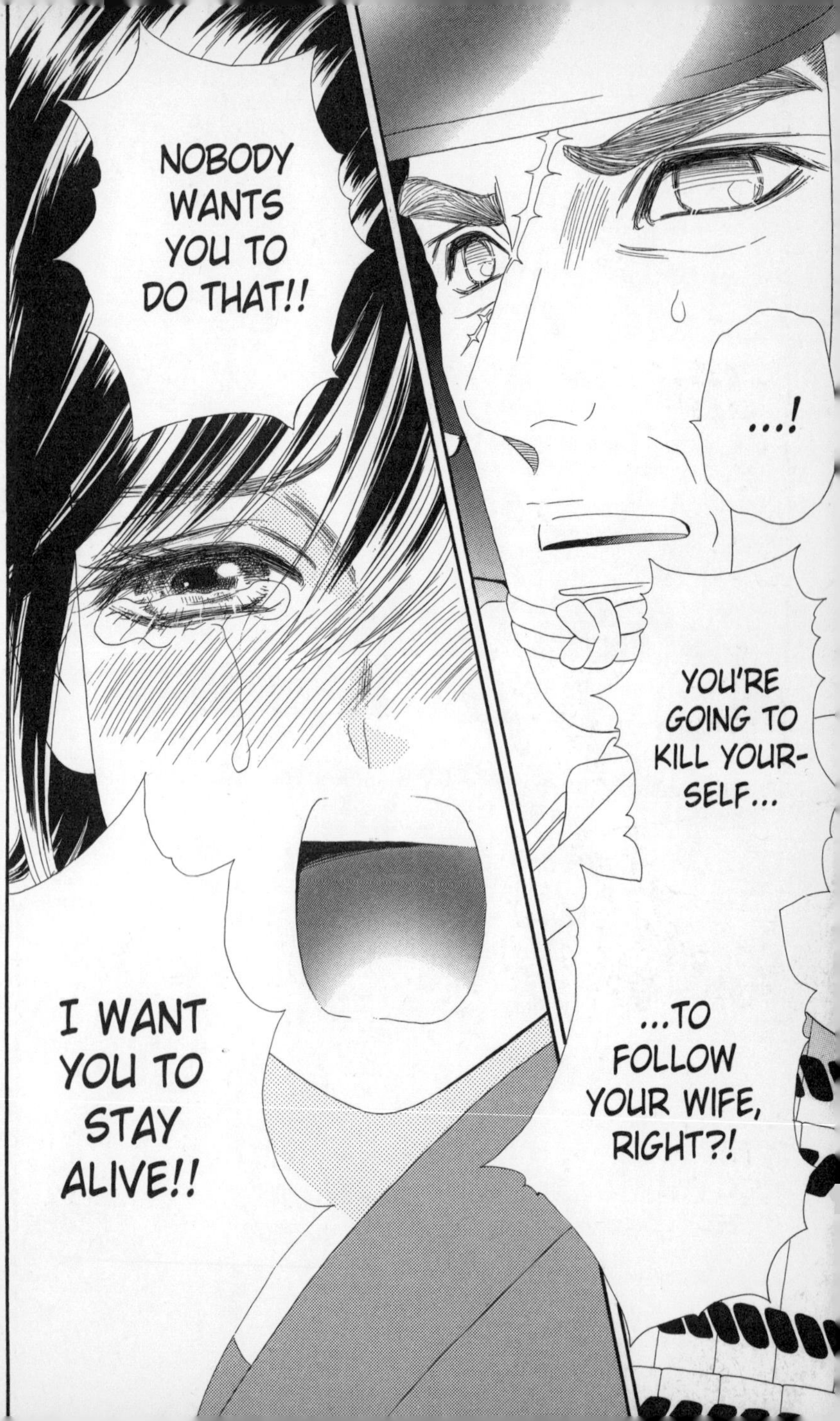
...!
YOU'RE GOING TO KILL YOUR-SELF...
...TO FOLLOW YOUR WIFE, RIGHT?!
NOBODY WANTS YOU TO DO THAT!!
I WANT YOU TO STAY ALIVE!!

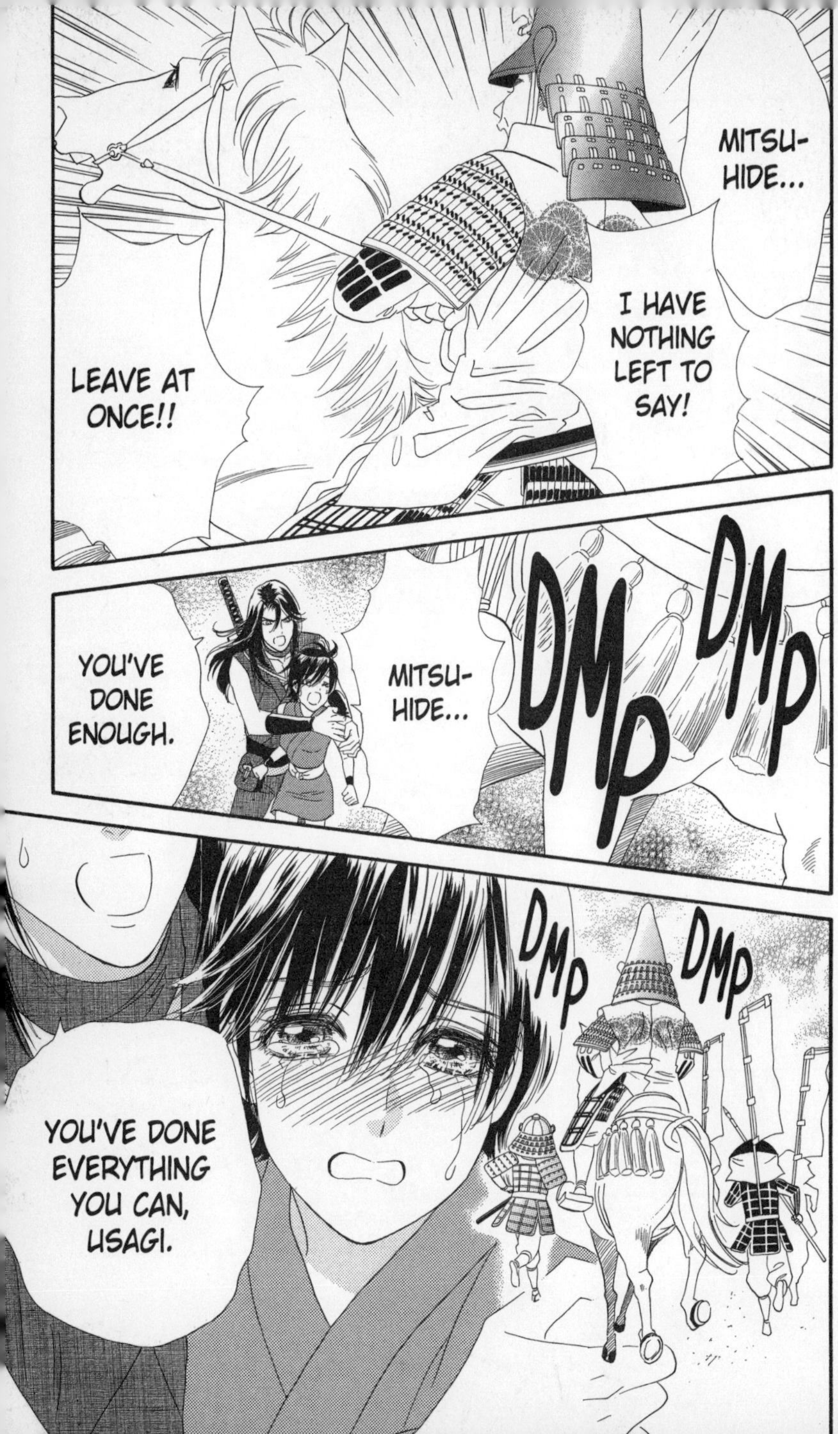
MITSU-HIDE...
I HAVE NOTHING LEFT TO SAY!
LEAVE AT ONCE!!
DMP
DMP
MITSU-HIDE...
YOU'VE DONE ENOUGH.
DMP
DMP
YOU'VE DONE EVERYTHING YOU CAN, USAGI.

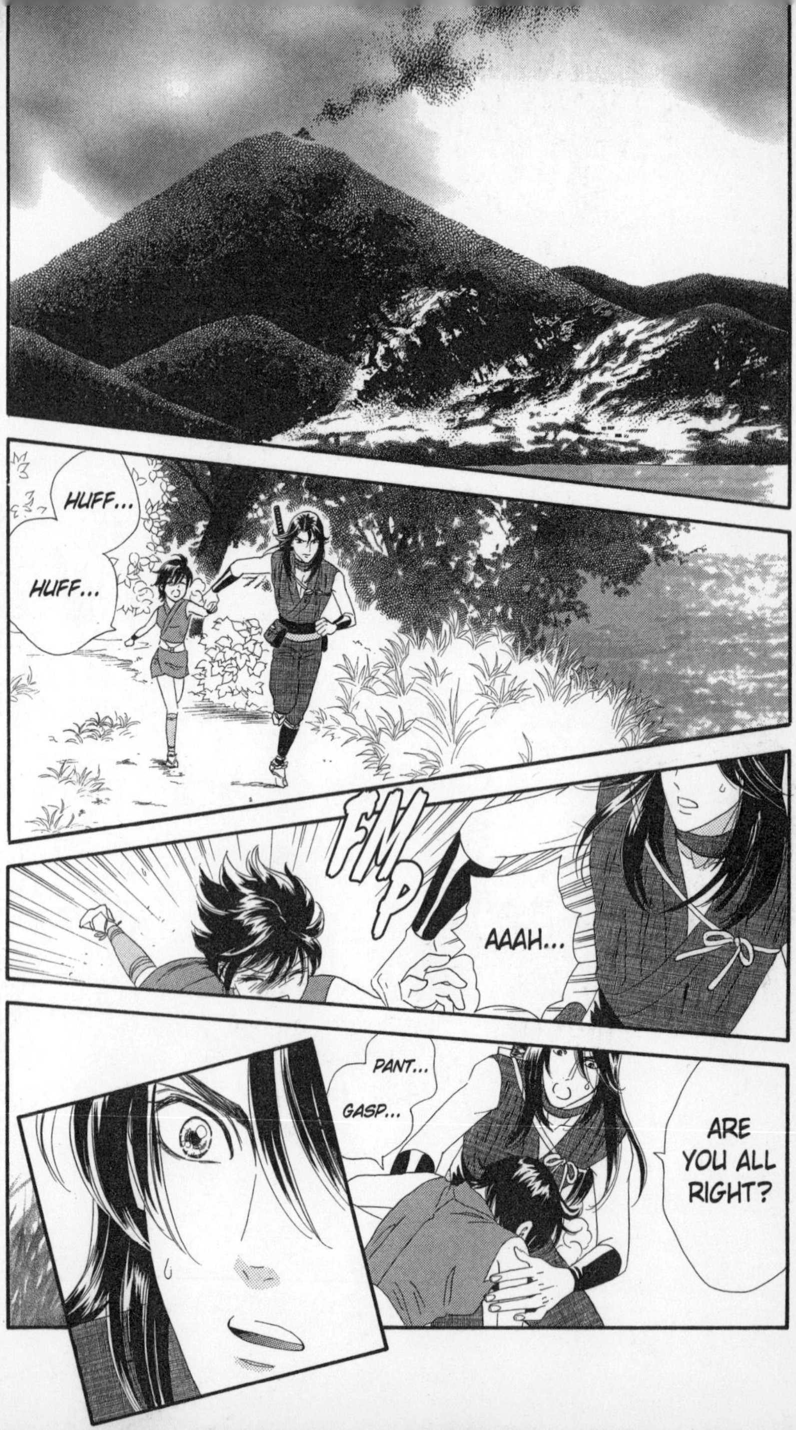
HUFF...
HUFF...
FMP
AAAH...
PANT...
GASP...
ARE YOU ALL RIGHT?

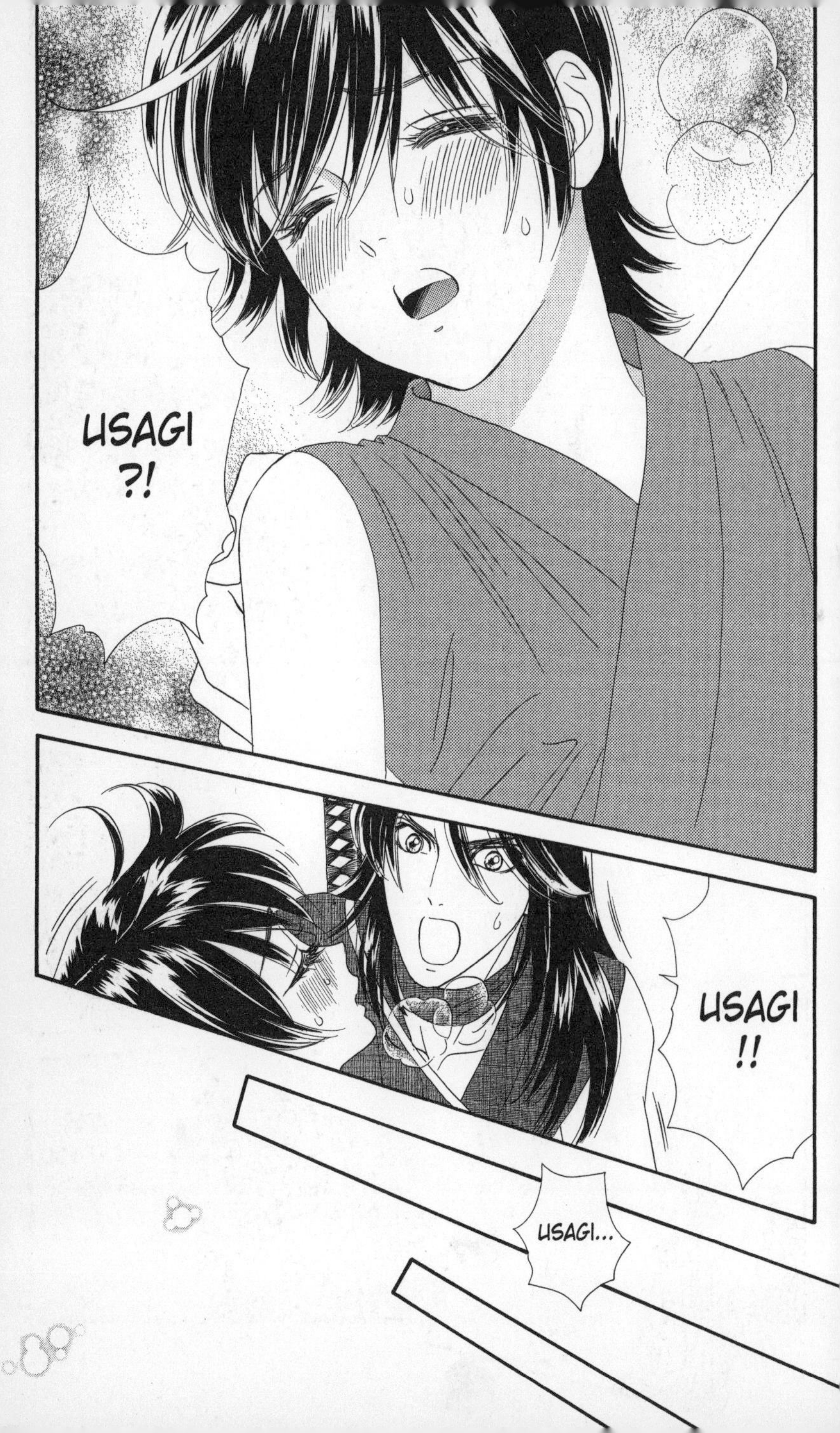
USAGI ?!
USAGI !!
USAGI...

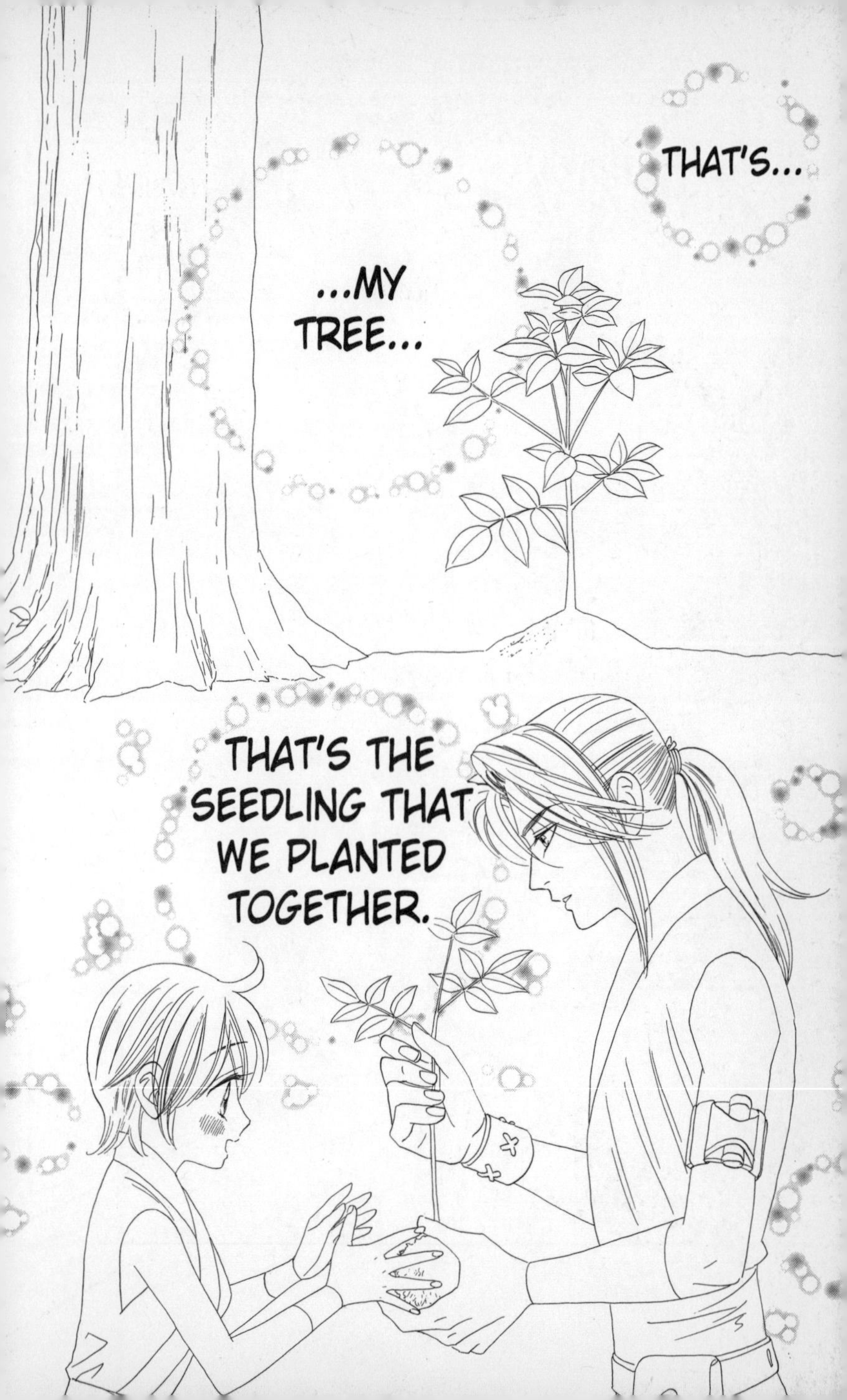
THAT'S...
...MY TREE...
THAT'S THE SEEDLING THAT WE PLANTED TOGETHER.

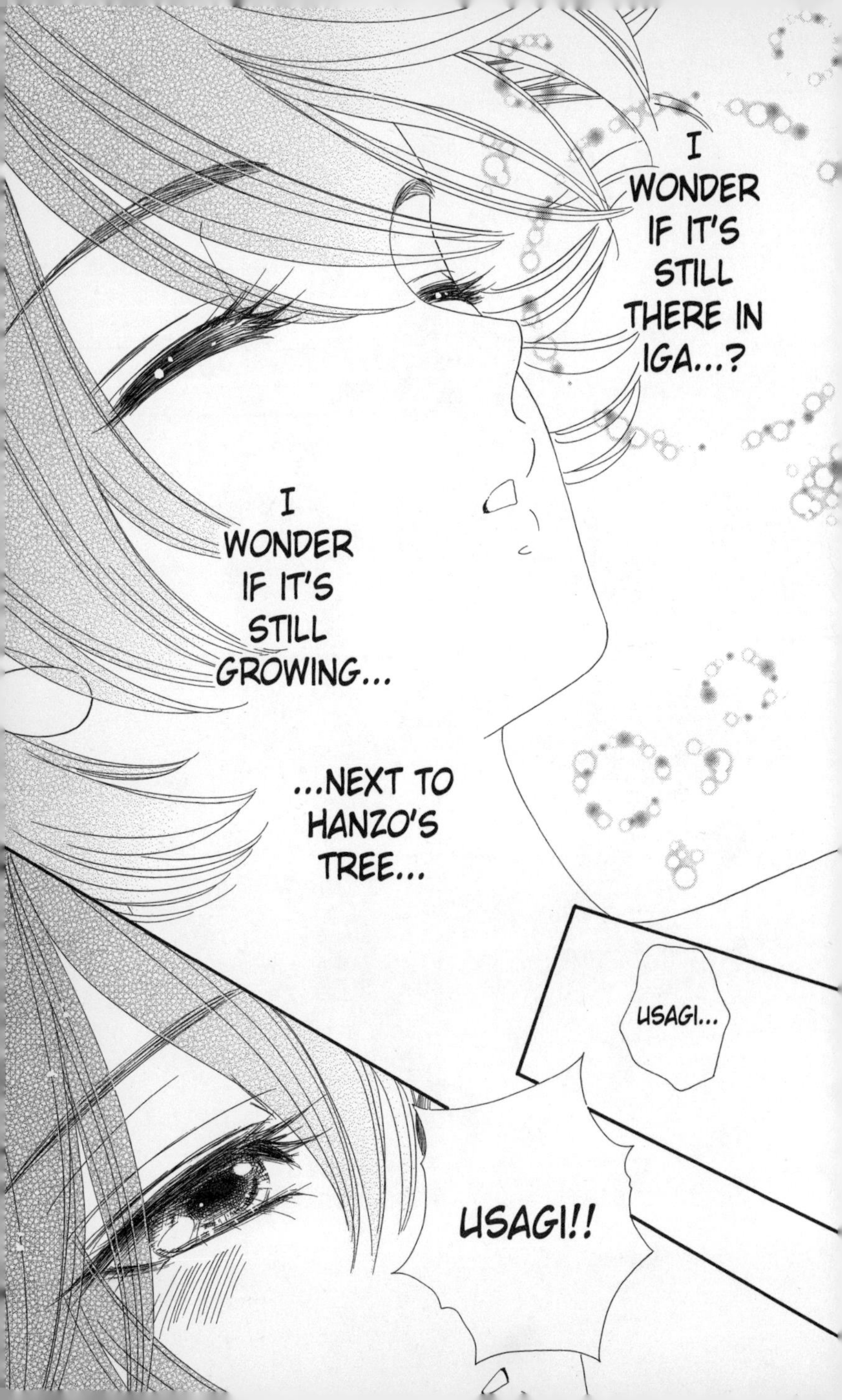

I WONDER IF IT'S STILL THERE IN IGA...?
I WONDER IF IT'S STILL GROWING...
...NEXT TO HANZO'S TREE...
USAGI...
USAGI!!

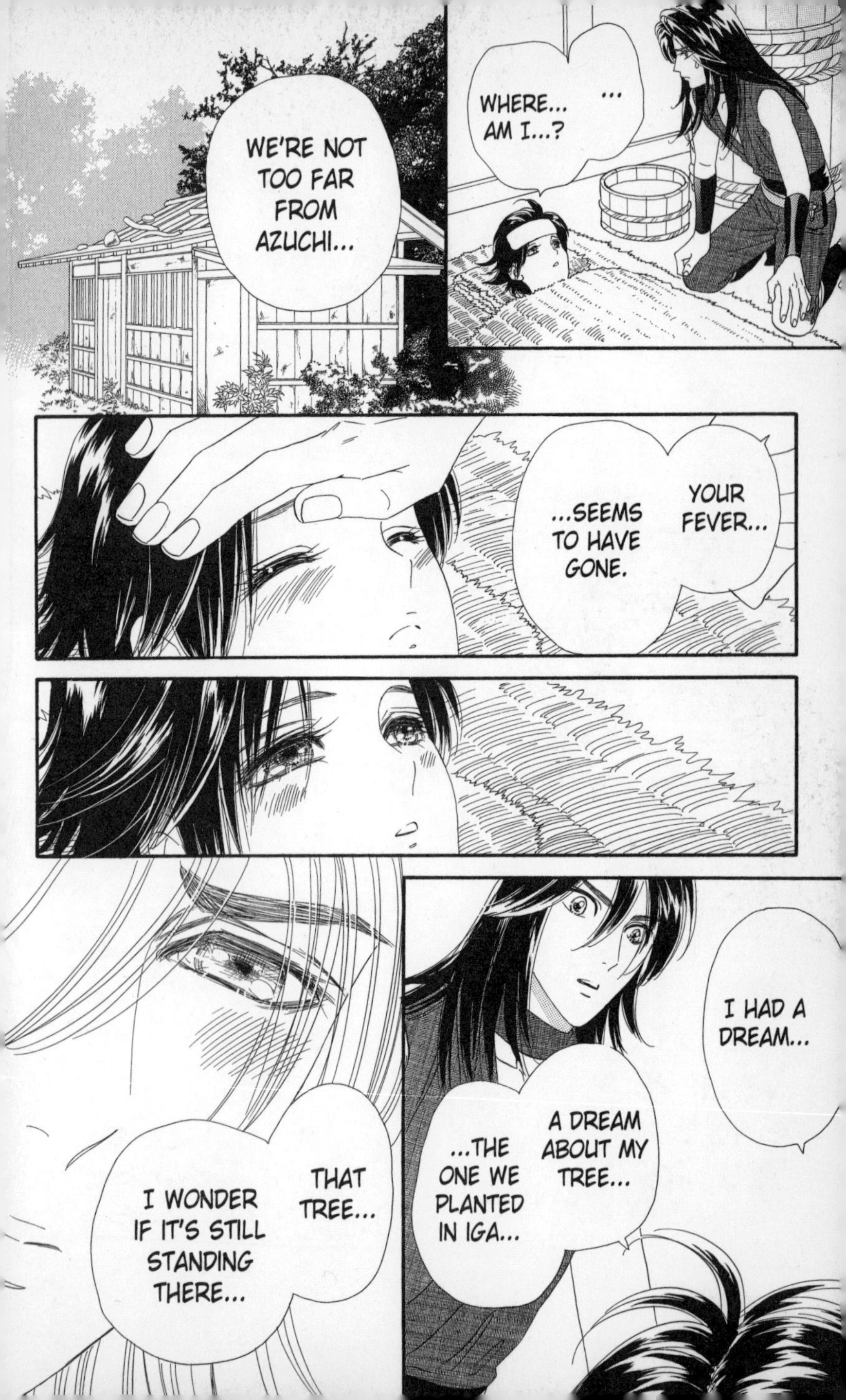

...
WHERE... AM I...?
WE'RE NOT TOO FAR FROM AZUCHI...
YOUR FEVER...
...SEEMS TO HAVE GONE.
I HAD A DREAM...
A DREAM ABOUT MY TREE...
...THE ONE WE PLANTED IN IGA...
THAT TREE...
I WONDER IF IT'S STILL STANDING THERE...

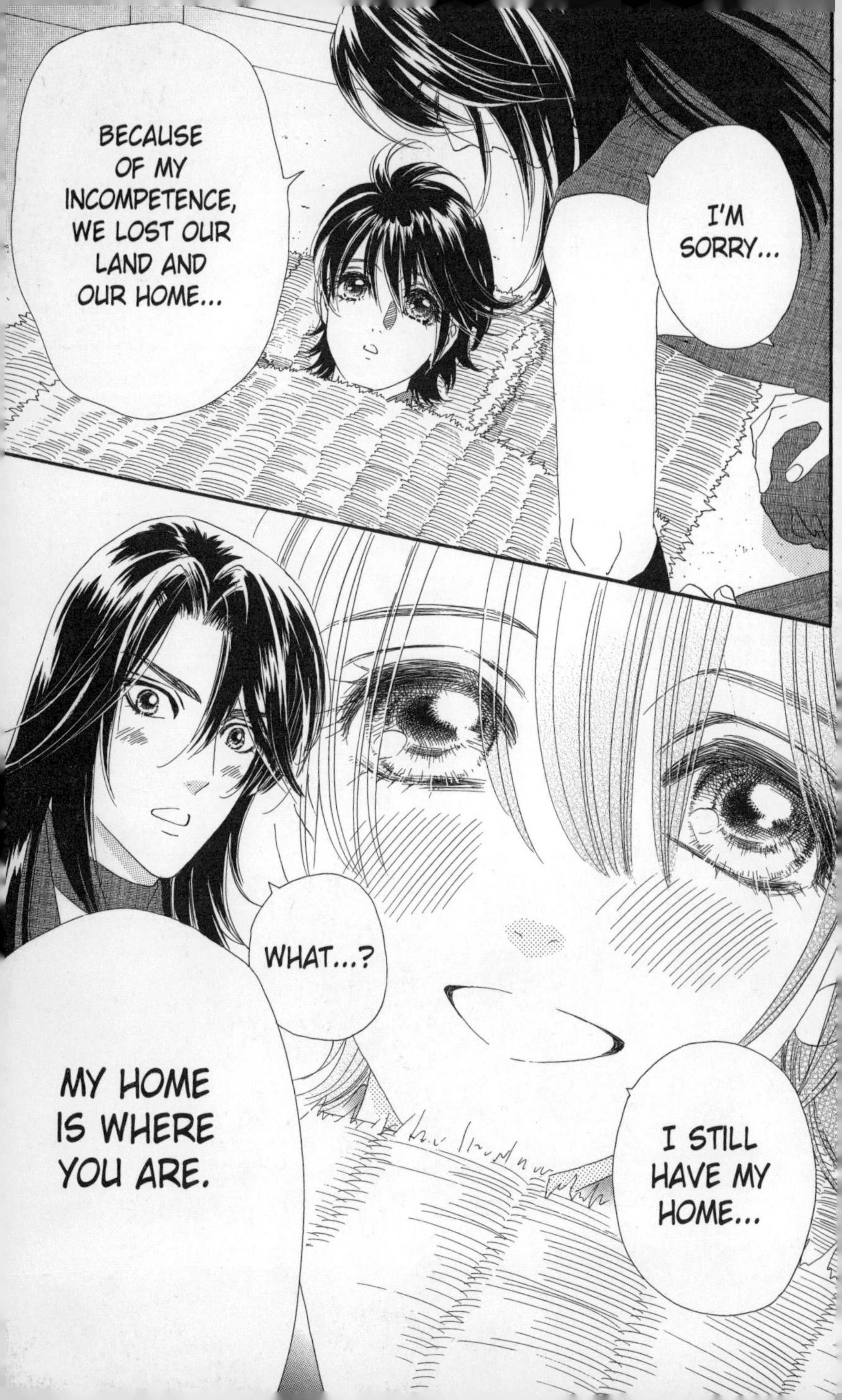
I'M SORRY...
BECAUSE OF MY INCOMPETENCE, WE LOST OUR LAND AND OUR HOME...
I STILL HAVE MY HOME...
WHAT...?
MY HOME IS WHERE YOU ARE.

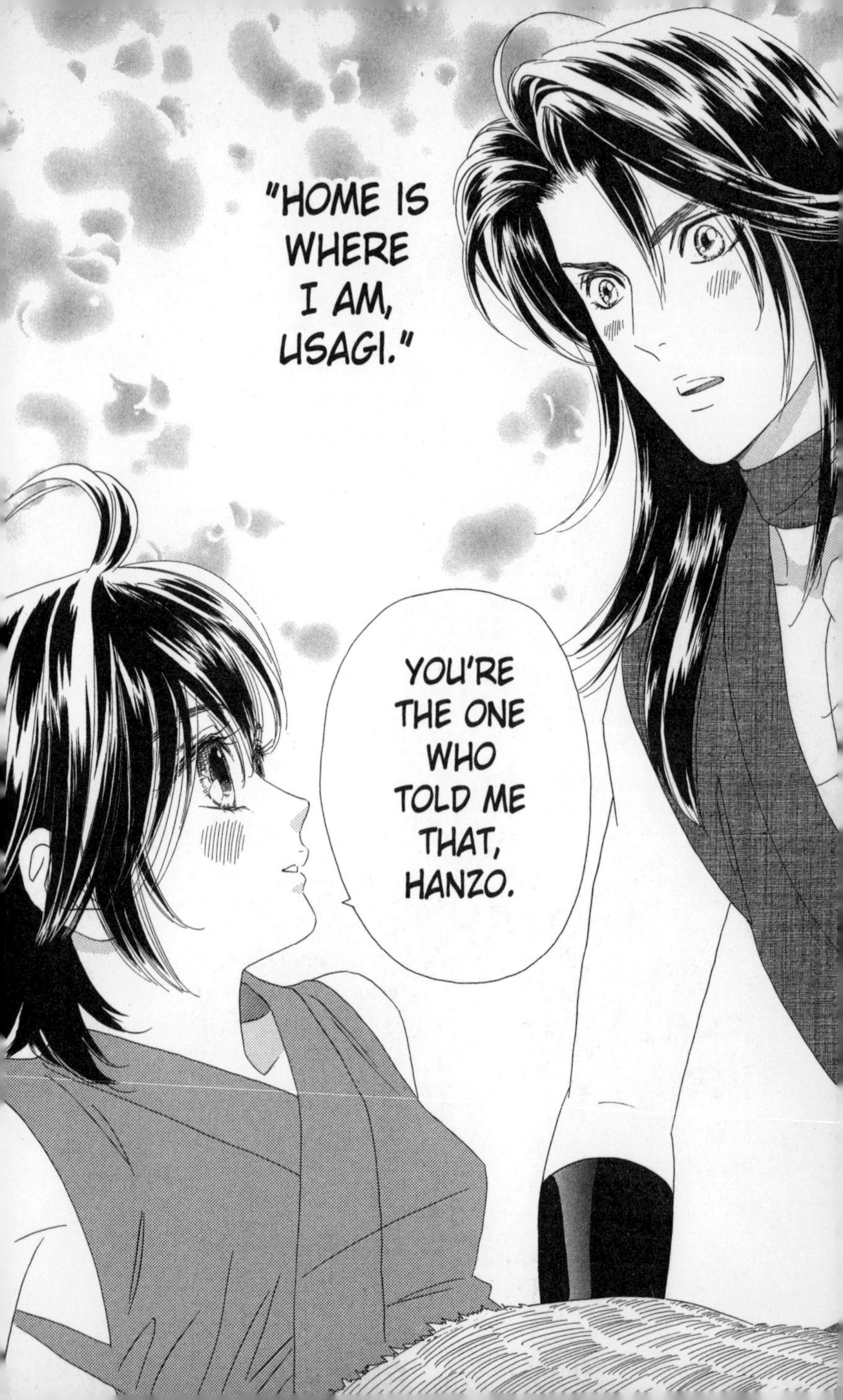
"HOME IS WHERE I AM, USAGI."
YOU'RE THE ONE WHO TOLD ME THAT, HANZO.

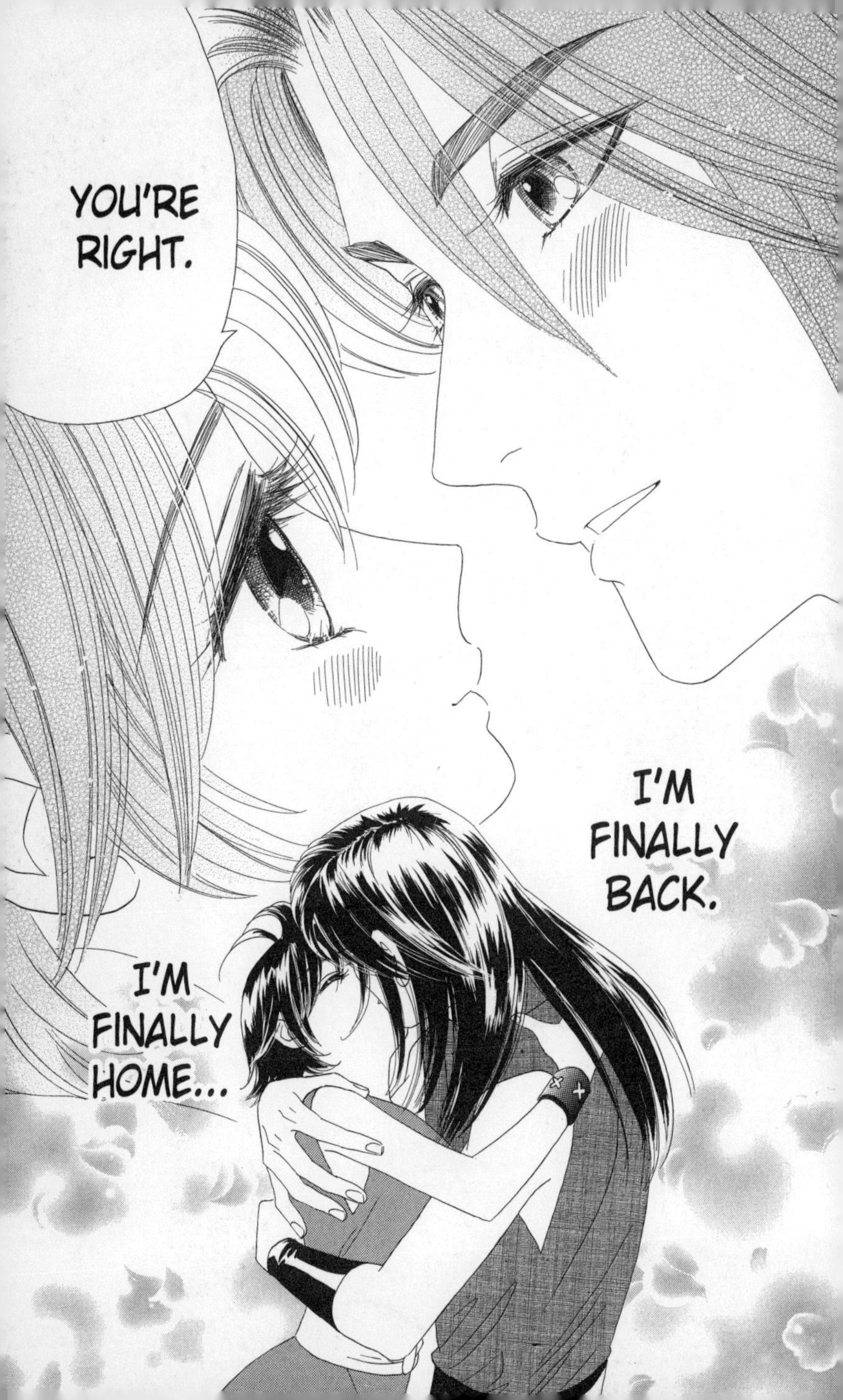
YOU'RE RIGHT.
I'M FINALLY BACK.
I'M FINALLY HOME...

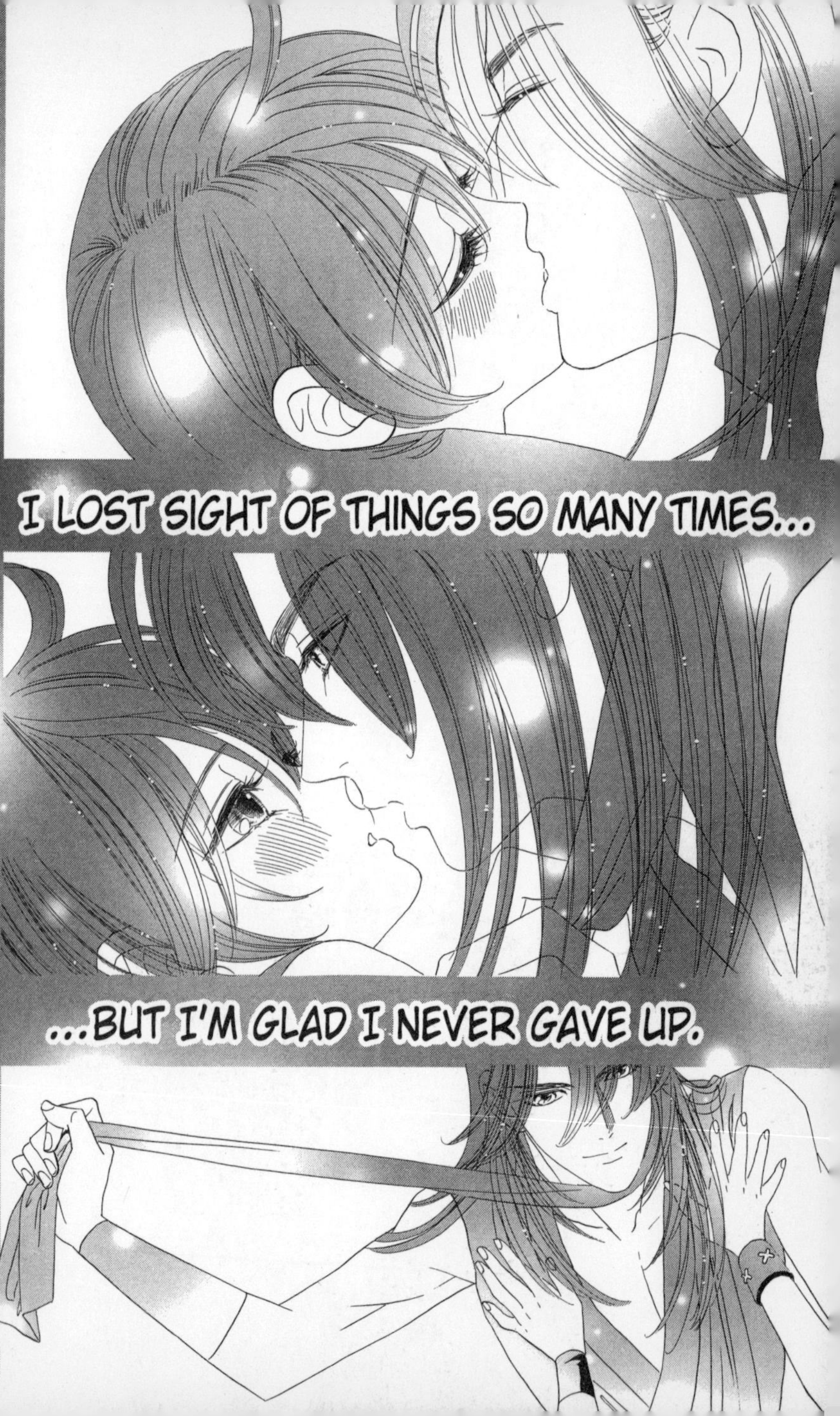
I LOST SIGHT OF THINGS SO MANY TIMES...
...BUT I'M GLAD I NEVER GAVE UP.

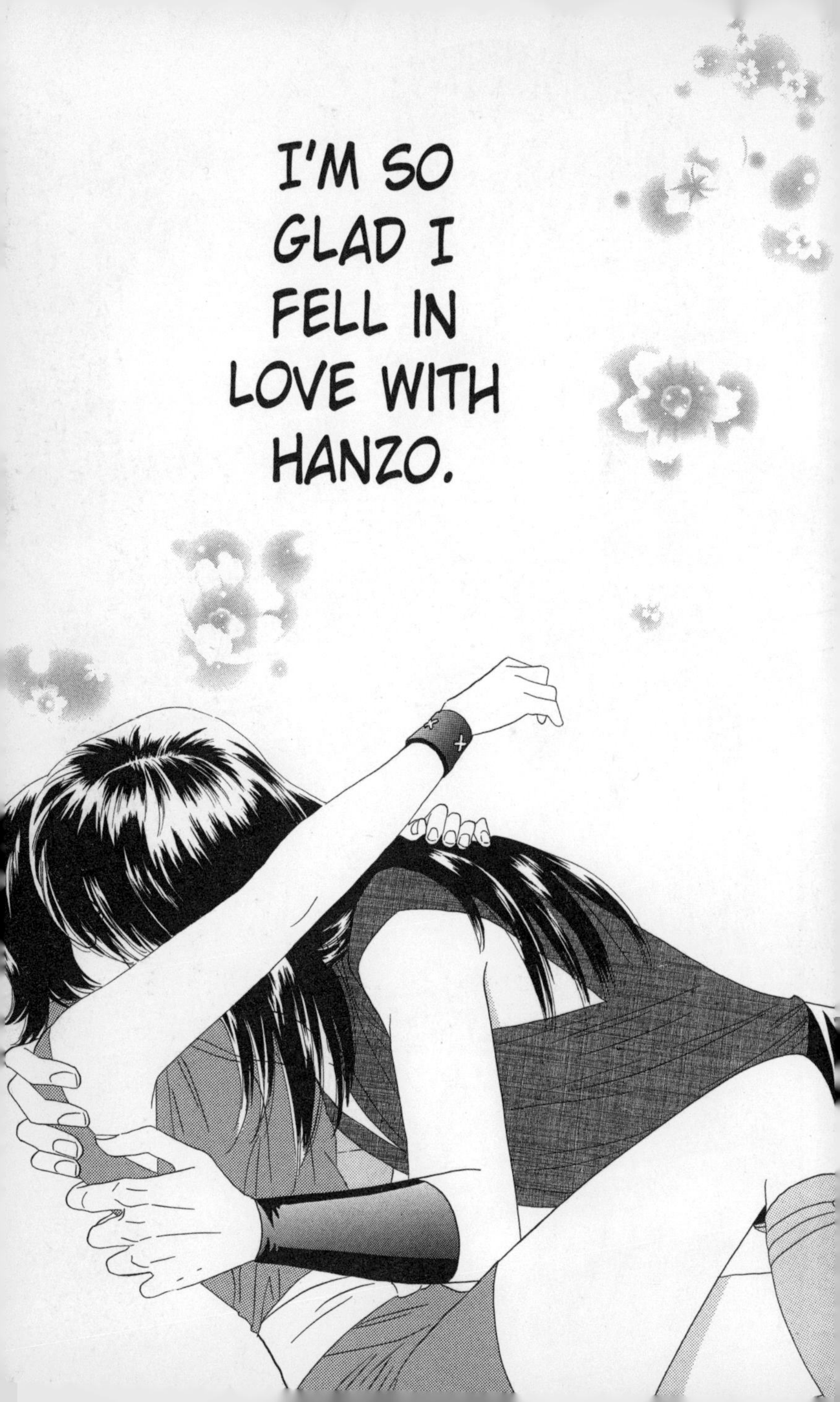
I'M SO GLAD I FELL IN LOVE WITH HANZO.

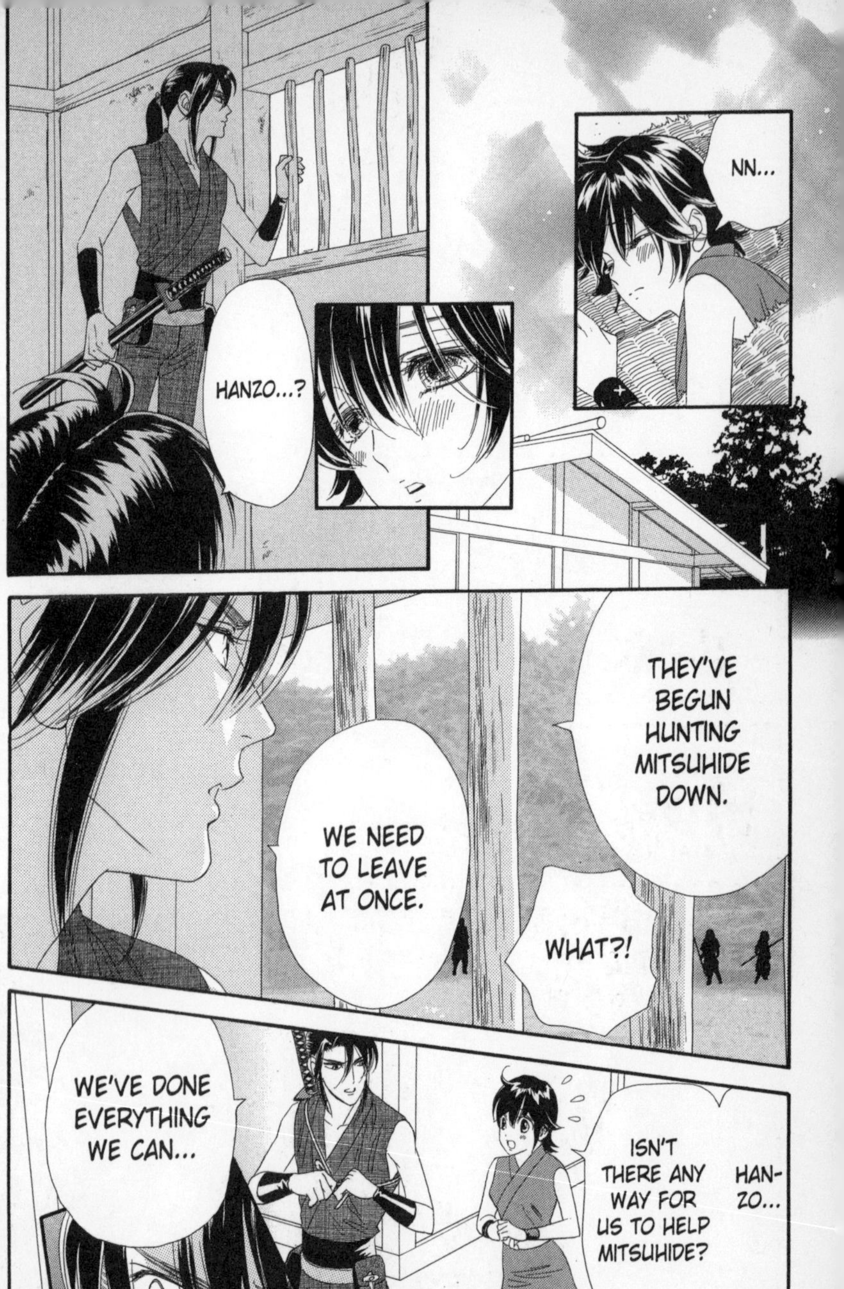
NN...
HANZO...?
THEY'VE BEGUN HUNTING MITSUHIDE DOWN.
WHAT?!
WE NEED TO LEAVE AT ONCE.
HANZO...
ISN'T THERE ANY WAY FOR US TO HELP MITSUHIDE?
WE'VE DONE EVERYTHING WE CAN...

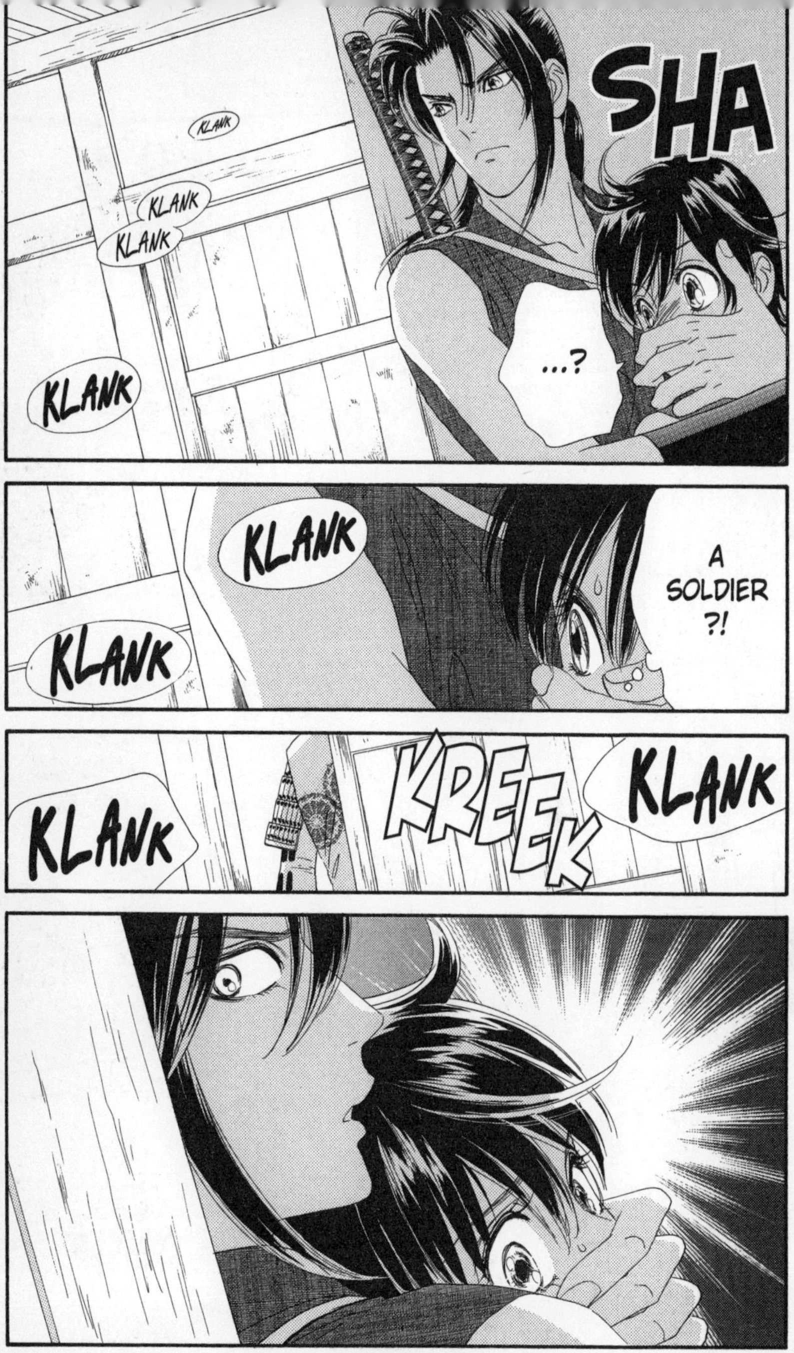
SHA
...?
KLANK
KLANK
KLANK
KLANK
A SOLDIER ?!
KLANK
KLANK
KLANK
KREEK
KLANK

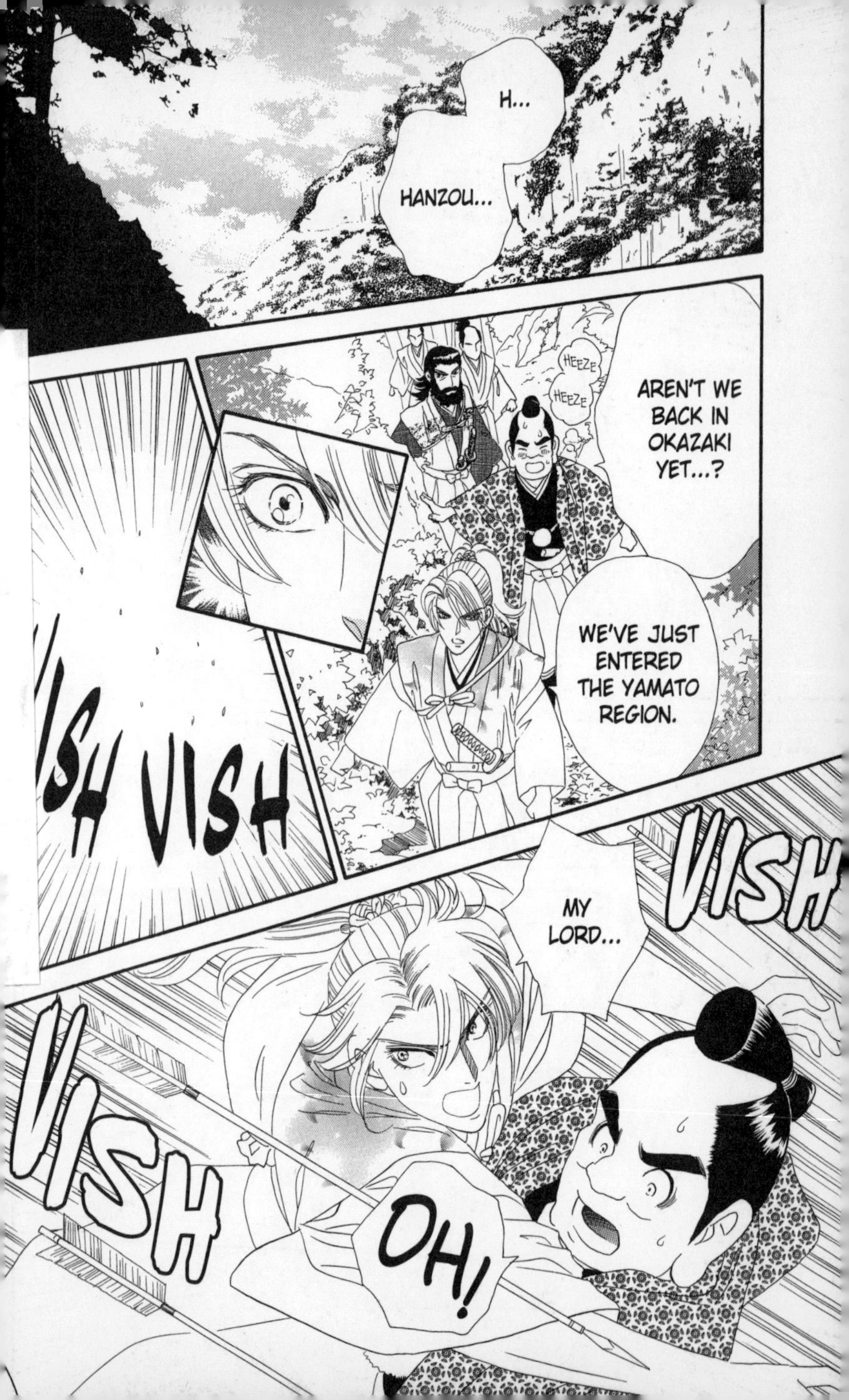

H...
HANZOU...
HEEZE
HEEZE
AREN'T WE BACK IN OKAZAKI YET...?
WE'VE JUST ENTERED THE YAMATO REGION.
ISH VISH
VISH
MY LORD...
OH!
VISH

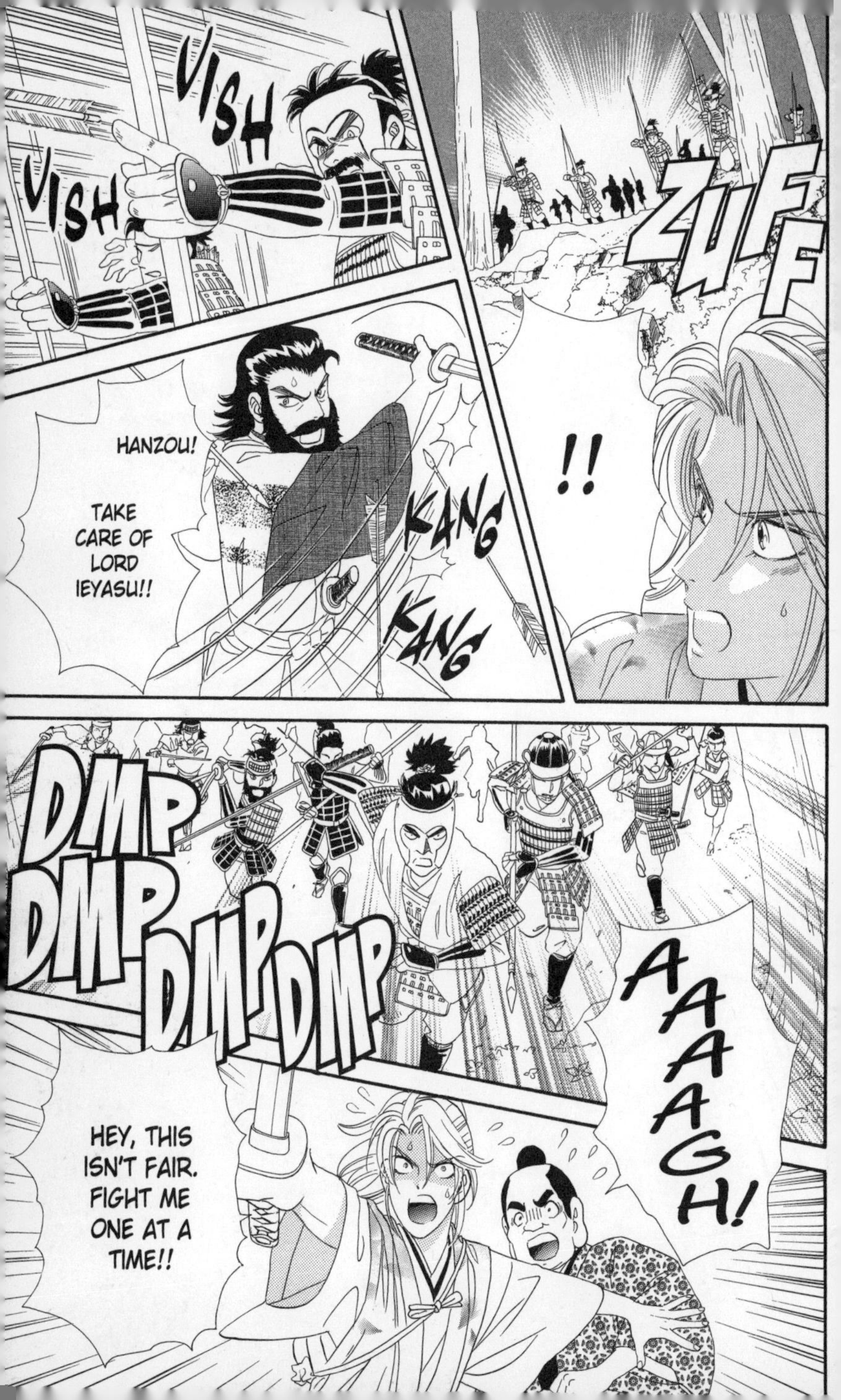
ZUFF
VISH
VISH
!!
HANZOU!
TAKE CARE OF LORD IEYASU!!
KANG
KANG
DMP DMP DMP DMP
AAAAGH!
HEY, THIS ISN'T FAIR. FIGHT ME ONE AT A TIME!!

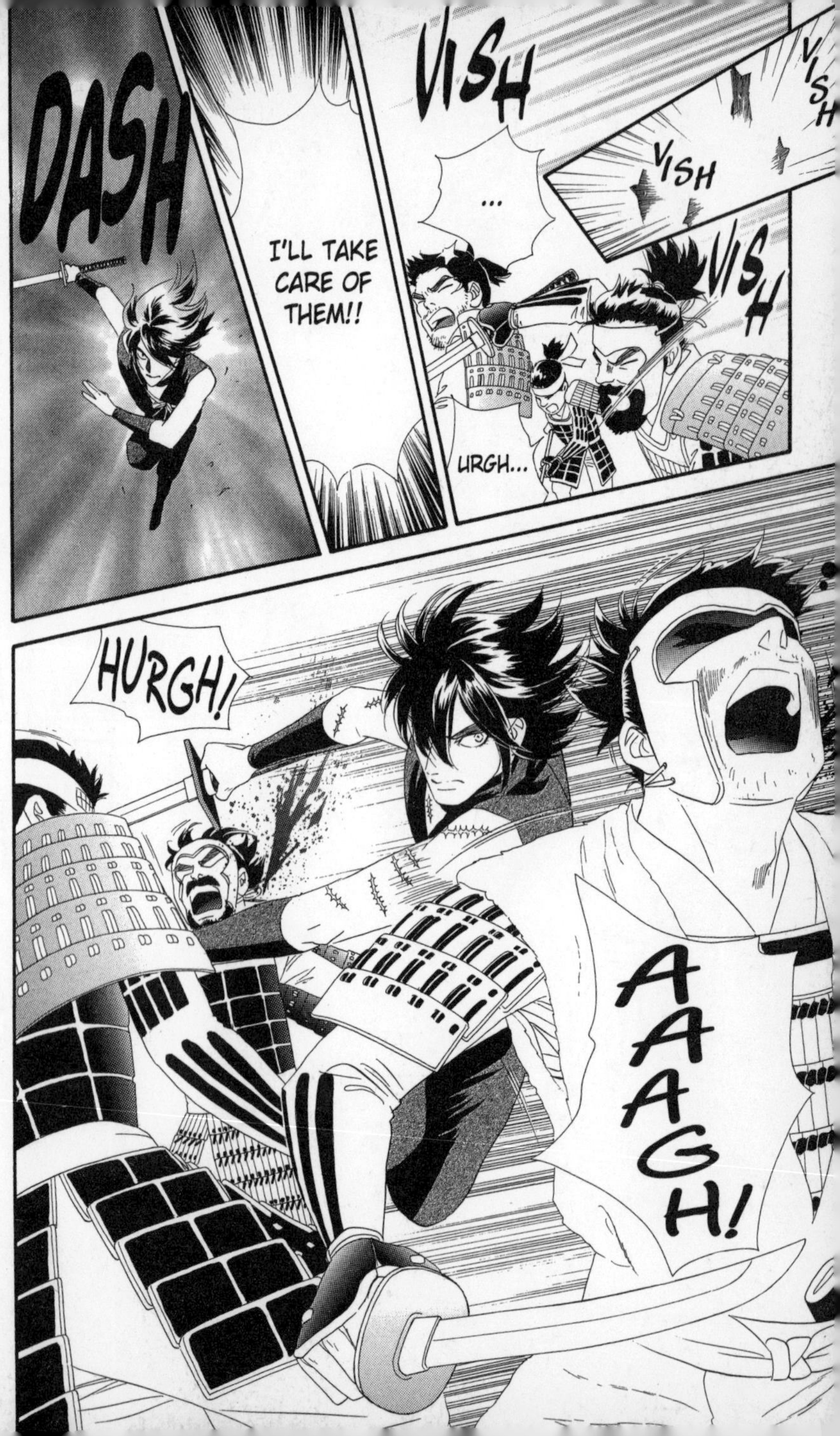

VISH
VISH
VISH
...
VISH
URGH...
I'LL TAKE CARE OF THEM!!
DASH
AAAGH!
HURGH!

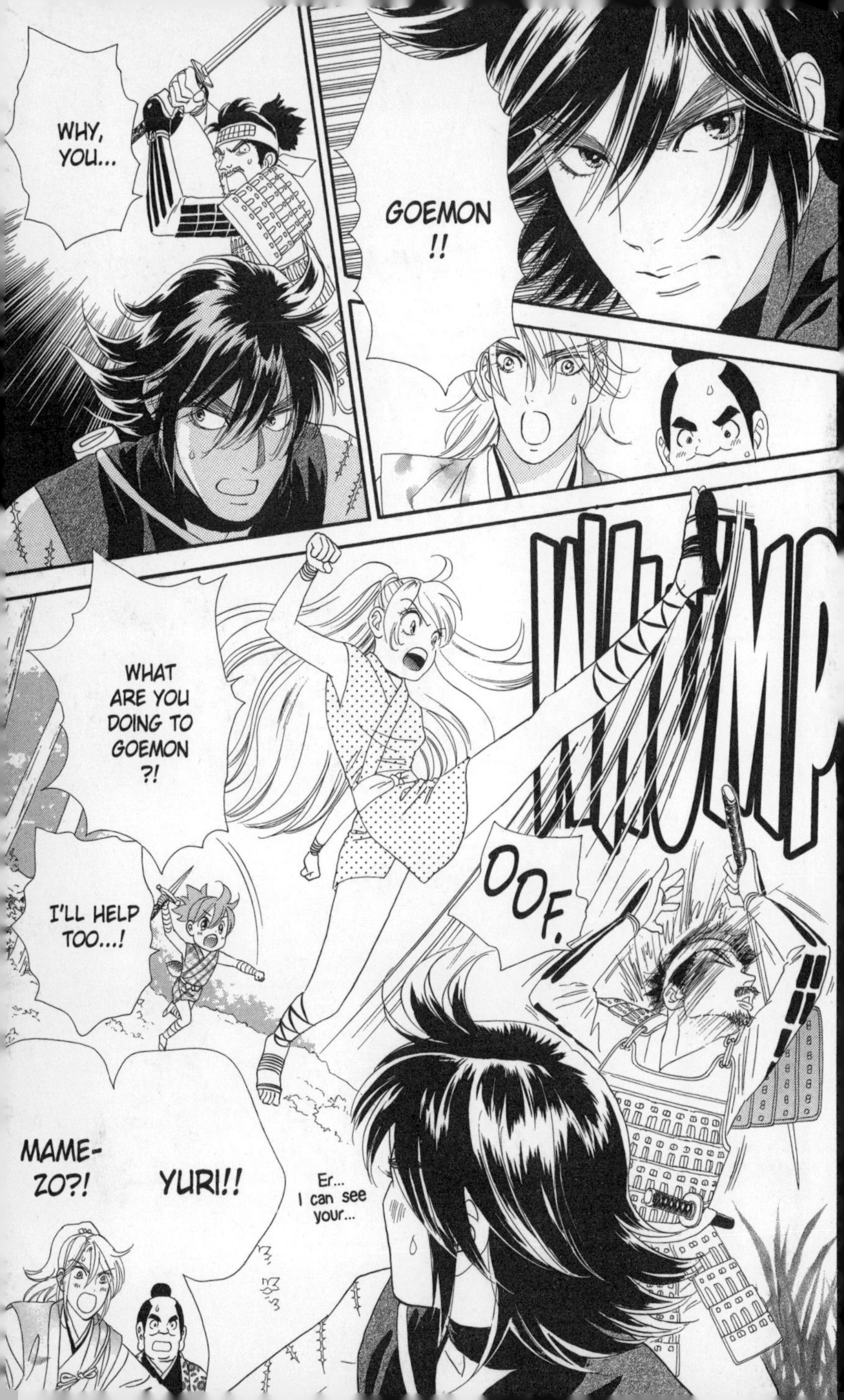
GOEMON !!
WHY, YOU...
WHUMP
WHAT ARE YOU DOING TO GOEMON ?!
OOF.
I'LL HELP TOO...!
Er... I can see your...
YURI!!
MAME-ZO?!

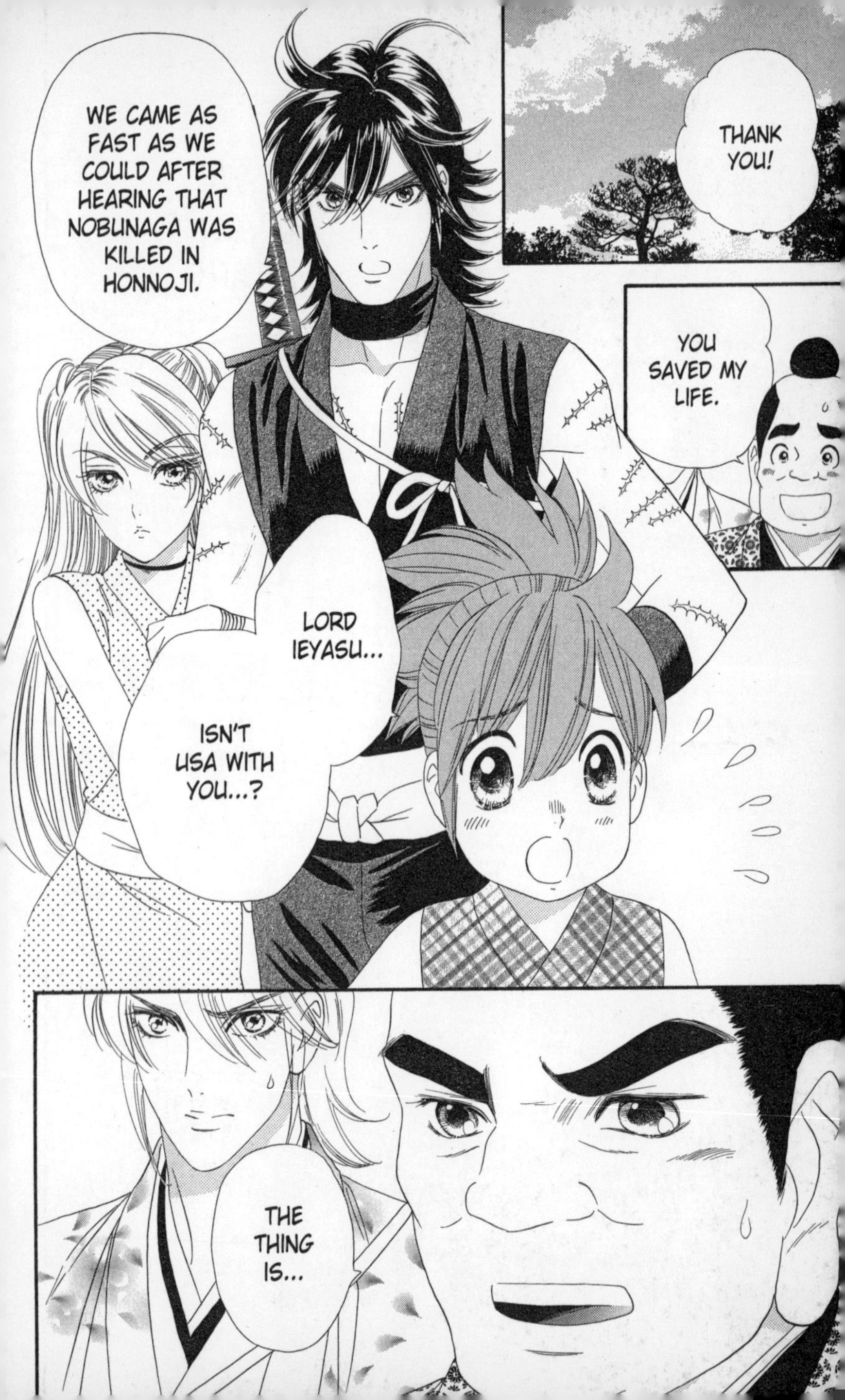
THANK YOU!
YOU SAVED MY LIFE.
WE CAME AS FAST AS WE COULD AFTER HEARING THAT NOBUNAGA WAS KILLED IN HONNOJI.
LORD IEYASU...
ISN'T USA WITH YOU...?
THE THING IS...

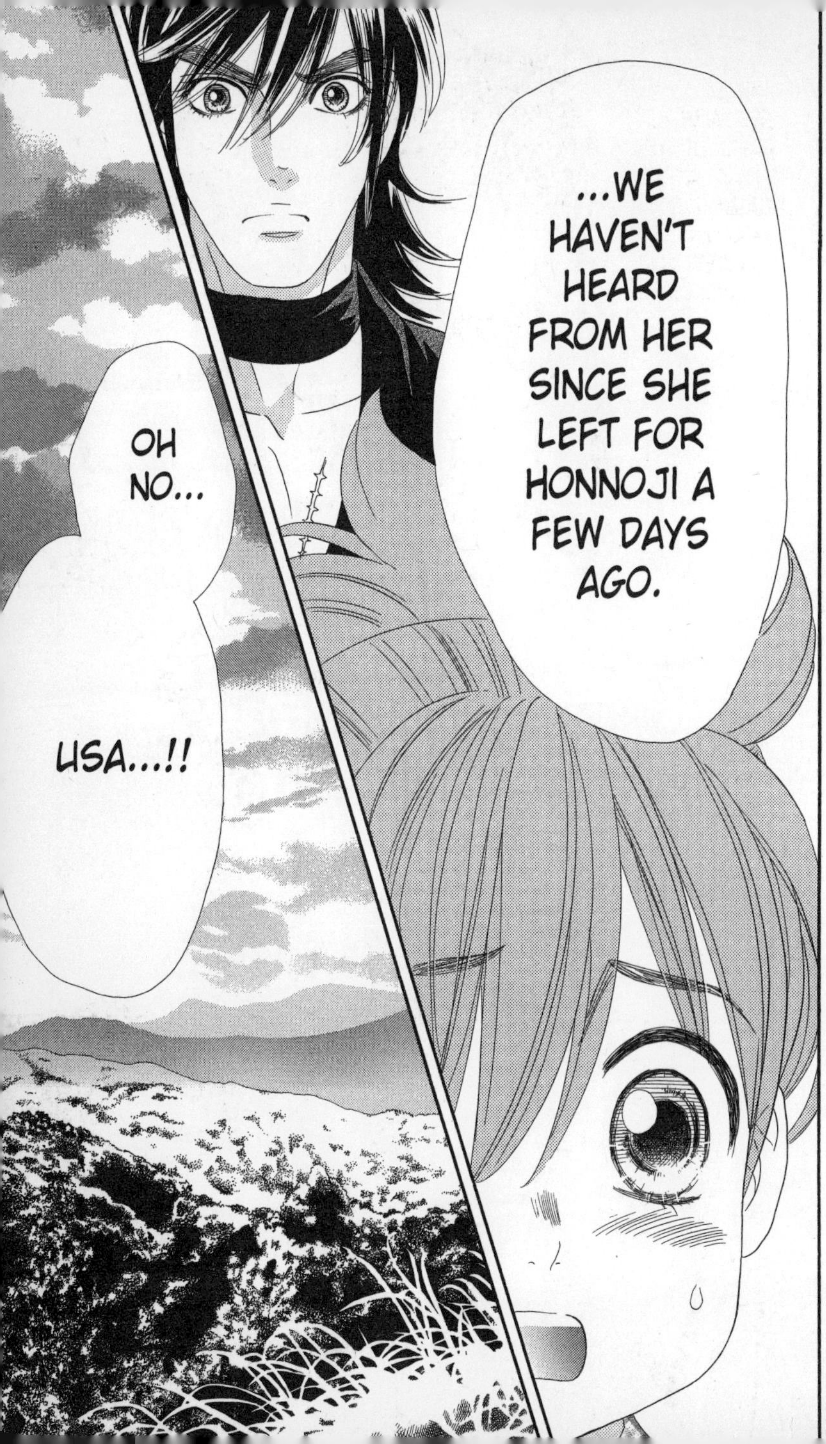
...WE HAVEN'T HEARD FROM HER SINCE SHE LEFT FOR HONNOJI A FEW DAYS AGO.
OH NO...
USA...!!

LET'S GO! LITTLE HANZO

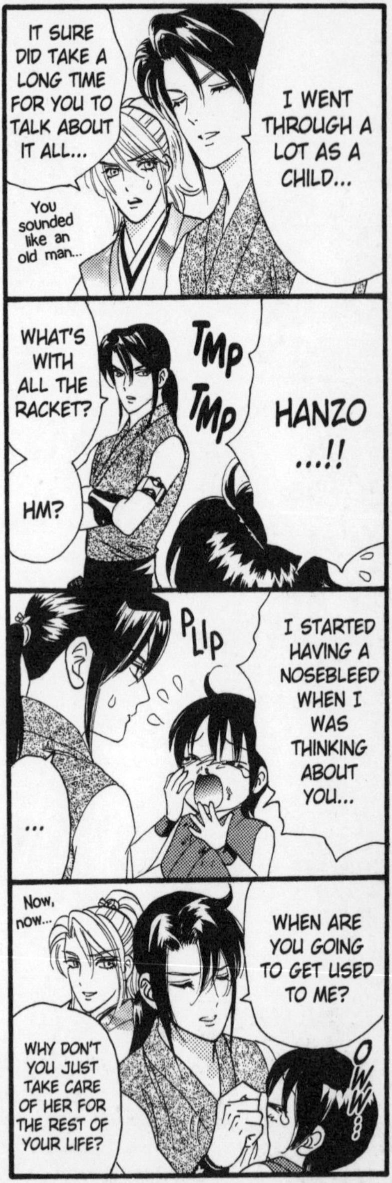
I WENT THROUGH A LOT AS A CHILD...
IT SURE DID TAKE A LONG TIME FOR YOU TO TALK ABOUT IT ALL...
You sounded like an old man...
HANZO ...!!
TMP TMP
WHAT'S WITH ALL THE RACKET?
HM?
I STARTED HAVING A NOSEBLEED WHEN I WAS THINKING ABOUT YOU...
PLIP
...
OWW!!
WHEN ARE YOU GOING TO GET USED TO ME?
Now, now...
WHY DON'T YOU JUST TAKE CARE OF HER FOR THE REST OF YOUR LIFE?

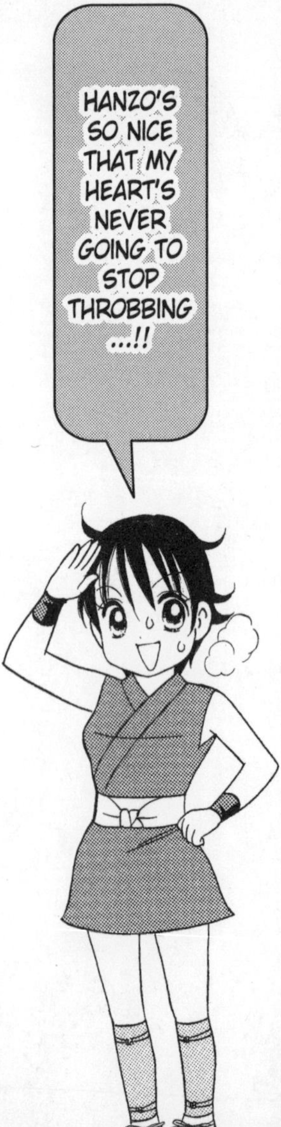
HANZO'S SO NICE THAT MY HEART'S NEVER GOING TO STOP THROBBING ...!!

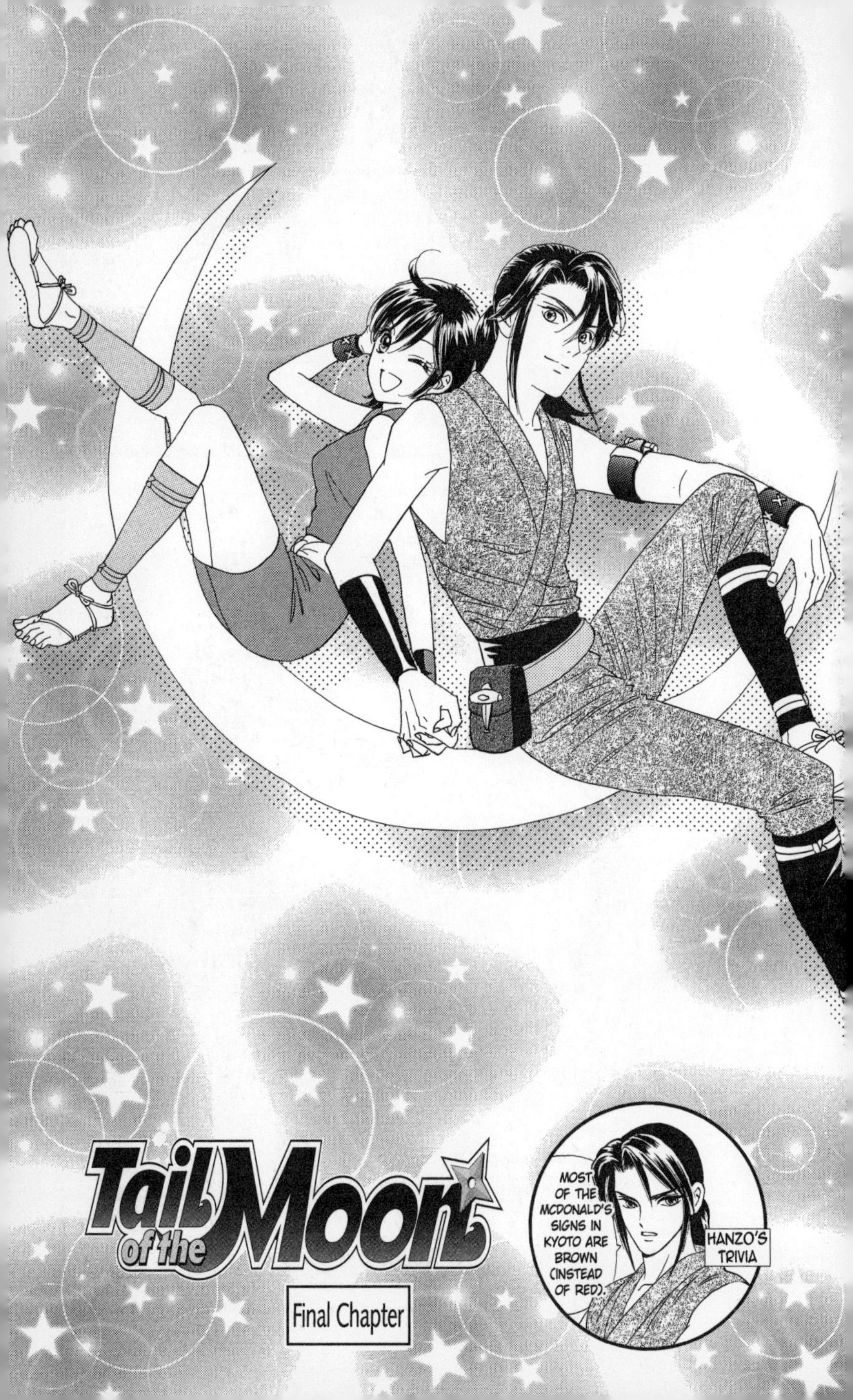
Tail of the Moon
Final Chapter
MOST OF THE MCDONALD'S SIGNS IN KYOTO ARE BROWN (INSTEAD OF RED).
HANZO'S TRIVIA

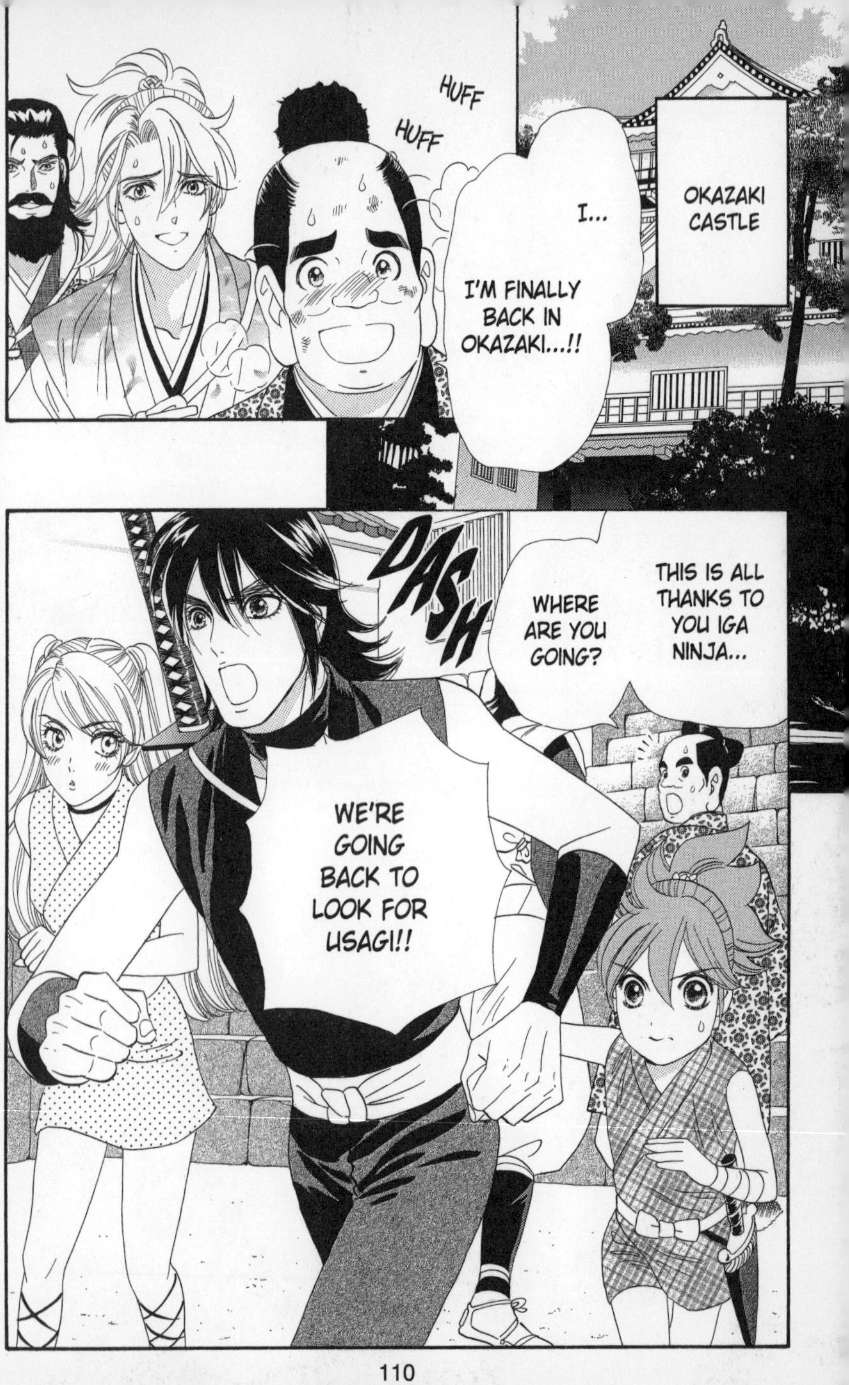
OKAZAKI CASTLE
HUFF
HUFF
I...
I'M FINALLY BACK IN OKAZAKI...!!
THIS IS ALL THANKS TO YOU IGA NINJA...
WHERE ARE YOU GOING?
DASH
WE'RE GOING BACK TO LOOK FOR USAGI!!

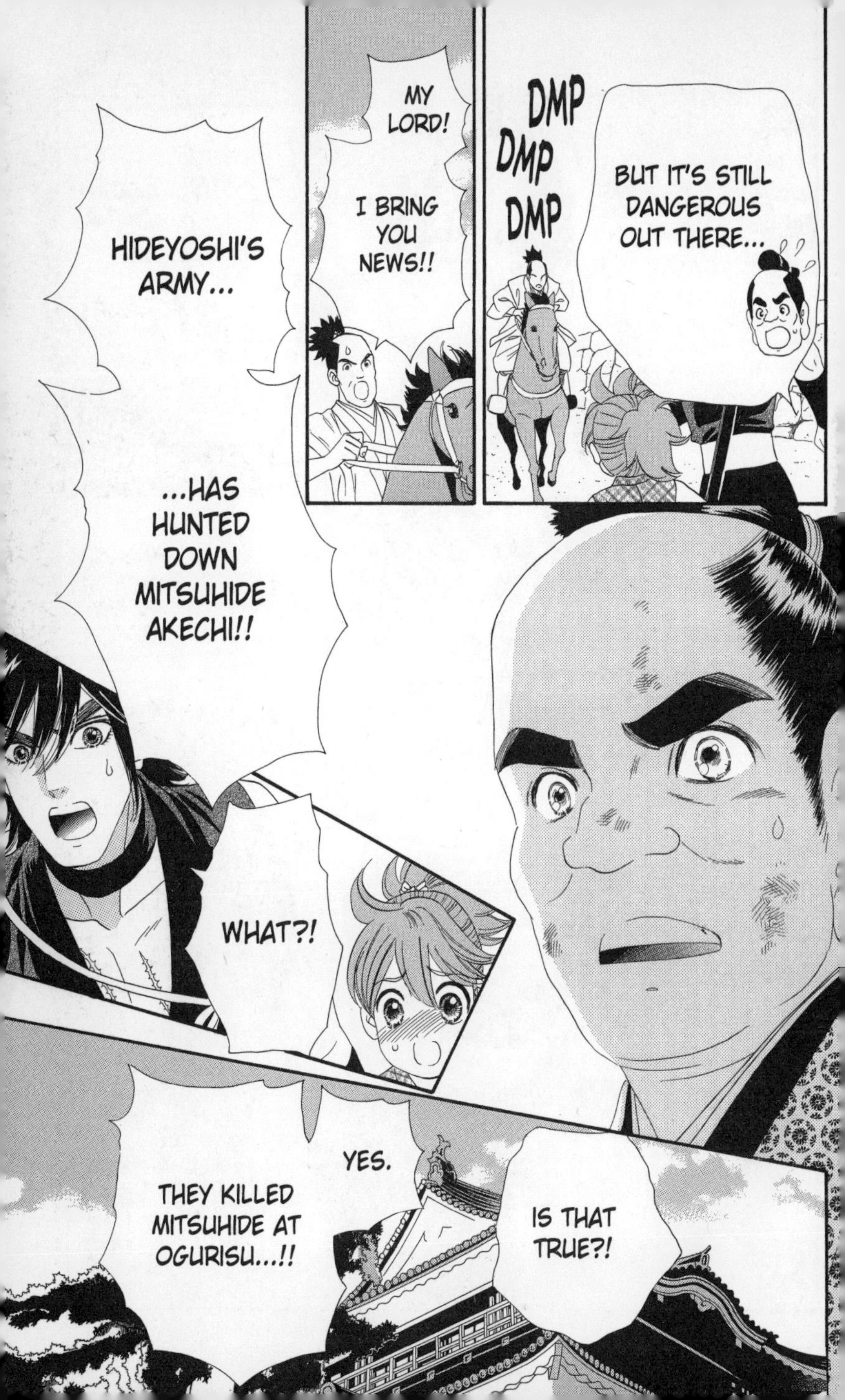
BUT IT'S STILL DANGEROUS OUT THERE...
DMP DMP DMP
MY LORD!
I BRING YOU NEWS!!
HIDEYOSHI'S ARMY...
...HAS HUNTED DOWN MITSUHIDE AKECHI!!
WHAT?!
IS THAT TRUE?!
YES.
THEY KILLED MITSUHIDE AT OGURISU...!!

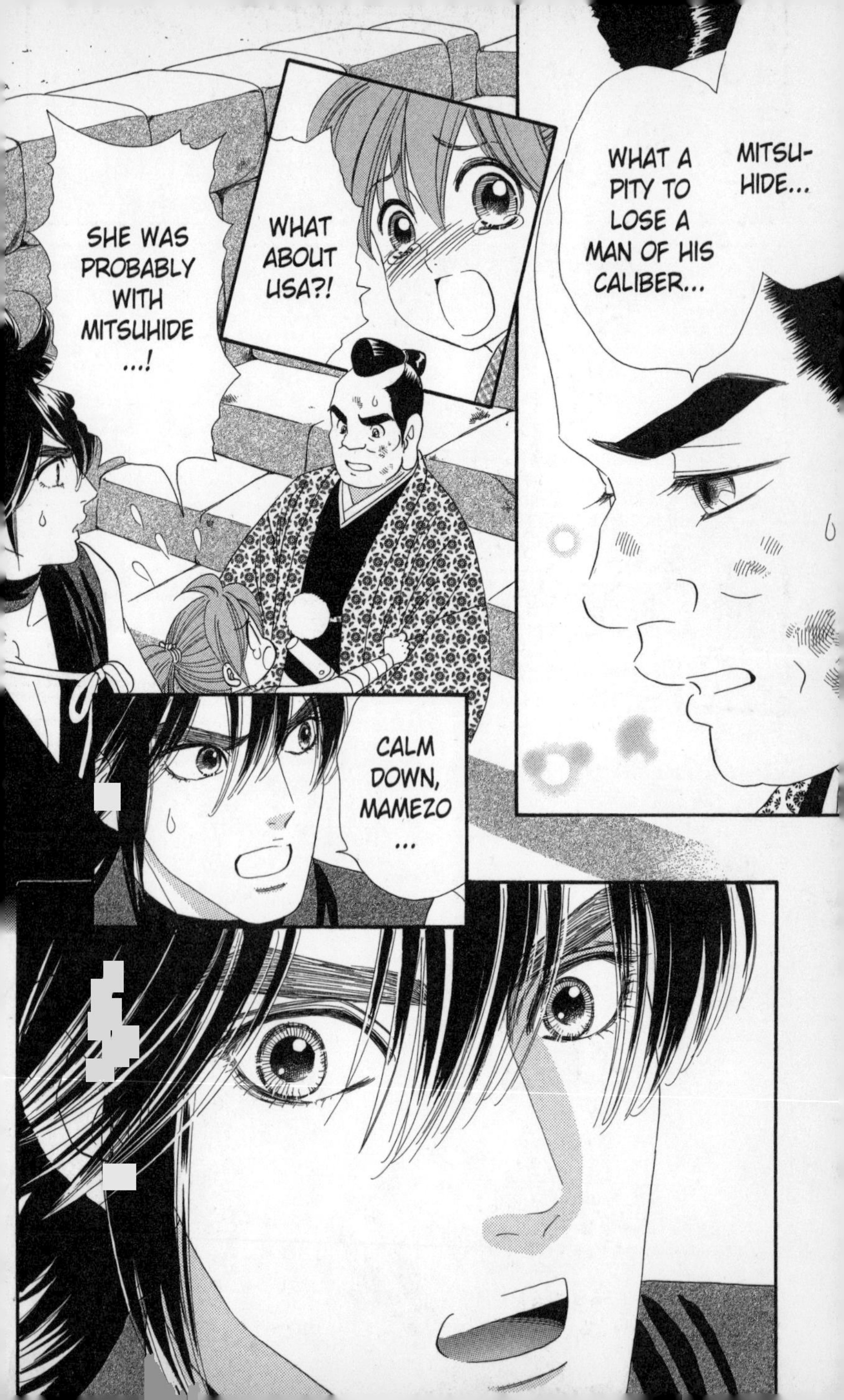
MITSU-HIDE...
WHAT A PITY TO LOSE A MAN OF HIS CALIBER...
WHAT ABOUT USA?!
SHE WAS PROBABLY WITH MITSUHIDE ...!
CALM DOWN, MAMEZO ...

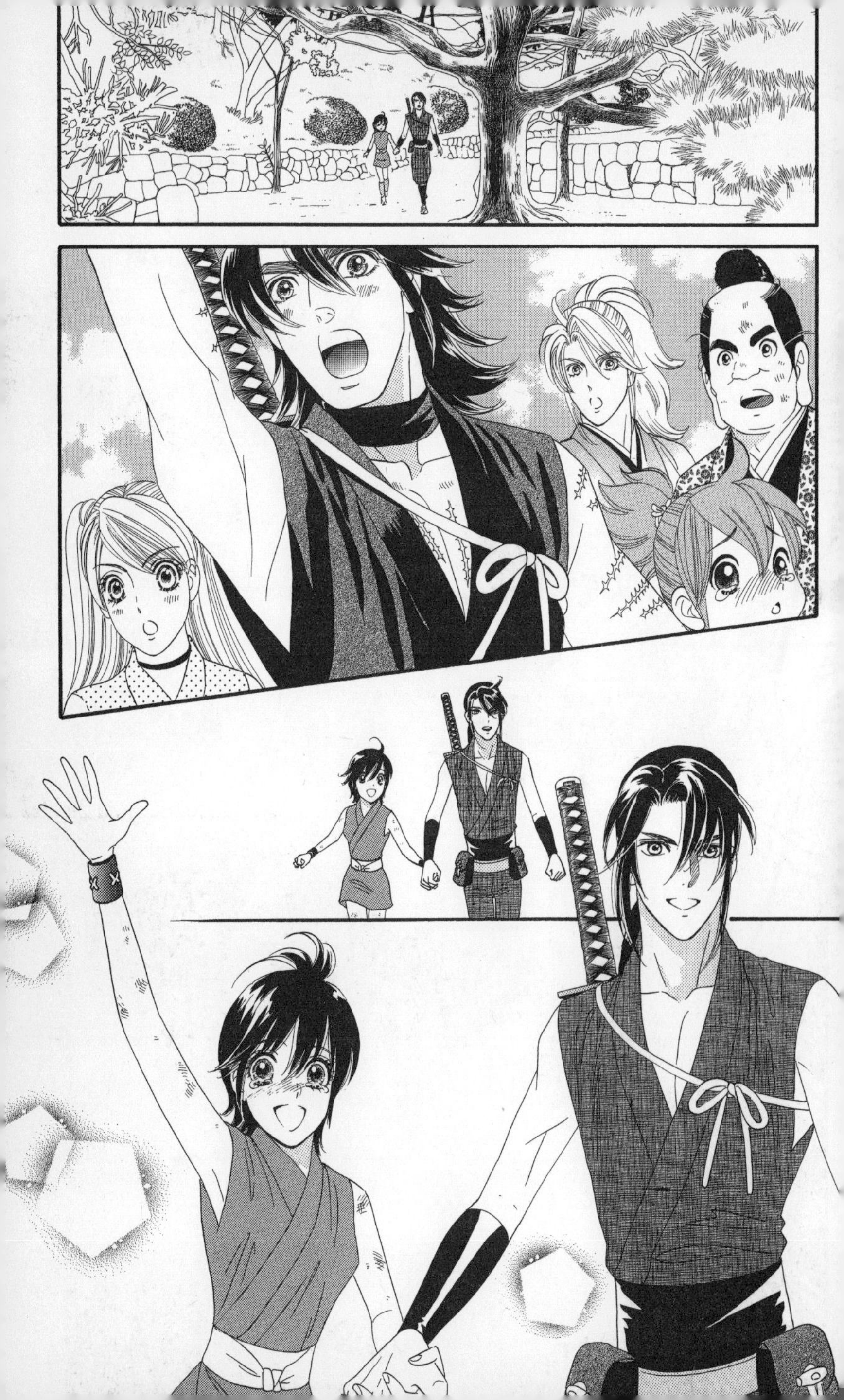

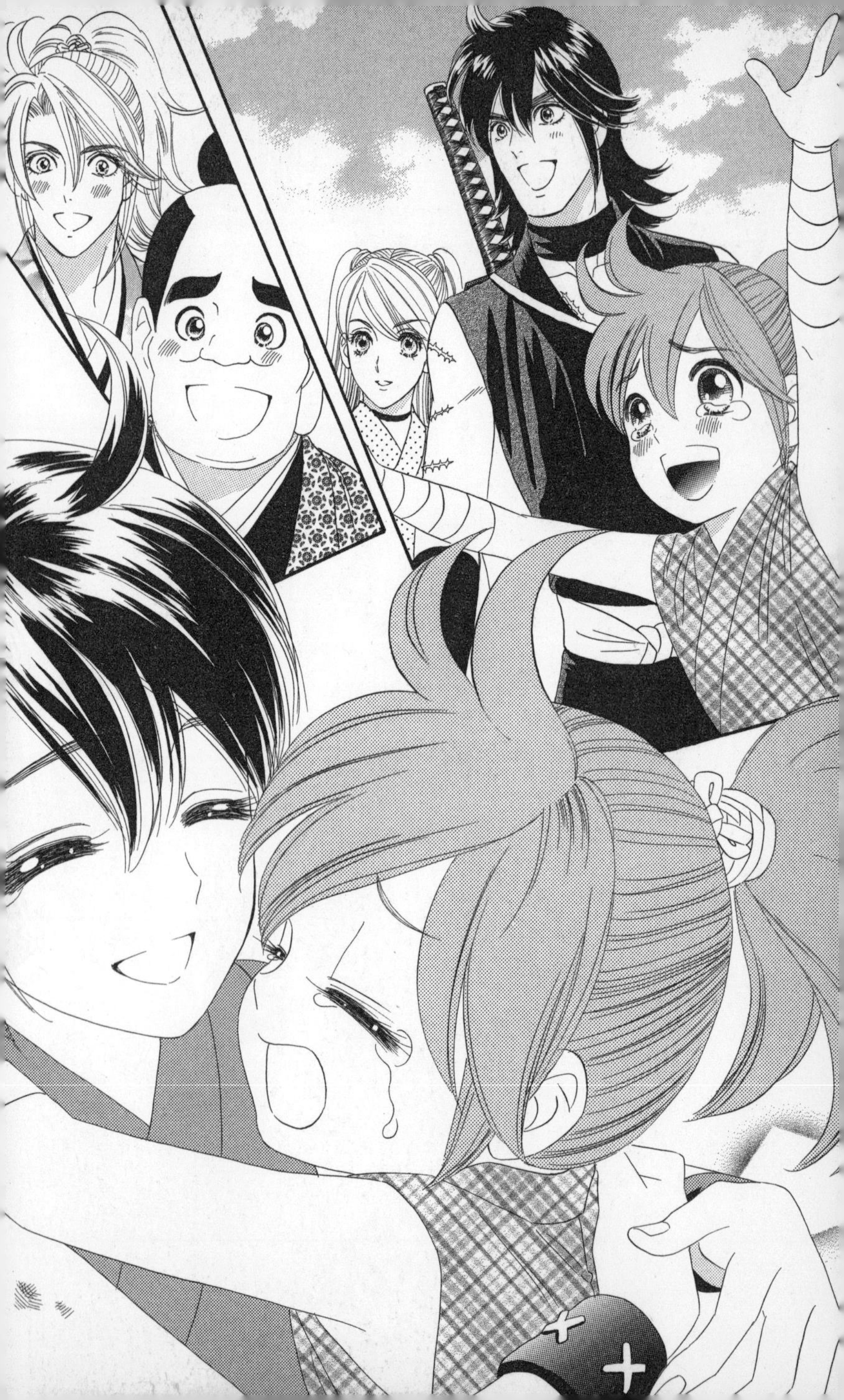

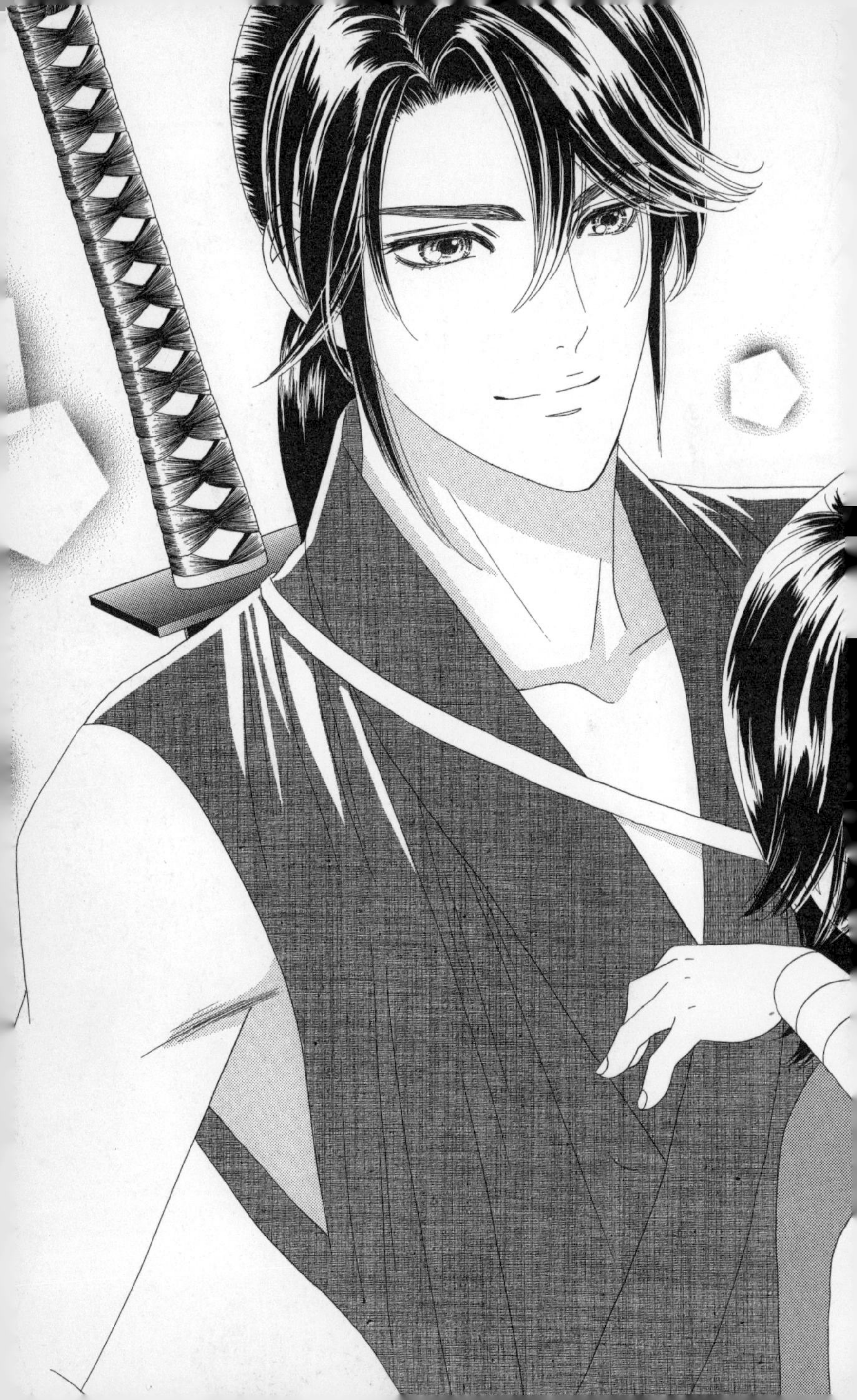

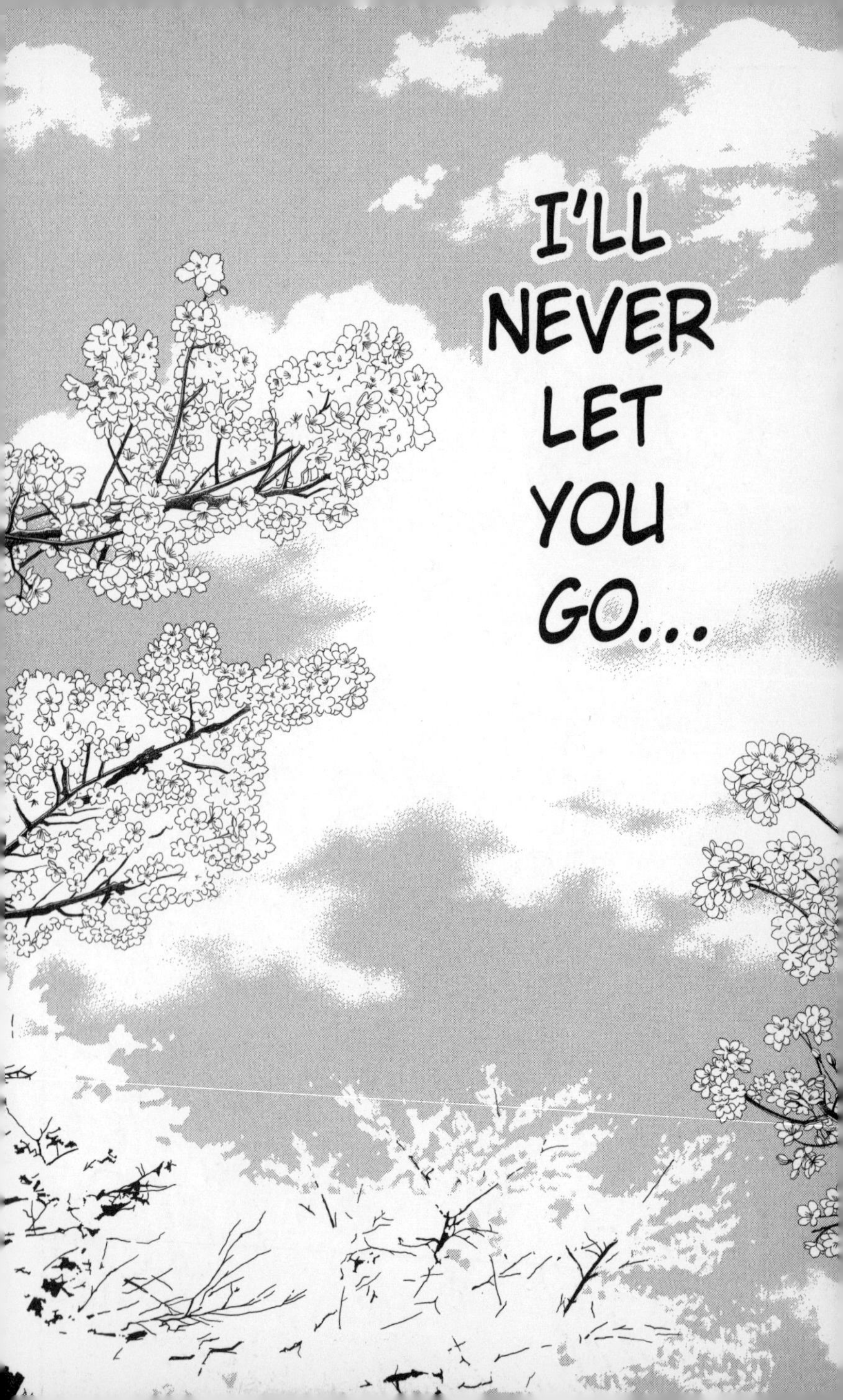
I'LL NEVER LET YOU GO...

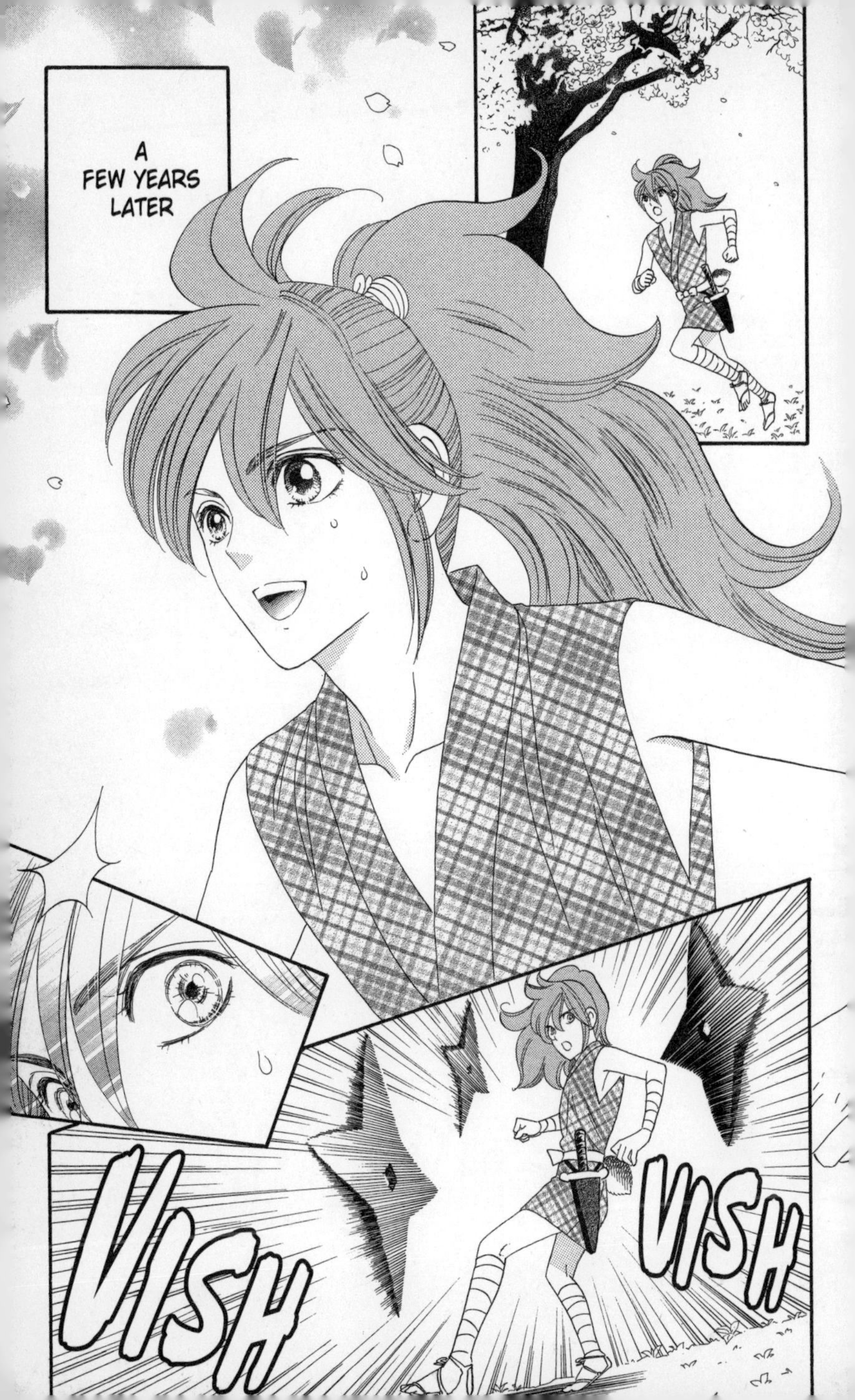
A FEW YEARS LATER
VISH
VISH

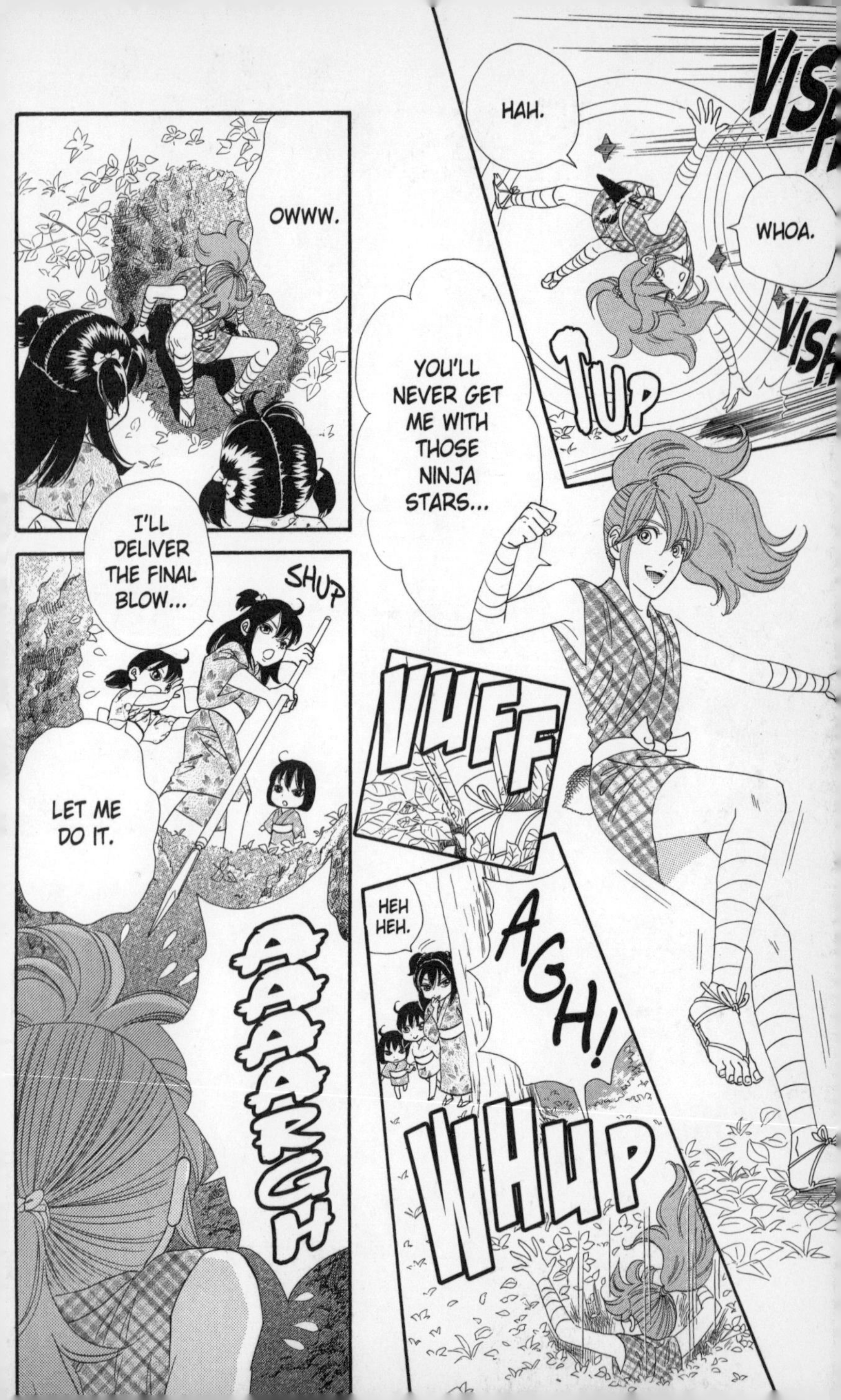

VISH
WHOA.
HAH.
VISH
TUP
YOU'LL NEVER GET ME WITH THOSE NINJA STARS...
VUFF
HEH HEH.
AGH!
WHUP
OWWW.
I'LL DELIVER THE FINAL BLOW...
SHUP
LET ME DO IT.
AAAARGH

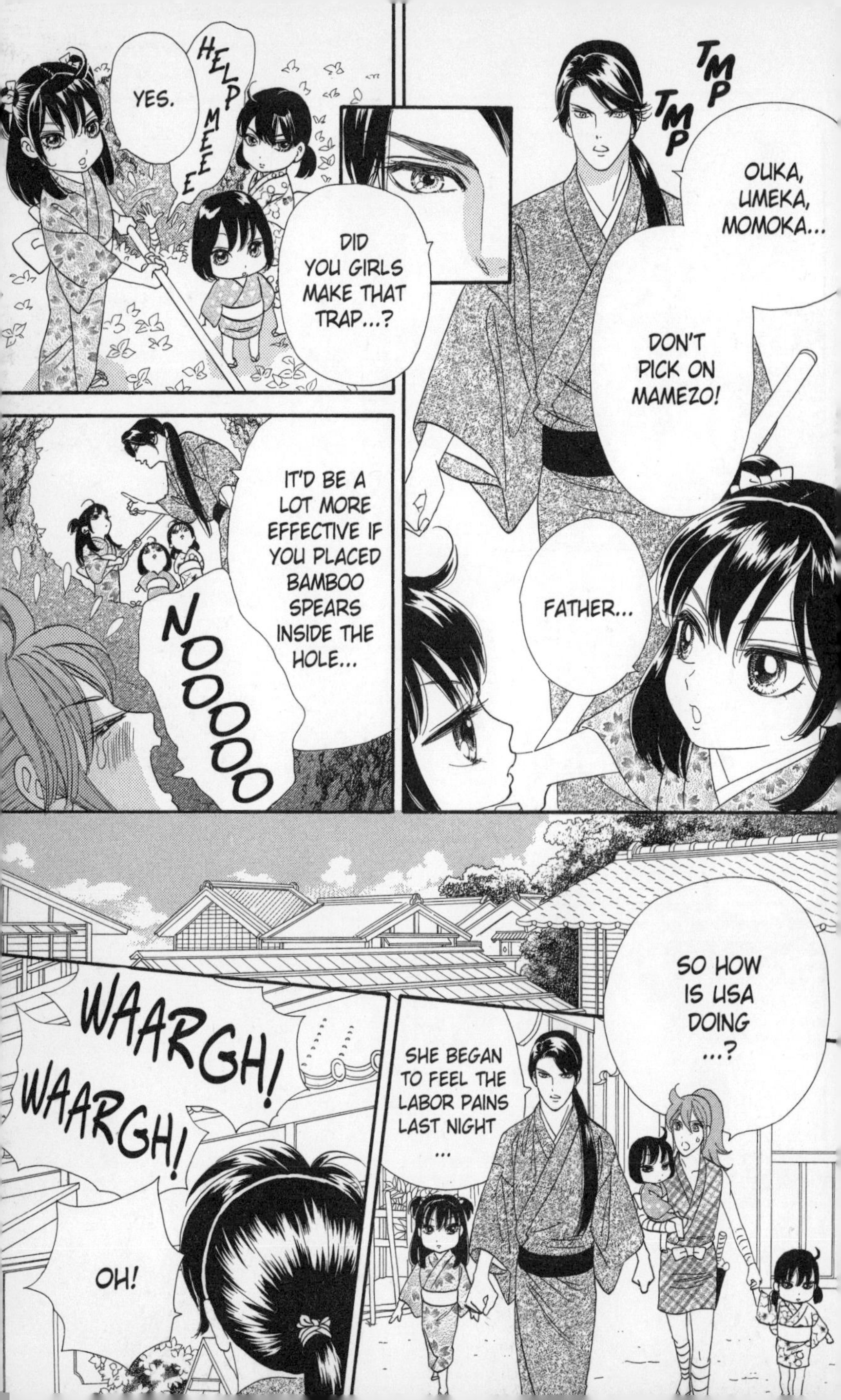
TMP TMP
OUKA, UMEKA, MOMOKA...
DON'T PICK ON MAMEZO!
FATHER...
DID YOU GIRLS MAKE THAT TRAP...?
HELP MEEE
YES.
IT'D BE A LOT MORE EFFECTIVE IF YOU PLACED BAMBOO SPEARS INSIDE THE HOLE...
NOOOOOO
SO HOW IS USA DOING ...?
SHE BEGAN TO FEEL THE LABOR PAINS LAST NIGHT ...
WAARGH! WAARGH!
OH!

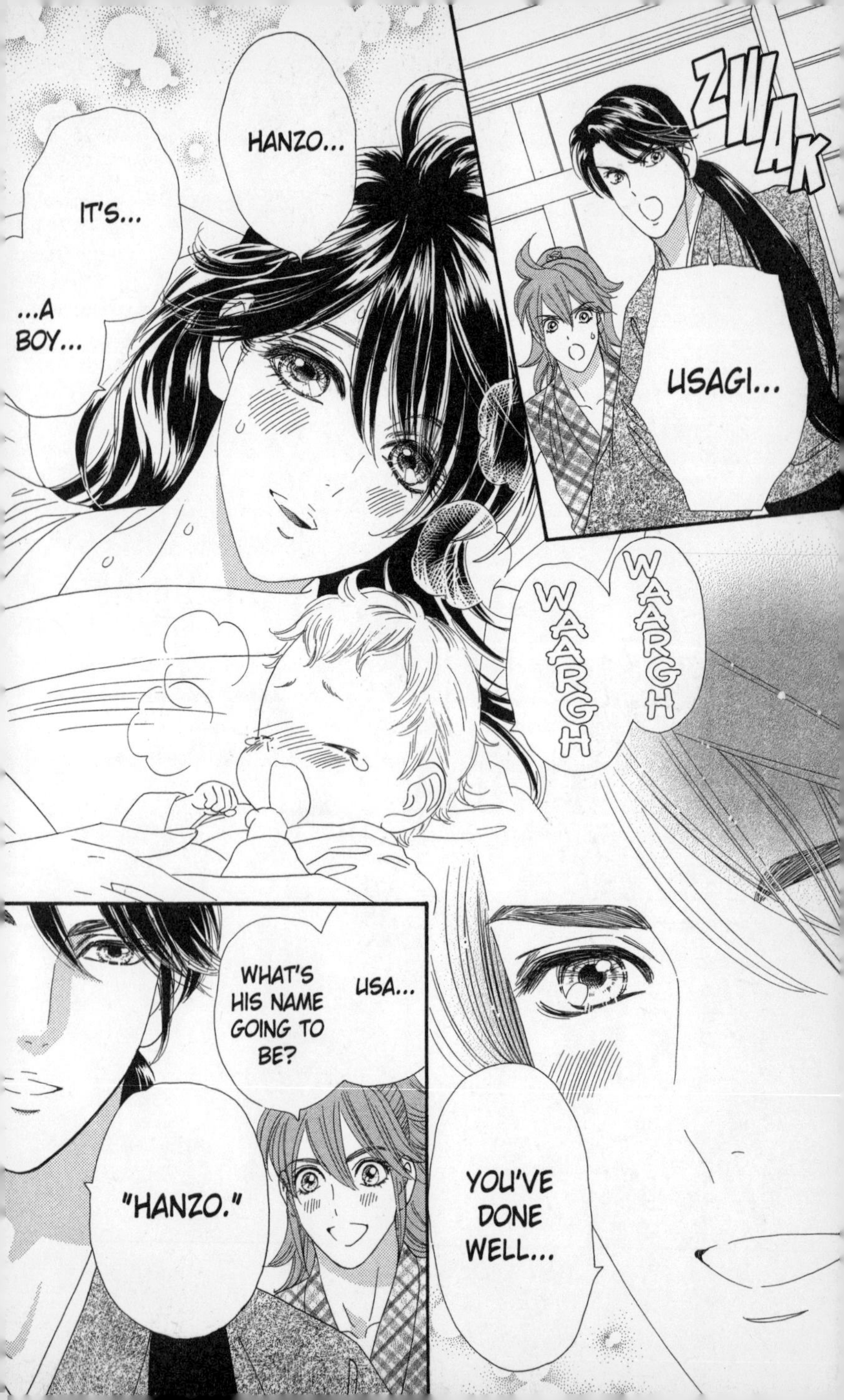
ZWAK
USAGI...
HANZO...
IT'S...
...A BOY...
WARGH WARGH
YOU'VE DONE WELL...
USA...
WHAT'S HIS NAME GOING TO BE?
"HANZO."

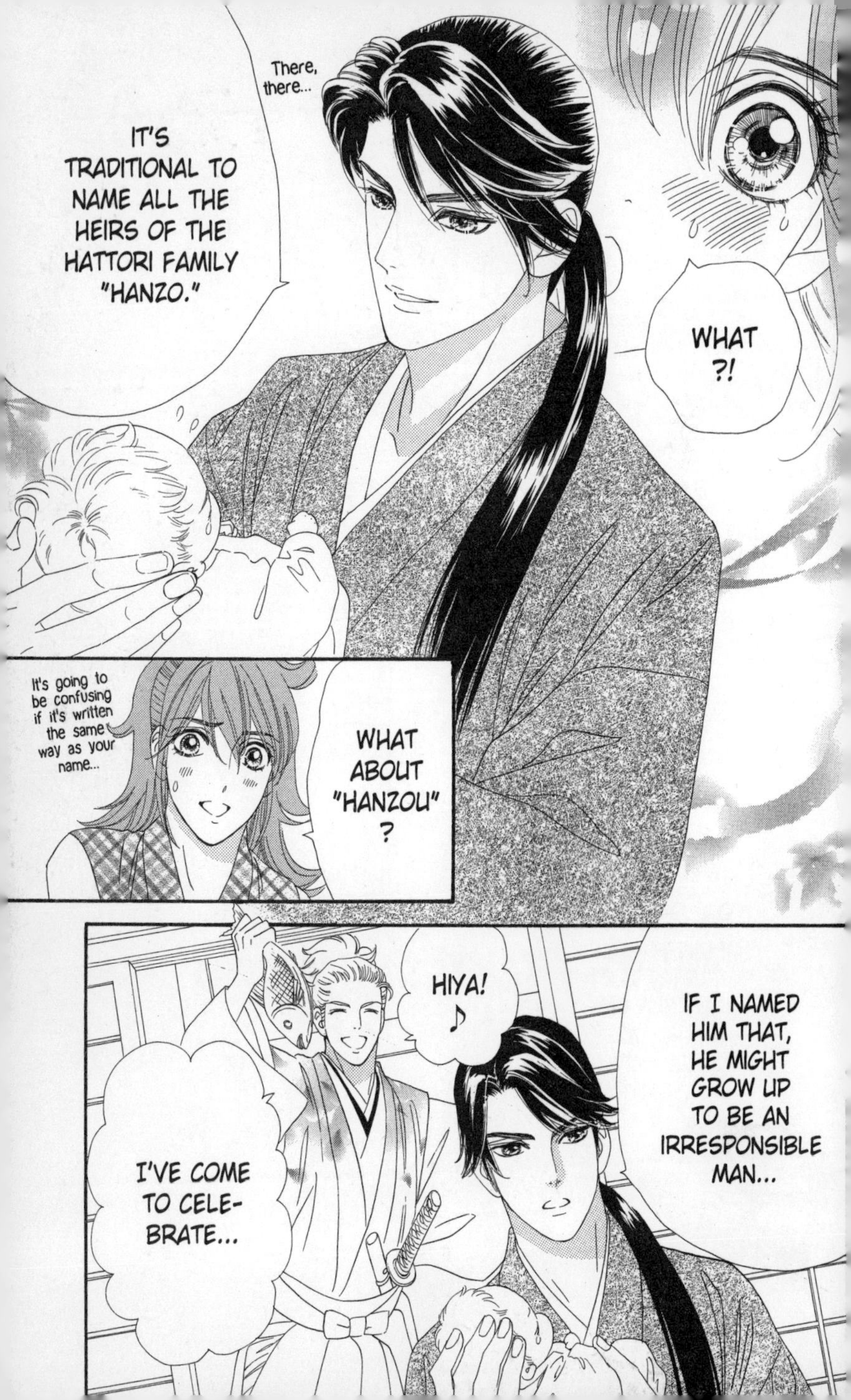
There, there...
IT'S TRADITIONAL TO NAME ALL THE HEIRS OF THE HATTORI FAMILY "HANZO."
WHAT ?!
WHAT ABOUT "HANZOU" ?
It's going to be confusing if it's written the same way as your name...
IF I NAMED HIM THAT, HE MIGHT GROW UP TO BE AN IRRESPONSIBLE MAN...
HIYA! ♪
I'VE COME TO CELE-BRATE...

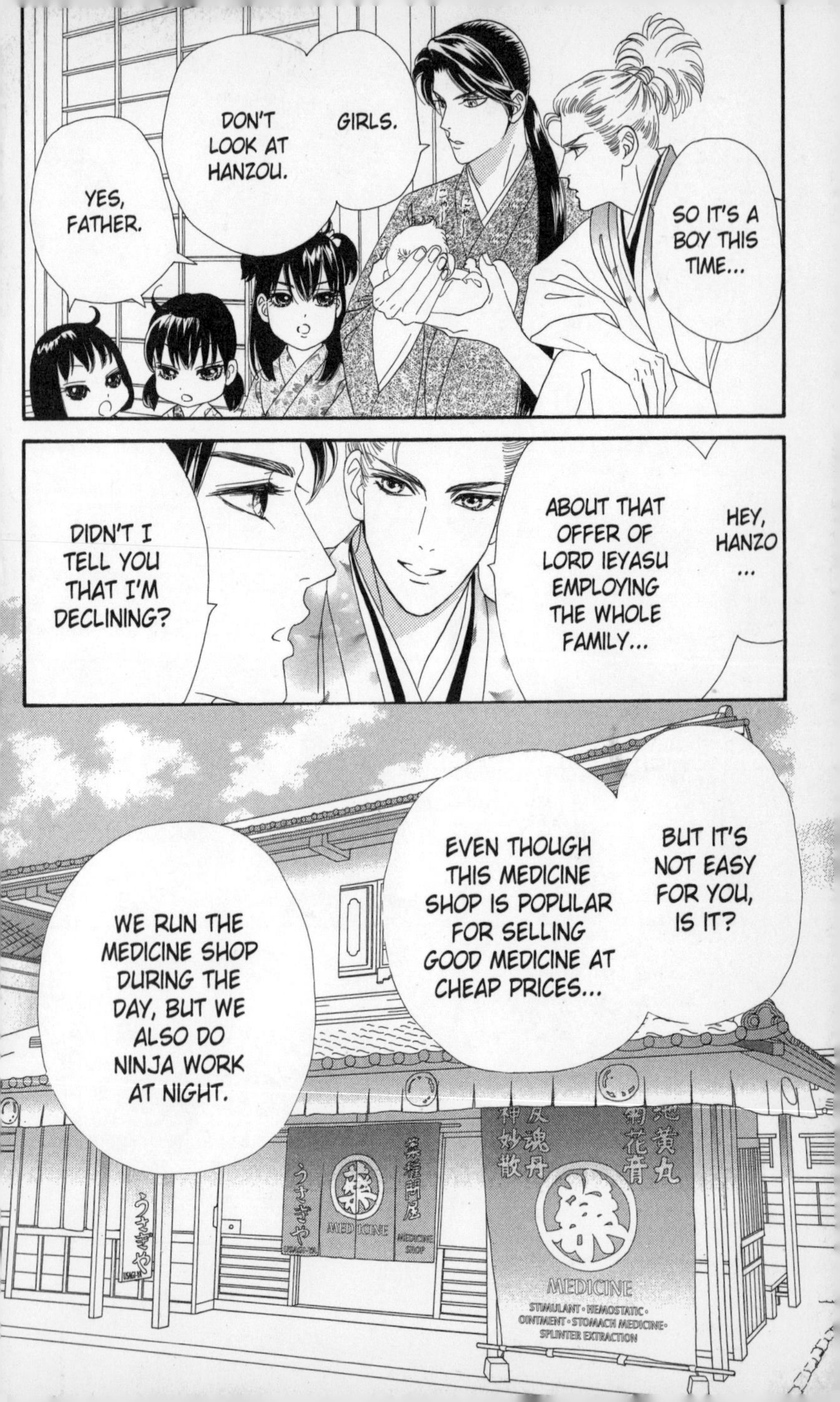
SO IT'S A BOY THIS TIME...
GIRLS.
DON'T LOOK AT HANZOU.
YES, FATHER.
HEY, HANZO ...
ABOUT THAT OFFER OF LORD IEYASU EMPLOYING THE WHOLE FAMILY...
DIDN'T I TELL YOU THAT I'M DECLINING?
BUT IT'S NOT EASY FOR YOU, IS IT?
EVEN THOUGH THIS MEDICINE SHOP IS POPULAR FOR SELLING GOOD MEDICINE AT CHEAP PRICES...
WE RUN THE MEDICINE SHOP DURING THE DAY, BUT WE ALSO DO NINJA WORK AT NIGHT.
MEDICINE
STIMULANT • HEMOSTATIC • OINTMENT • STOMACH MEDICINE • SPLINTER EXTRACTION
MEDICINE
MEDICINE SHOP
うさぎや
USAGI-YA

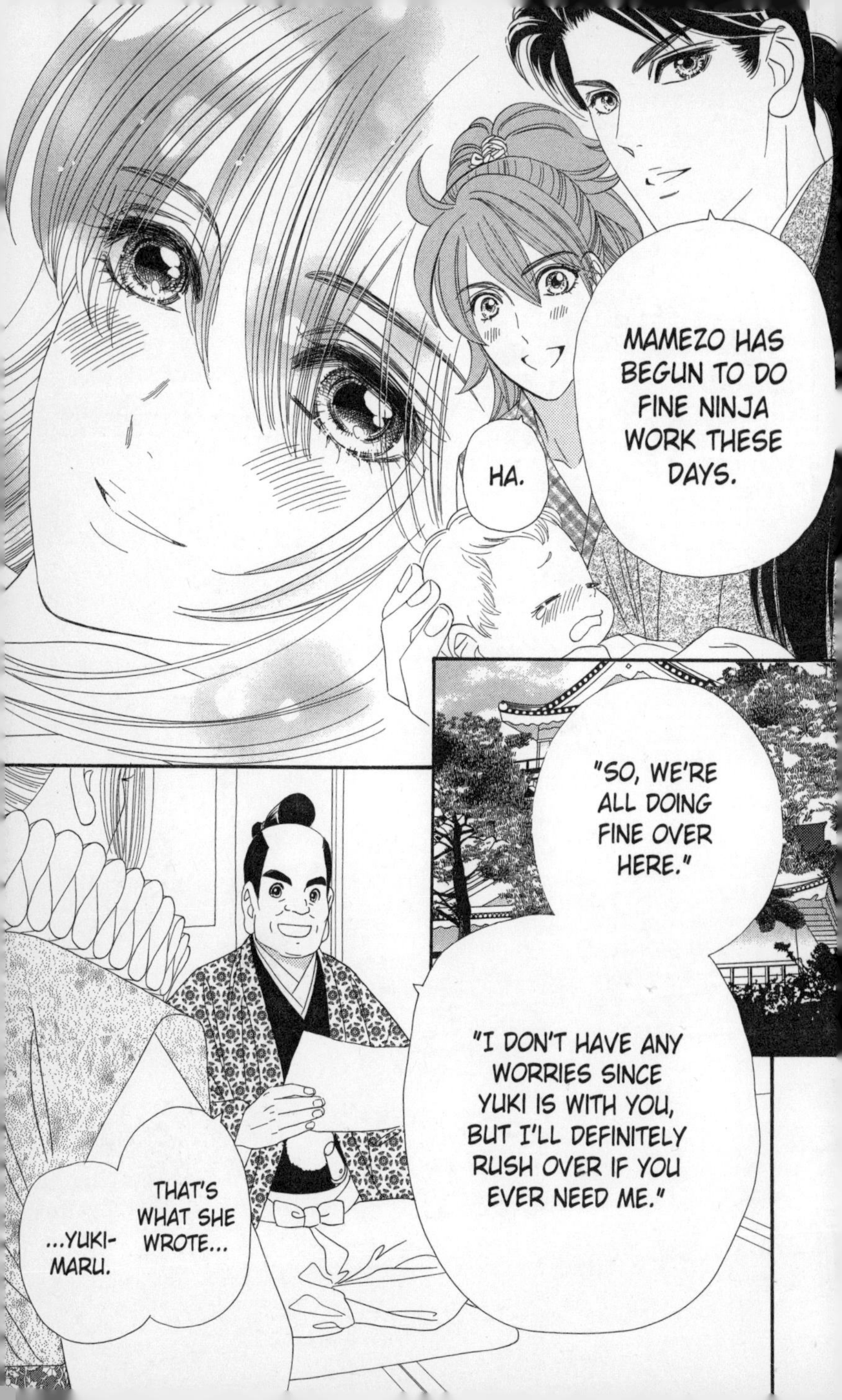
MAMEZO HAS BEGUN TO DO FINE NINJA WORK THESE DAYS.
HA.
"SO, WE'RE ALL DOING FINE OVER HERE."
"I DON'T HAVE ANY WORRIES SINCE YUKI IS WITH YOU, BUT I'LL DEFINITELY RUSH OVER IF YOU EVER NEED ME."
THAT'S WHAT SHE WROTE...
...YUKI-MARU.

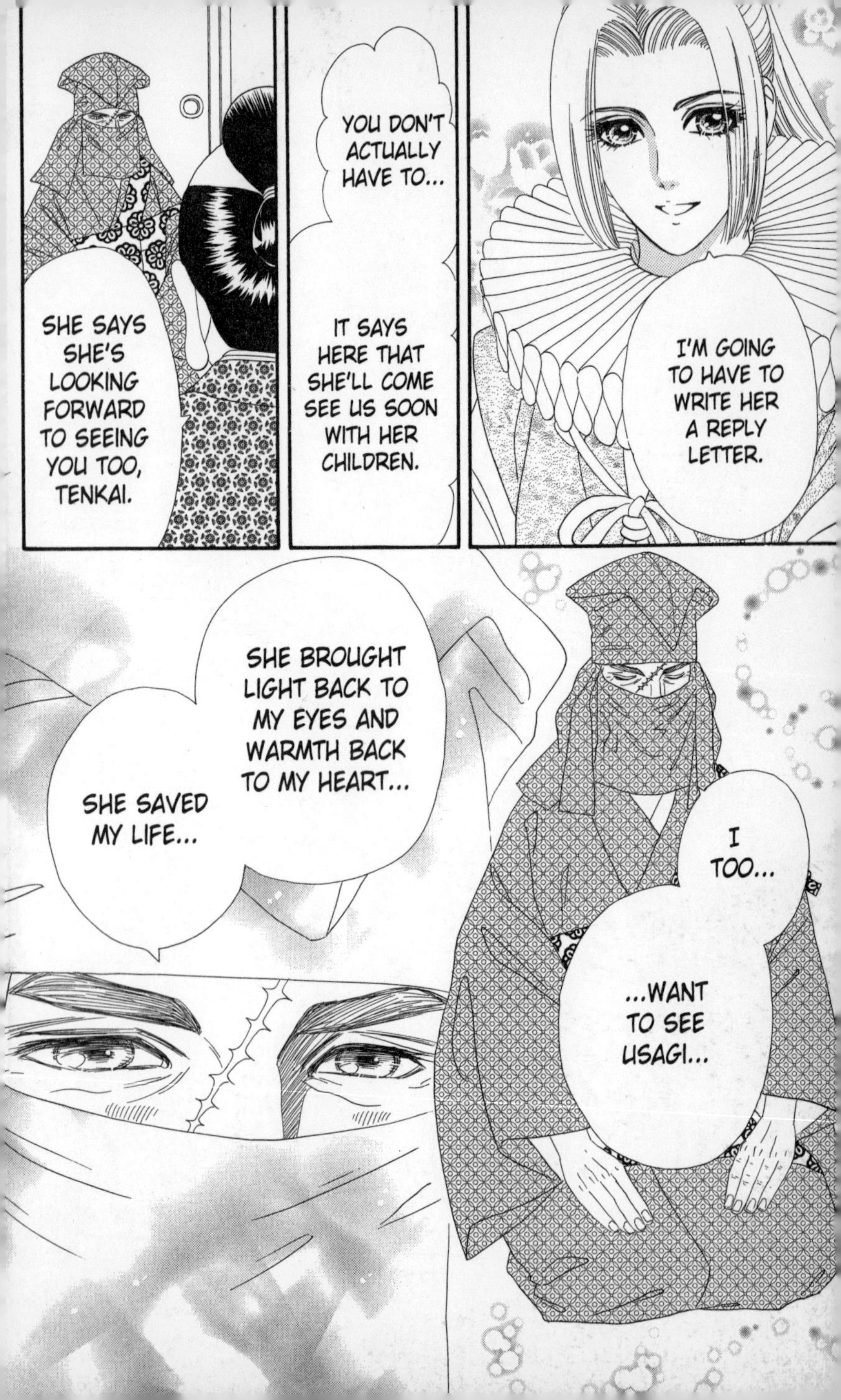

I'M GOING TO HAVE TO WRITE HER A REPLY LETTER.
YOU DON'T ACTUALLY HAVE TO...
IT SAYS HERE THAT SHE'LL COME SEE US SOON WITH HER CHILDREN.
SHE SAYS SHE'S LOOKING FORWARD TO SEEING YOU TOO, TENKAI.
I TOO...
...WANT TO SEE USAGI...
SHE BROUGHT LIGHT BACK TO MY EYES AND WARMTH BACK TO MY HEART...
SHE SAVED MY LIFE...

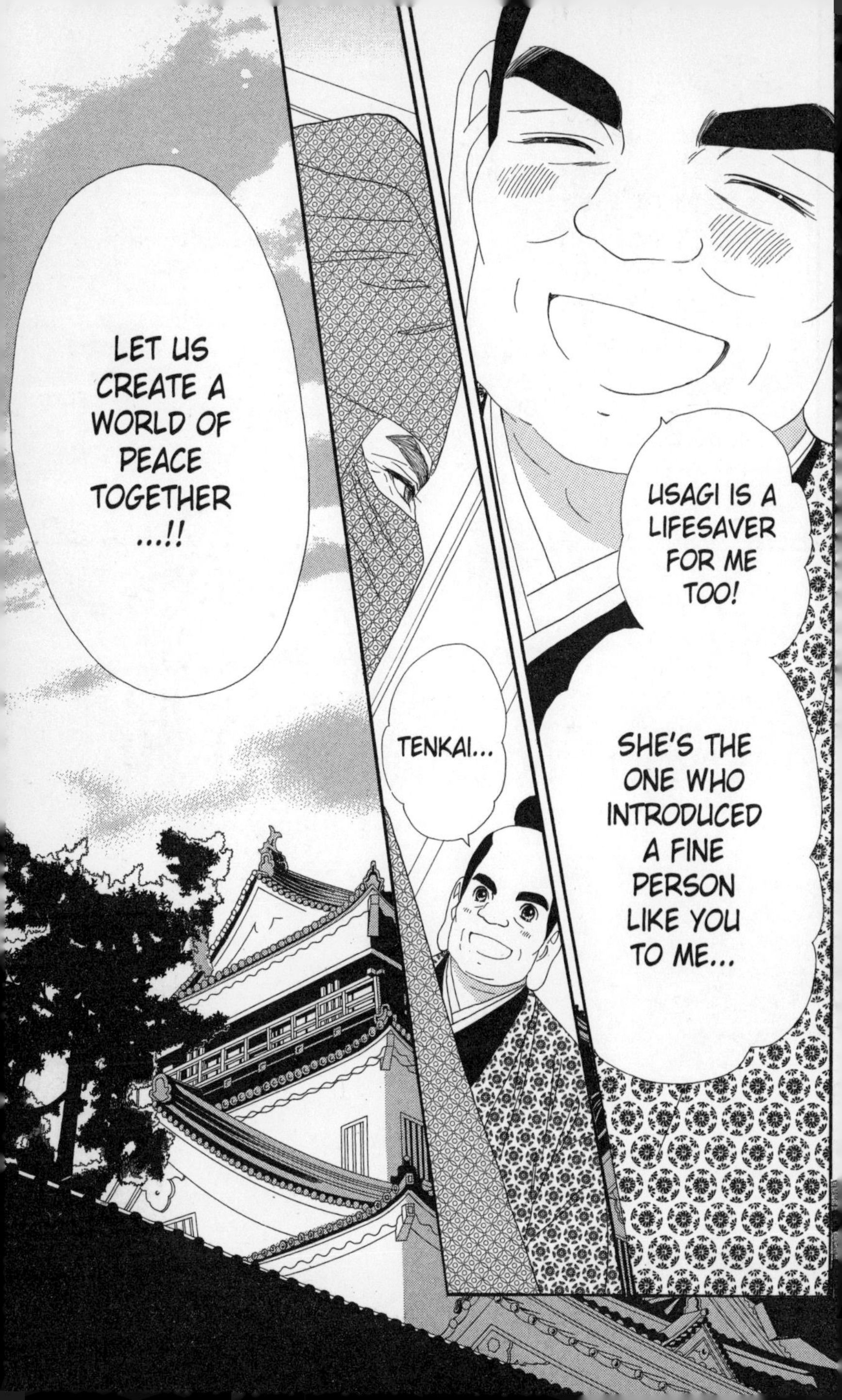
USAGI IS A LIFESAVER FOR ME TOO!
SHE'S THE ONE WHO INTRODUCED A FINE PERSON LIKE YOU TO ME...
TENKAI...
LET US CREATE A WORLD OF PEACE TOGETHER ...!!

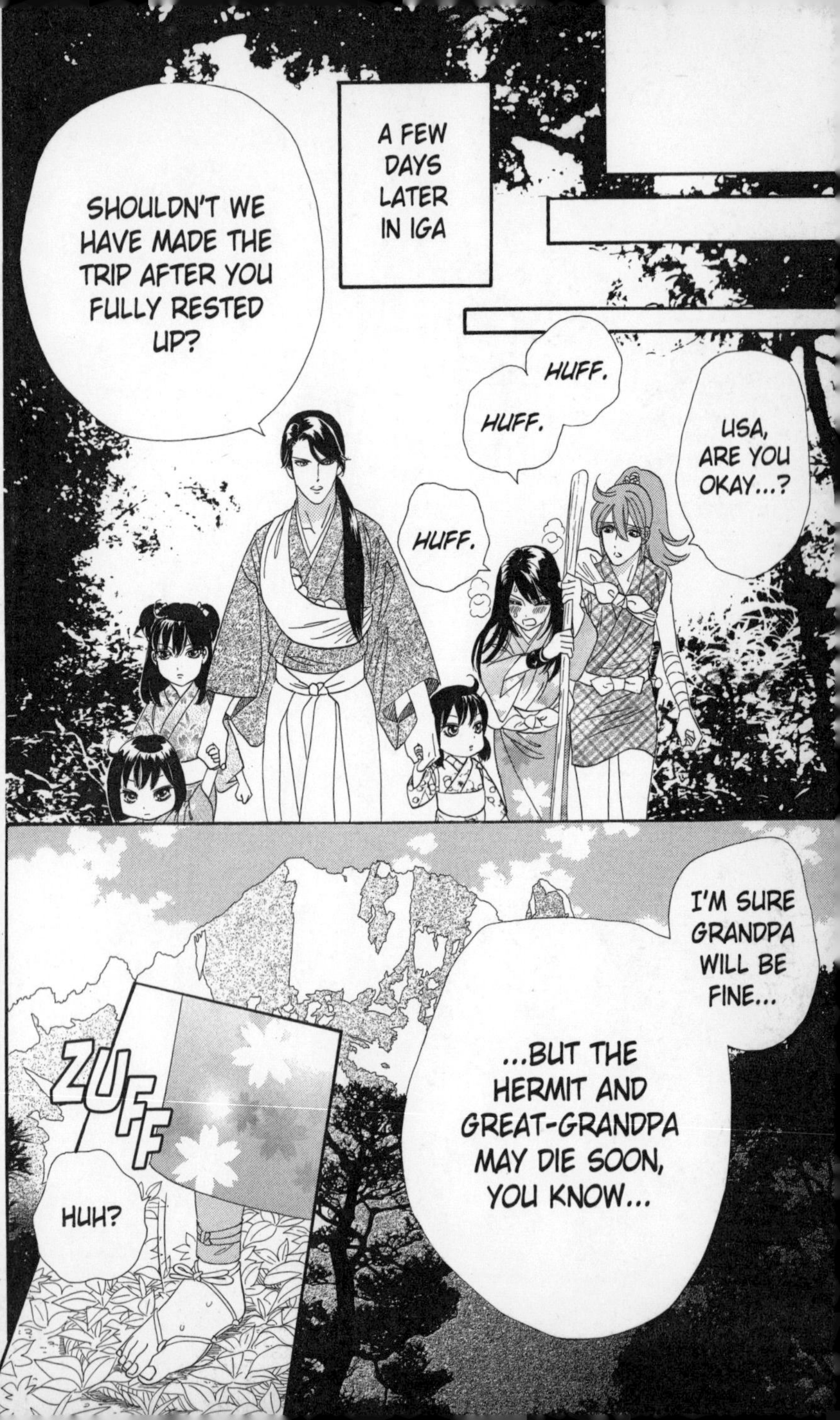
A FEW DAYS LATER IN IGA
SHOULDN'T WE HAVE MADE THE TRIP AFTER YOU FULLY RESTED UP?
USA, ARE YOU OKAY...?
HUFF.
HUFF.
HUFF.
I'M SURE GRANDPA WILL BE FINE...
...BUT THE HERMIT AND GREAT-GRANDPA MAY DIE SOON, YOU KNOW...
ZUFF
HUH?

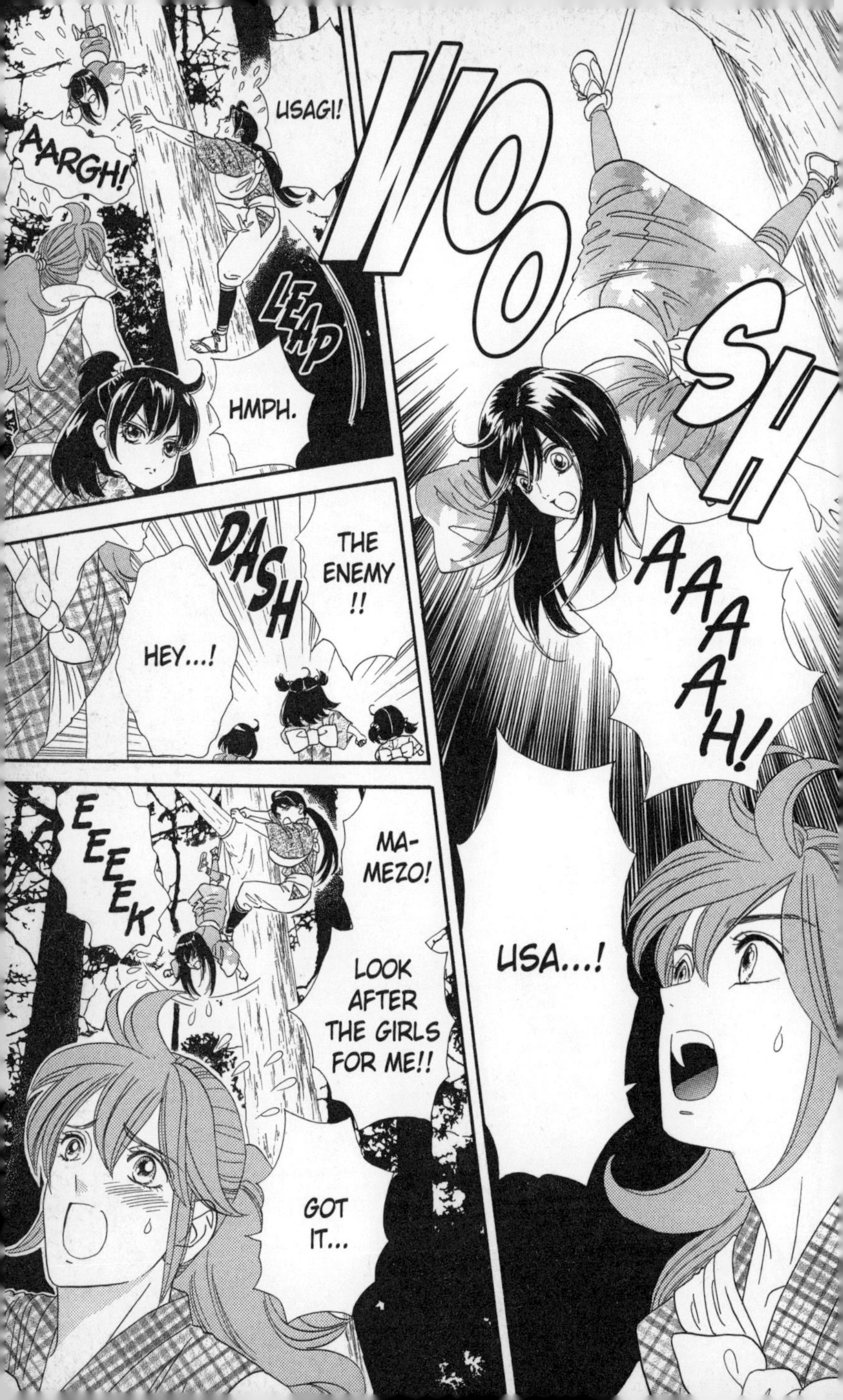
WHOOSH
AAAAH!
USA...!
USAGI!
AARGH!
LEAP
HMPH.
THE ENEMY!!
DASH
HEY...!
MA-MEZO!
LOOK AFTER THE GIRLS FOR ME!!
EEEEK
GOT IT...

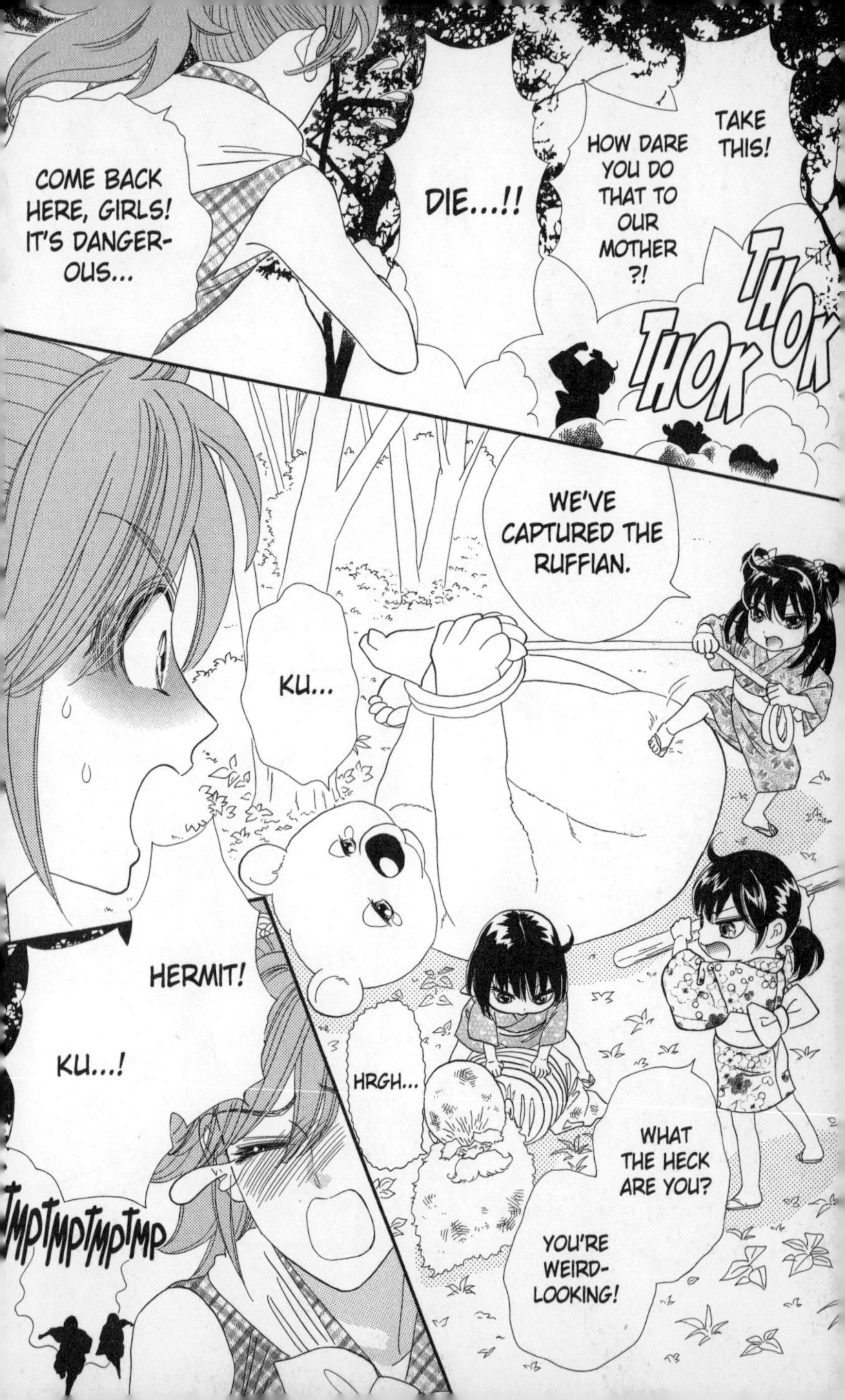
TAKE THIS!
HOW DARE YOU DO THAT TO OUR MOTHER?!
THOK THOK
DIE...!!
COME BACK HERE, GIRLS! IT'S DANGER-OUS...
WE'VE CAPTURED THE RUFFIAN.
KU...
WHAT THE HECK ARE YOU?
YOU'RE WEIRD-LOOKING!
HRGH...
HERMIT!
KU...!
TMPTMPTMPTMP

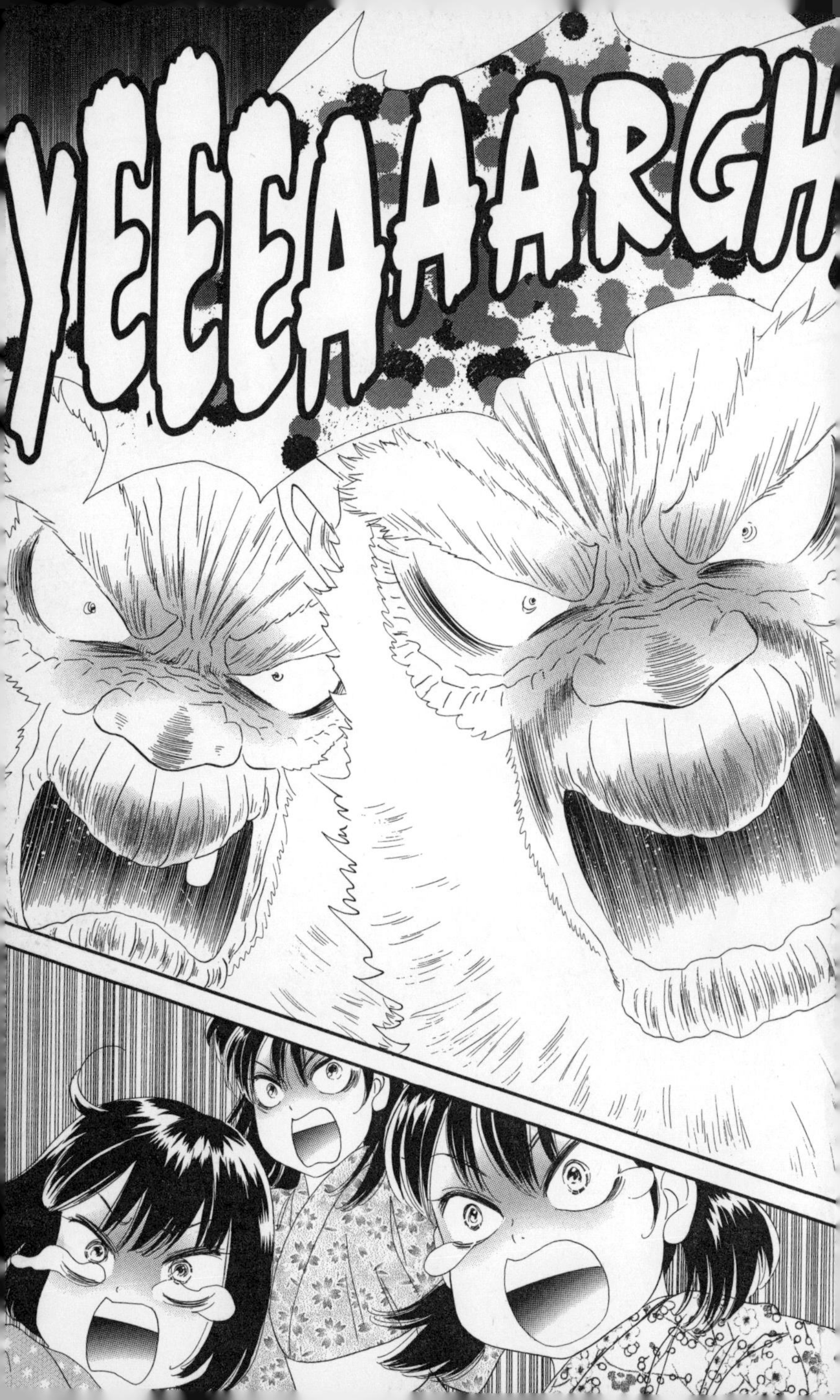
YEEEAAARGH

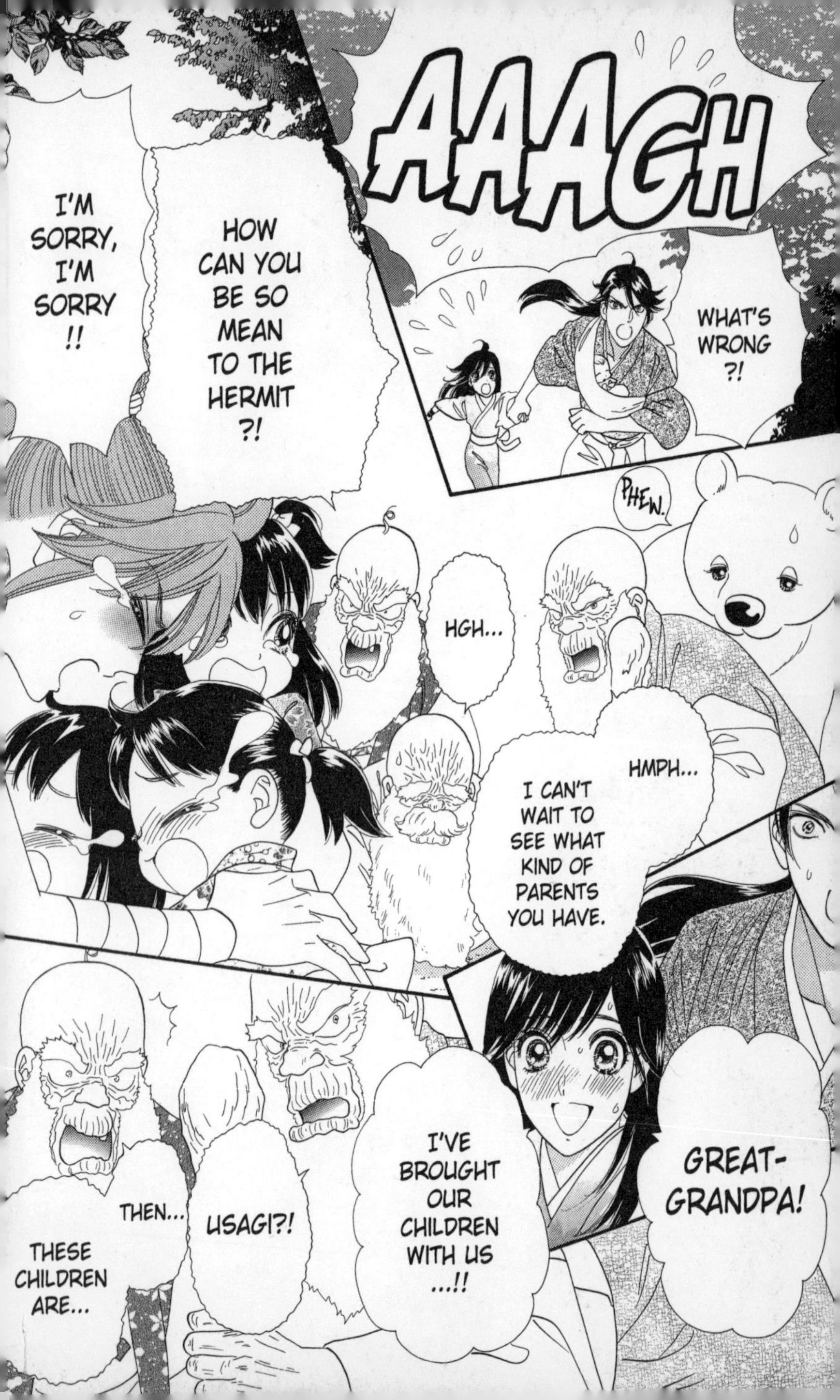
AAACH
WHAT'S WRONG?!
HOW CAN YOU BE SO MEAN TO THE HERMIT?!
I'M SORRY, I'M SORRY!!
PHEW.
HGH...
HMPH...
I CAN'T WAIT TO SEE WHAT KIND OF PARENTS YOU HAVE.
GREAT-GRANDPA!
I'VE BROUGHT OUR CHILDREN WITH US...!!
USAGI?!
THEN...
THESE CHILDREN ARE...

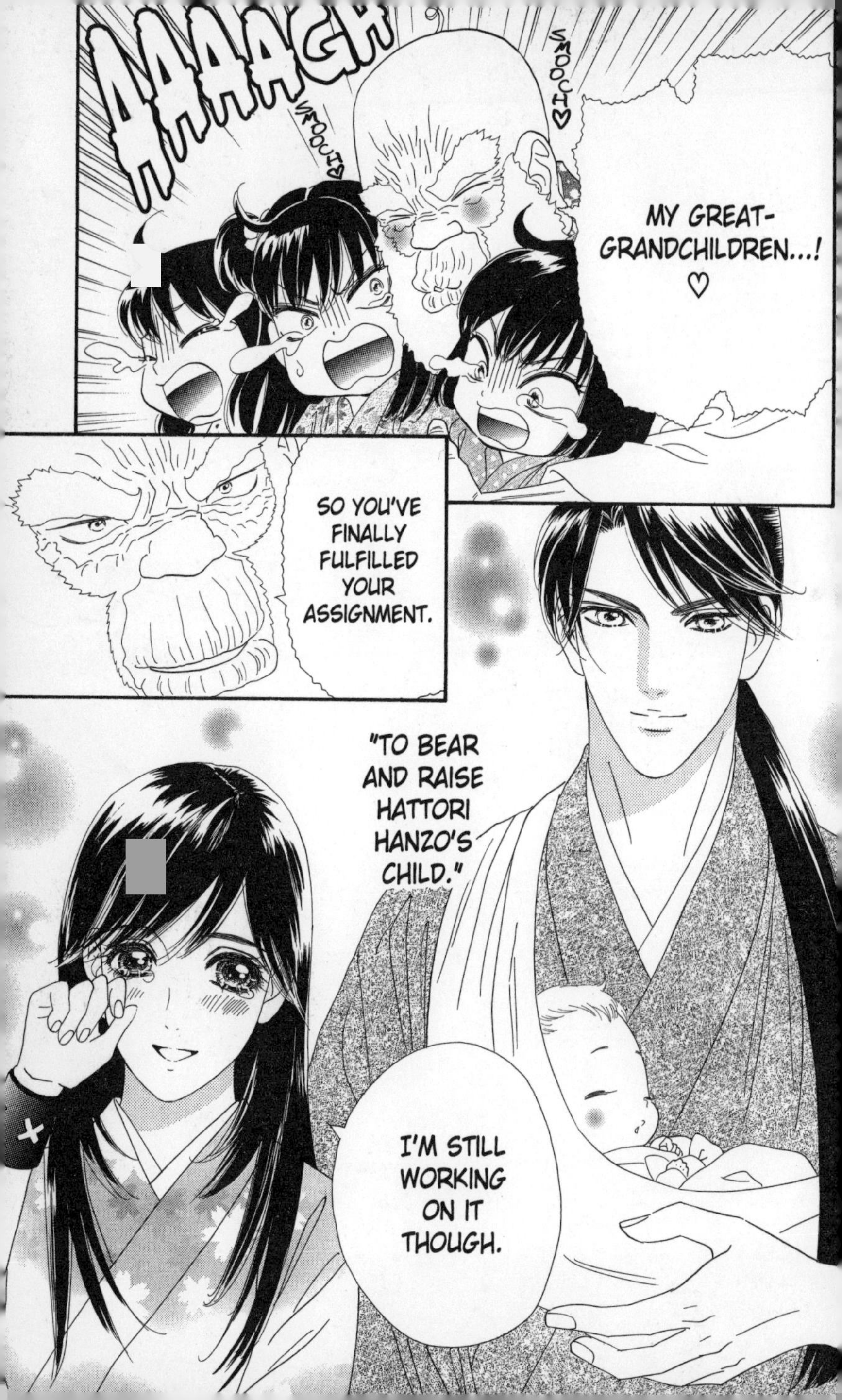
SMOOCH♡
MY GREAT-GRANDCHILDREN...! ♡
AAAAGH
SMOOCH♡
SO YOU'VE FINALLY FULFILLED YOUR ASSIGNMENT.
"TO BEAR AND RAISE HATTORI HANZO'S CHILD."
I'M STILL WORKING ON IT THOUGH.

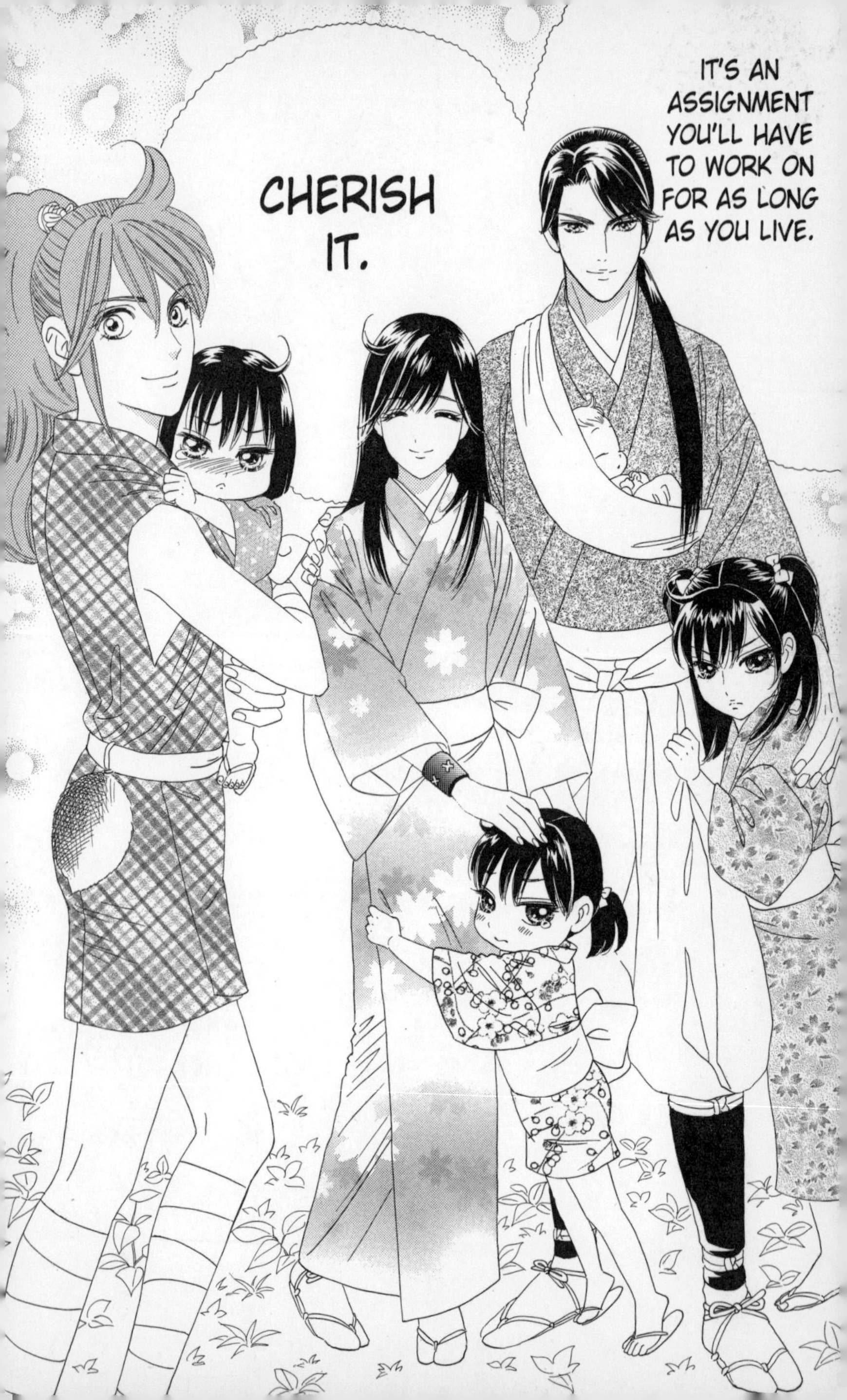
IT'S AN ASSIGNMENT YOU'LL HAVE TO WORK ON FOR AS LONG AS YOU LIVE.
CHERISH IT.

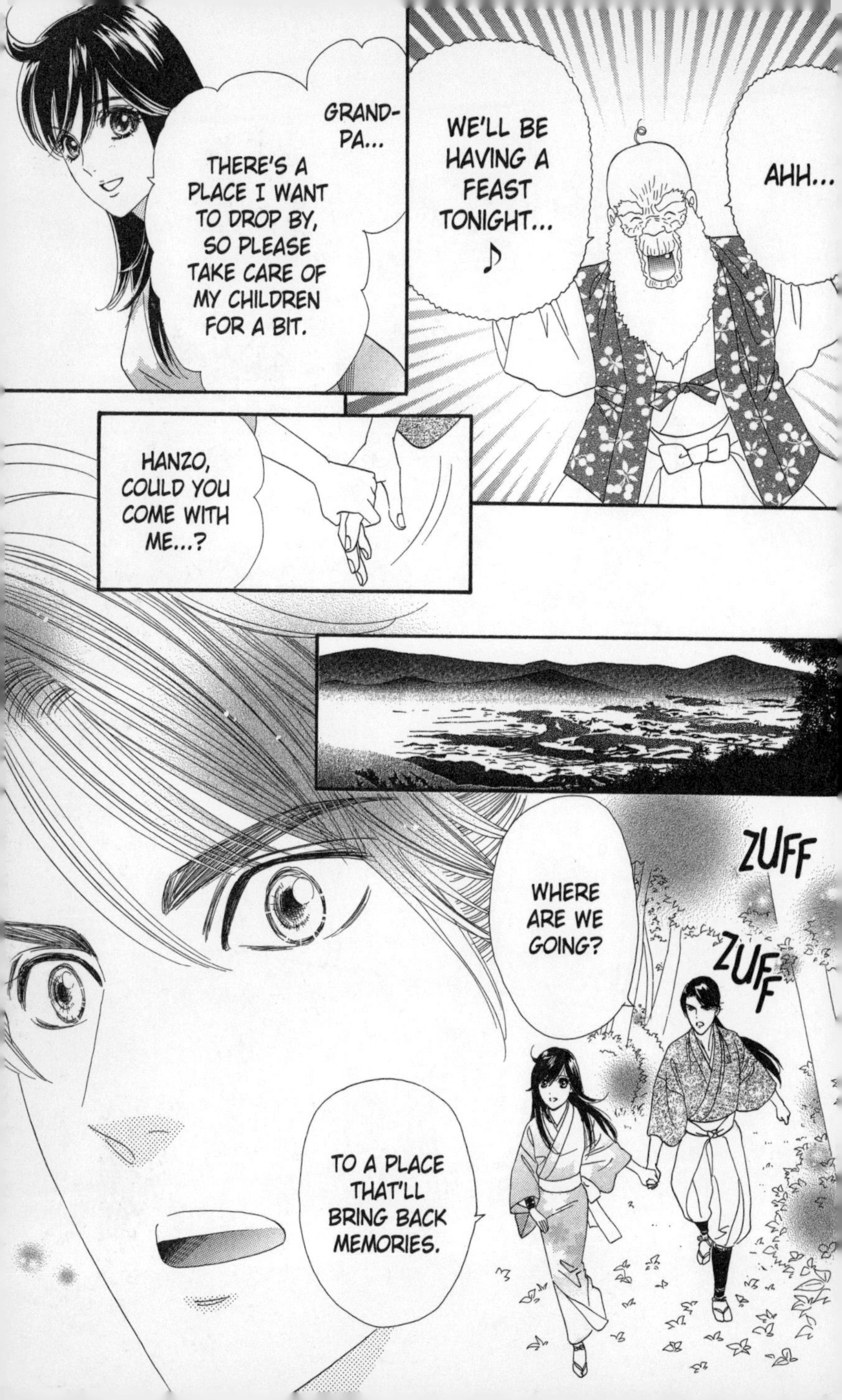
AHH...
WE'LL BE HAVING A FEAST TONIGHT... ♪
GRAND-PA...
THERE'S A PLACE I WANT TO DROP BY, SO PLEASE TAKE CARE OF MY CHILDREN FOR A BIT.
HANZO, COULD YOU COME WITH ME...?
ZUFF
ZUFF
WHERE ARE WE GOING?
TO A PLACE THAT'LL BRING BACK MEMORIES.

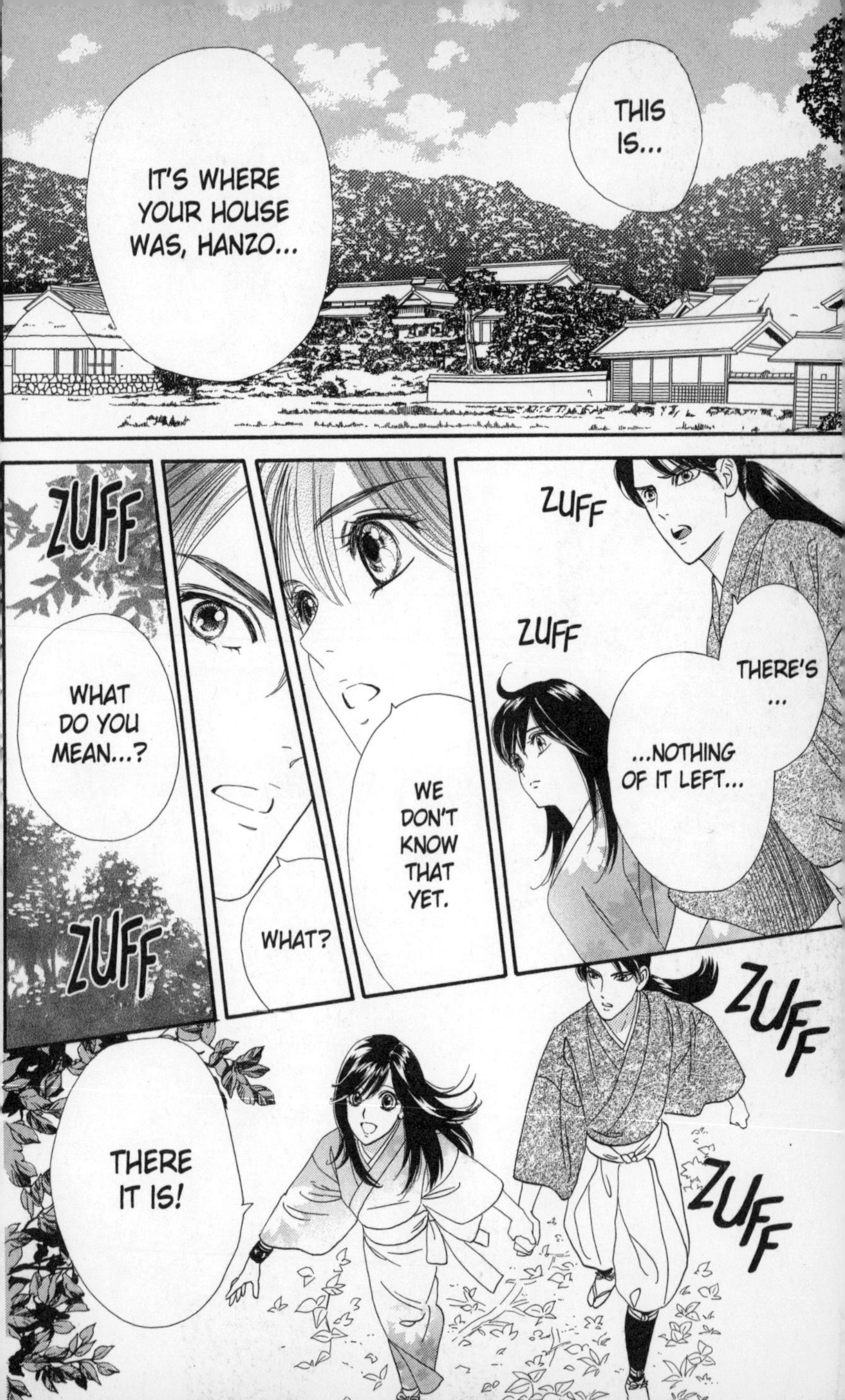
THIS IS...
IT'S WHERE YOUR HOUSE WAS, HANZO...
ZUFF
ZUFF
THERE'S ... ...NOTHING OF IT LEFT...
WE DON'T KNOW THAT YET.
WHAT?
ZUFF
WHAT DO YOU MEAN...?
ZUFF
ZUFF
ZUFF
THERE IT IS!

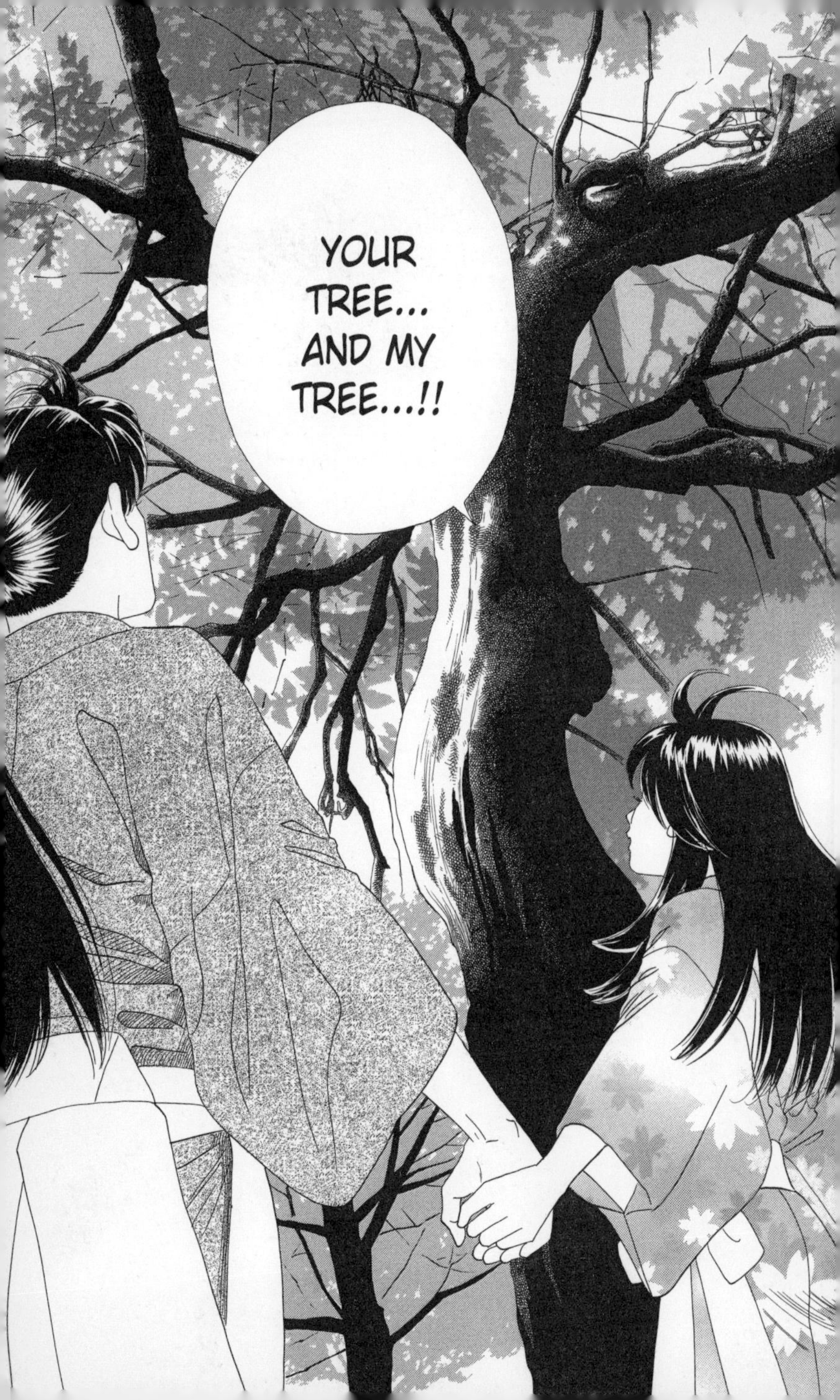
YOUR TREE... AND MY TREE...!!

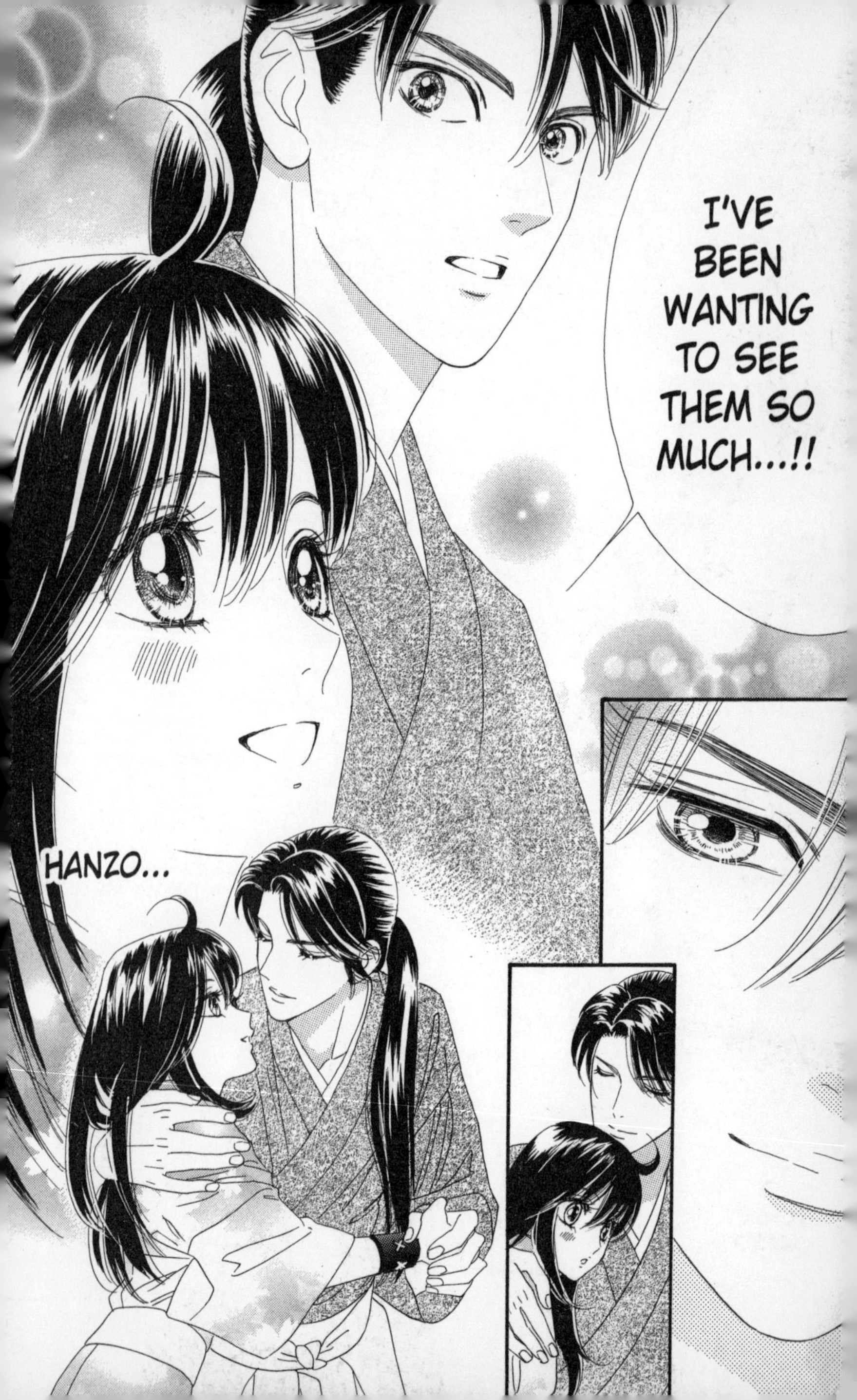
I'VE BEEN WANTING TO SEE THEM SO MUCH...!!
HANZO...

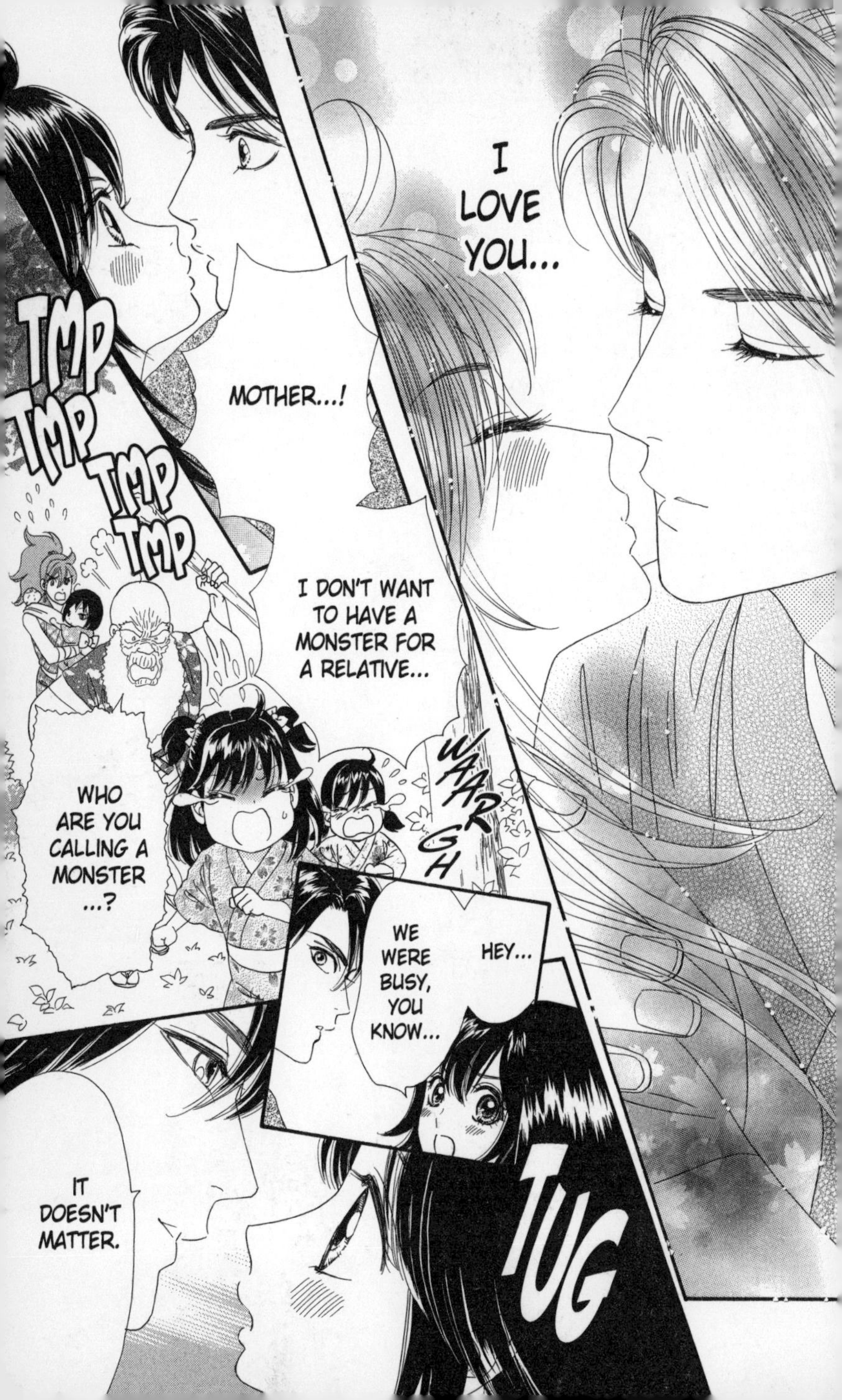
I LOVE YOU...
MOTHER...!
I DON'T WANT TO HAVE A MONSTER FOR A RELATIVE...
WAAARGH
TMP TMP TMP TMP
WHO ARE YOU CALLING A MONSTER ...?
HEY...
WE WERE BUSY, YOU KNOW...
TUG
IT DOESN'T MATTER.

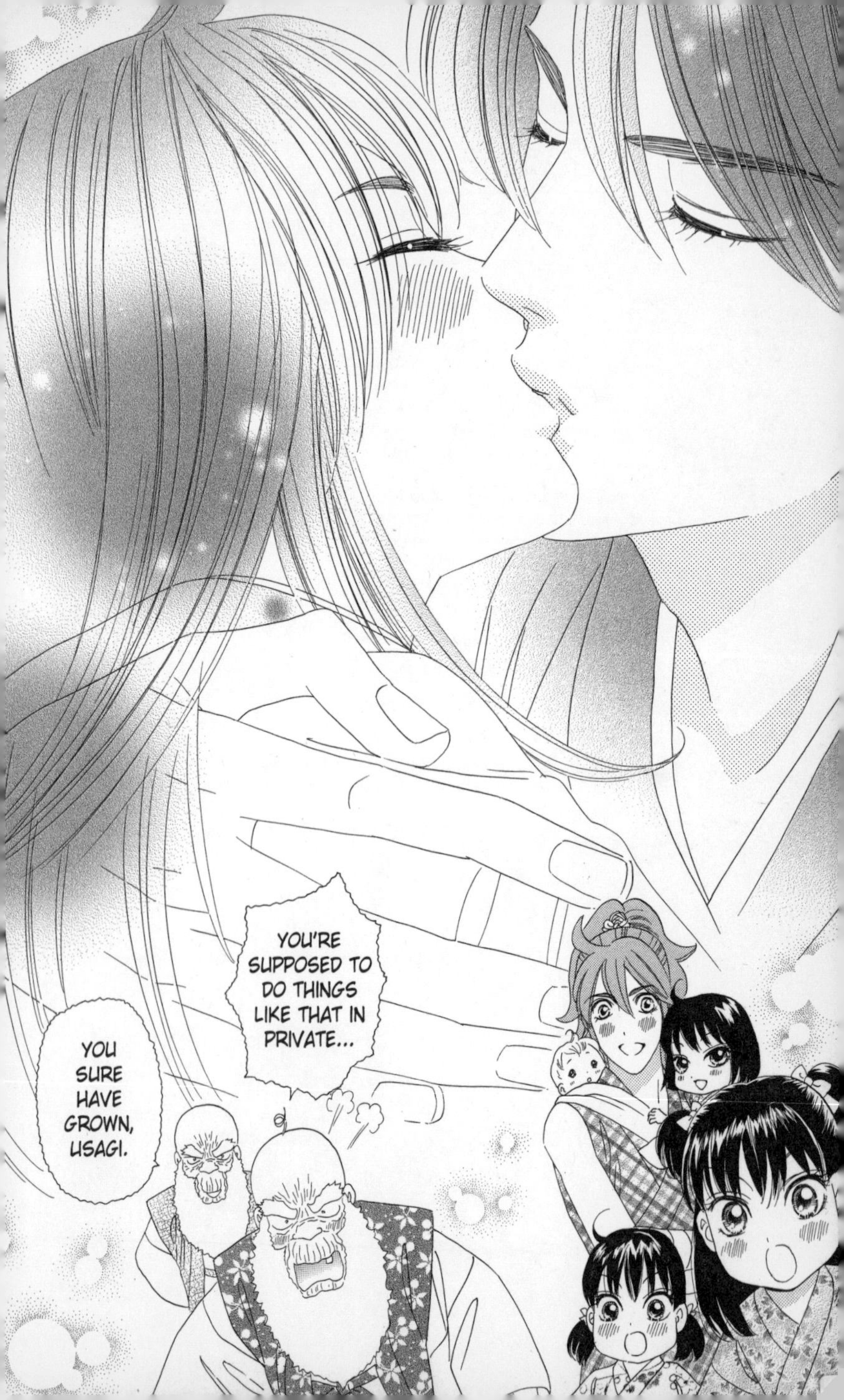
YOU'RE SUPPOSED TO DO THINGS LIKE THAT IN PRIVATE...
YOU SURE HAVE GROWN, USAGI.

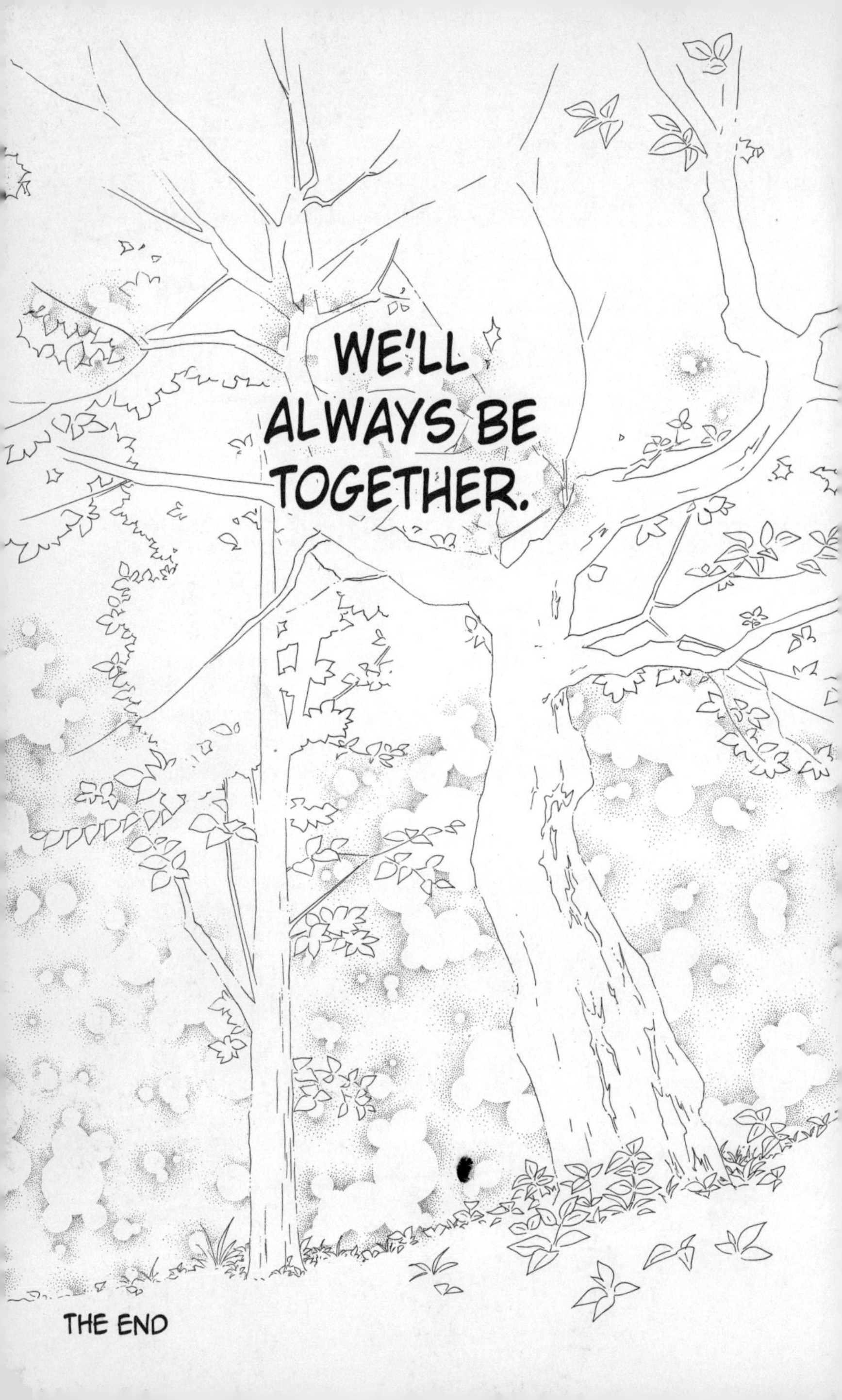
WE'LL ALWAYS BE TOGETHER.
THE END

SPECIAL PROJECT PART 1

FROM UE-RIN TO ALL THE READERS

A MESSAGE OF GRATITUDE
TO THE READERS FROM UE-RIN!!

THANK YOU VERY MUCH FOR READING THIS SERIES!!

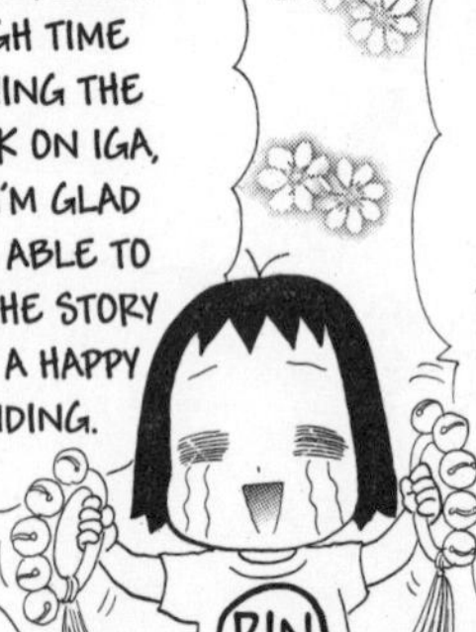
I STARTED WRITING *TAIL OF THE MOON* WITH A LIGHTHEARTED FEELING AS A SEQUEL TO *TSUKI NO TOIKI, AI NO KIZU* (WHICH I CREATED FOR *THE MARGARET*). THANKS TO ALL OF YOUR SUPPORT, IT HAS BECOME MY LONGEST SERIES EVER.
I HAD A REALLY TOUGH TIME DRAWING THE ATTACK ON IGA, BUT I'M GLAD I WAS ABLE TO END THE STORY WITH A HAPPY ENDING.
I WAS SO HAPPY TO BE ABLE TO DRAW USAGI AND HANZO'S CHILDREN...
I'M THINKING ABOUT CREATING AN EXTRA STORY FOR *TAIL OF THE MOON*, SO PLEASE CHECK IT OUT IF YOU SEE IT IN THE MAGAZINE!!
RIN

I'M A VERY HAPPY PERSON...!♡

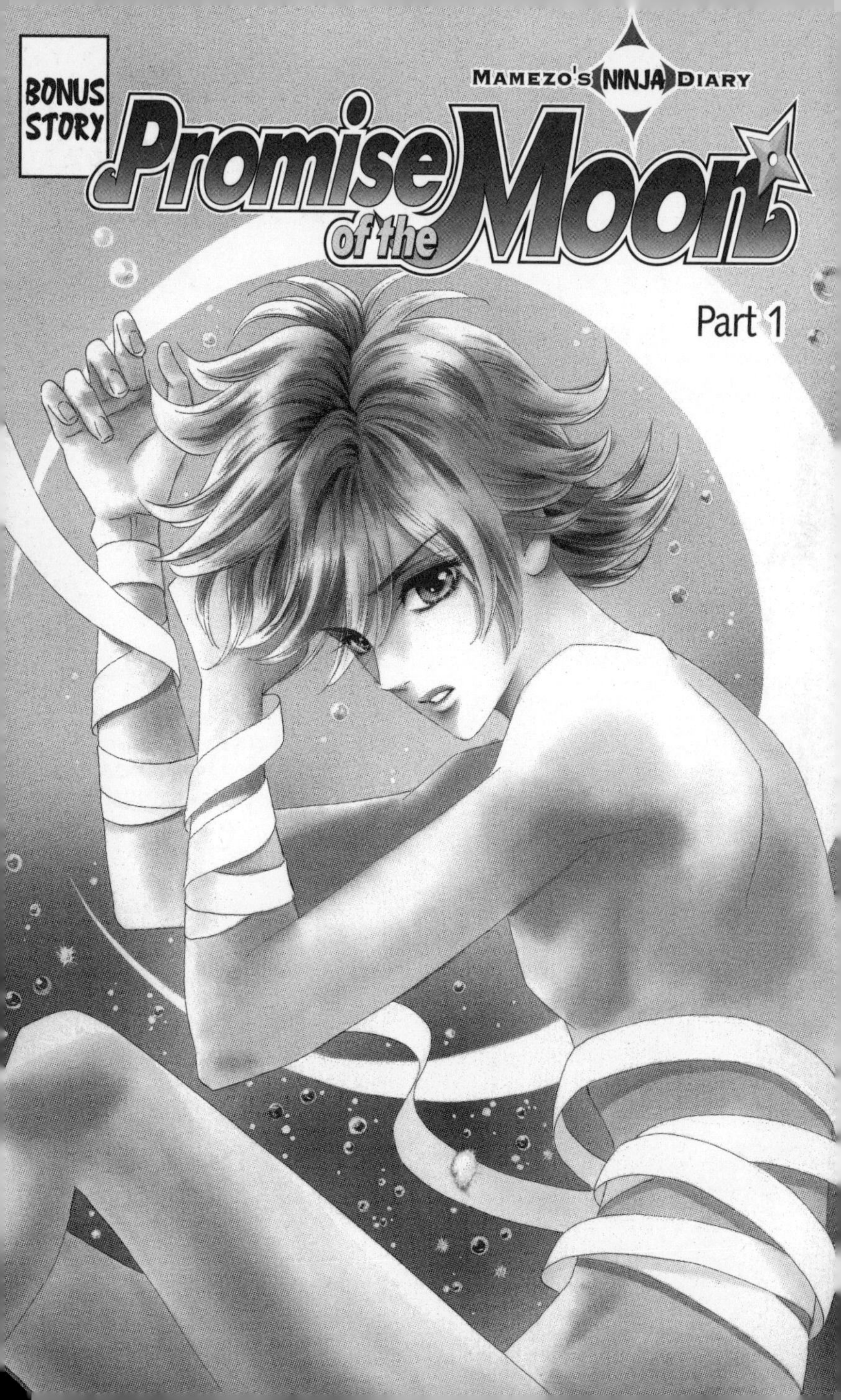
BONUS STORY
MAMEZO'S NINJA DIARY
Promise of the Moon
Part 1

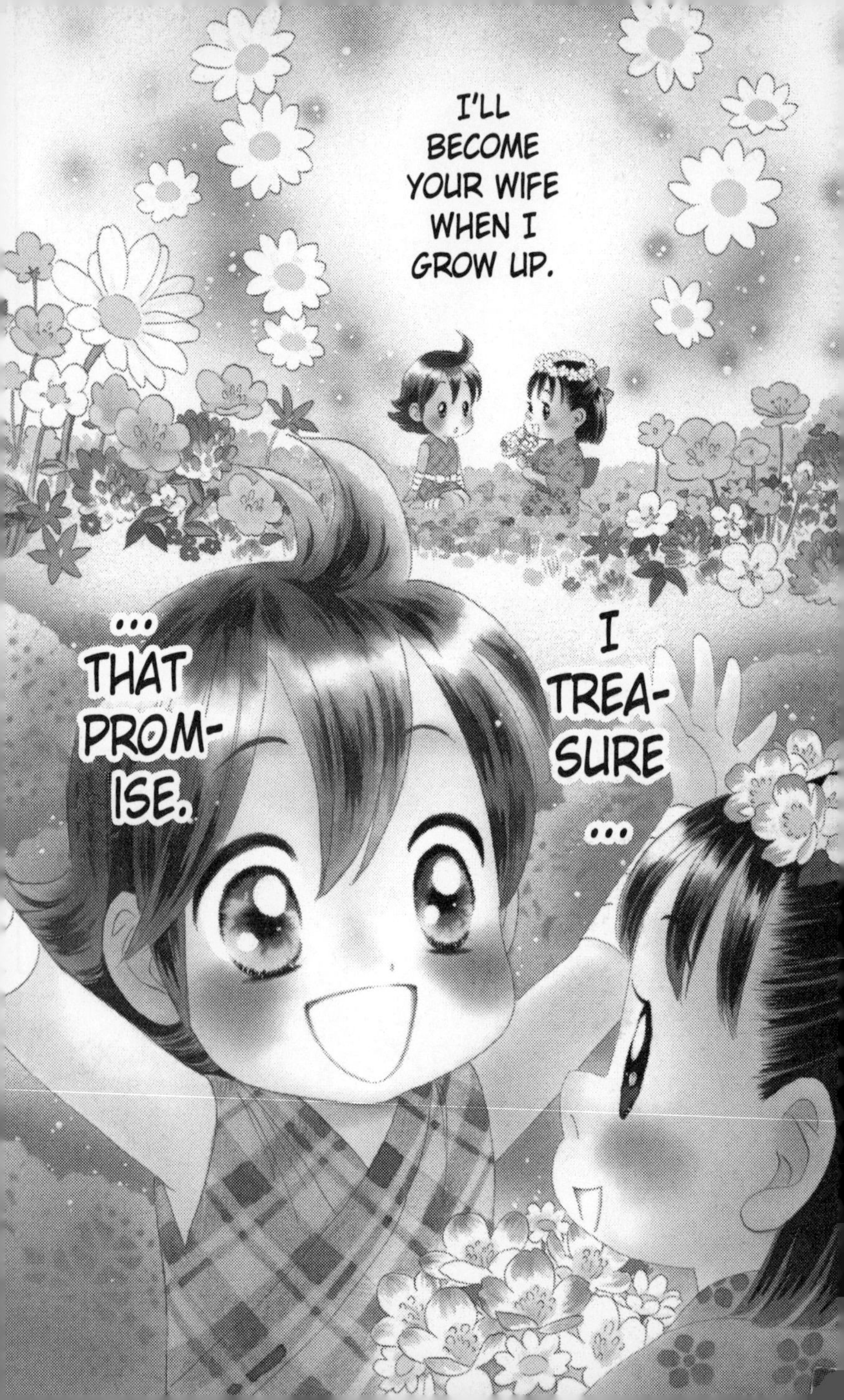
I'LL BECOME YOUR WIFE WHEN I GROW UP.
I TREASURE...
...THAT PROMISE.

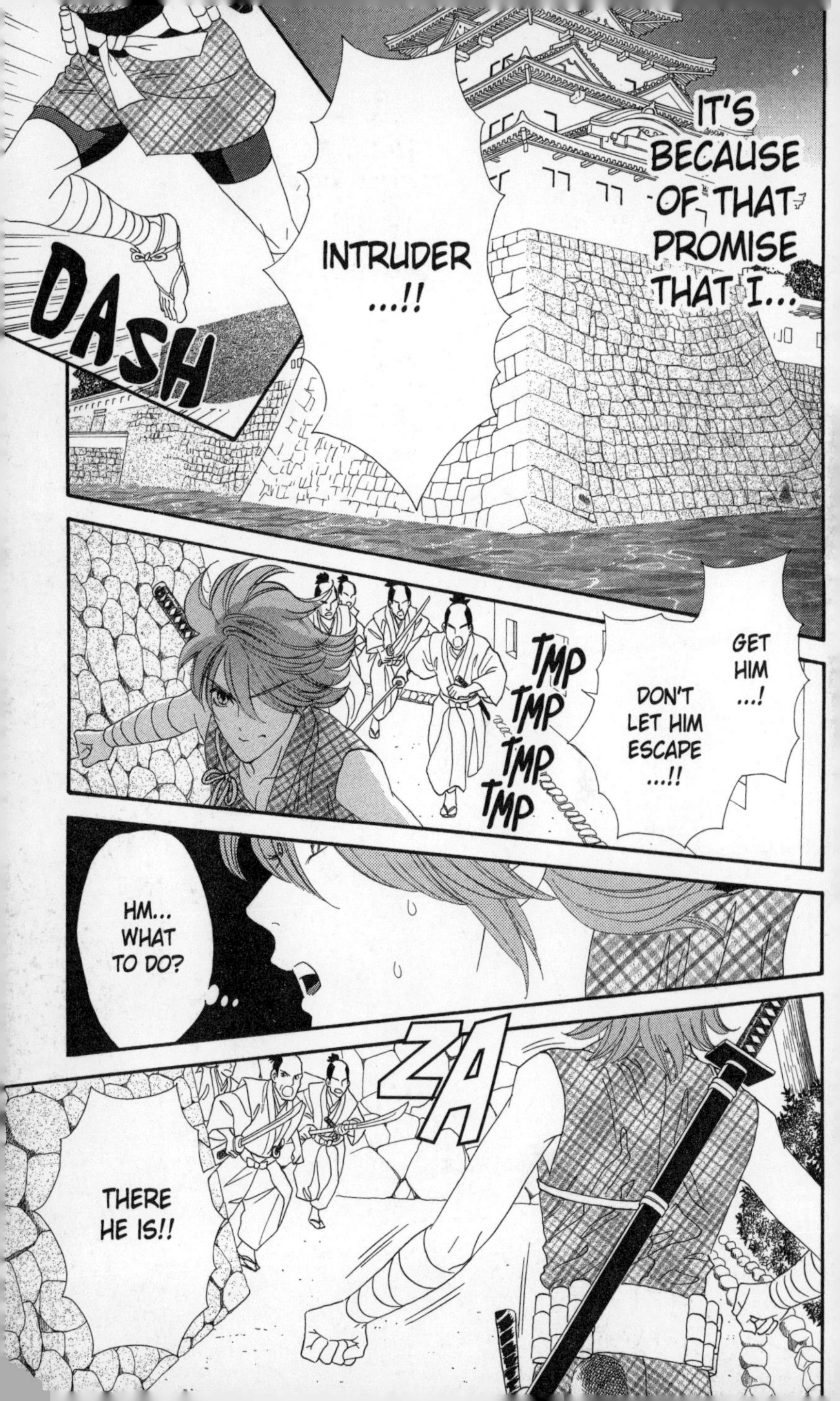
IT'S BECAUSE OF THAT PROMISE THAT I...
INTRUDER ...!!
DASH
GET HIM ...!
DON'T LET HIM ESCAPE ...!!
TMP TMP TMP TMP
HM... WHAT TO DO?
ZA
THERE HE IS!!

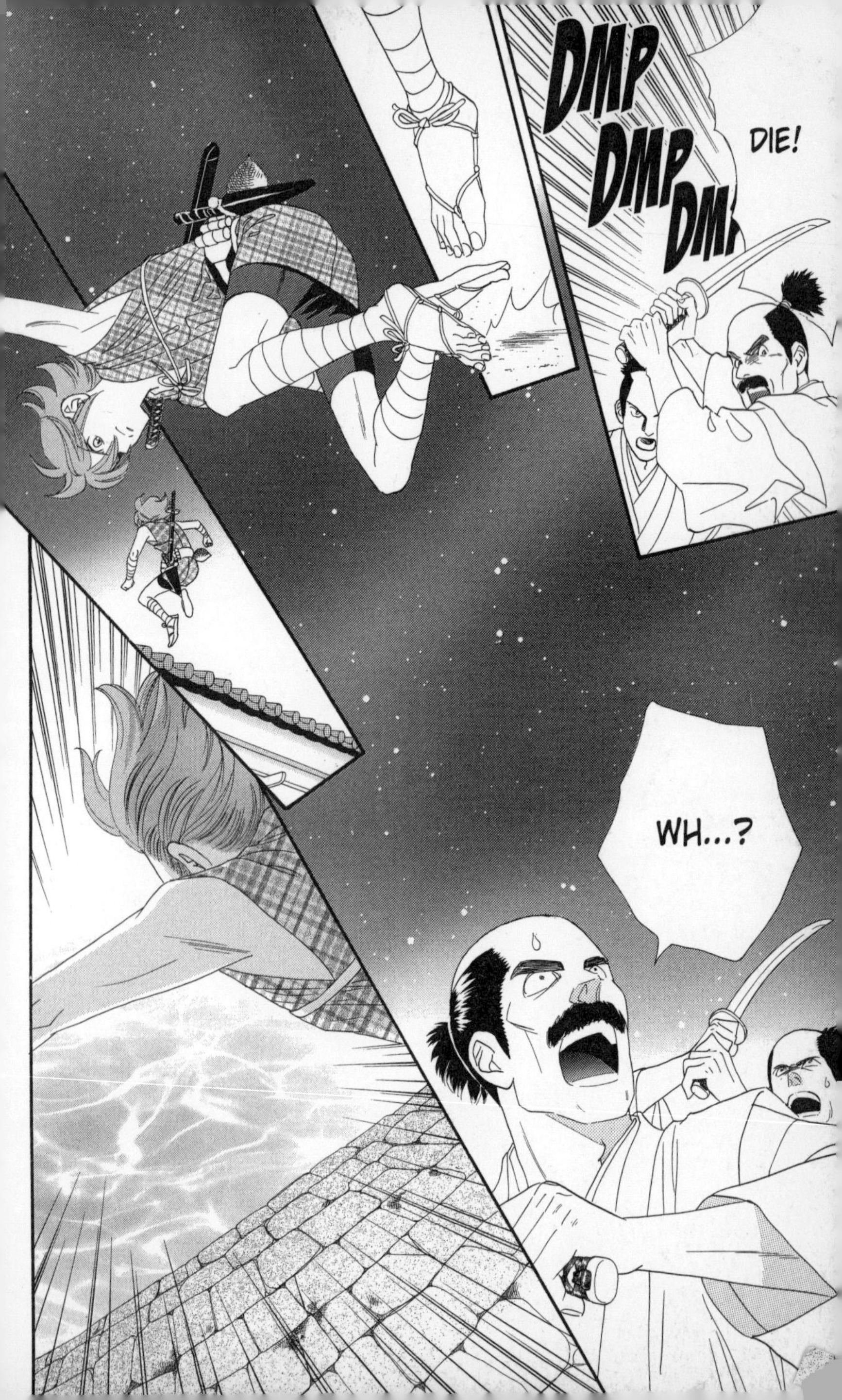
DMP
DMP
DM
DIE!
WH...?

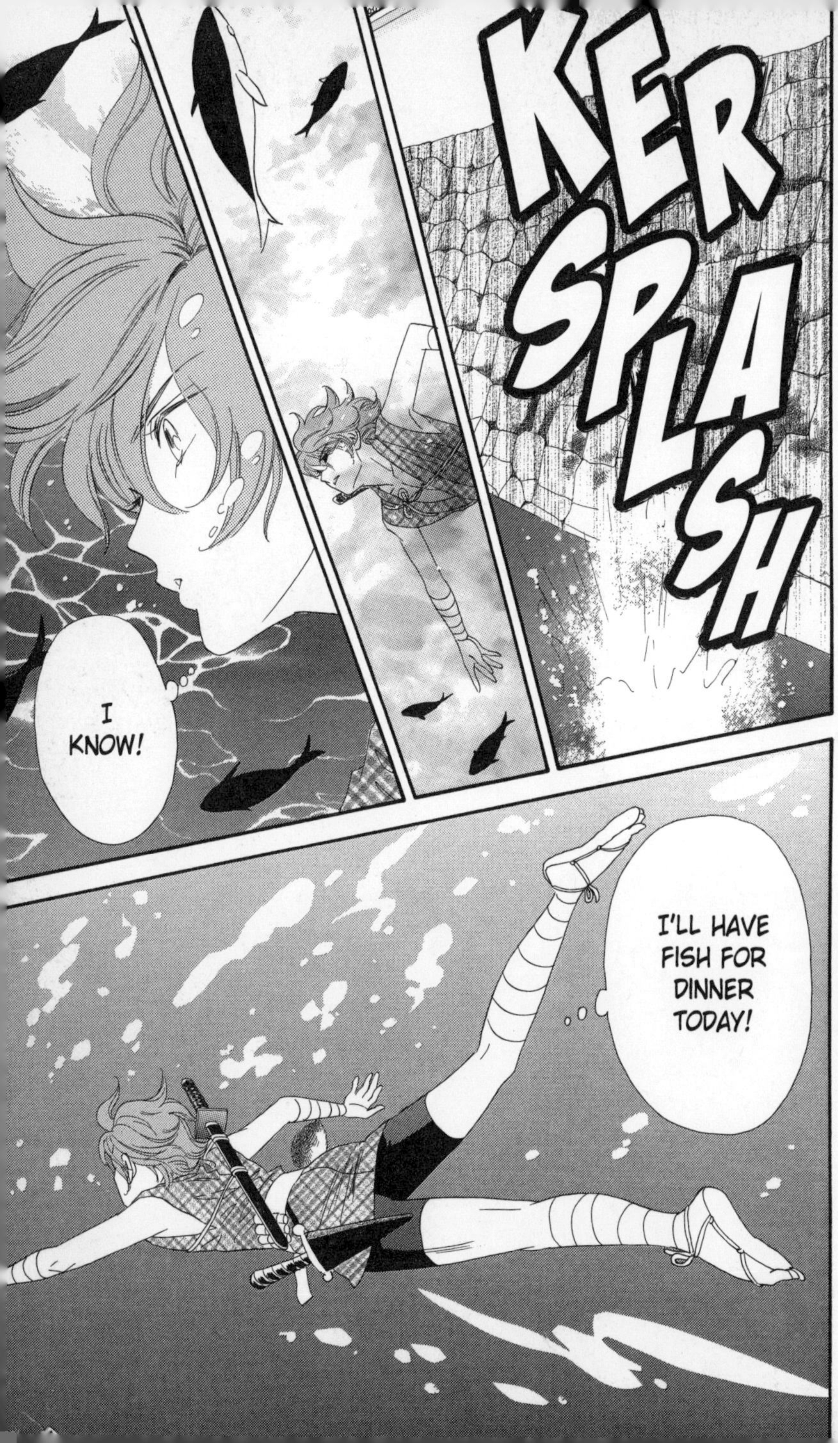
KER SPLASH
I KNOW!
I'LL HAVE FISH FOR DINNER TODAY!

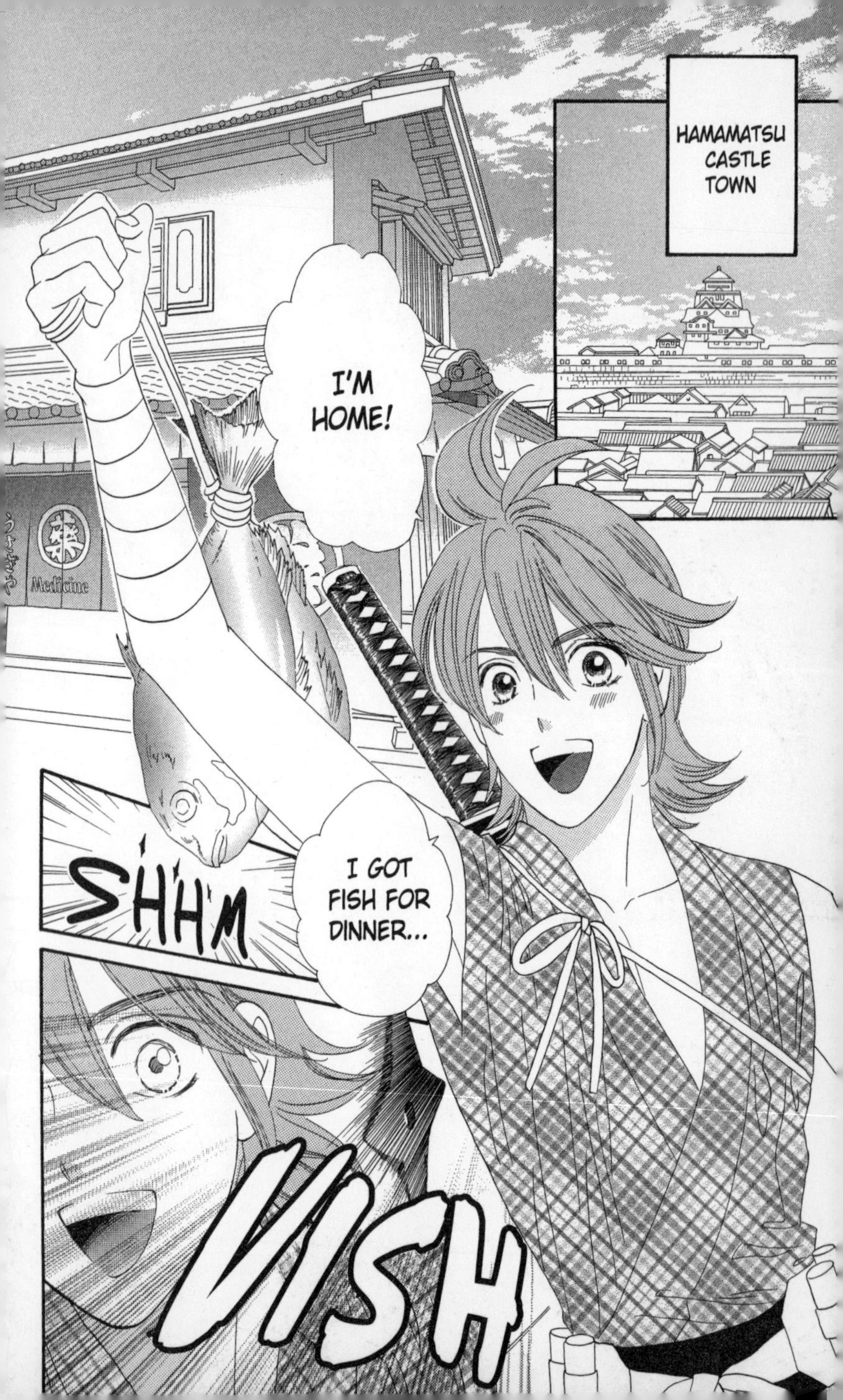
HAMAMATSU CASTLE TOWN
I'M HOME!
I GOT FISH FOR DINNER...
Medicine
SHHM
VISH

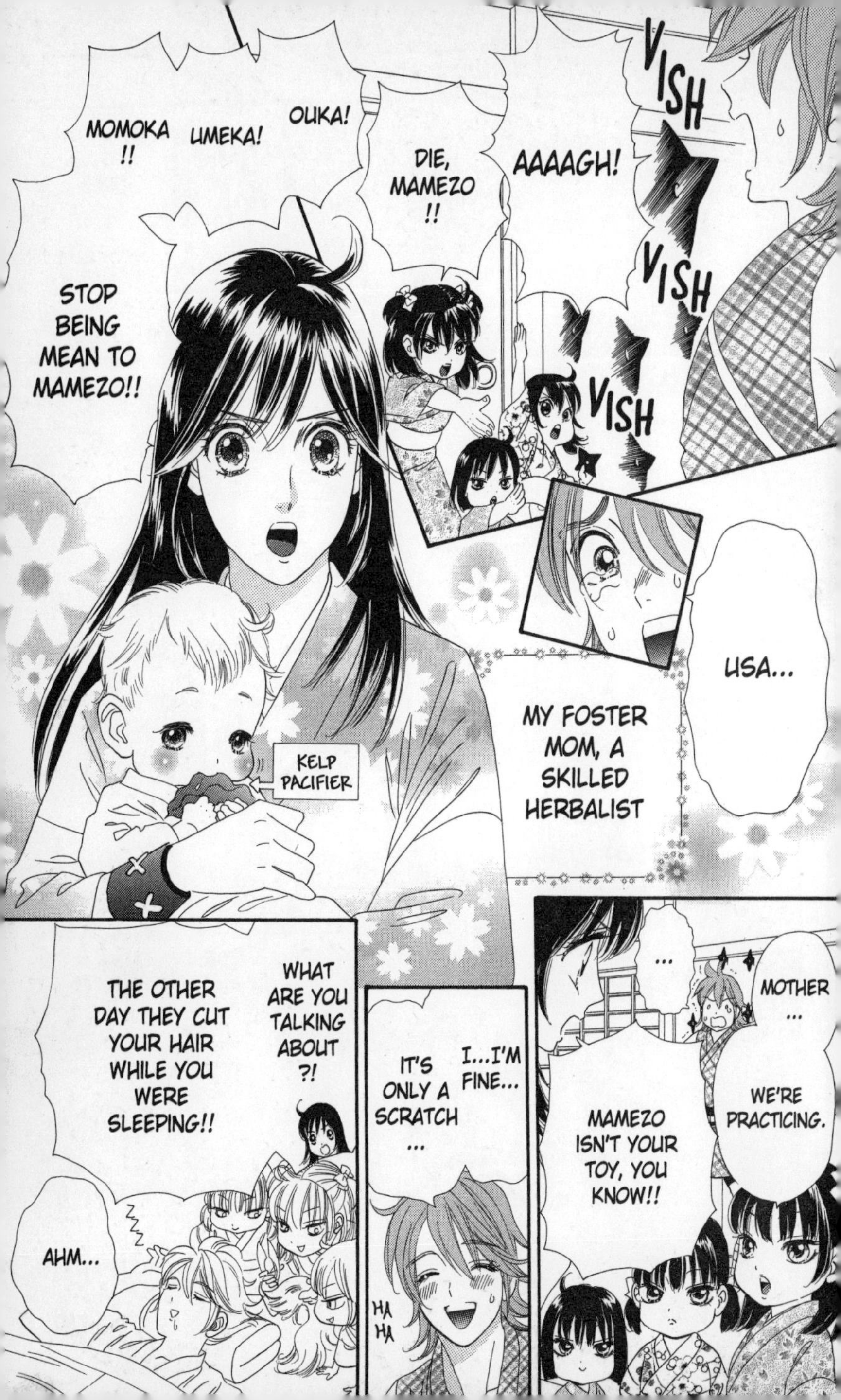
VISH
AAAAGH!
DIE, MAMEZO!!
OUKA!
UMEKA!
MOMOKA!!
VISH
VISH
STOP BEING MEAN TO MAMEZO!!
USA...
MY FOSTER MOM, A SKILLED HERBALIST
KELP PACIFIER
...
MOTHER...
WE'RE PRACTICING.
MAMEZO ISN'T YOUR TOY, YOU KNOW!!
I...I'M FINE...
IT'S ONLY A SCRATCH...
HA HA
WHAT ARE YOU TALKING ABOUT?!
THE OTHER DAY THEY CUT YOUR HAIR WHILE YOU WERE SLEEPING!!
ZZZ
AHM...

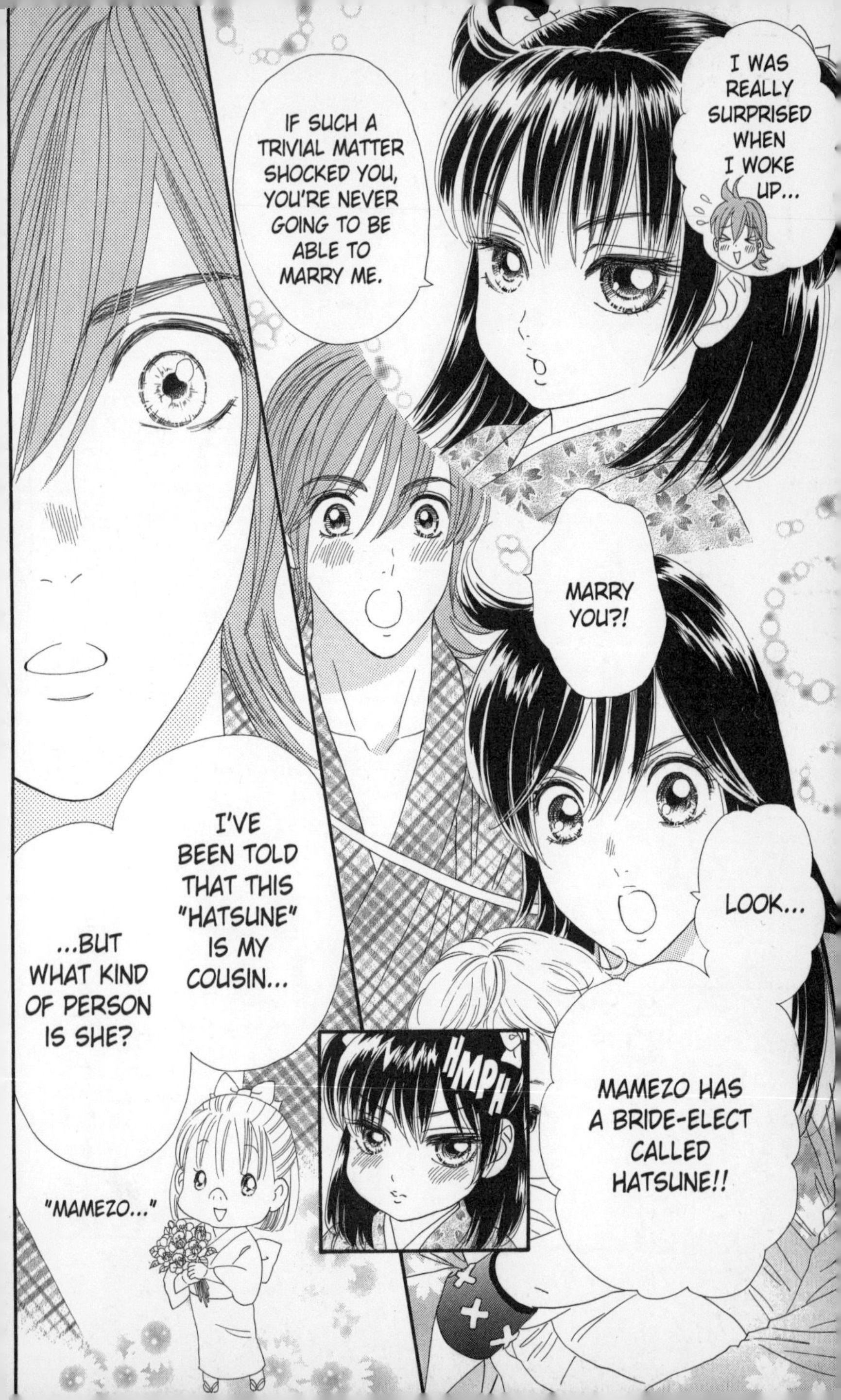
I WAS REALLY SURPRISED WHEN I WOKE UP...
IF SUCH A TRIVIAL MATTER SHOCKED YOU, YOU'RE NEVER GOING TO BE ABLE TO MARRY ME.
MARRY YOU?!
LOOK...
MAMEZO HAS A BRIDE-ELECT CALLED HATSUNE!!
HMPH
I'VE BEEN TOLD THAT THIS "HATSUNE" IS MY COUSIN...
...BUT WHAT KIND OF PERSON IS SHE?
"MAMEZO..."

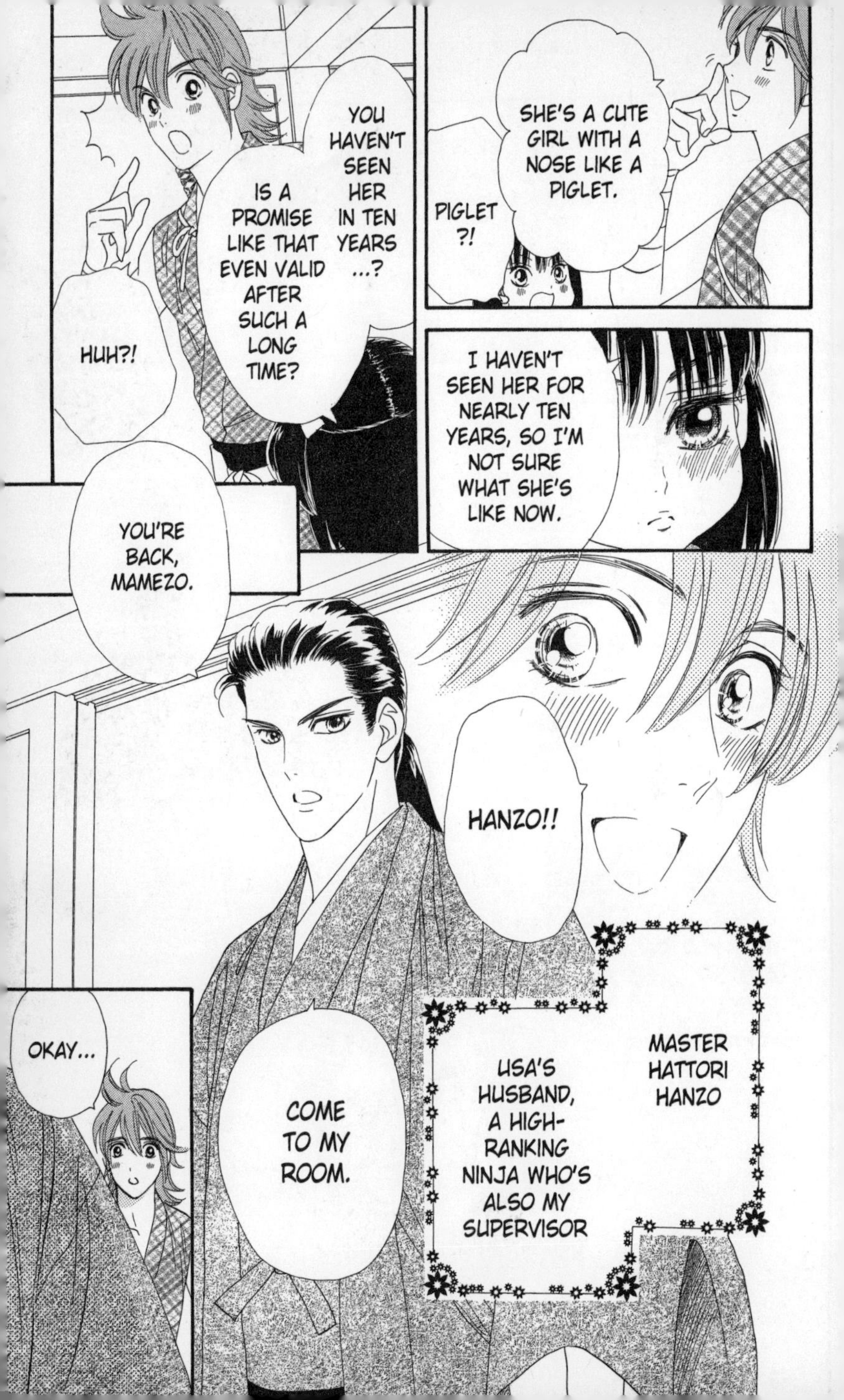
SHE'S A CUTE GIRL WITH A NOSE LIKE A PIGLET.
PIGLET ?!
I HAVEN'T SEEN HER FOR NEARLY TEN YEARS, SO I'M NOT SURE WHAT SHE'S LIKE NOW.
YOU HAVEN'T SEEN HER IN TEN YEARS ...?
IS A PROMISE LIKE THAT EVEN VALID AFTER SUCH A LONG TIME?
HUH?!
YOU'RE BACK, MAMEZO.
HANZO!!
MASTER HATTORI HANZO
USA'S HUSBAND, A HIGH-RANKING NINJA WHO'S ALSO MY SUPERVISOR
COME TO MY ROOM.
OKAY...

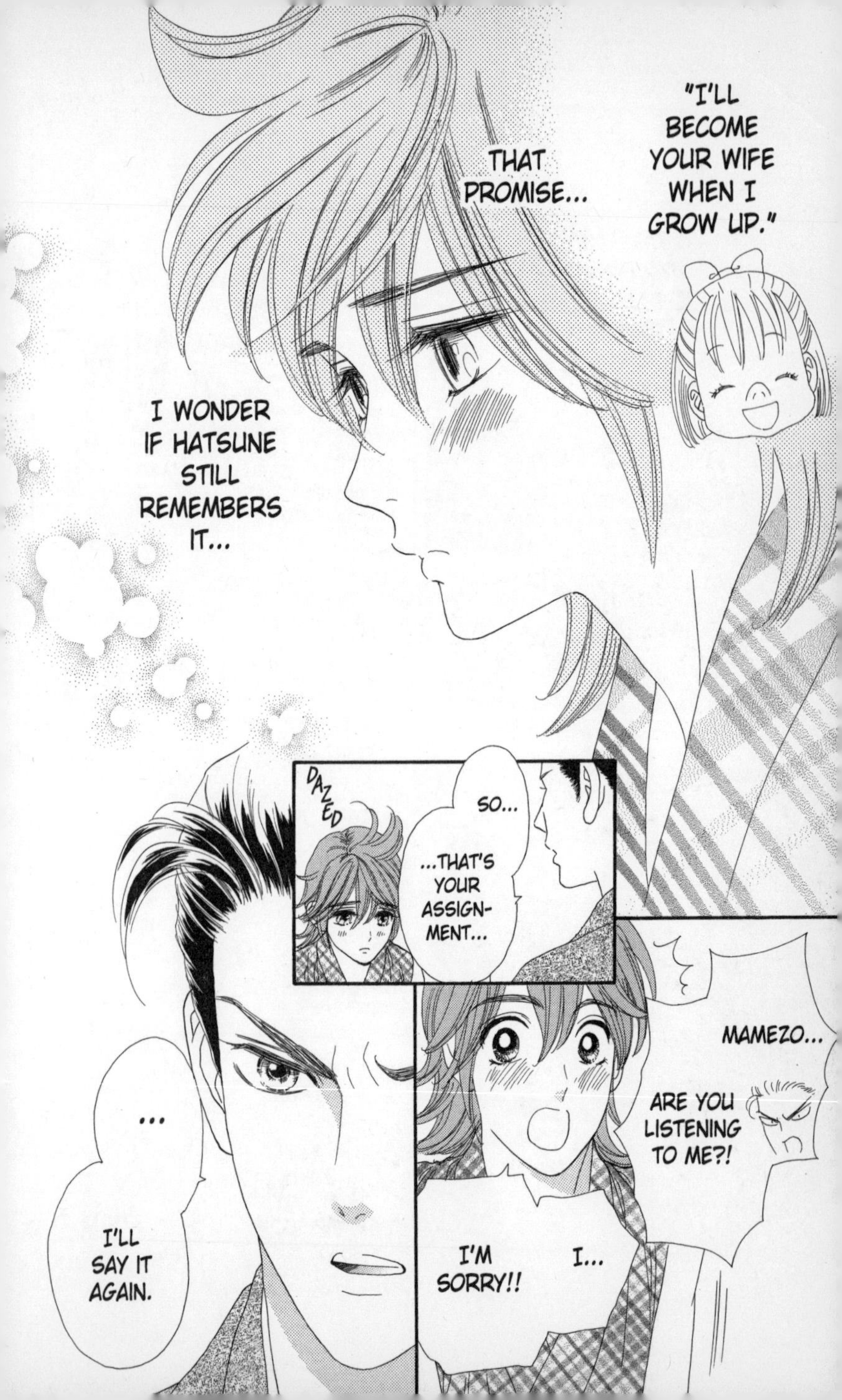
"I'LL BECOME YOUR WIFE WHEN I GROW UP."
THAT PROMISE...
I WONDER IF HATSUNE STILL REMEMBERS IT...
SO...
...THAT'S YOUR ASSIGNMENT...
DAZED
MAMEZO...
ARE YOU LISTENING TO ME?!
I...
I'M SORRY!!
...
I'LL SAY IT AGAIN.

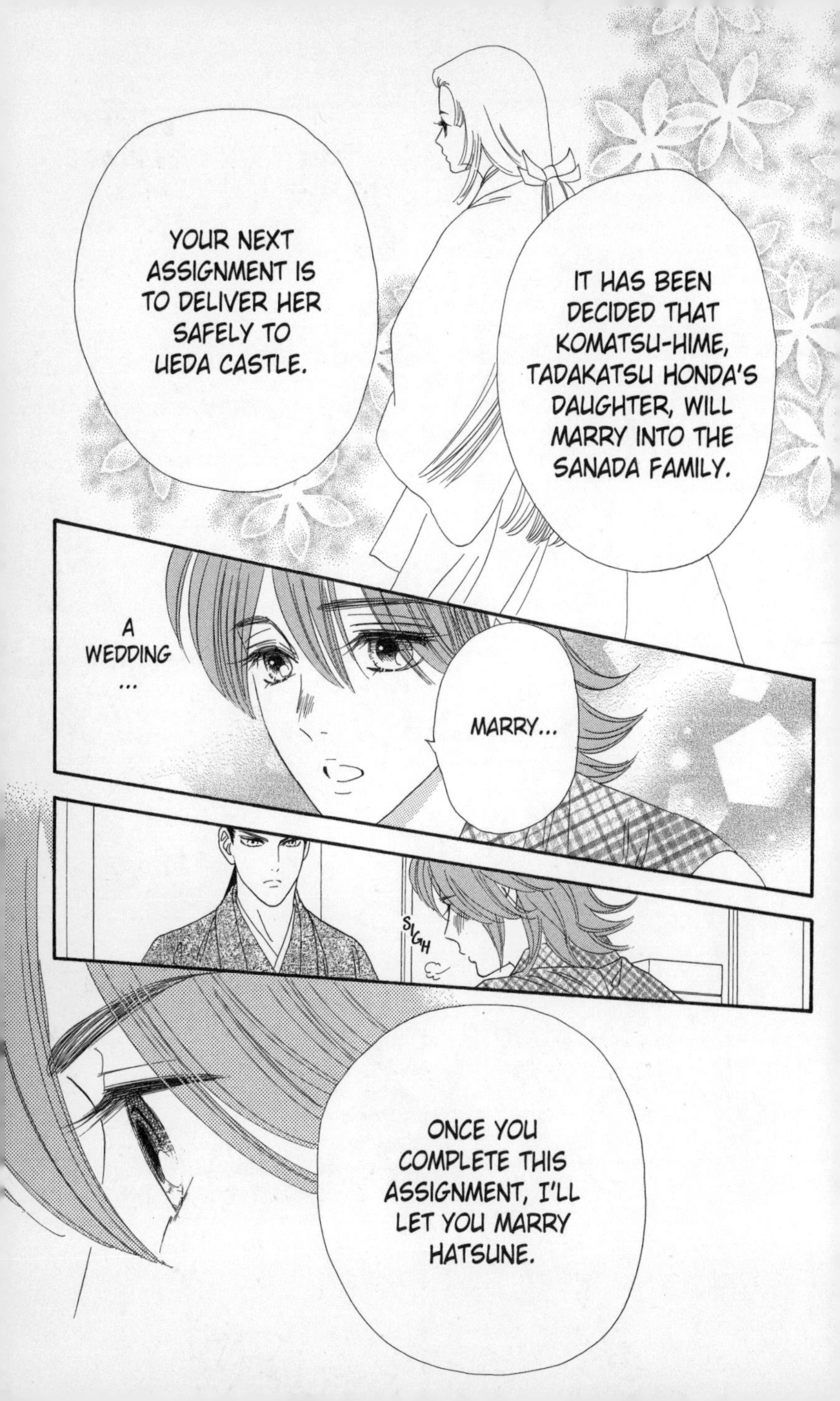
IT HAS BEEN DECIDED THAT KOMATSU-HIME, TADAKATSU HONDA'S DAUGHTER, WILL MARRY INTO THE SANADA FAMILY.
YOUR NEXT ASSIGNMENT IS TO DELIVER HER SAFELY TO UEDA CASTLE.
MARRY...
A WEDDING ...
SIGH
ONCE YOU COMPLETE THIS ASSIGNMENT, I'LL LET YOU MARRY HATSUNE.

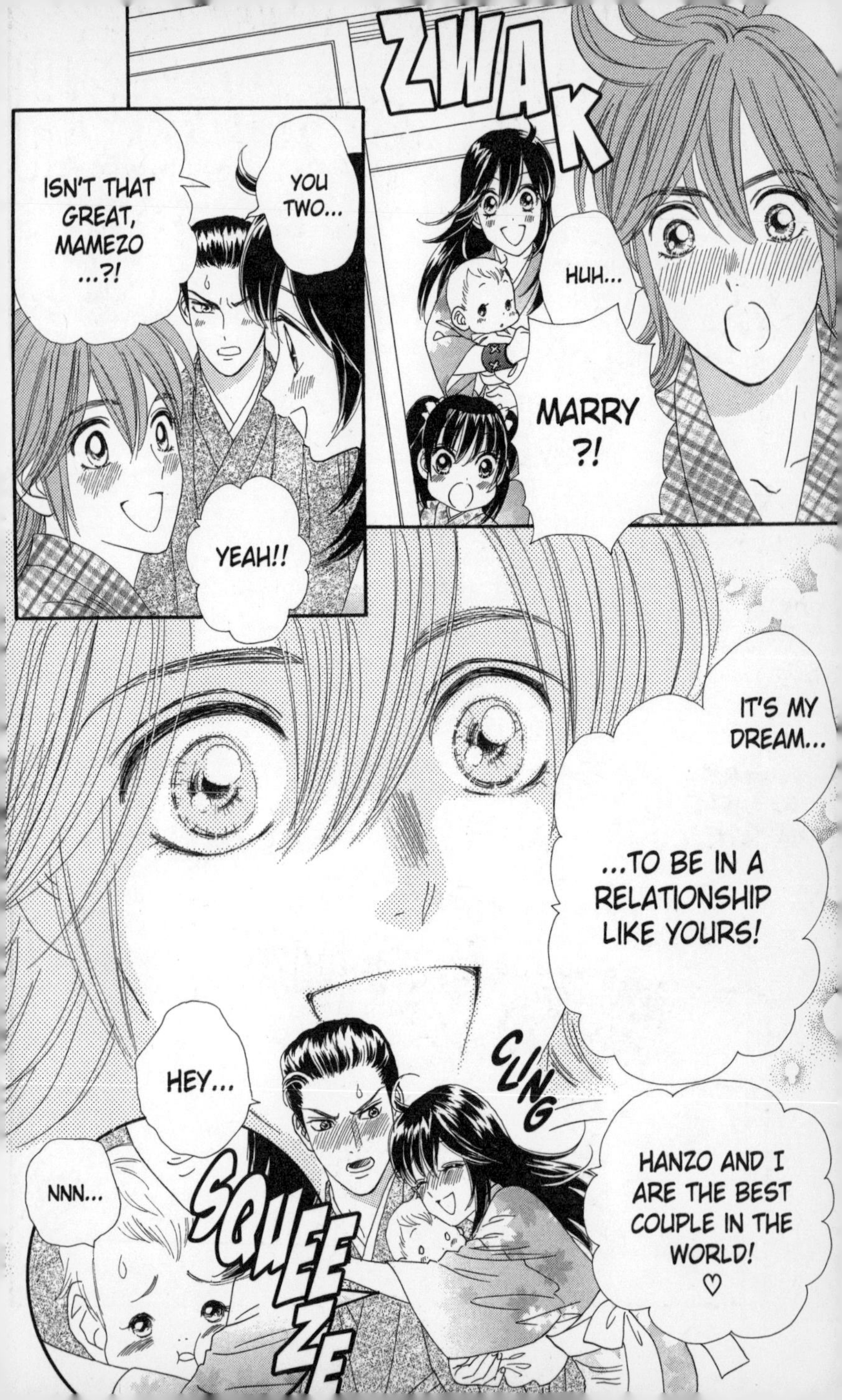
ZWAK
HUH...
MARRY ?!
YOU TWO...
ISN'T THAT GREAT, MAMEZO ...?!
YEAH!!
IT'S MY DREAM...
...TO BE IN A RELATIONSHIP LIKE YOURS!
CLING
HANZO AND I ARE THE BEST COUPLE IN THE WORLD! ♡
HEY...
SQUEEZE
NNN...

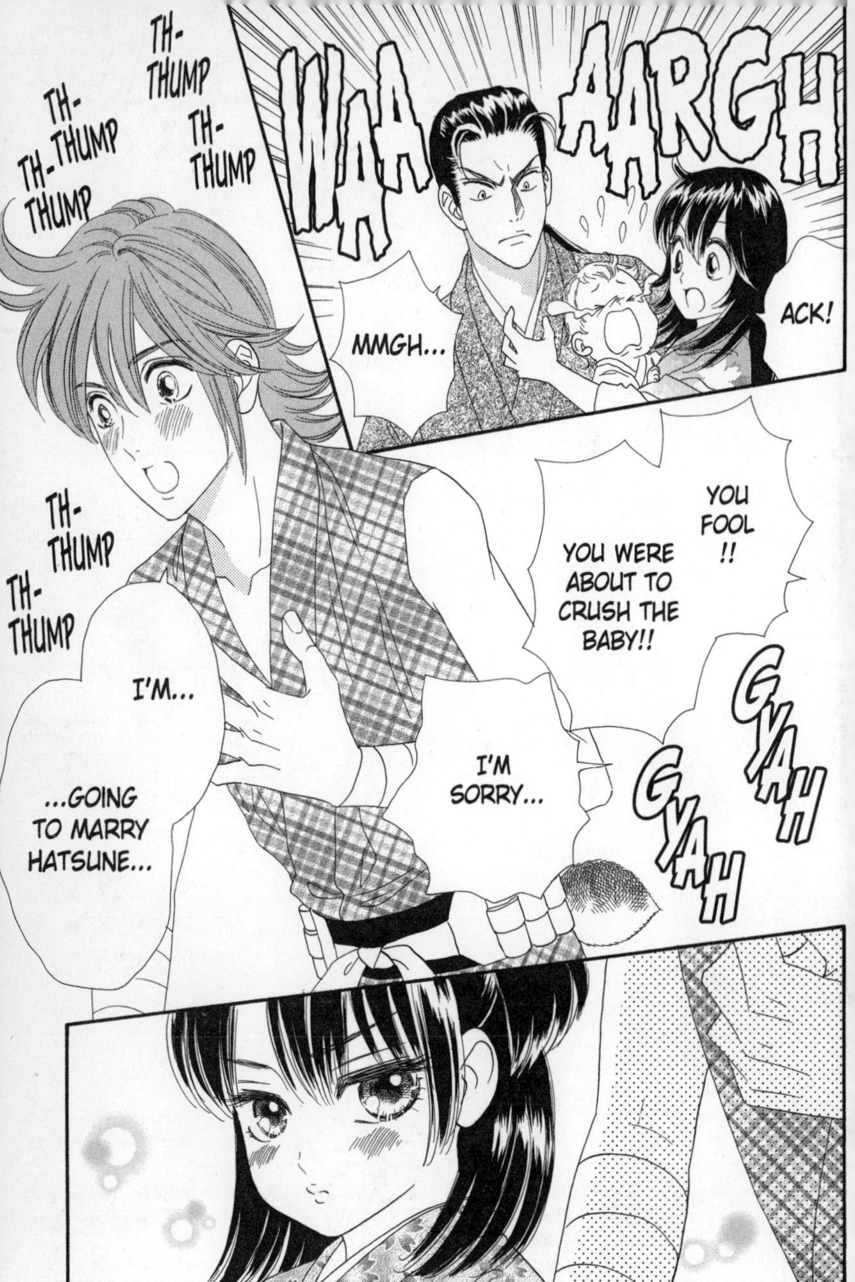
WAAARGH
ACK!
MMGH...
YOU FOOL!!
YOU WERE ABOUT TO CRUSH THE BABY!!
GYAH GYAH
I'M SORRY...
TH-THUMP TH-THUMP TH-THUMP TH-THUMP
TH-THUMP TH-THUMP
I'M...
...GOING TO MARRY HATSUNE...

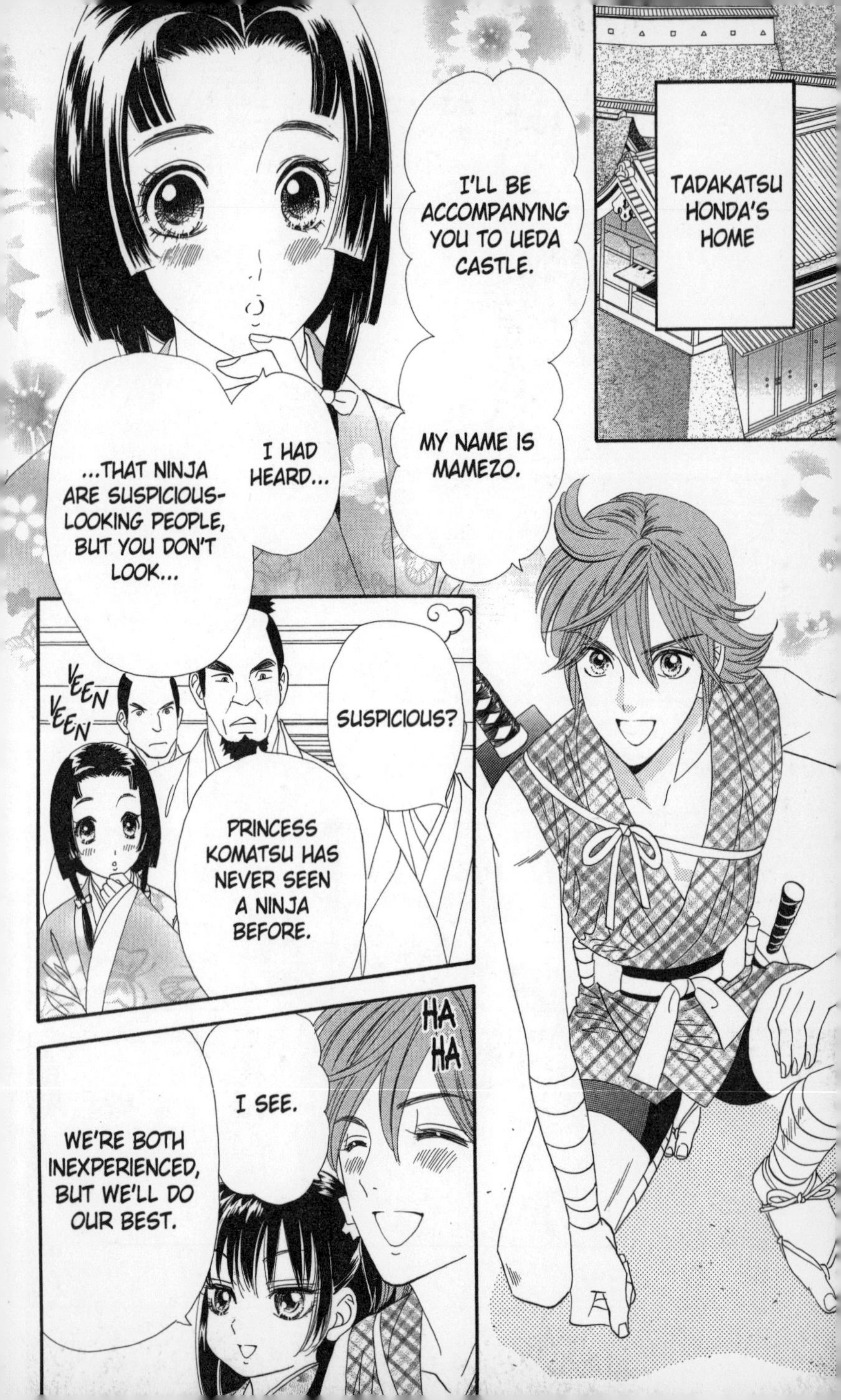

TADAKATSU HONDA'S HOME
I'LL BE ACCOMPANYING YOU TO UEDA CASTLE.
MY NAME IS MAMEZO.
I HAD HEARD...
...THAT NINJA ARE SUSPICIOUS-LOOKING PEOPLE, BUT YOU DON'T LOOK...
SUSPICIOUS?
VEEN VEEN
PRINCESS KOMATSU HAS NEVER SEEN A NINJA BEFORE.
HA HA
I SEE.
WE'RE BOTH INEXPERIENCED, BUT WE'LL DO OUR BEST.

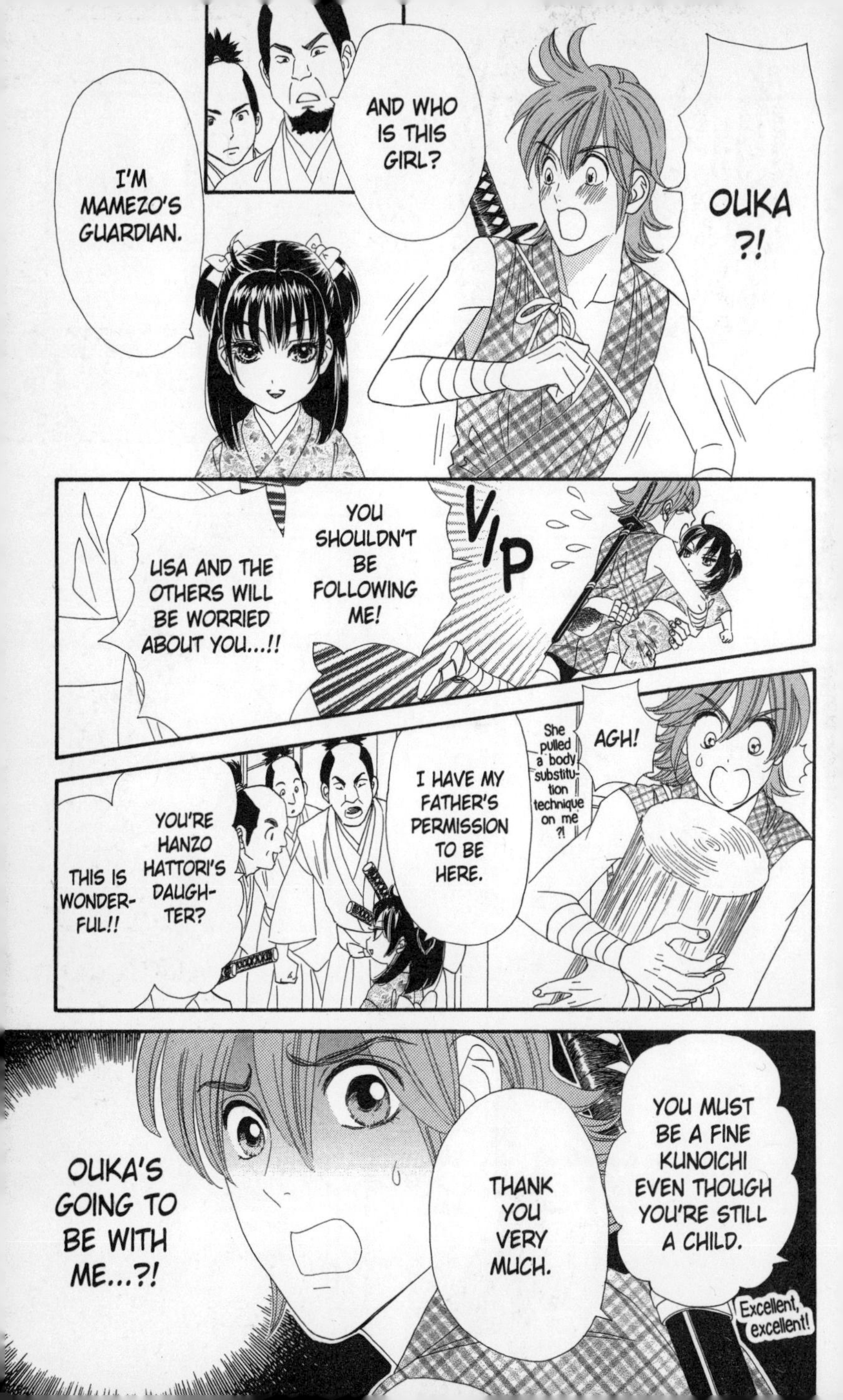
OUKA ?!
AND WHO IS THIS GIRL?
I'M MAMEZO'S GUARDIAN.
VIP
YOU SHOULDN'T BE FOLLOWING ME!
USA AND THE OTHERS WILL BE WORRIED ABOUT YOU...!!
AGH!
She pulled a body substitution technique on me ?!
I HAVE MY FATHER'S PERMISSION TO BE HERE.
YOU'RE HANZO HATTORI'S DAUGHTER?
THIS IS WONDERFUL!!
YOU MUST BE A FINE KUNOICHI EVEN THOUGH YOU'RE STILL A CHILD.
Excellent, excellent!
THANK YOU VERY MUCH.
OUKA'S GOING TO BE WITH ME...?!

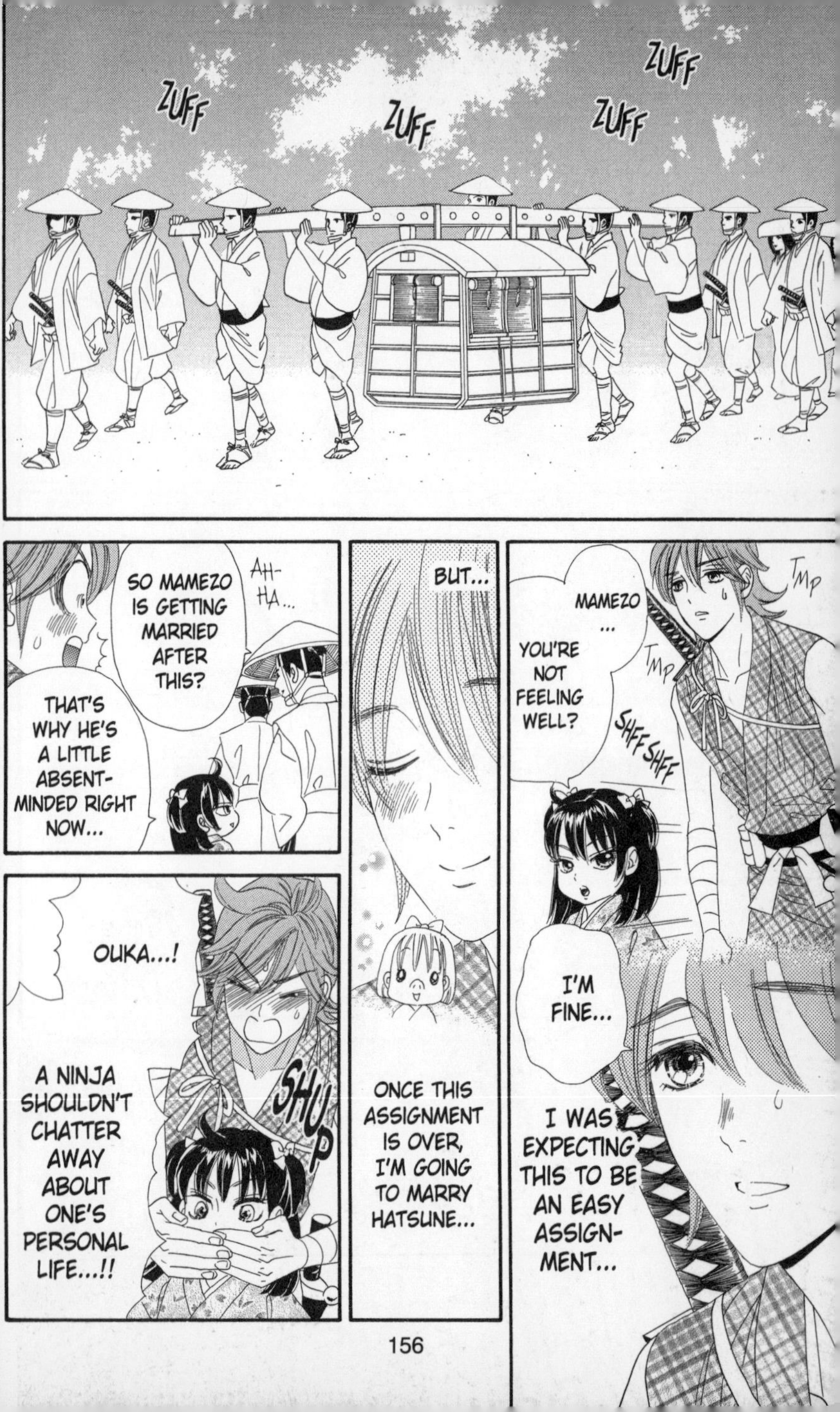
ZUFF
ZUFF
ZUFF
ZUFF
TMP
TMP
MAMEZO ... YOU'RE NOT FEELING WELL?
SHFF SHFF
I'M FINE...
I WAS EXPECTING THIS TO BE AN EASY ASSIGNMENT...
BUT...!
ONCE THIS ASSIGNMENT IS OVER, I'M GOING TO MARRY HATSUNE...
AH-HA...
SO MAMEZO IS GETTING MARRIED AFTER THIS?
THAT'S WHY HE'S A LITTLE ABSENT-MINDED RIGHT NOW...
OUKA...!
SHUP
A NINJA SHOULDN'T CHATTER AWAY ABOUT ONE'S PERSONAL LIFE...!!

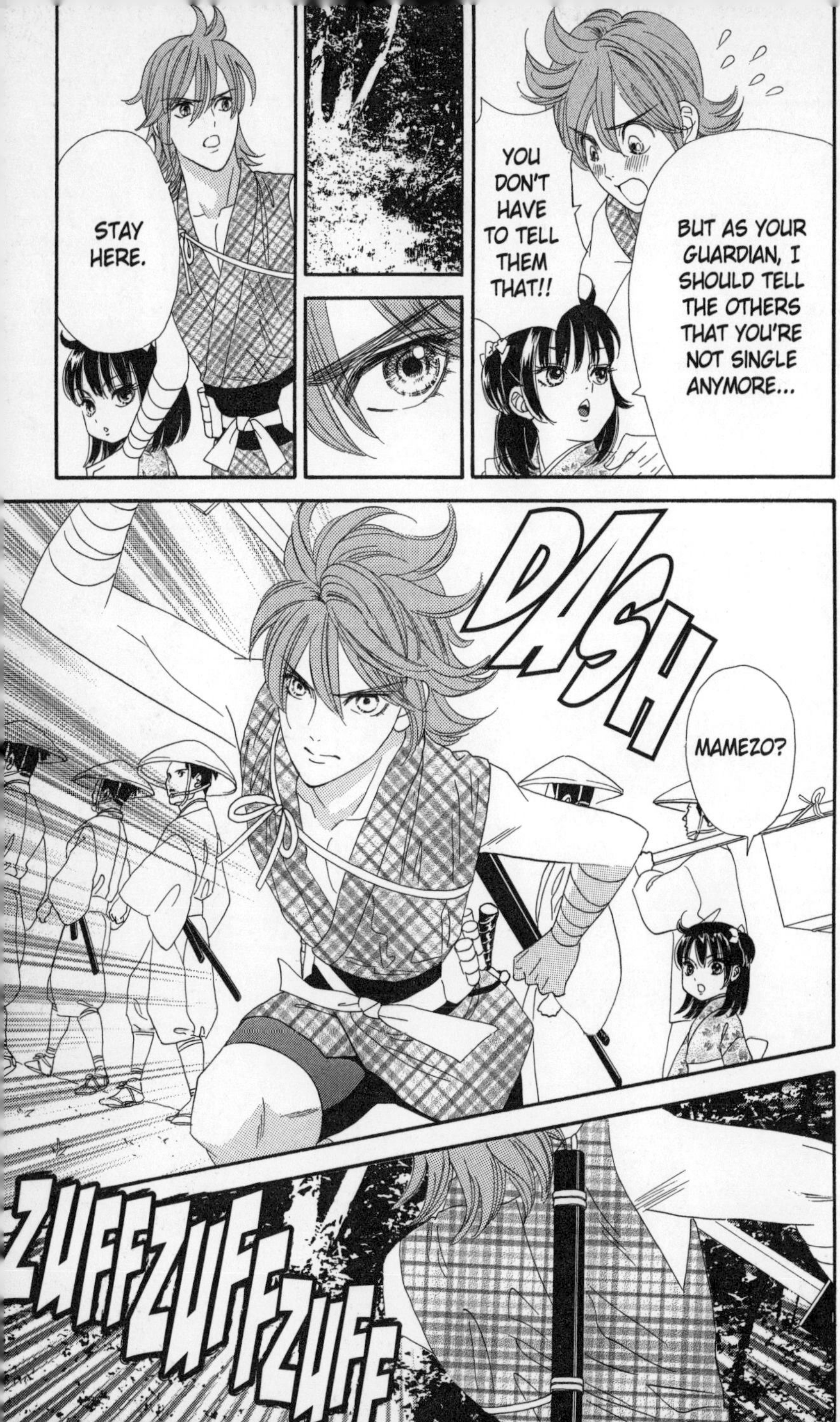
BUT AS YOUR GUARDIAN, I SHOULD TELL THE OTHERS THAT YOU'RE NOT SINGLE ANYMORE...
YOU DON'T HAVE TO TELL THEM THAT!!
STAY HERE.
DASH
MAMEZO?
ZUFF ZUFF ZUFF

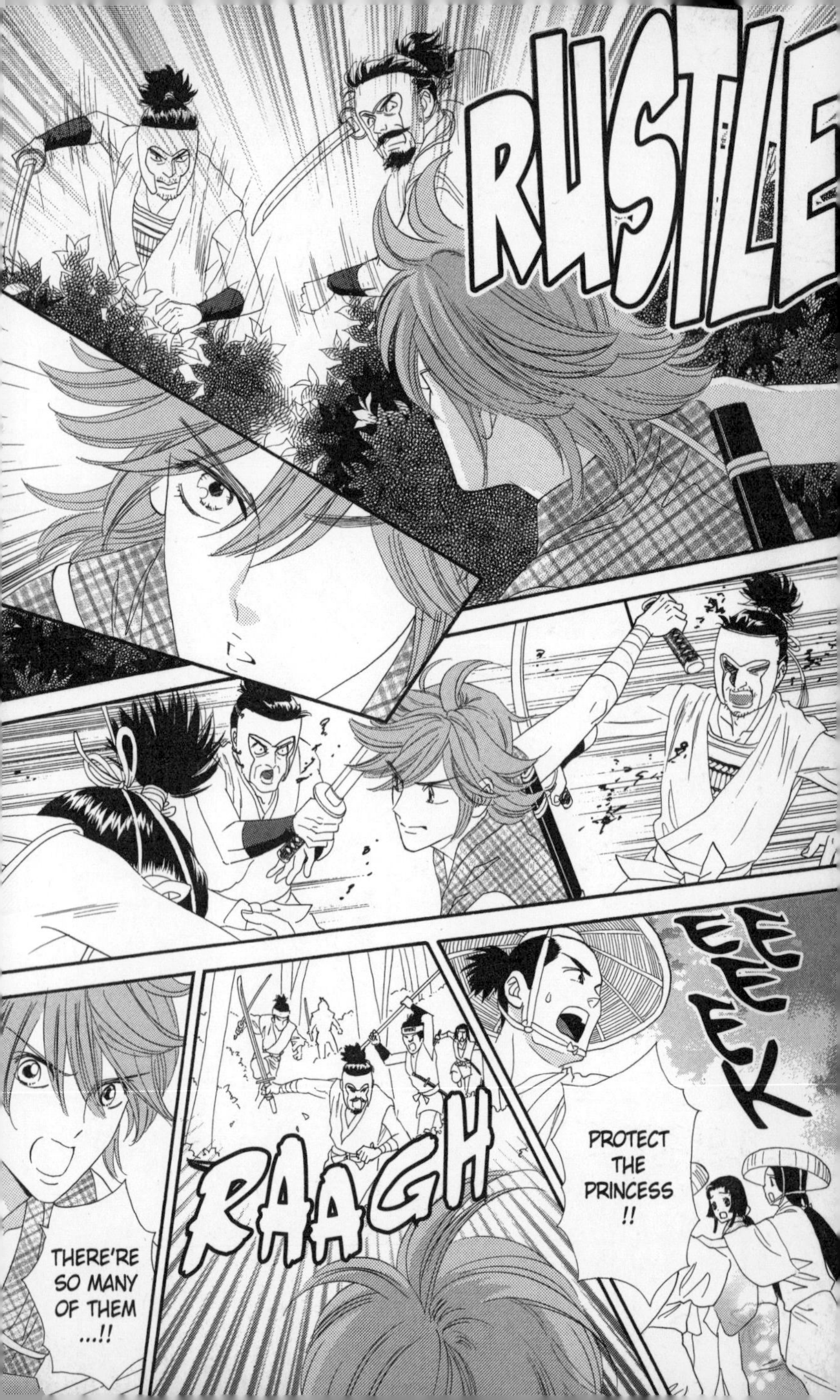
RUSTLE
EEEEK
PROTECT THE PRINCESS!!
RAAGH
THERE'RE SO MANY OF THEM ...!!

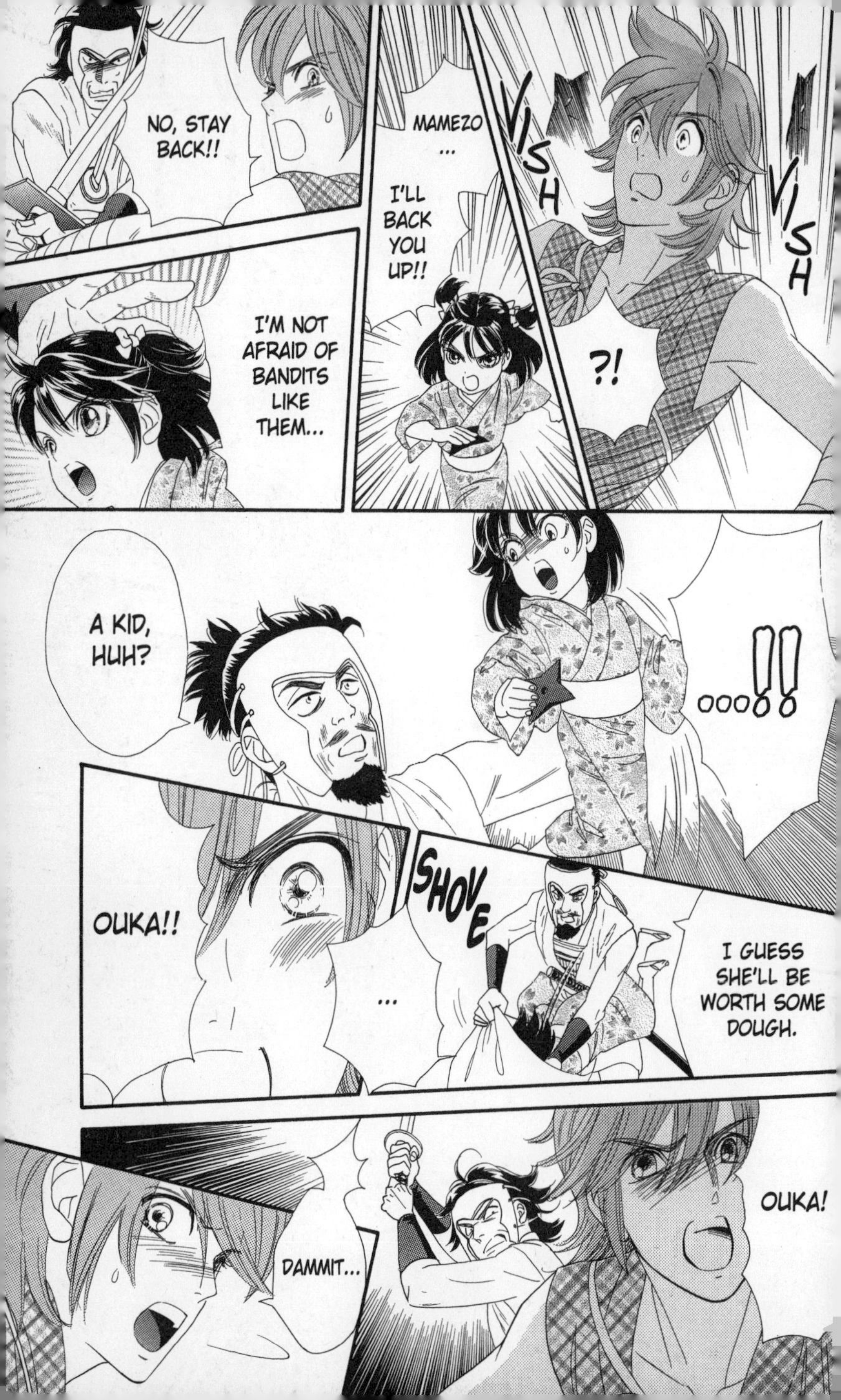

VISH
?!
VISH
MAMEZO ...
I'LL BACK YOU UP!!
NO, STAY BACK!!
I'M NOT AFRAID OF BANDITS LIKE THEM...
OOO!!
A KID, HUH?
SHOVE
I GUESS SHE'LL BE WORTH SOME DOUGH.
...
OUKA!!
OUKA!
DAMMIT...

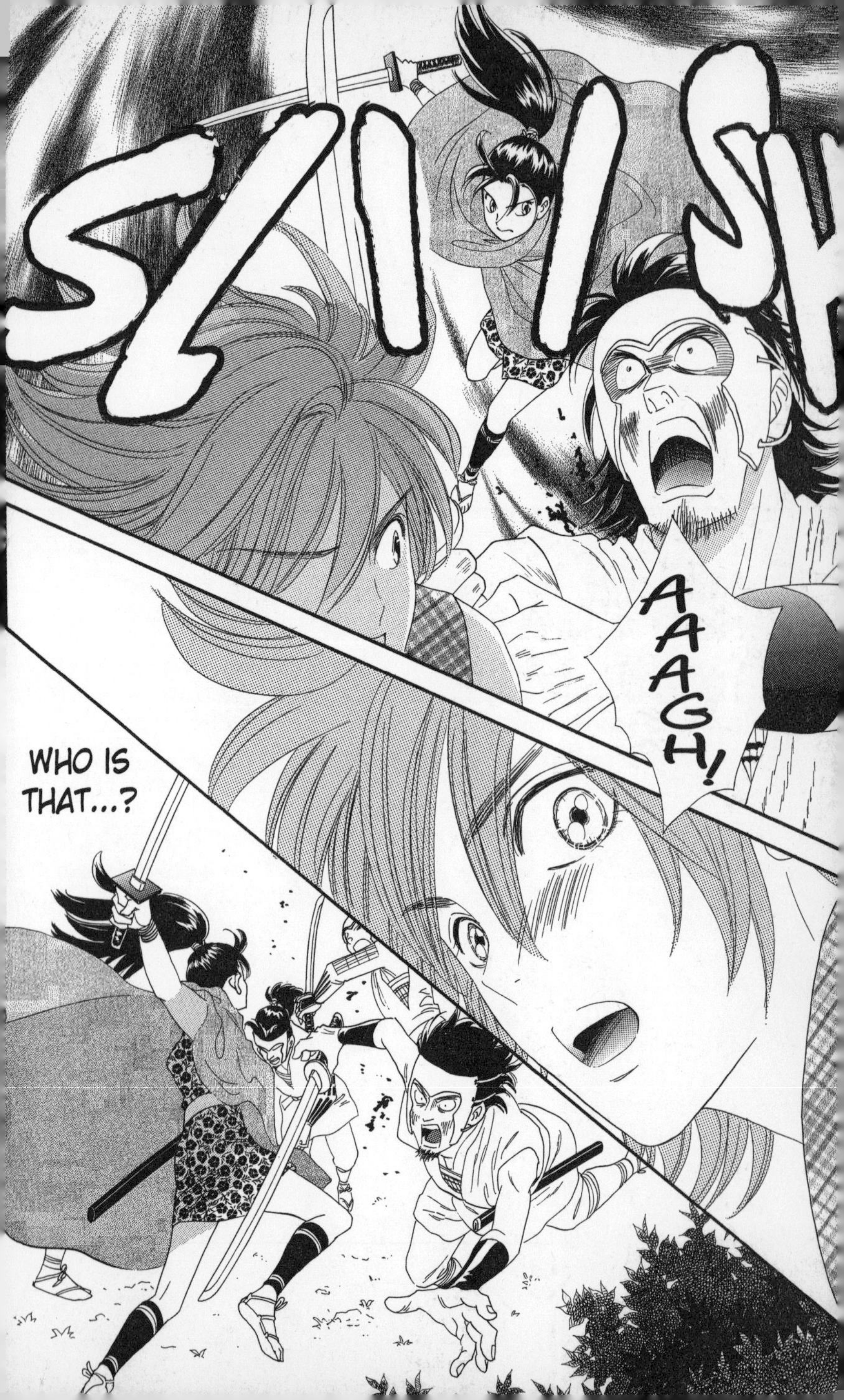

SLIISH
AAAAGH!
WHO IS THAT...?

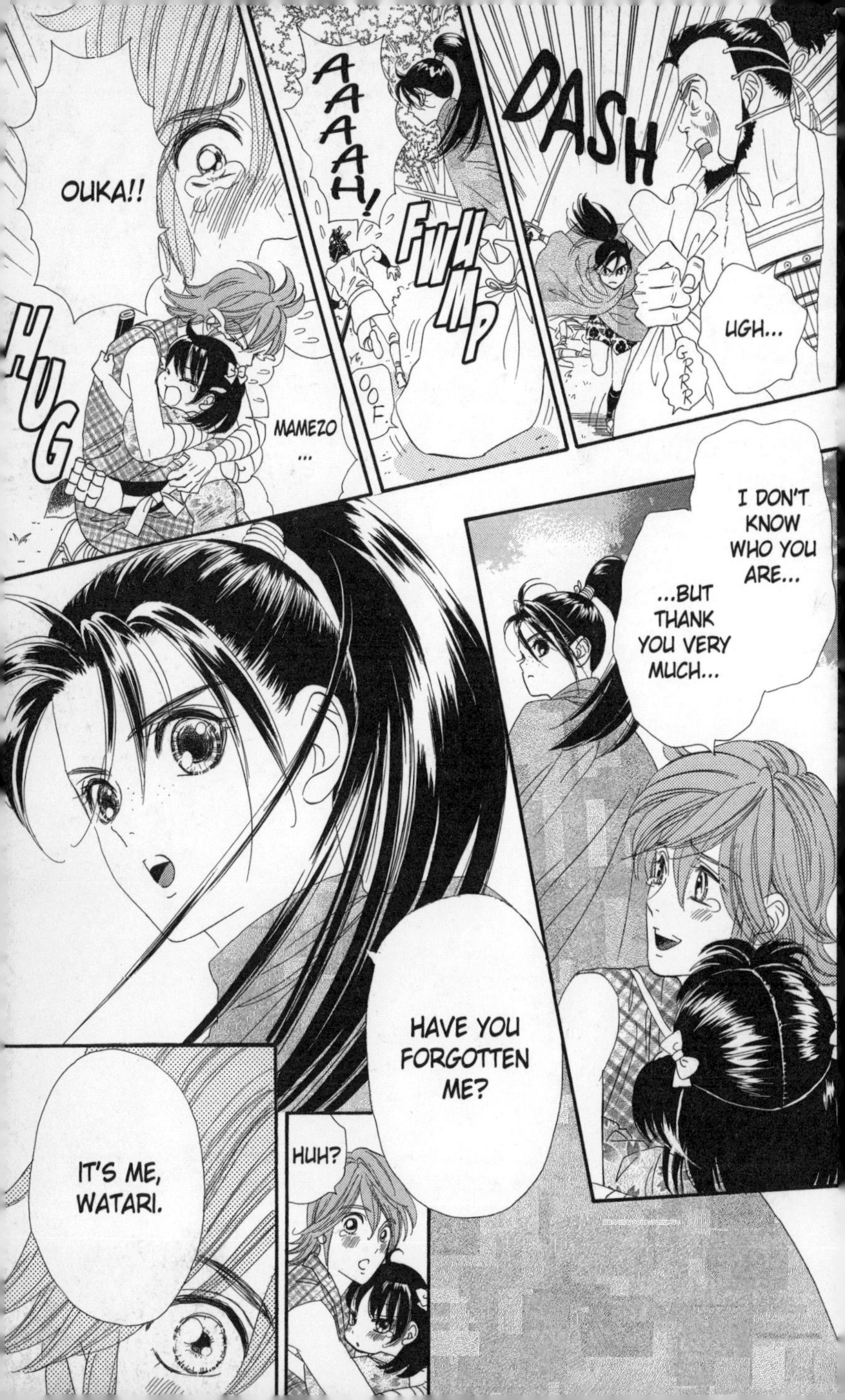
DASH
UGH...
GRRR
AAAAH!
FWUMP
OOF.
OUKA!!
HUG
MAMEZO...
I DON'T KNOW WHO YOU ARE...
...BUT THANK YOU VERY MUCH...
HAVE YOU FORGOTTEN ME?
HUH?
IT'S ME, WATARI.

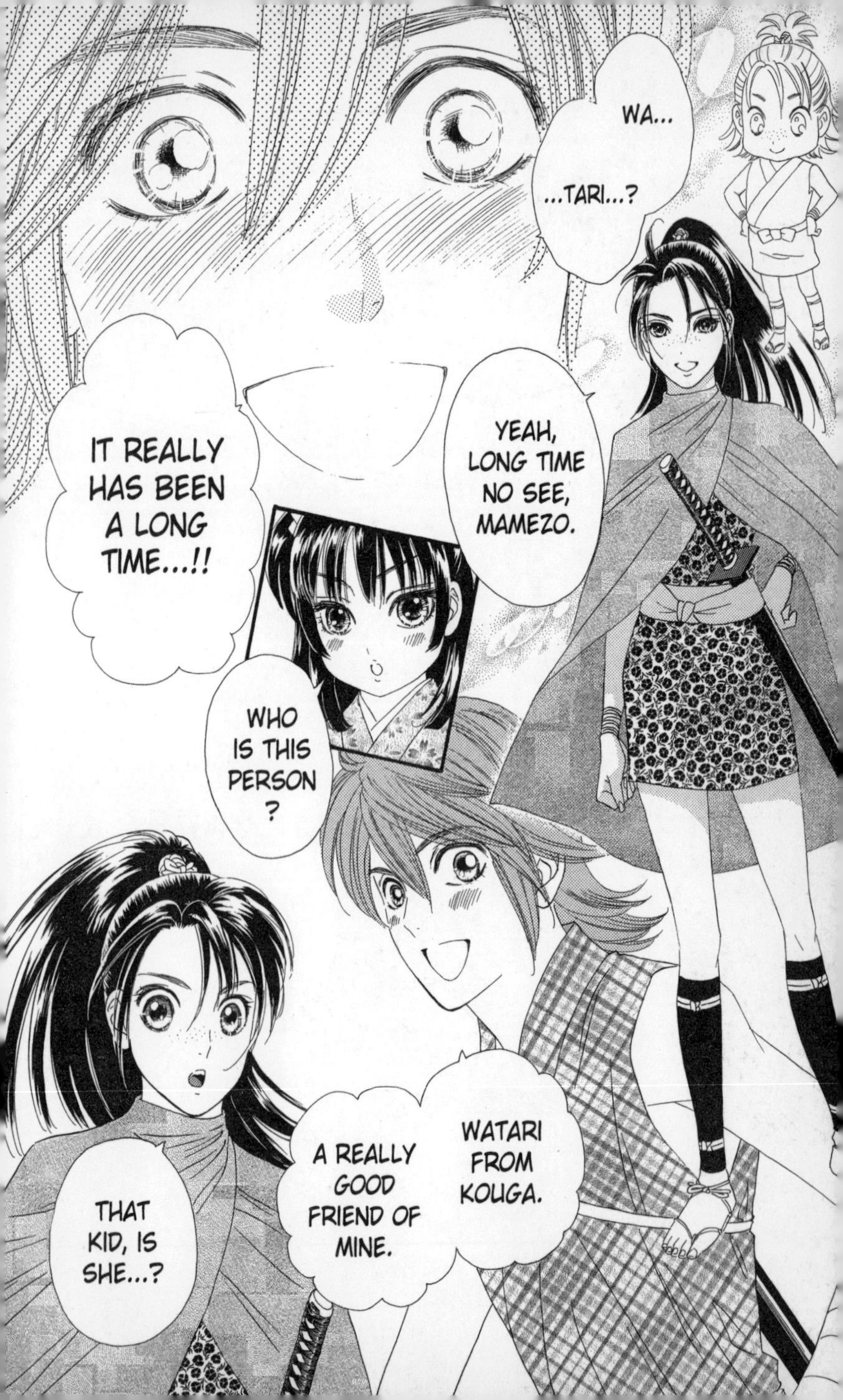
WA...
...TARI...?
YEAH, LONG TIME NO SEE, MAMEZO.
IT REALLY HAS BEEN A LONG TIME...!!
WHO IS THIS PERSON?
WATARI FROM KOUGA.
A REALLY GOOD FRIEND OF MINE.
THAT KID, IS SHE...?

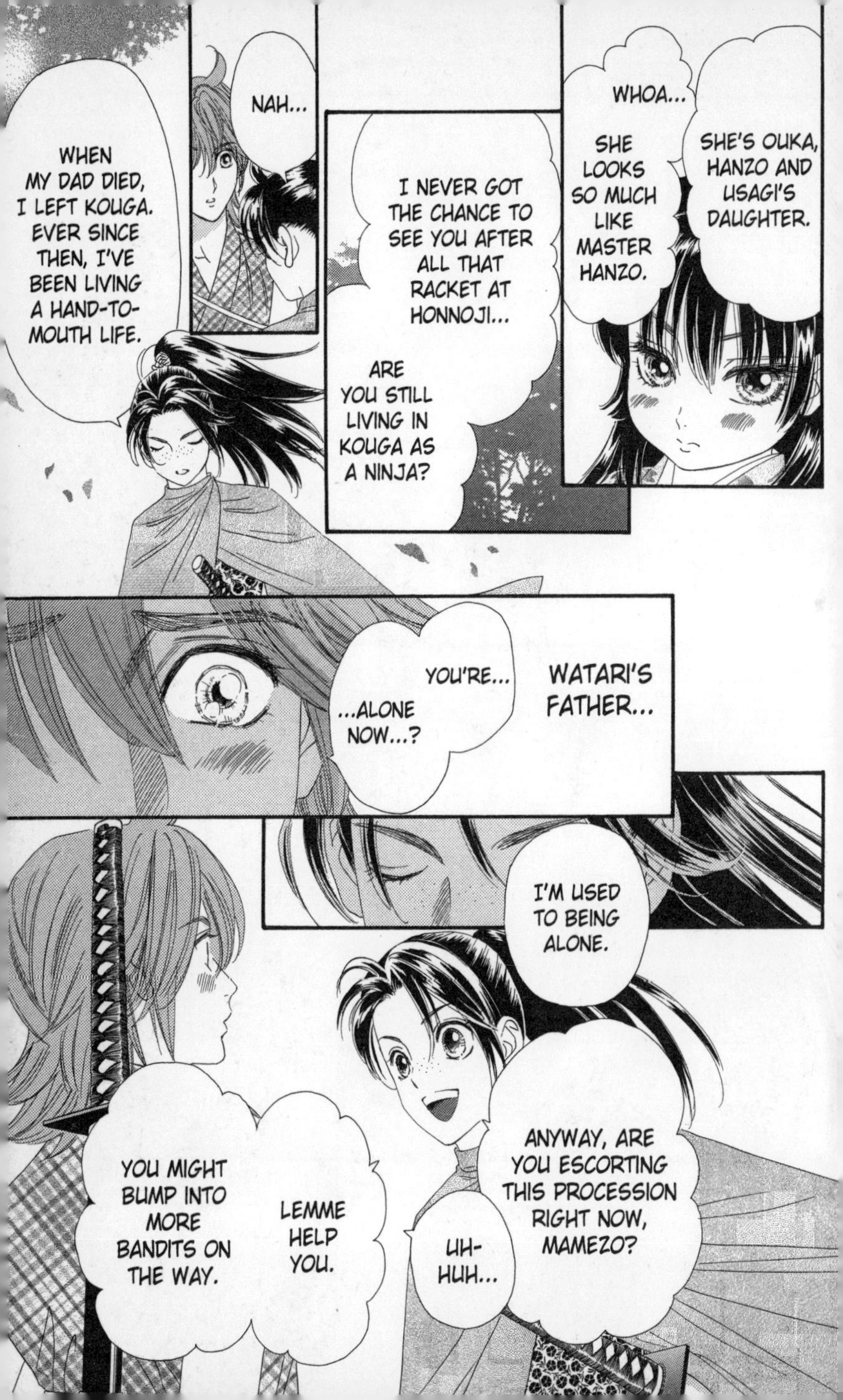
SHE'S OUKA, HANZO AND USAGI'S DAUGHTER.
WHOA...
SHE LOOKS SO MUCH LIKE MASTER HANZO.
I NEVER GOT THE CHANCE TO SEE YOU AFTER ALL THAT RACKET AT HONNOJI...
ARE YOU STILL LIVING IN KOUGA AS A NINJA?
NAH...
WHEN MY DAD DIED, I LEFT KOUGA. EVER SINCE THEN, I'VE BEEN LIVING A HAND-TO-MOUTH LIFE.
WATARI'S FATHER...
YOU'RE...
...ALONE NOW...?
I'M USED TO BEING ALONE.
ANYWAY, ARE YOU ESCORTING THIS PROCESSION RIGHT NOW, MAMEZO?
UH-HUH...
LEMME HELP YOU.
YOU MIGHT BUMP INTO MORE BANDITS ON THE WAY.

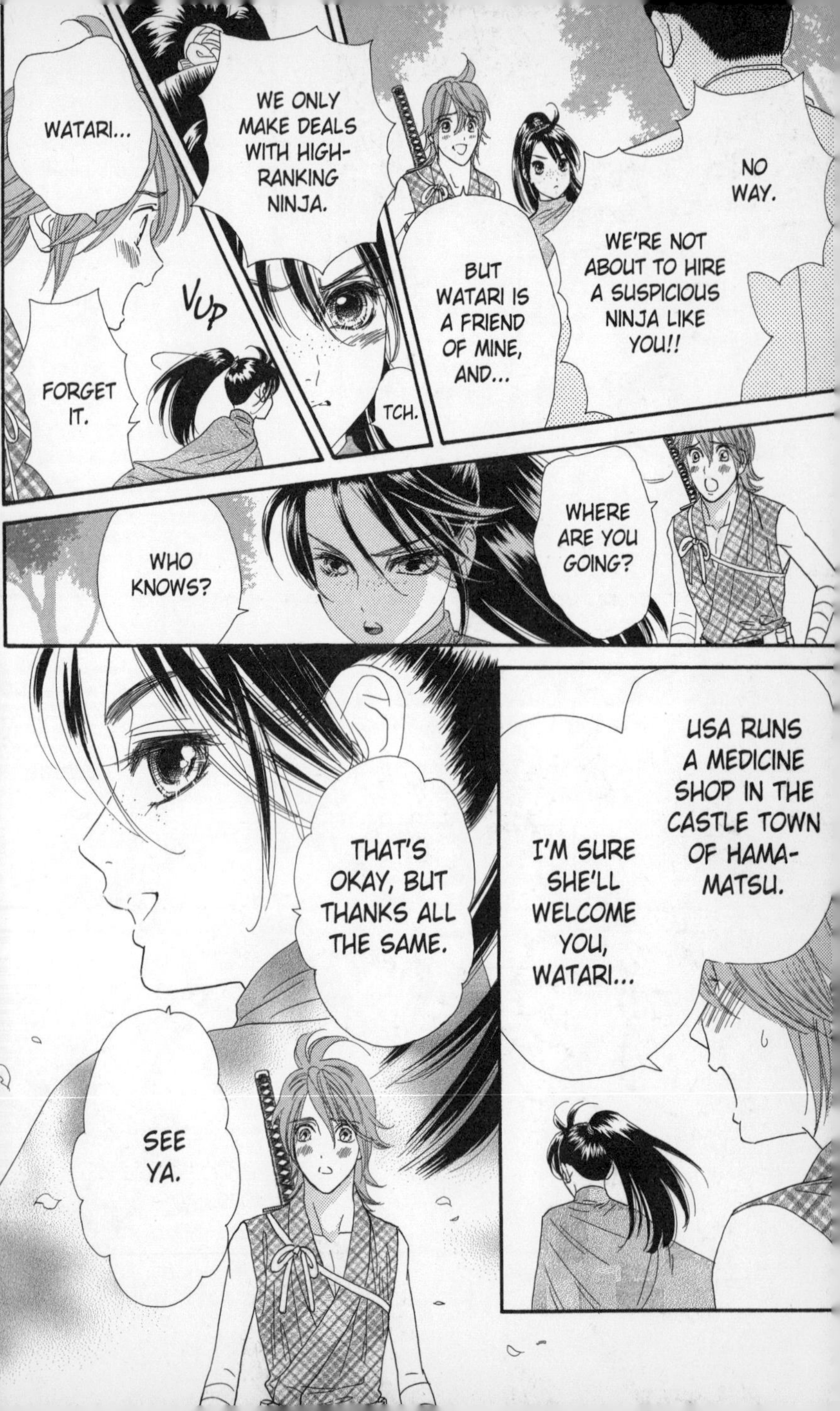
NO WAY.
WE'RE NOT ABOUT TO HIRE A SUSPICIOUS NINJA LIKE YOU!!
BUT WATARI IS A FRIEND OF MINE, AND...
WE ONLY MAKE DEALS WITH HIGH-RANKING NINJA.
TCH.
WATARI...
VUP
FORGET IT.
WHERE ARE YOU GOING?
WHO KNOWS?
USA RUNS A MEDICINE SHOP IN THE CASTLE TOWN OF HAMA-MATSU.
I'M SURE SHE'LL WELCOME YOU, WATARI...
THAT'S OKAY, BUT THANKS ALL THE SAME.
SEE YA.

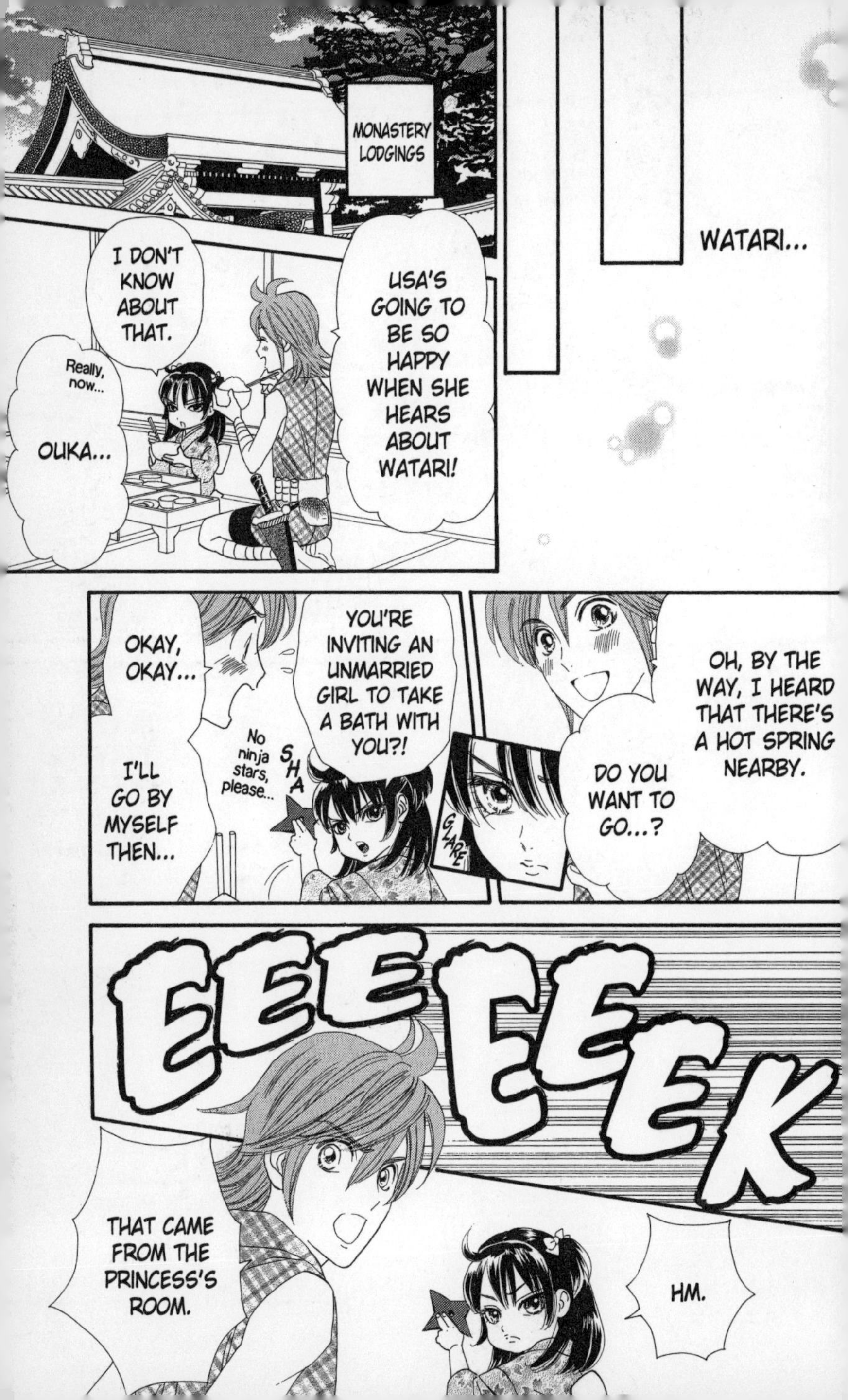

WATARI...
MONASTERY LODGINGS
USA'S GOING TO BE SO HAPPY WHEN SHE HEARS ABOUT WATARI!
I DON'T KNOW ABOUT THAT.
Really, now...
OUKA...
OH, BY THE WAY, I HEARD THAT THERE'S A HOT SPRING NEARBY.
DO YOU WANT TO GO...?
GLARE
YOU'RE INVITING AN UNMARRIED GIRL TO TAKE A BATH WITH YOU?!
SHA
No ninja stars, please...
OKAY, OKAY...
I'LL GO BY MYSELF THEN...
EEEEEEK
HM.
THAT CAME FROM THE PRINCESS'S ROOM.

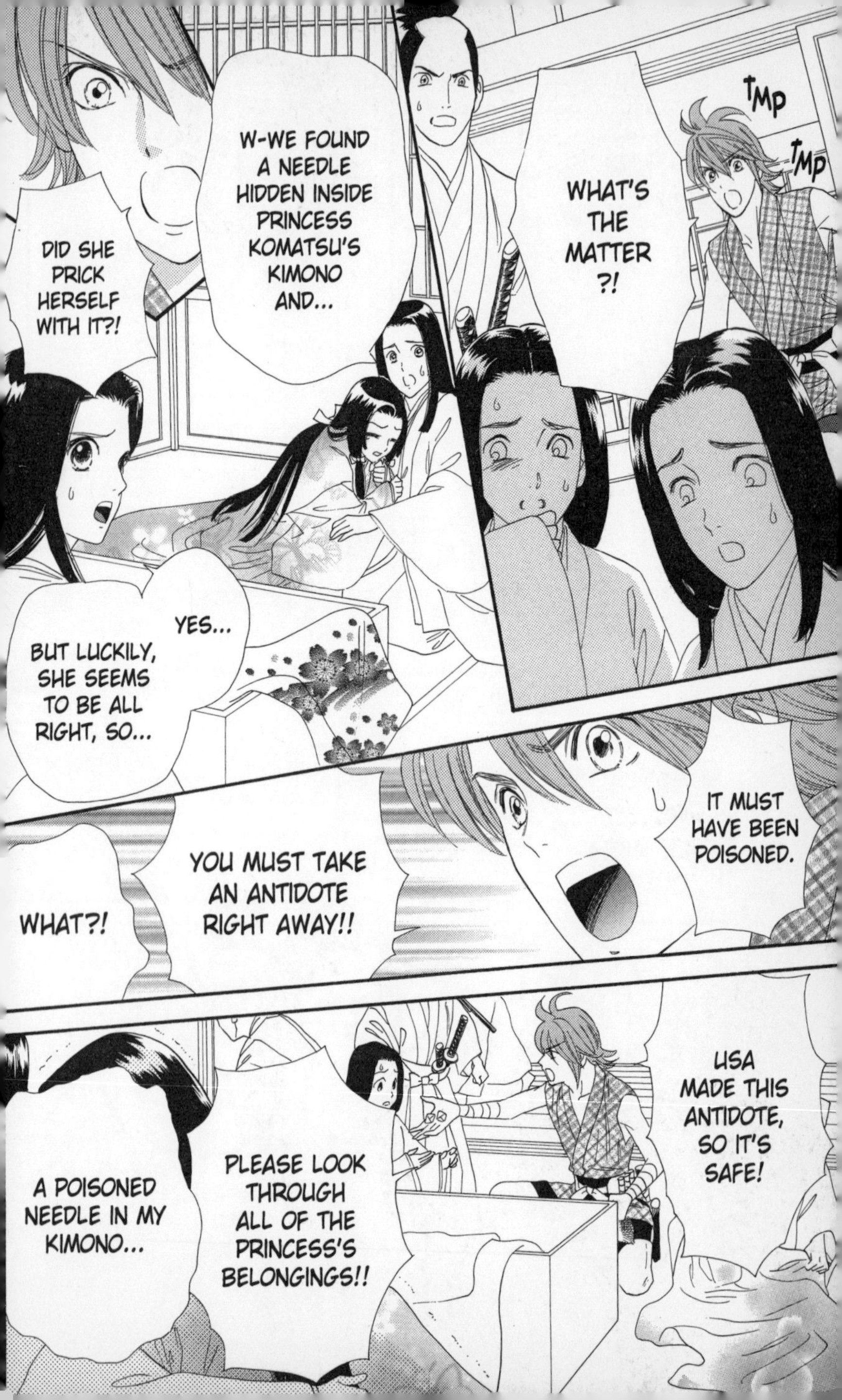
TMP
TMP
WHAT'S THE MATTER ?!
W-WE FOUND A NEEDLE HIDDEN INSIDE PRINCESS KOMATSU'S KIMONO AND...
DID SHE PRICK HERSELF WITH IT?!
YES...
BUT LUCKILY, SHE SEEMS TO BE ALL RIGHT, SO...
IT MUST HAVE BEEN POISONED.
YOU MUST TAKE AN ANTIDOTE RIGHT AWAY!!
WHAT?!
USA MADE THIS ANTIDOTE, SO IT'S SAFE!
PLEASE LOOK THROUGH ALL OF THE PRINCESS'S BELONGINGS!!
A POISONED NEEDLE IN MY KIMONO...

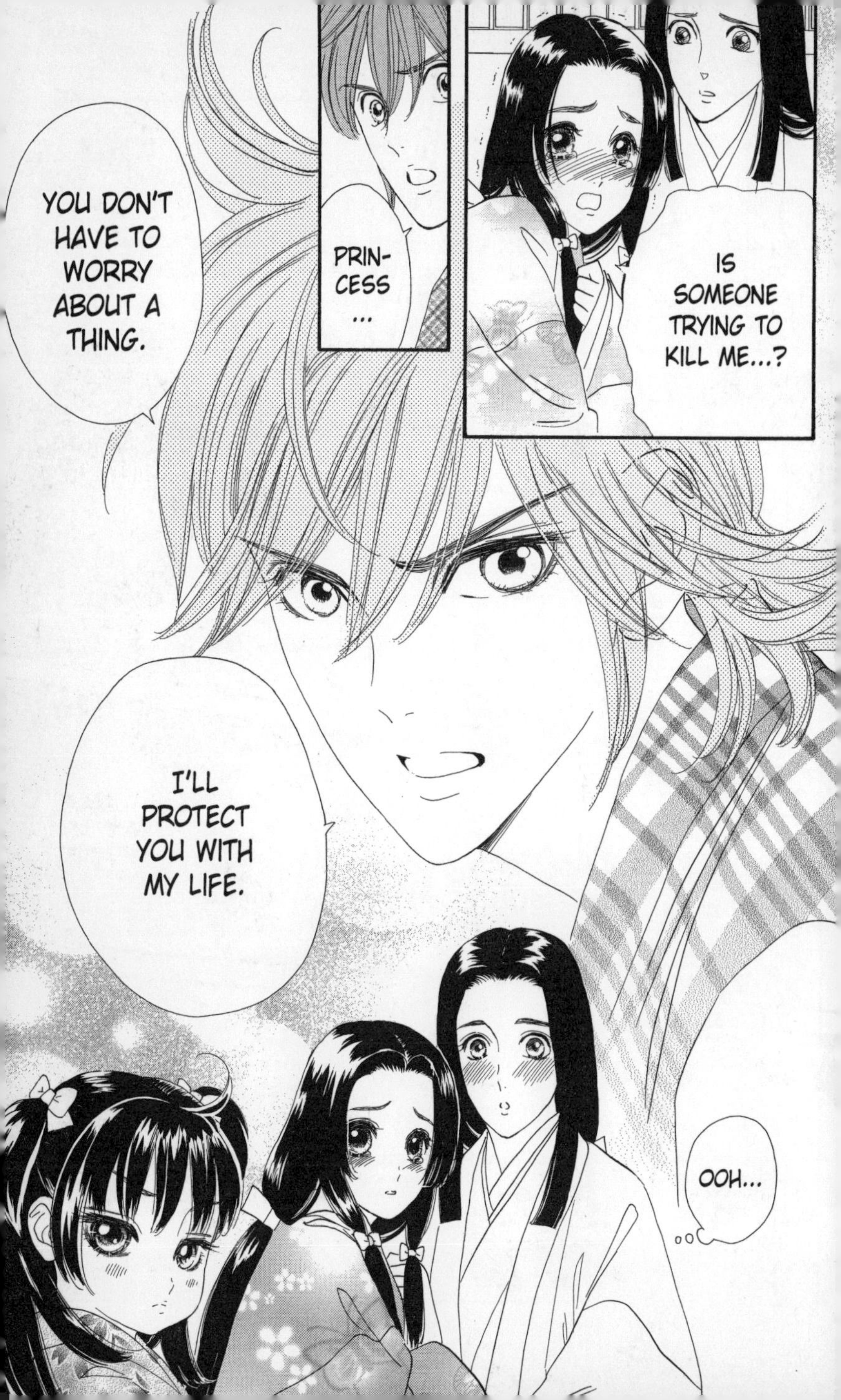
IS SOMEONE TRYING TO KILL ME...?
PRIN-CESS ...
YOU DON'T HAVE TO WORRY ABOUT A THING.
I'LL PROTECT YOU WITH MY LIFE.
OOH...

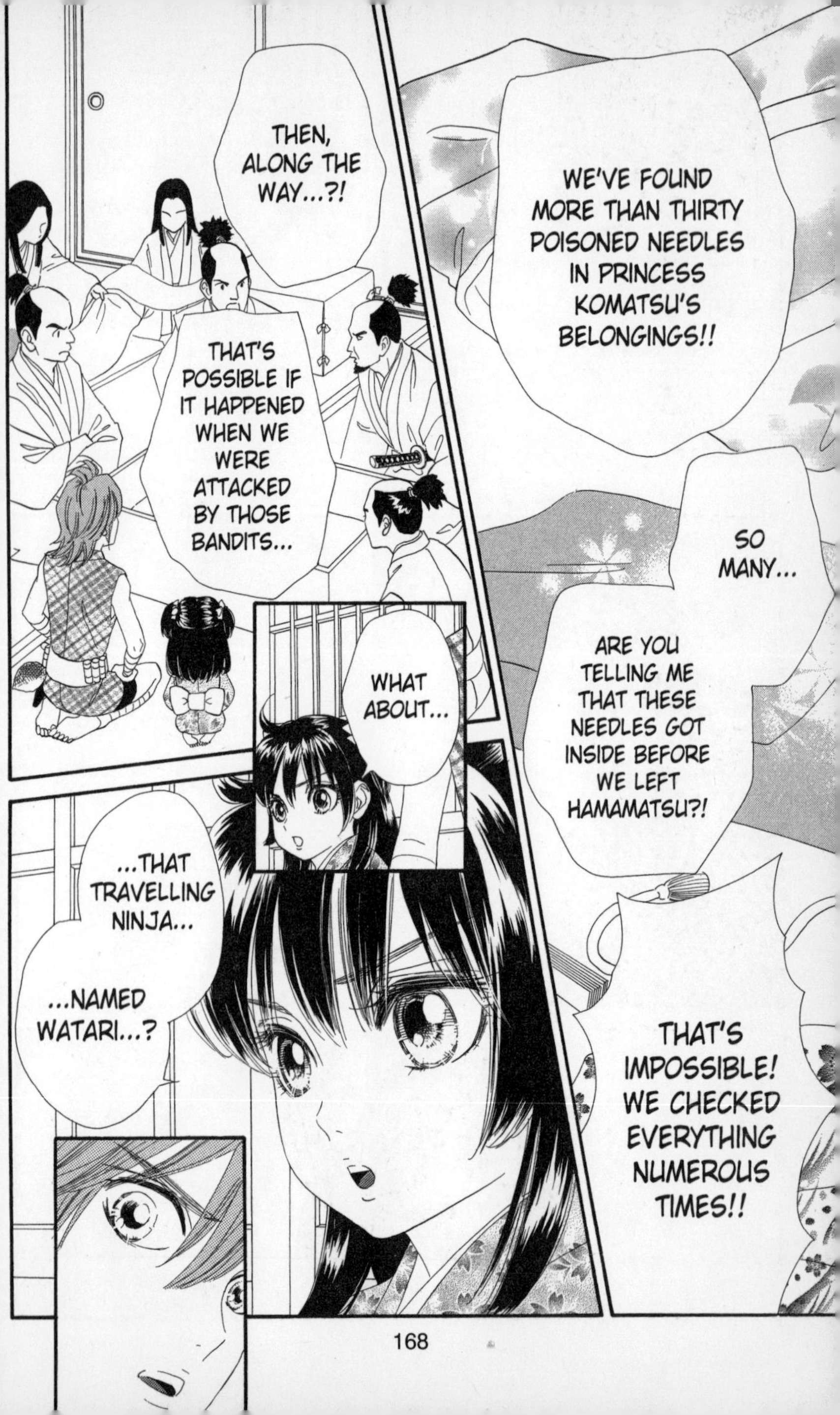
WE'VE FOUND MORE THAN THIRTY POISONED NEEDLES IN PRINCESS KOMATSU'S BELONGINGS!!
SO MANY...
ARE YOU TELLING ME THAT THESE NEEDLES GOT INSIDE BEFORE WE LEFT HAMAMATSU?!
THAT'S IMPOSSIBLE! WE CHECKED EVERYTHING NUMEROUS TIMES!!
THEN, ALONG THE WAY...?!
THAT'S POSSIBLE IF IT HAPPENED WHEN WE WERE ATTACKED BY THOSE BANDITS...
WHAT ABOUT...
...THAT TRAVELLING NINJA...
...NAMED WATARI...?

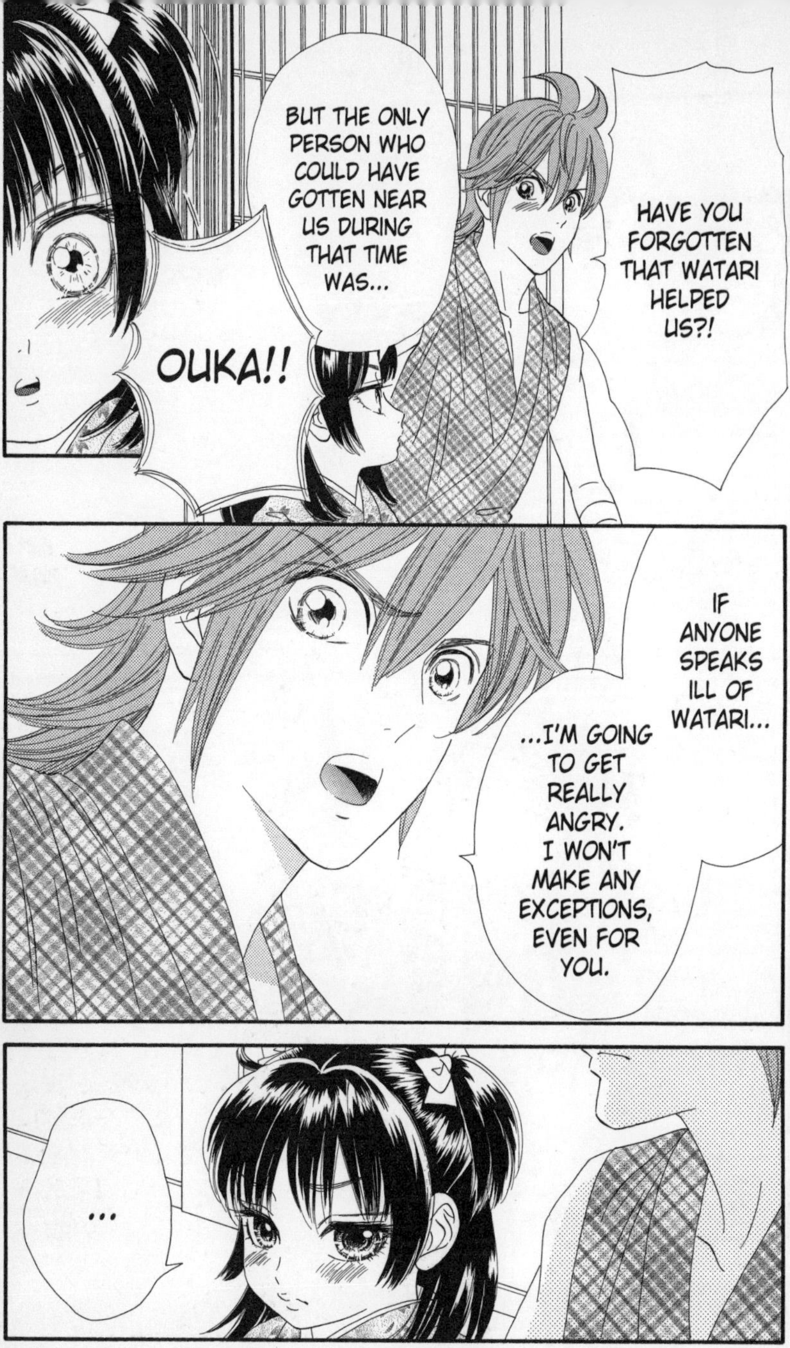
BUT THE ONLY PERSON WHO COULD HAVE GOTTEN NEAR US DURING THAT TIME WAS...
OUKA!!
HAVE YOU FORGOTTEN THAT WATARI HELPED US?!
IF ANYONE SPEAKS ILL OF WATARI...
...I'M GOING TO GET REALLY ANGRY. I WON'T MAKE ANY EXCEPTIONS, EVEN FOR YOU.
...

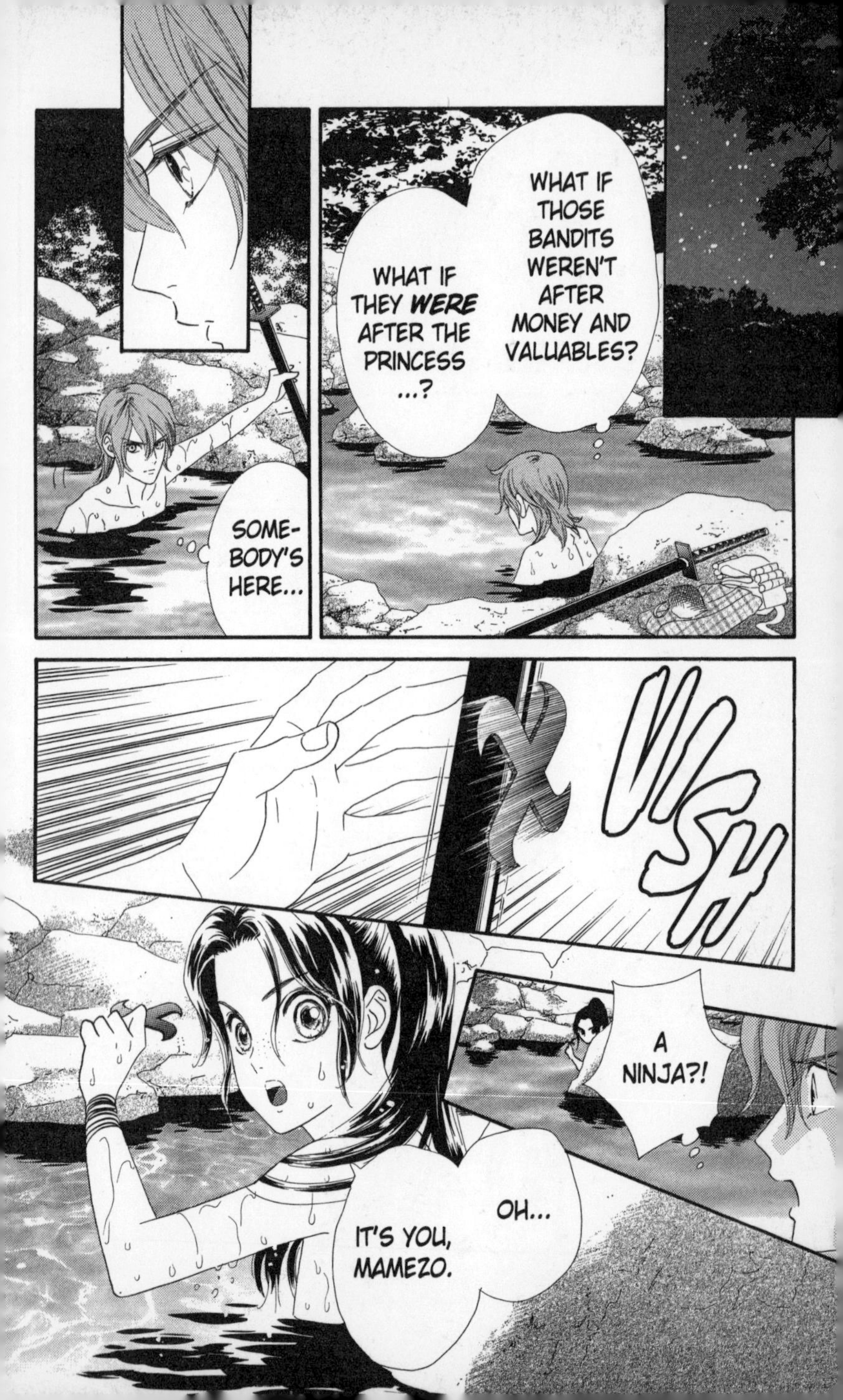
WHAT IF THOSE BANDITS WEREN'T AFTER MONEY AND VALUABLES?
WHAT IF THEY *WERE* AFTER THE PRINCESS ...?
SOME-BODY'S HERE...
VISH
A NINJA?!
OH...
IT'S YOU, MAMEZO.

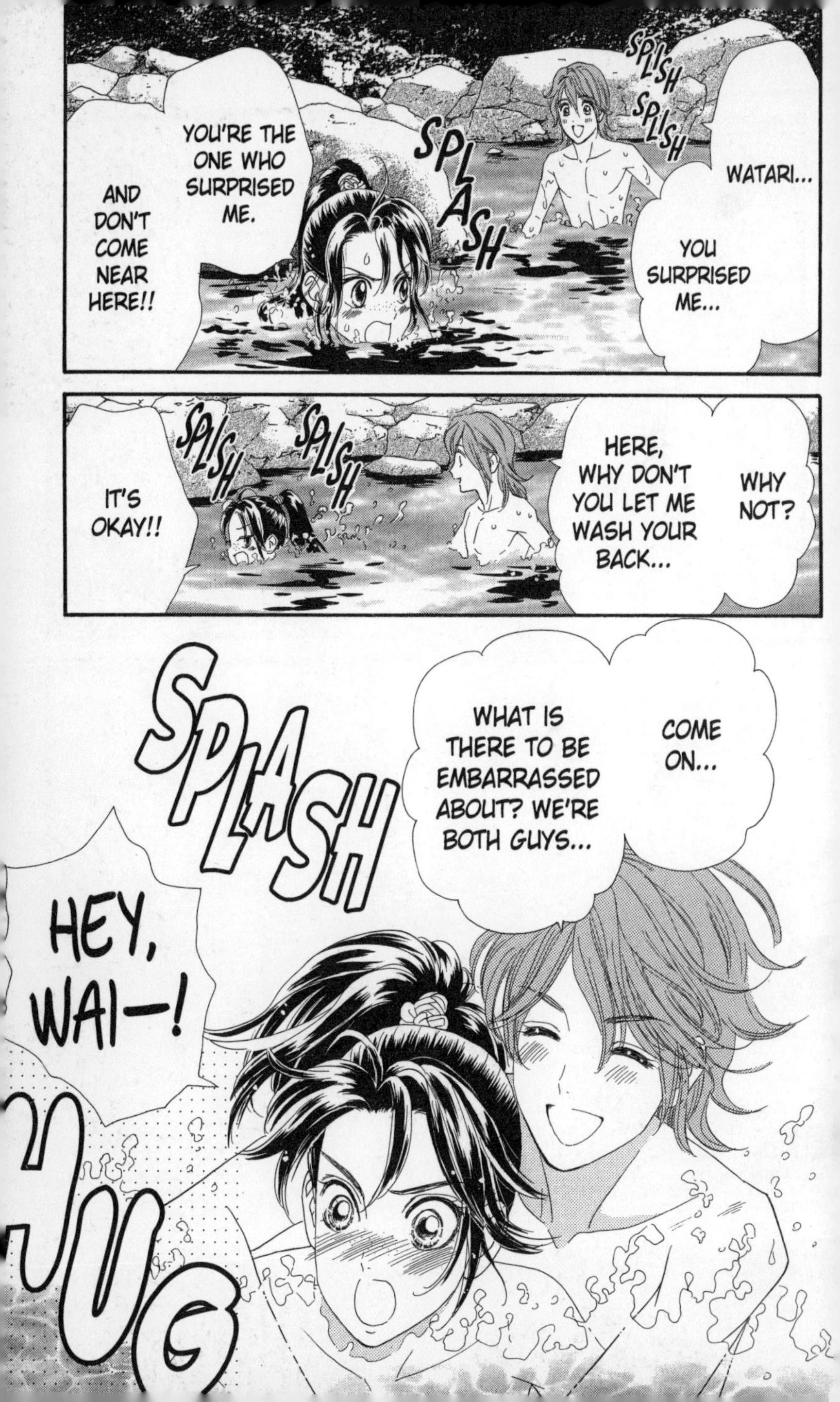
SPLISH SPLISH
WATARI...
YOU SURPRISED ME...
SPLASH
YOU'RE THE ONE WHO SURPRISED ME.
AND DON'T COME NEAR HERE!!
WHY NOT?
HERE, WHY DON'T YOU LET ME WASH YOUR BACK...
SPLISH
SPLISH
IT'S OKAY!!
COME ON...
WHAT IS THERE TO BE EMBARRASSED ABOUT? WE'RE BOTH GUYS...
SPLASH
HEY, WAI—!
HUG

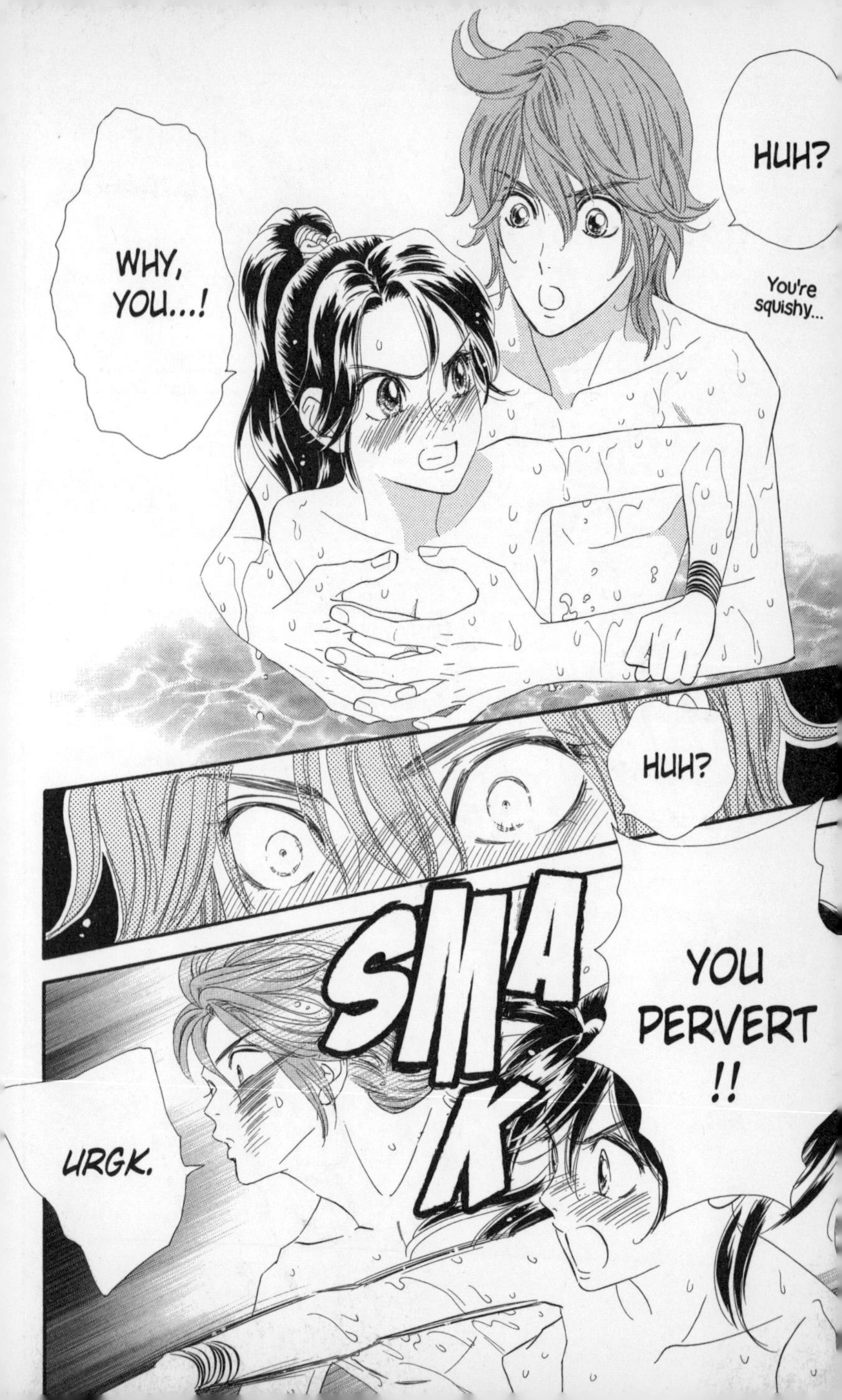
HUH?
You're squishy...
WHY, YOU...!
HUH?
YOU PERVERT !!
SMAK
URGK.

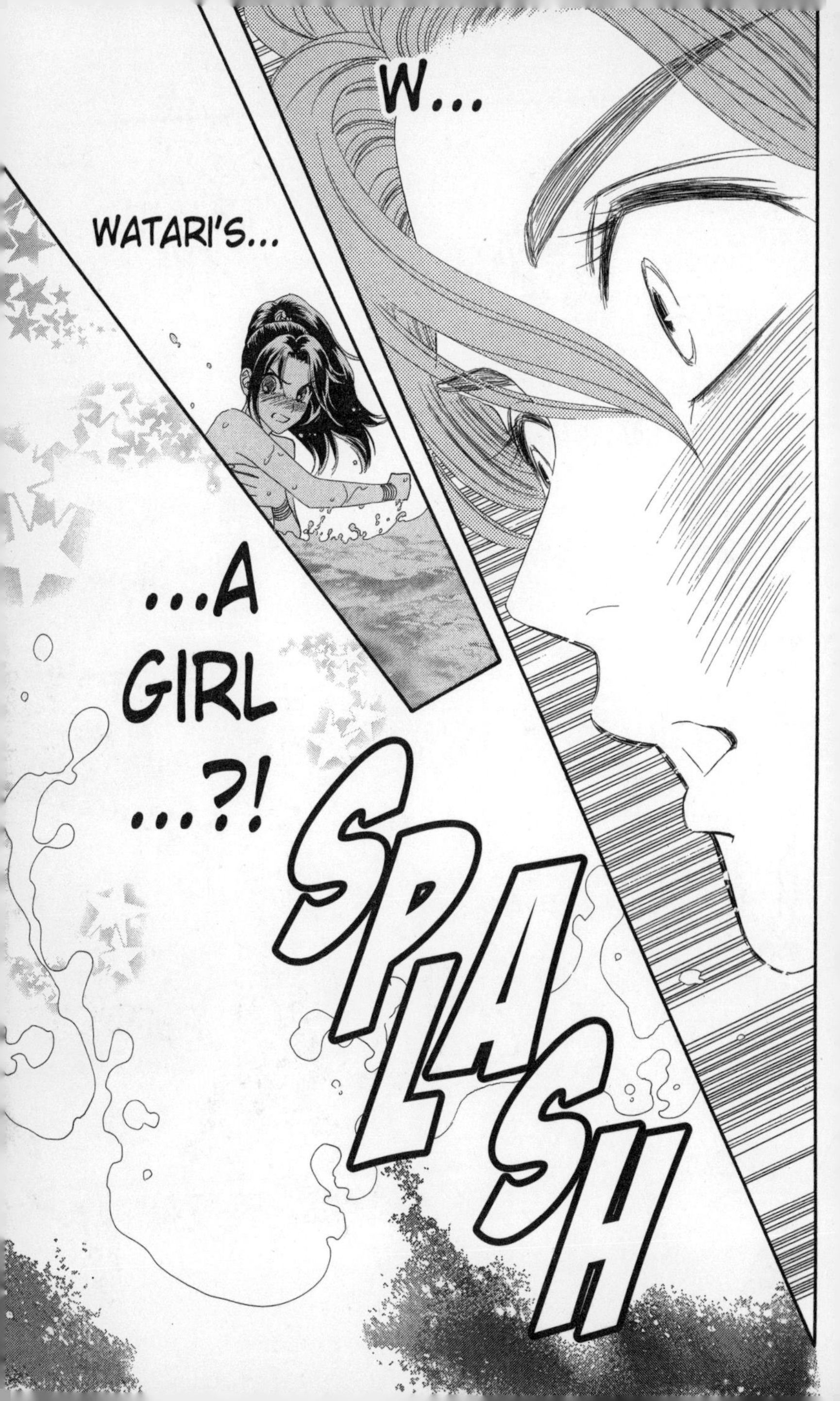
W...
WATARI'S...
...A GIRL ...?!
SPLASH

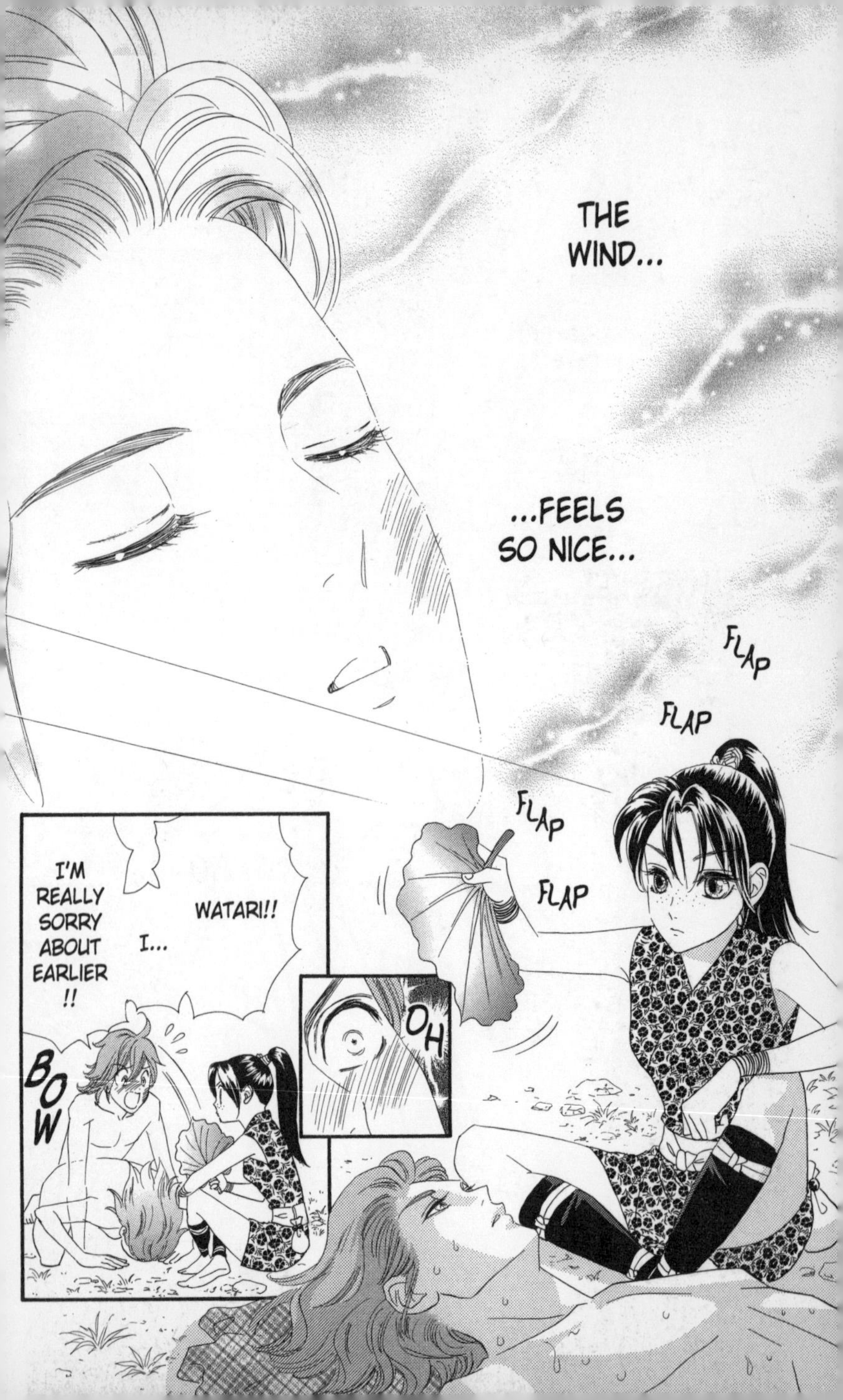
THE WIND...
...FEELS SO NICE...
FLAP
FLAP
FLAP
FLAP
OH
WATARI!!
I...
I'M REALLY SORRY ABOUT EARLIER!!
BOW

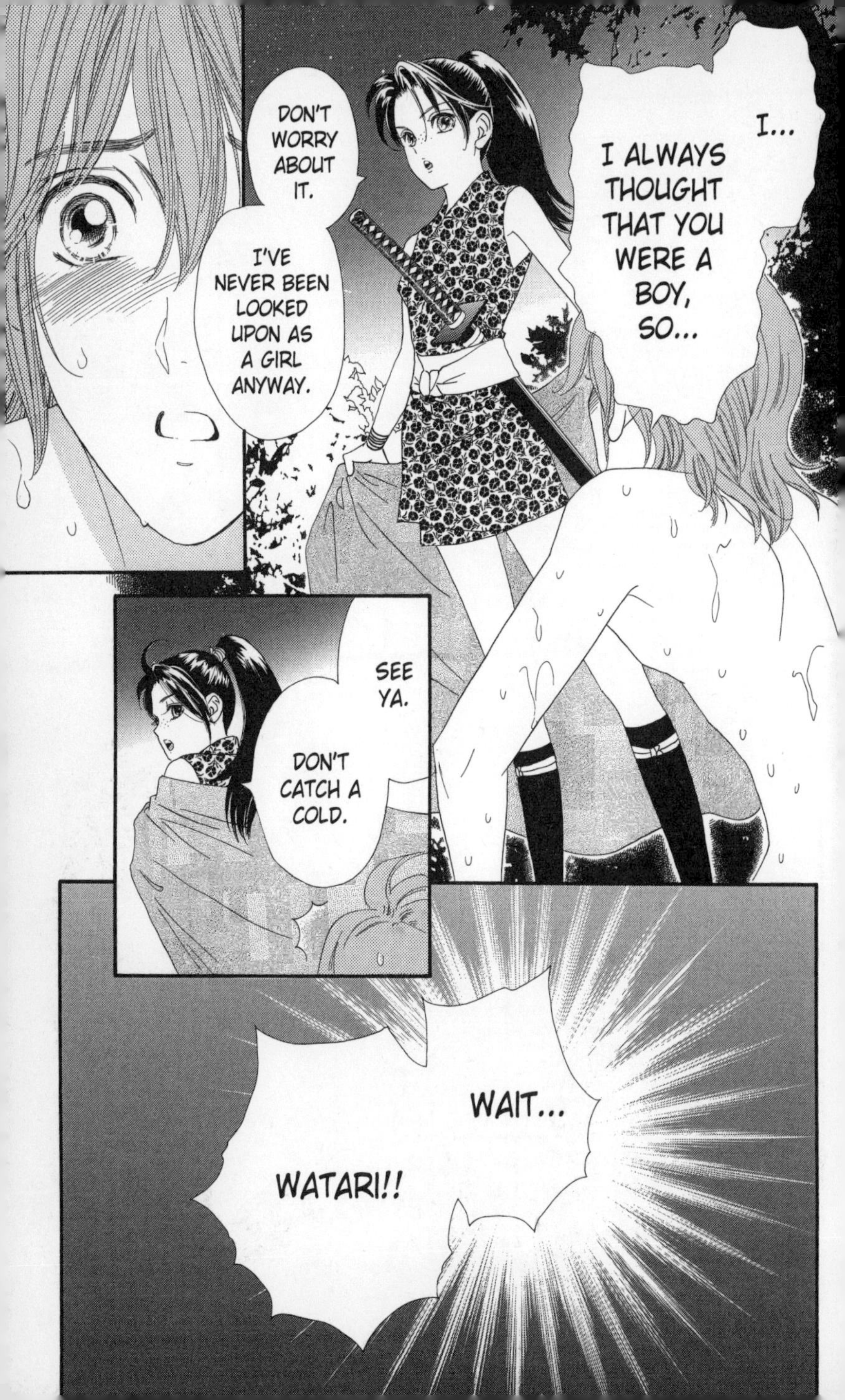
I...
I ALWAYS THOUGHT THAT YOU WERE A BOY, SO...
DON'T WORRY ABOUT IT.
I'VE NEVER BEEN LOOKED UPON AS A GIRL ANYWAY.
SEE YA.
DON'T CATCH A COLD.
WAIT...
WATARI!!

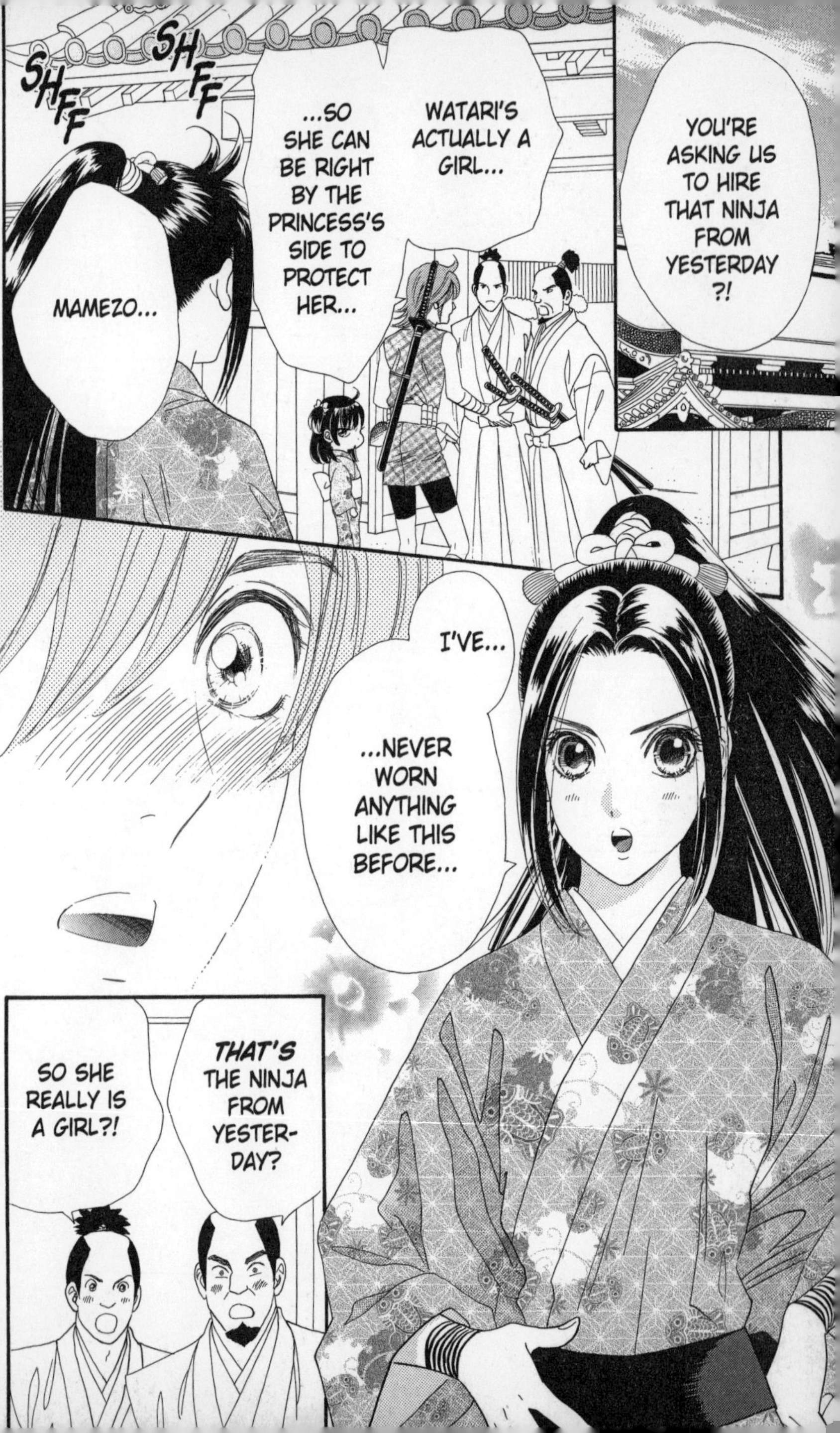
YOU'RE ASKING US TO HIRE THAT NINJA FROM YESTERDAY ?!
SHFF
WATARI'S ACTUALLY A GIRL...
...SO SHE CAN BE RIGHT BY THE PRINCESS'S SIDE TO PROTECT HER...
SHFF
MAMEZO...
I'VE...
...NEVER WORN ANYTHING LIKE THIS BEFORE...
THAT'S THE NINJA FROM YESTER-DAY?
SO SHE REALLY IS A GIRL?!

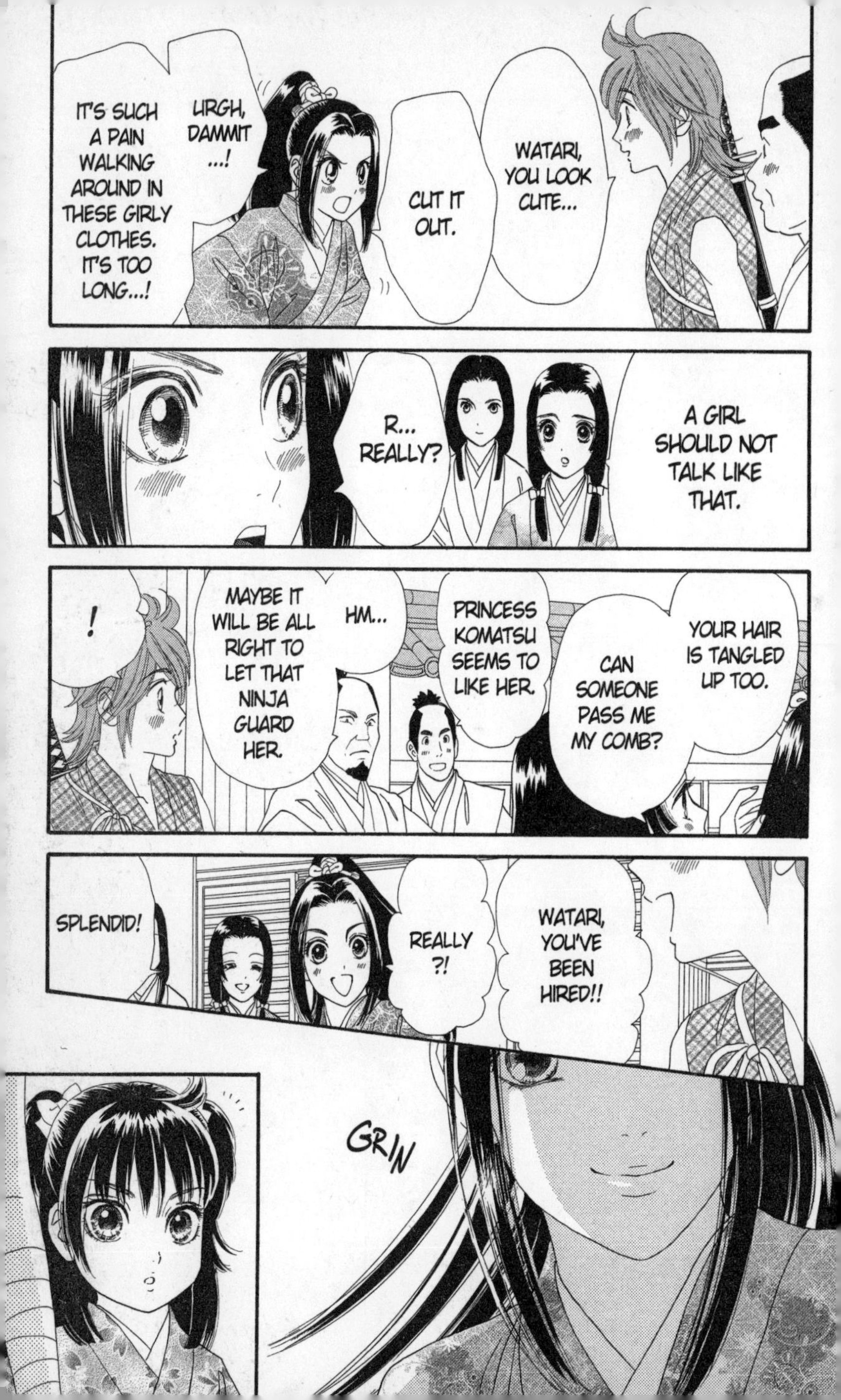
WATARI, YOU LOOK CUTE...
CUT IT OUT.
URGH, DAMMIT ...!
IT'S SUCH A PAIN WALKING AROUND IN THESE GIRLY CLOTHES. IT'S TOO LONG...!
A GIRL SHOULD NOT TALK LIKE THAT.
R... REALLY?
YOUR HAIR IS TANGLED UP TOO.
CAN SOMEONE PASS ME MY COMB?
PRINCESS KOMATSU SEEMS TO LIKE HER.
HM...
MAYBE IT WILL BE ALL RIGHT TO LET THAT NINJA GUARD HER.
!
WATARI, YOU'VE BEEN HIRED!!
REALLY ?!
SPLENDID!
GRIN

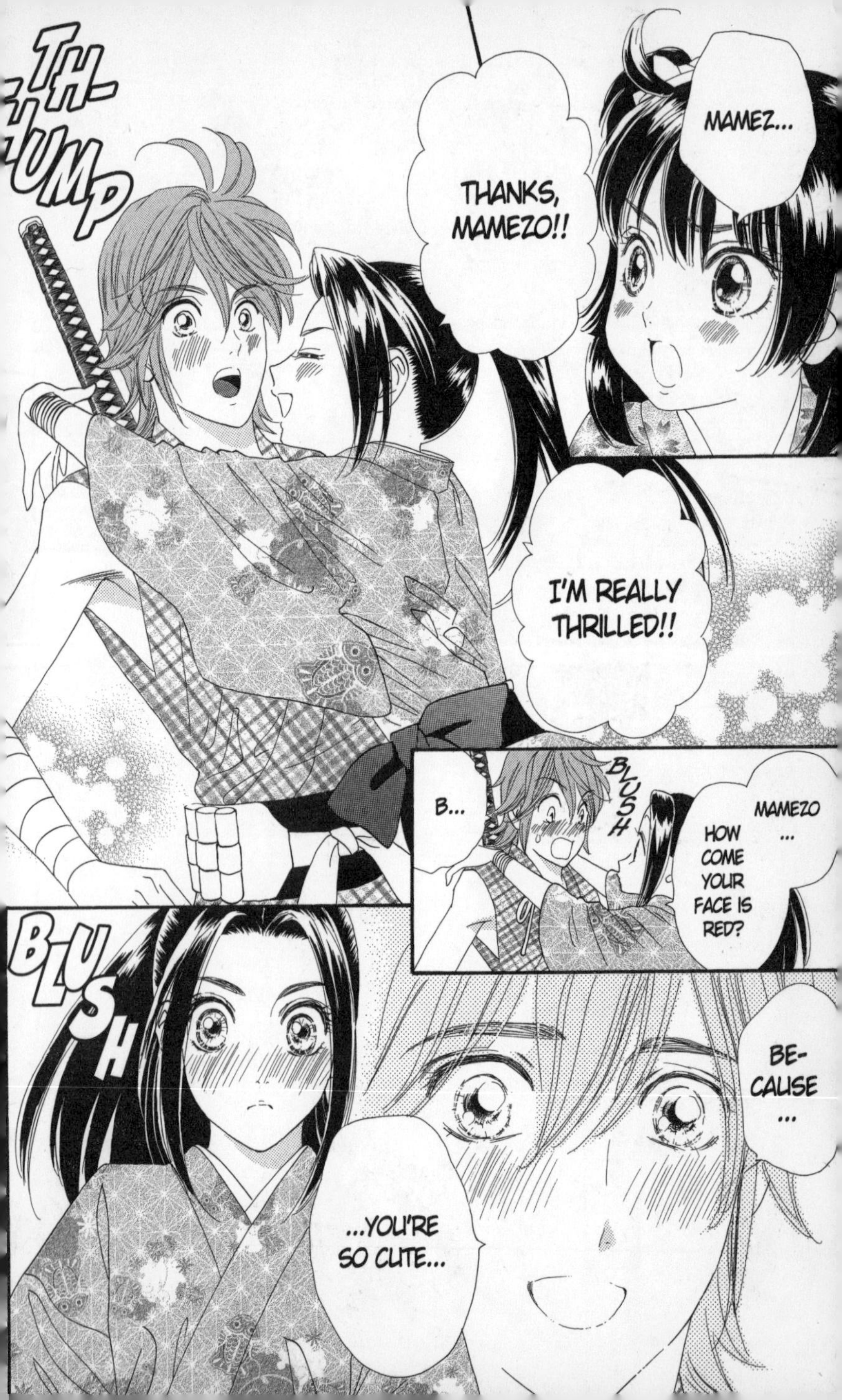
MAMEZ...
THANKS, MAMEZO!!
TH-THUMP
I'M REALLY THRILLED!!
MAMEZO ... HOW COME YOUR FACE IS RED?
BLUSH
B...
BE-CAUSE ...
...YOU'RE SO CUTE...
BLUSH

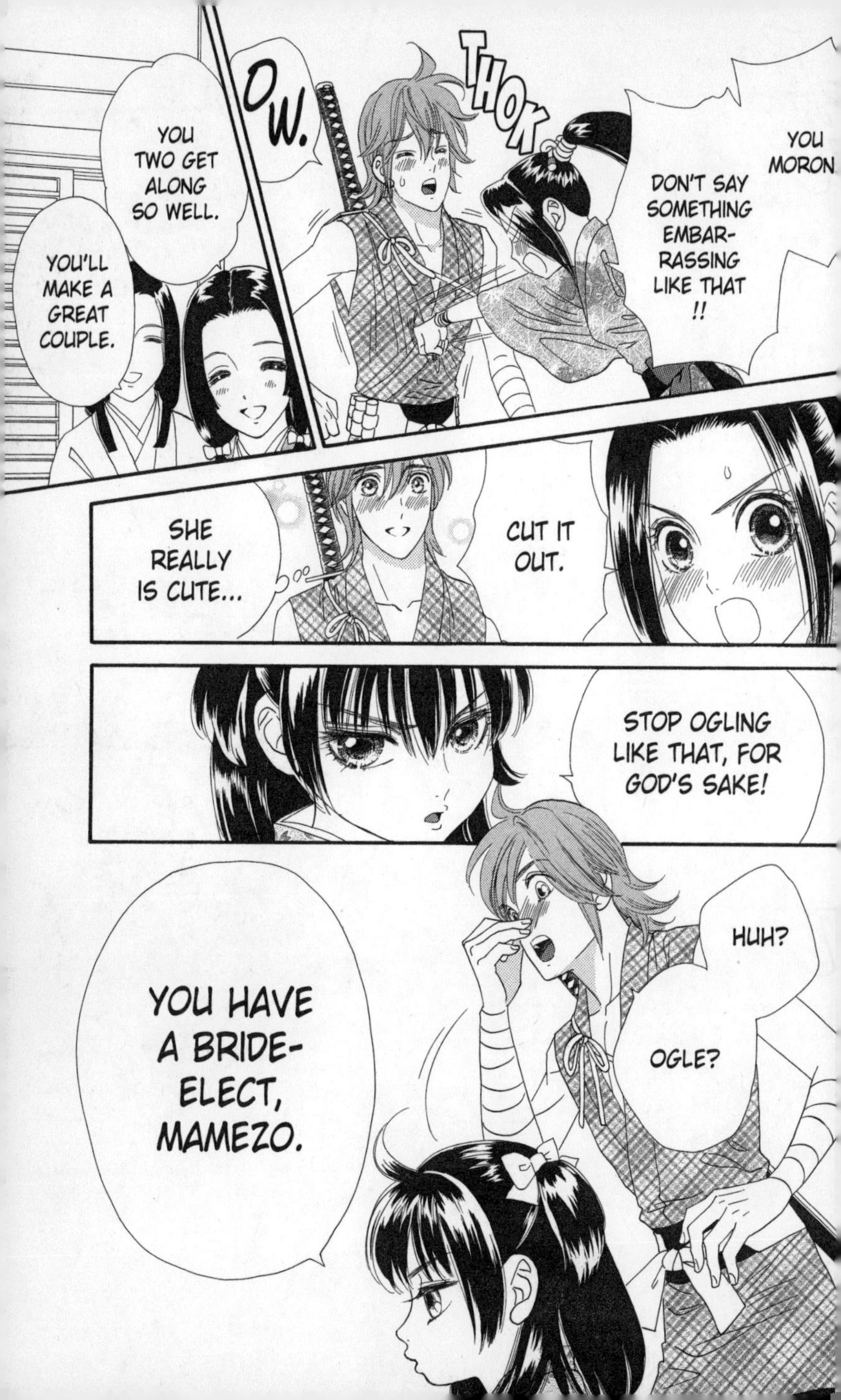
YOU MORON.
DON'T SAY SOMETHING EMBARRASSING LIKE THAT!!
THOK
OW.
YOU TWO GET ALONG SO WELL.
YOU'LL MAKE A GREAT COUPLE.
CUT IT OUT.
SHE REALLY IS CUTE...
STOP OGLING LIKE THAT, FOR GOD'S SAKE!
HUH?
OGLE?
YOU HAVE A BRIDE-ELECT, MAMEZO.

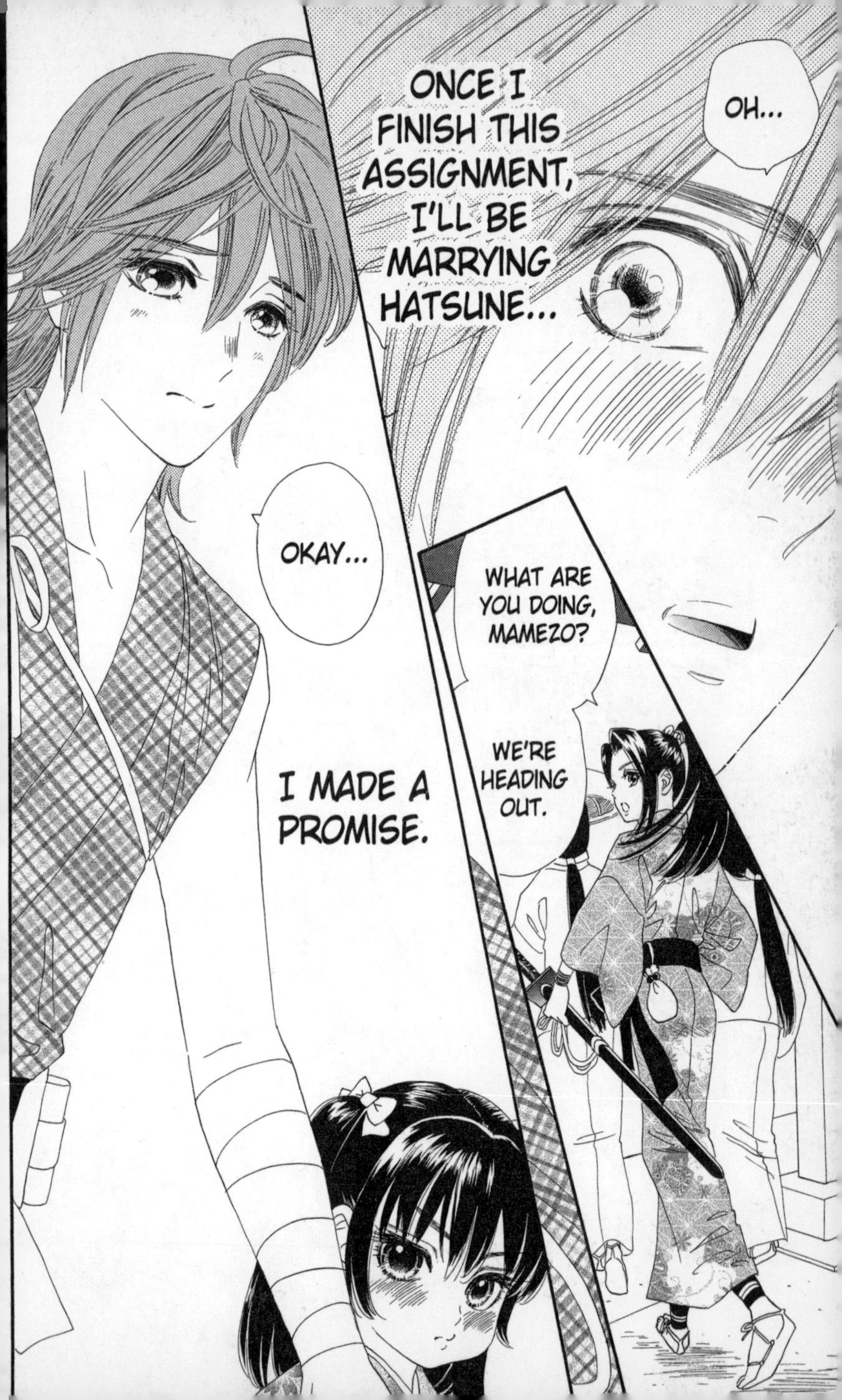
OH...
ONCE I FINISH THIS ASSIGNMENT, I'LL BE MARRYING HATSUNE...
WHAT ARE YOU DOING, MAMEZO?
WE'RE HEADING OUT.
OKAY...
I MADE A PROMISE.

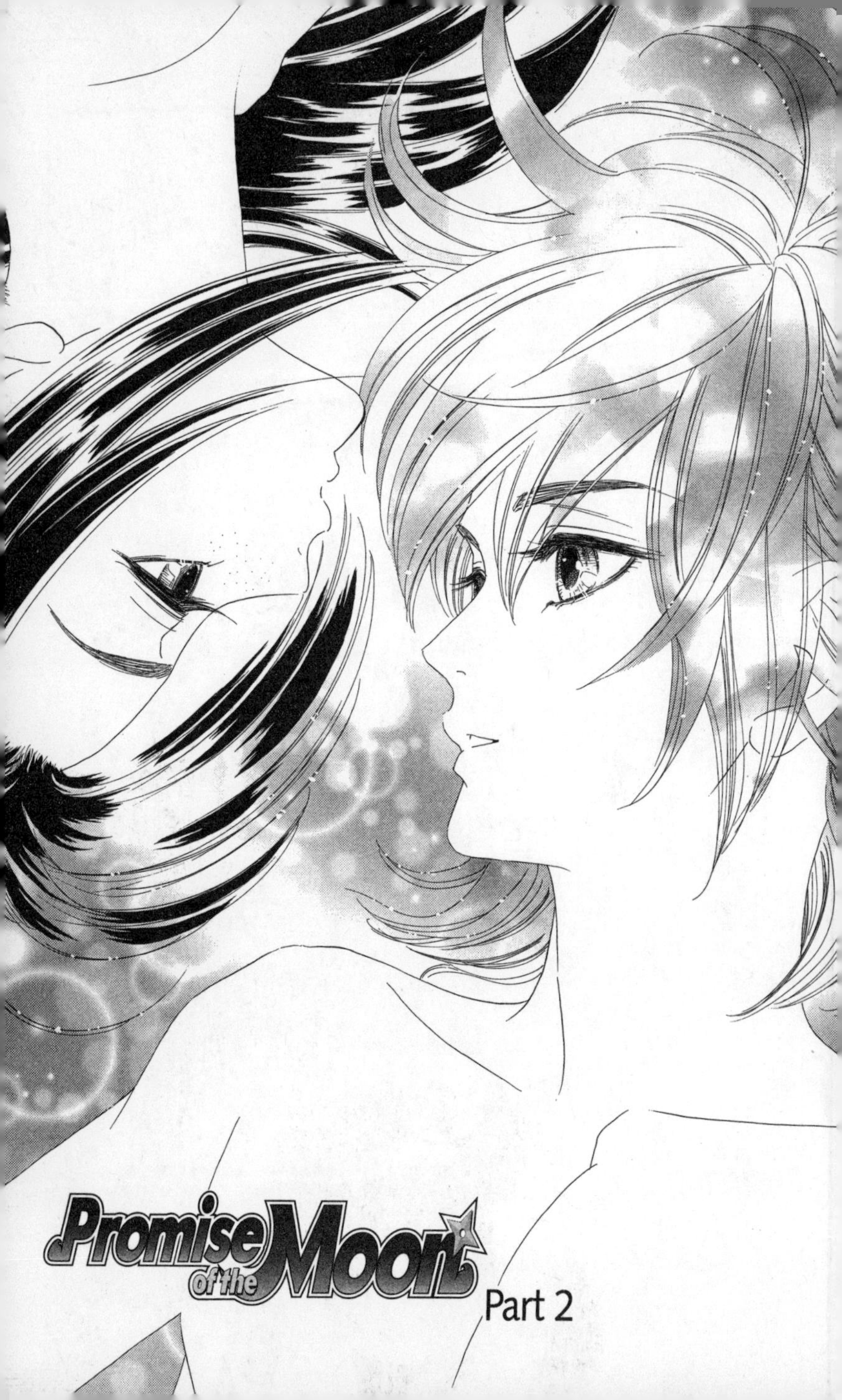
Promise of the Moon
Part 2

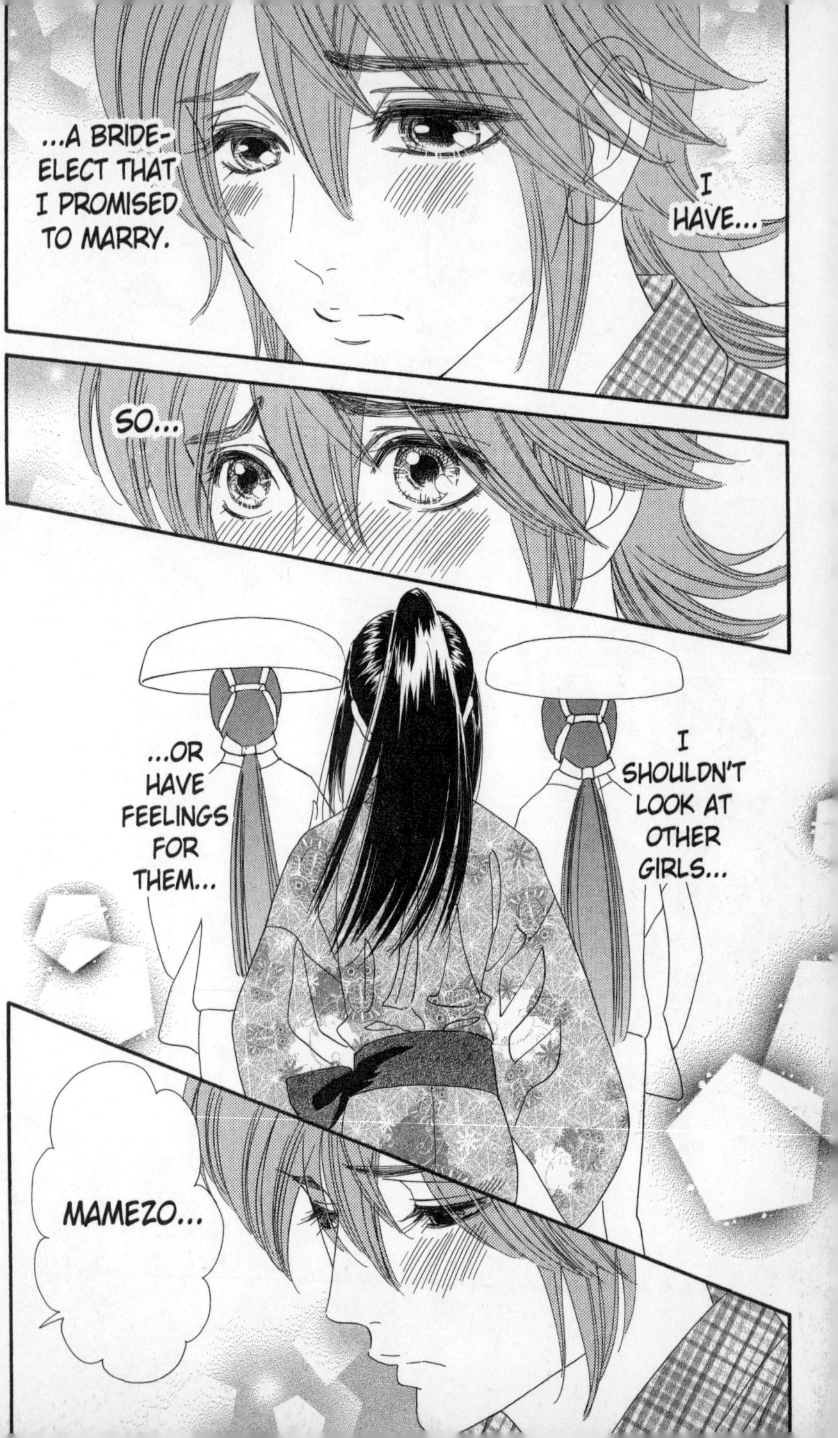
I HAVE...
...A BRIDE-ELECT THAT I PROMISED TO MARRY.
SO...
I SHOULDN'T LOOK AT OTHER GIRLS...
...OR HAVE FEELINGS FOR THEM...
MAMEZO...

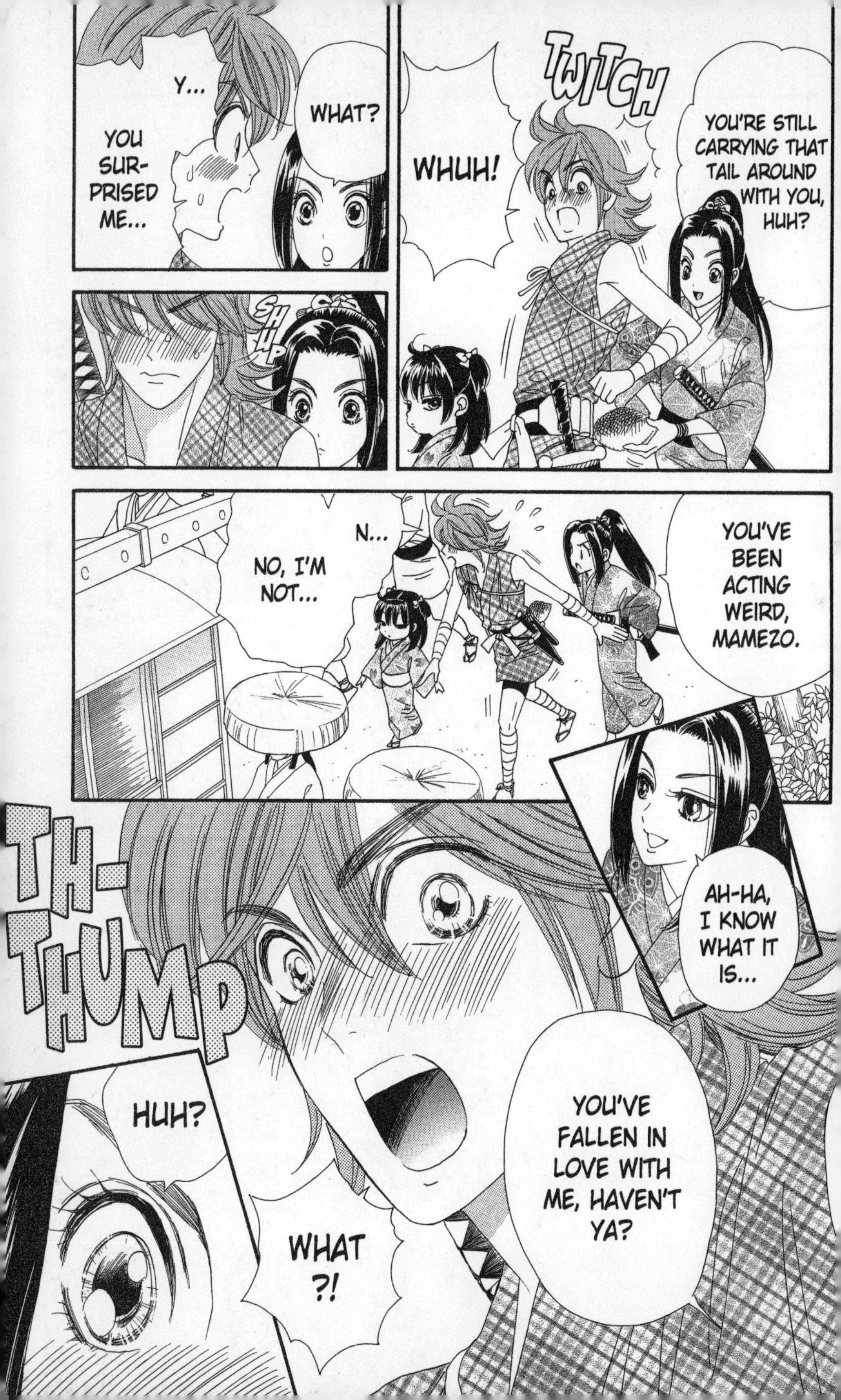
TWITCH
YOU'RE STILL CARRYING THAT TAIL AROUND WITH YOU, HUH?
WHUH!
WHAT?
Y...
YOU SURPRISED ME...
SHUP
YOU'VE BEEN ACTING WEIRD, MAMEZO.
N...
NO, I'M NOT...
AH-HA, I KNOW WHAT IT IS...
YOU'VE FALLEN IN LOVE WITH ME, HAVEN'T YA?
TH-THUMP
WHAT ?!
HUH?

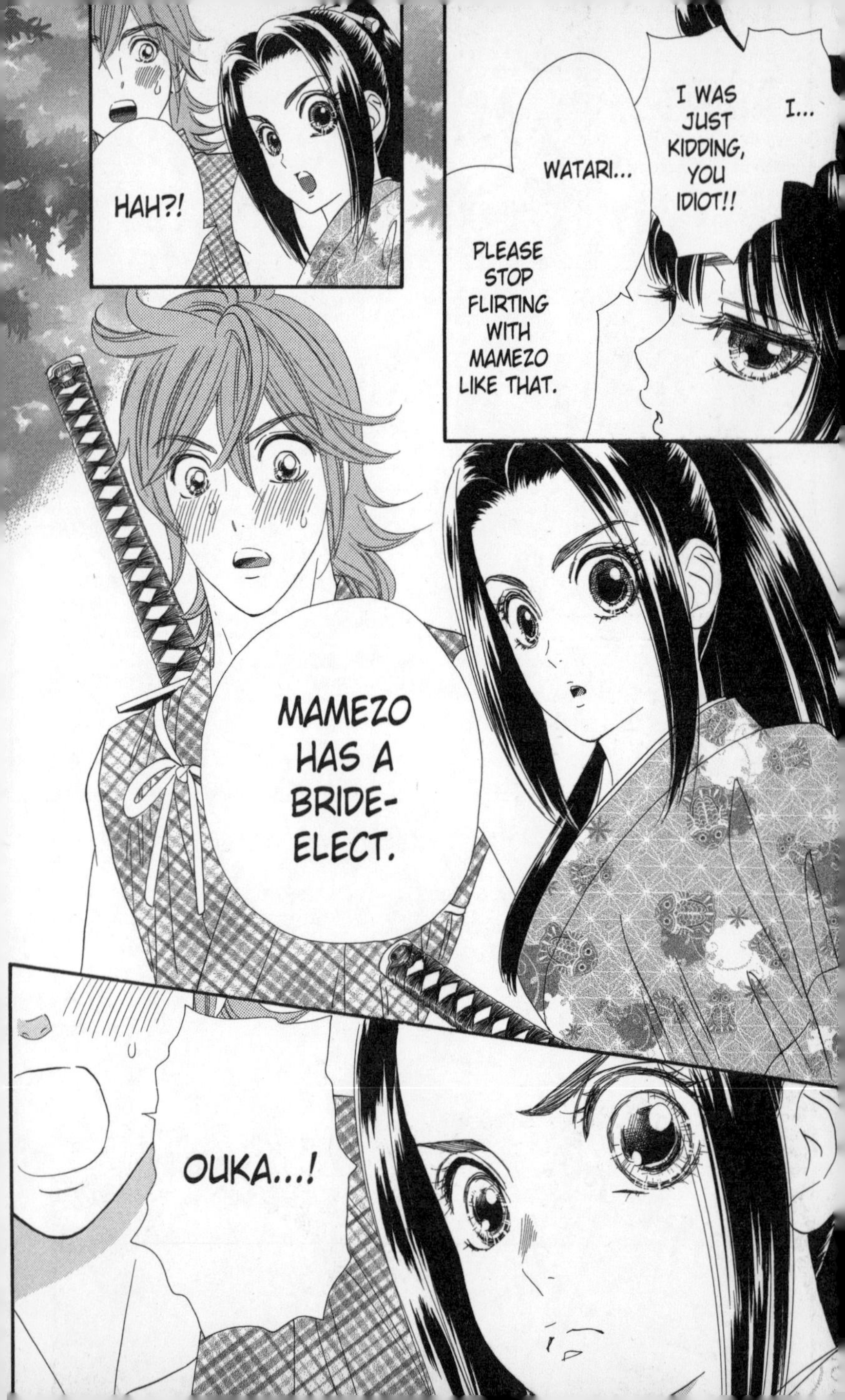
I...
I WAS JUST KIDDING, YOU IDIOT!!
WATARI...
PLEASE STOP FLIRTING WITH MAMEZO LIKE THAT.
HAH?!
MAMEZO HAS A BRIDE-ELECT.
OUKA...!

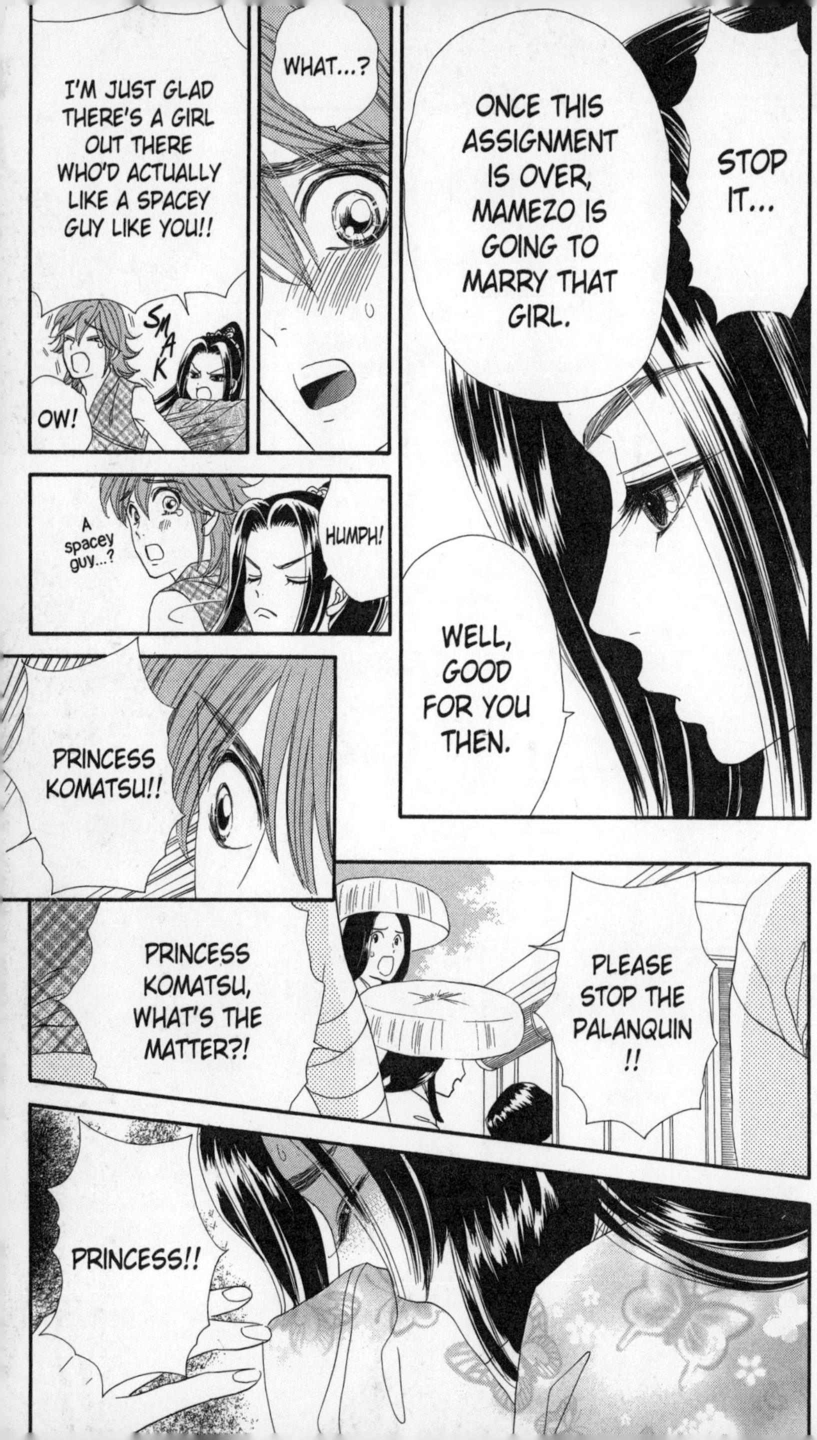
STOP IT...
ONCE THIS ASSIGNMENT IS OVER, MAMEZO IS GOING TO MARRY THAT GIRL.
WELL, GOOD FOR YOU THEN.
WHAT...?
I'M JUST GLAD THERE'S A GIRL OUT THERE WHO'D ACTUALLY LIKE A SPACEY GUY LIKE YOU!!
SMAK
OW!
HUMPH!
A spacey guy...?
PRINCESS KOMATSU!!
PLEASE STOP THE PALANQUIN!!
PRINCESS KOMATSU, WHAT'S THE MATTER?!
PRINCESS!!

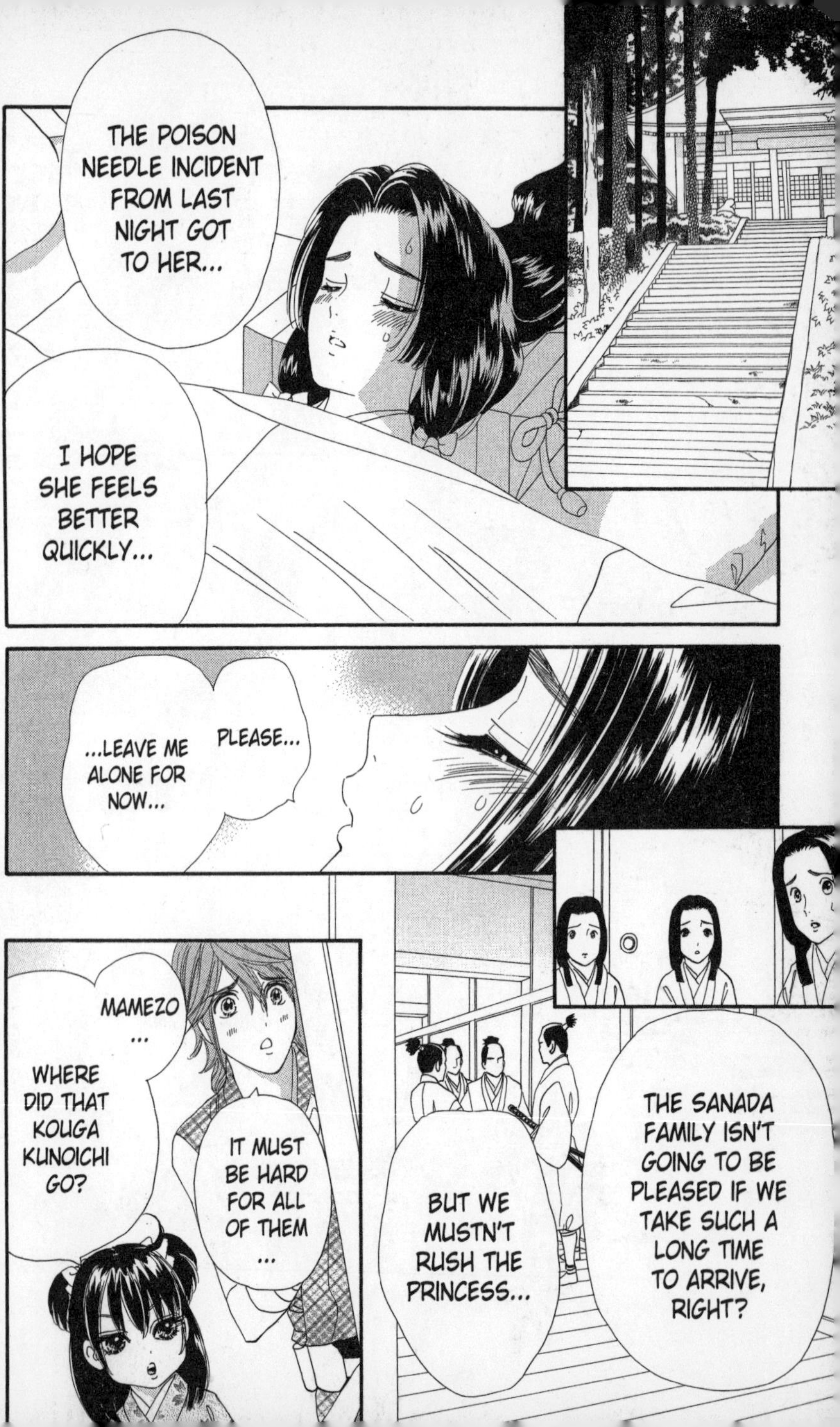
THE POISON NEEDLE INCIDENT FROM LAST NIGHT GOT TO HER...
I HOPE SHE FEELS BETTER QUICKLY...
PLEASE...
...LEAVE ME ALONE FOR NOW...
THE SANADA FAMILY ISN'T GOING TO BE PLEASED IF WE TAKE SUCH A LONG TIME TO ARRIVE, RIGHT?
BUT WE MUSTN'T RUSH THE PRINCESS...
MAMEZO...
WHERE DID THAT KOUGA KUNOICHI GO?
IT MUST BE HARD FOR ALL OF THEM...

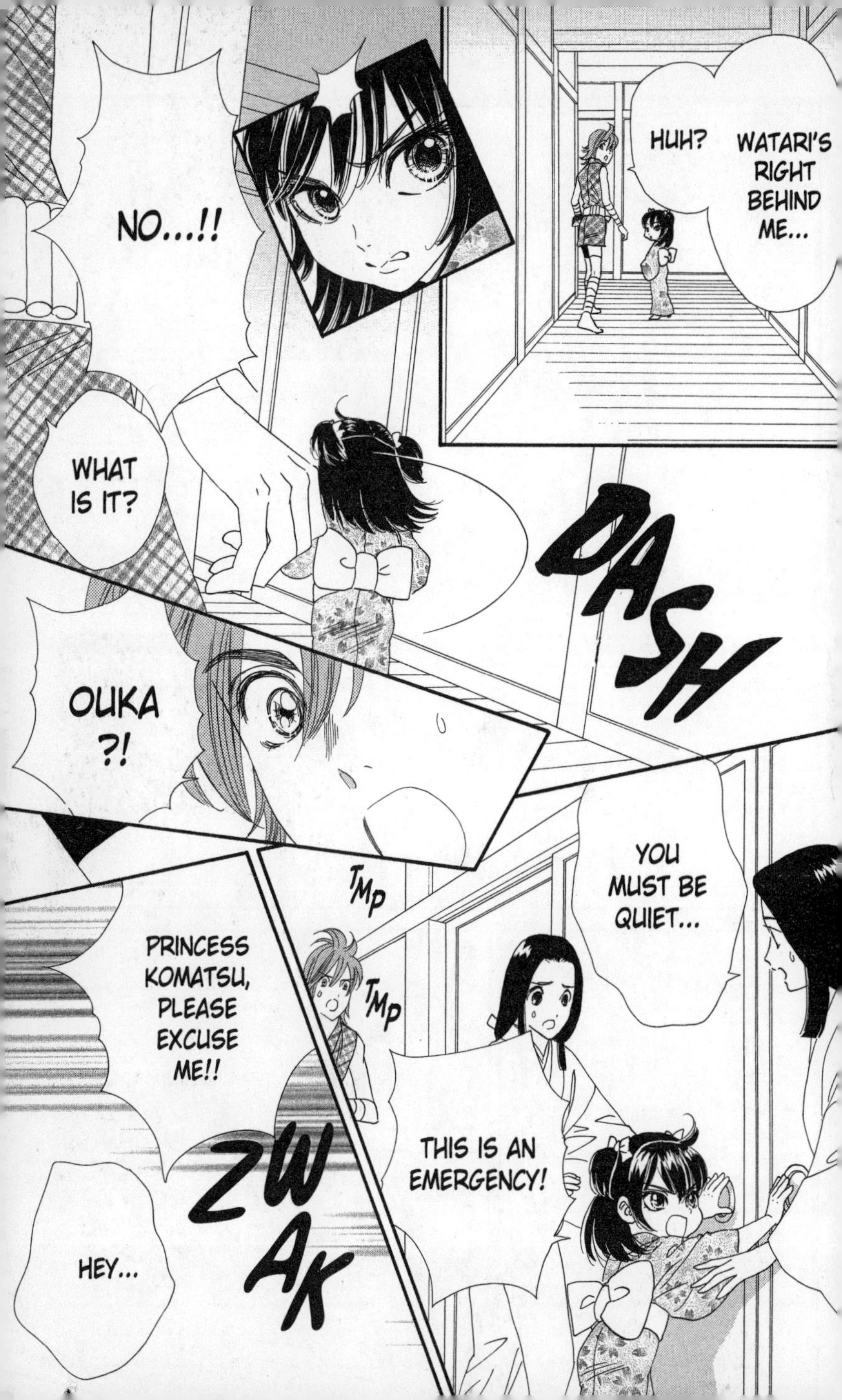
WATARI'S RIGHT BEHIND ME...
HUH?
NO...!!
WHAT IS IT?
DASH
OUKA ?!
YOU MUST BE QUIET...
THIS IS AN EMERGENCY!
TMP
TMP
PRINCESS KOMATSU, PLEASE EXCUSE ME!!
ZWAK
HEY...

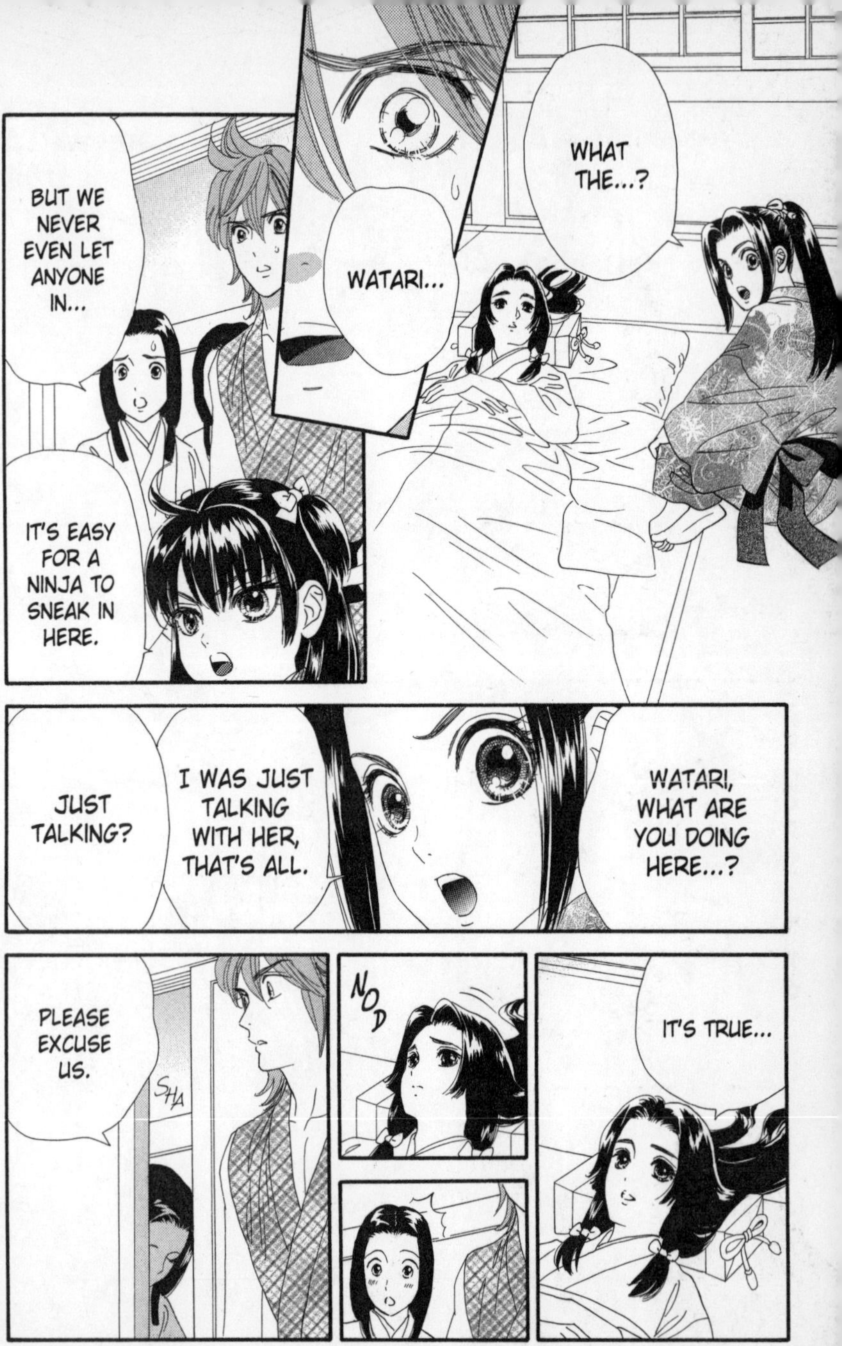
WHAT THE...?
WATARI...
BUT WE NEVER EVEN LET ANYONE IN...
IT'S EASY FOR A NINJA TO SNEAK IN HERE.
WATARI, WHAT ARE YOU DOING HERE...?
I WAS JUST TALKING WITH HER, THAT'S ALL.
JUST TALKING?
IT'S TRUE...
NOD
PLEASE EXCUSE US.
SHA

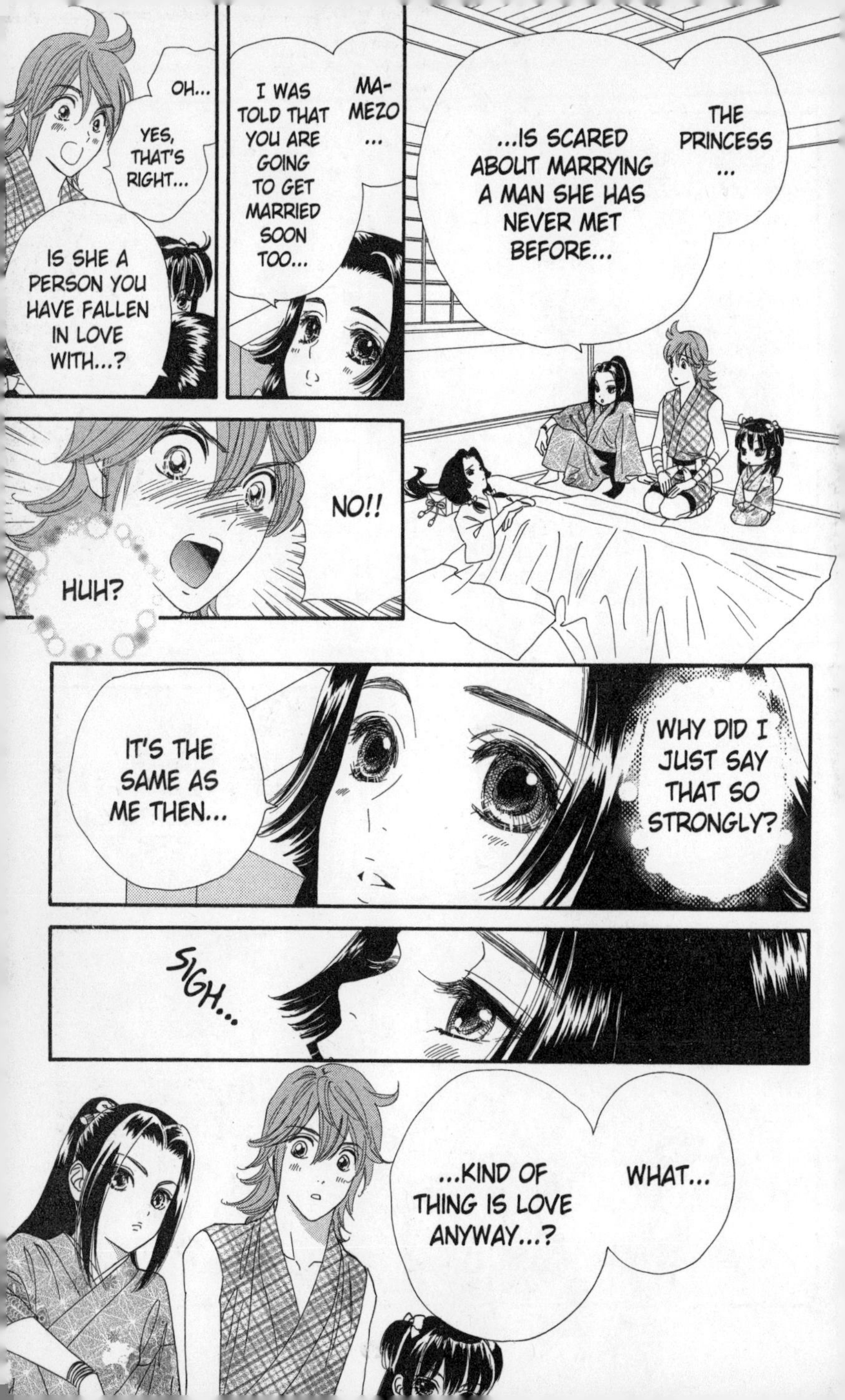
THE PRINCESS ...
...IS SCARED ABOUT MARRYING A MAN SHE HAS NEVER MET BEFORE...
MA-MEZO ...
I WAS TOLD THAT YOU ARE GOING TO GET MARRIED SOON TOO...
OH...
YES, THAT'S RIGHT...
IS SHE A PERSON YOU HAVE FALLEN IN LOVE WITH...?
NO!!
HUH?
WHY DID I JUST SAY THAT SO STRONGLY?
IT'S THE SAME AS ME THEN...
SIGH...
WHAT...
...KIND OF THING IS LOVE ANYWAY...?

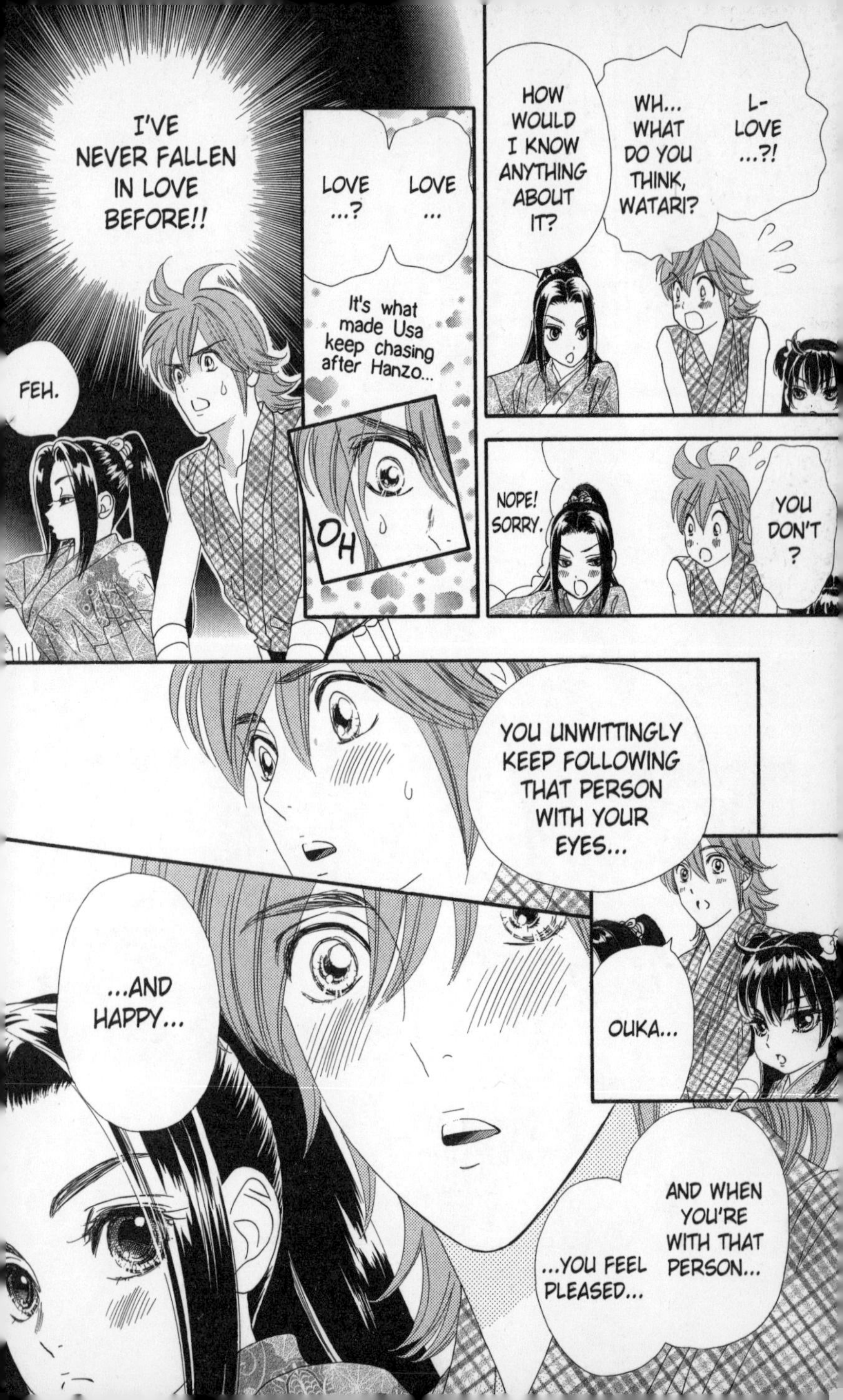
L-LOVE ...?!
WH... WHAT DO YOU THINK, WATARI?
HOW WOULD I KNOW ANYTHING ABOUT IT?
YOU DON'T ?
NOPE! SORRY.
LOVE ...
LOVE ...?
It's what made Usa keep chasing after Hanzo...
OH
I'VE NEVER FALLEN IN LOVE BEFORE!!
FEH.
YOU UNWITTINGLY KEEP FOLLOWING THAT PERSON WITH YOUR EYES...
OUKA...
AND WHEN YOU'RE WITH THAT PERSON...
...YOU FEEL PLEASED...
...AND HAPPY...

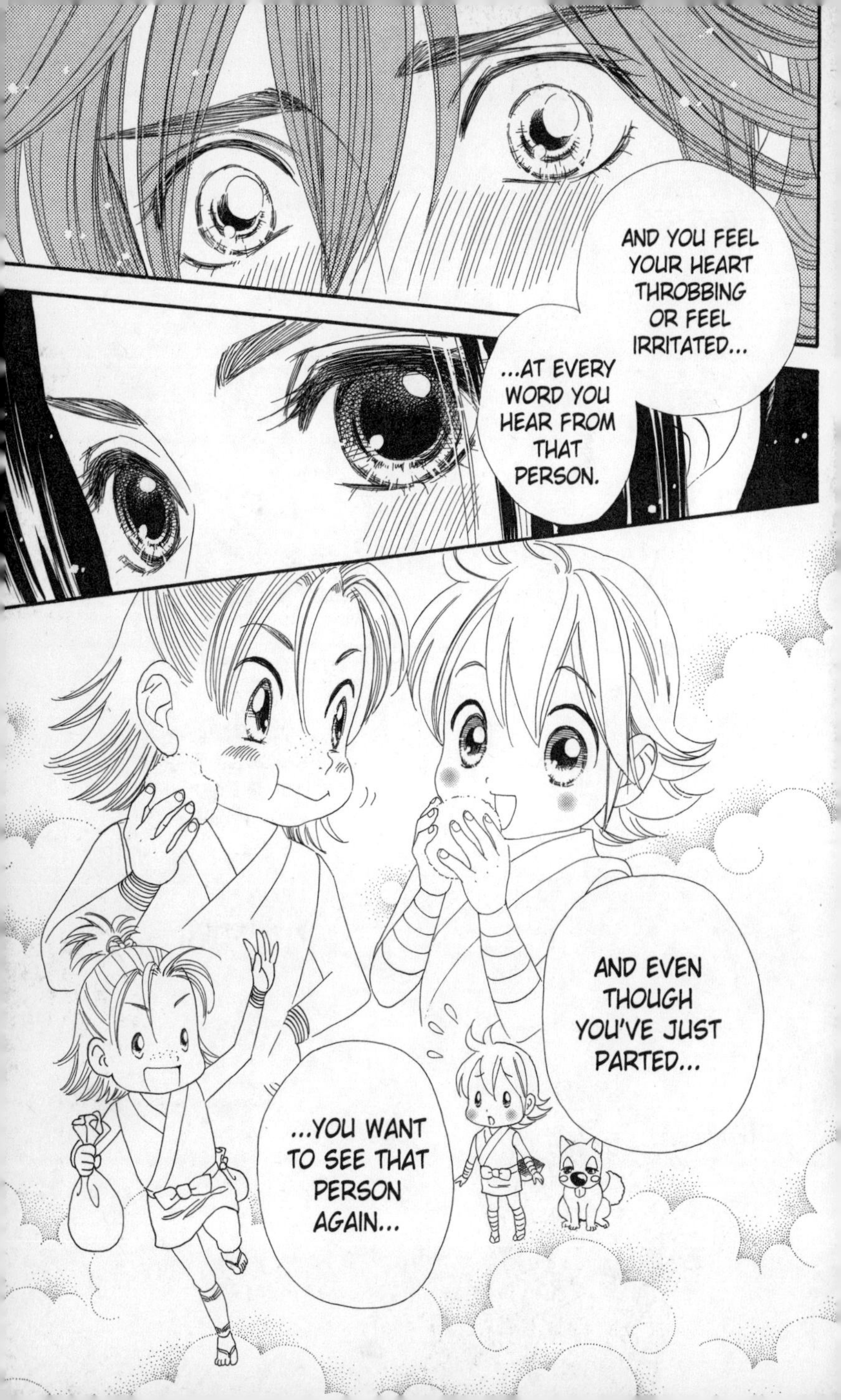

AND YOU FEEL YOUR HEART THROBBING OR FEEL IRRITATED...
...AT EVERY WORD YOU HEAR FROM THAT PERSON.
AND EVEN THOUGH YOU'VE JUST PARTED...
...YOU WANT TO SEE THAT PERSON AGAIN...

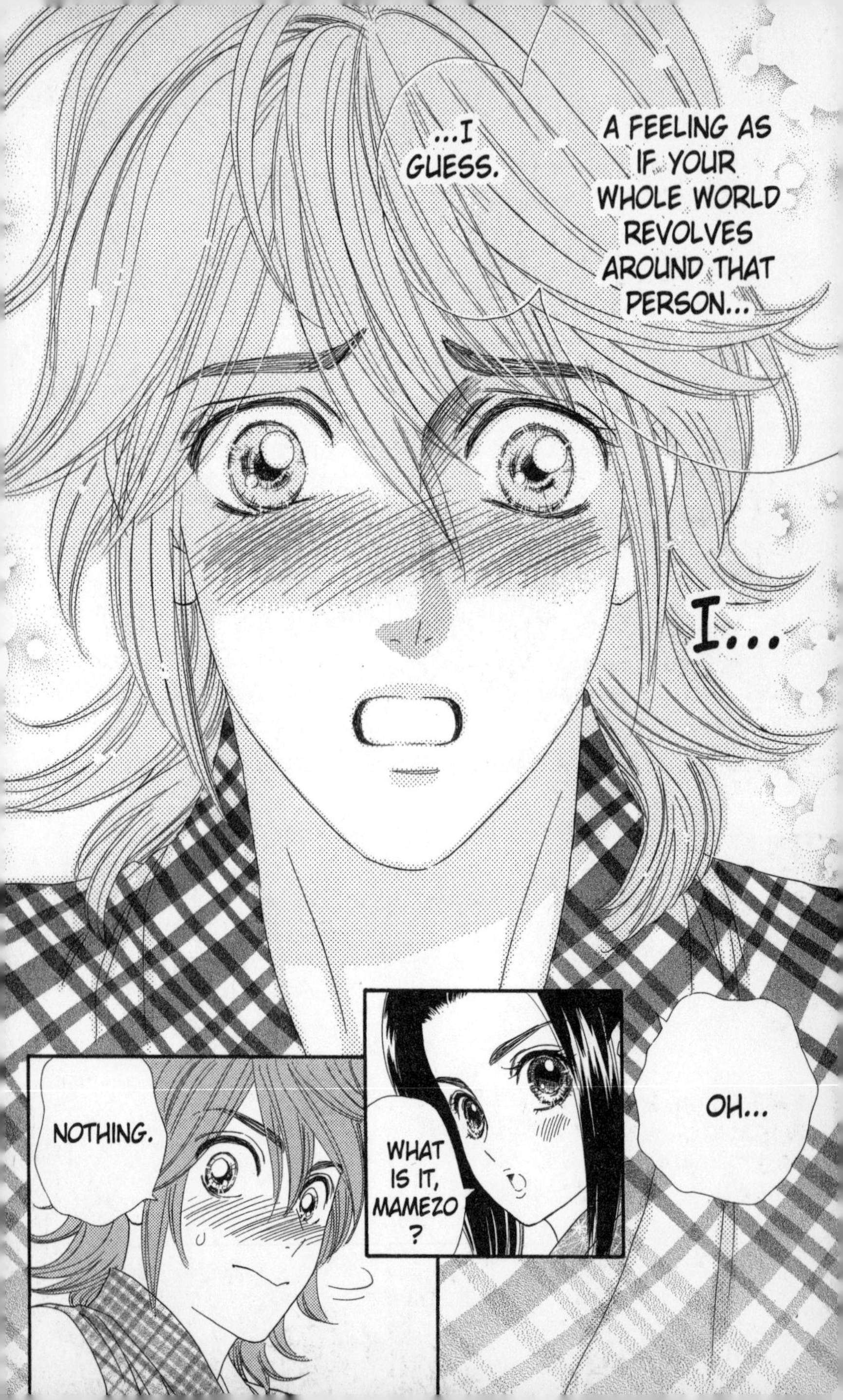
A FEELING AS IF YOUR WHOLE WORLD REVOLVES AROUND THAT PERSON...
...I GUESS.
I...
OH...
WHAT IS IT, MAMEZO?
NOTHING.

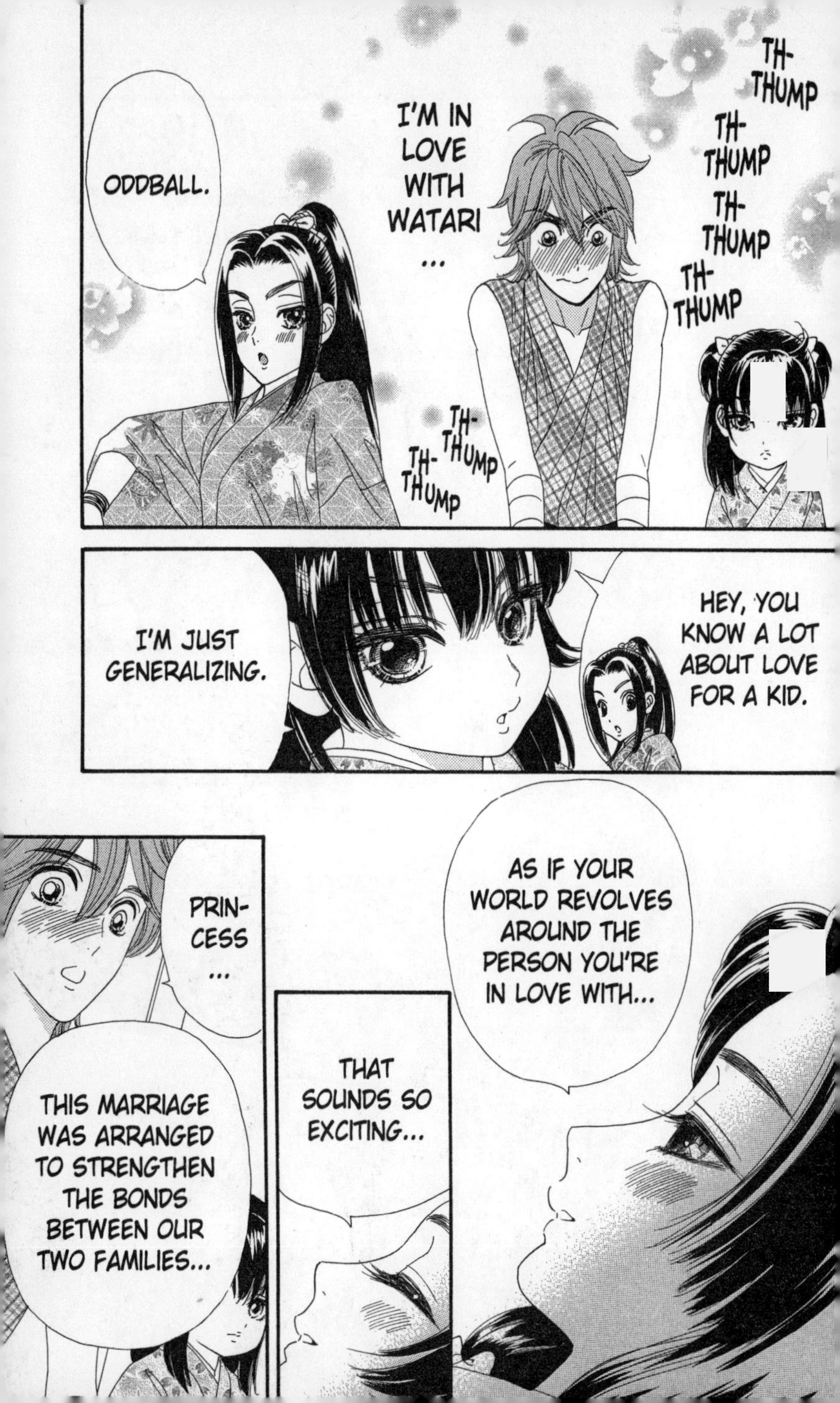
TH-THUMP
TH-THUMP
TH-THUMP
TH-THUMP
I'M IN LOVE WITH WATARI ...
ODDBALL.
TH-THUMP
TH-THUMP
HEY, YOU KNOW A LOT ABOUT LOVE FOR A KID.
I'M JUST GENERALIZING.
AS IF YOUR WORLD REVOLVES AROUND THE PERSON YOU'RE IN LOVE WITH...
THAT SOUNDS SO EXCITING...
PRIN-CESS ...
THIS MARRIAGE WAS ARRANGED TO STRENGTHEN THE BONDS BETWEEN OUR TWO FAMILIES...

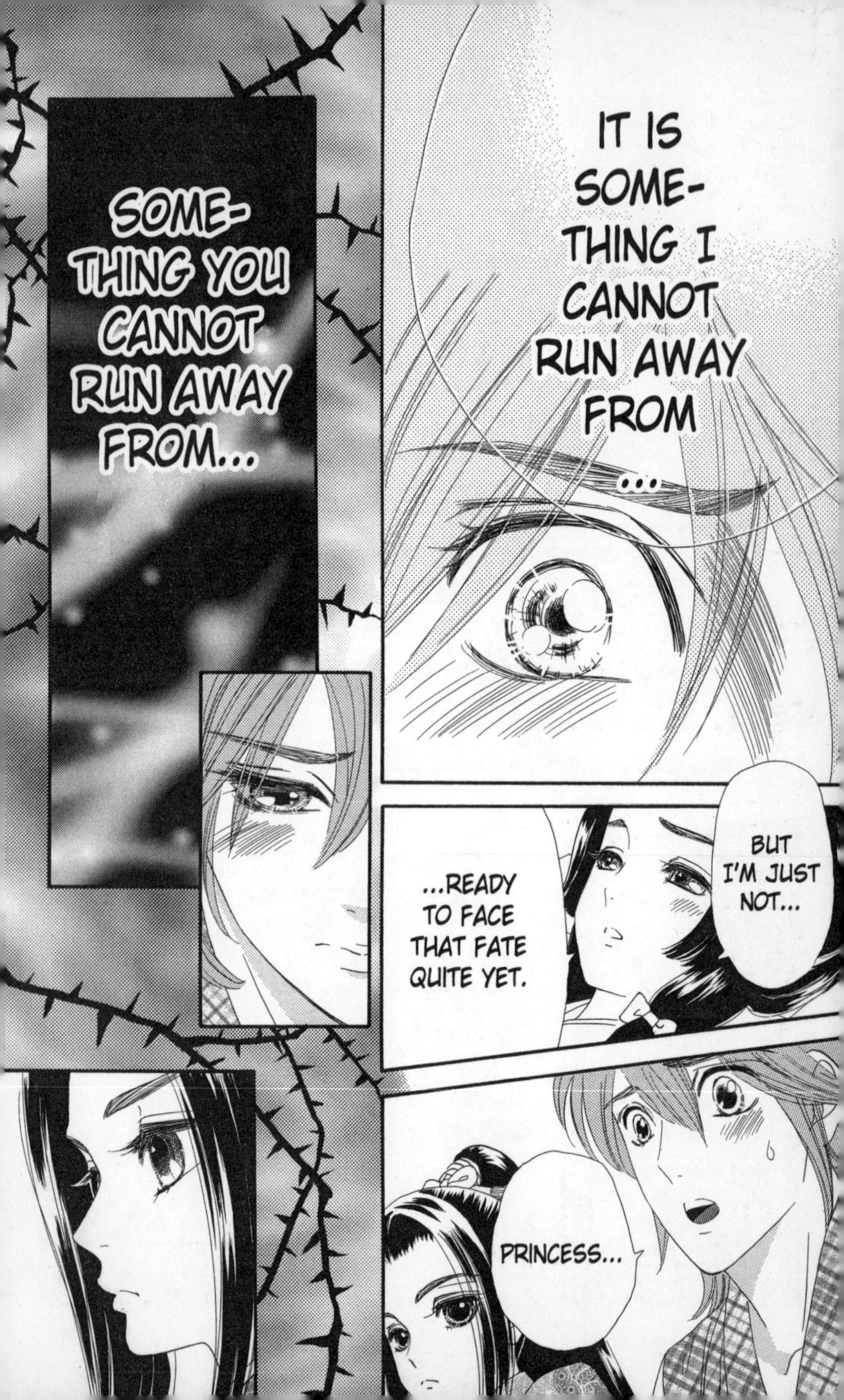
IT IS SOME-THING I CANNOT RUN AWAY FROM ...
SOME-THING YOU CANNOT RUN AWAY FROM...
BUT I'M JUST NOT...
...READY TO FACE THAT FATE QUITE YET.
PRINCESS...

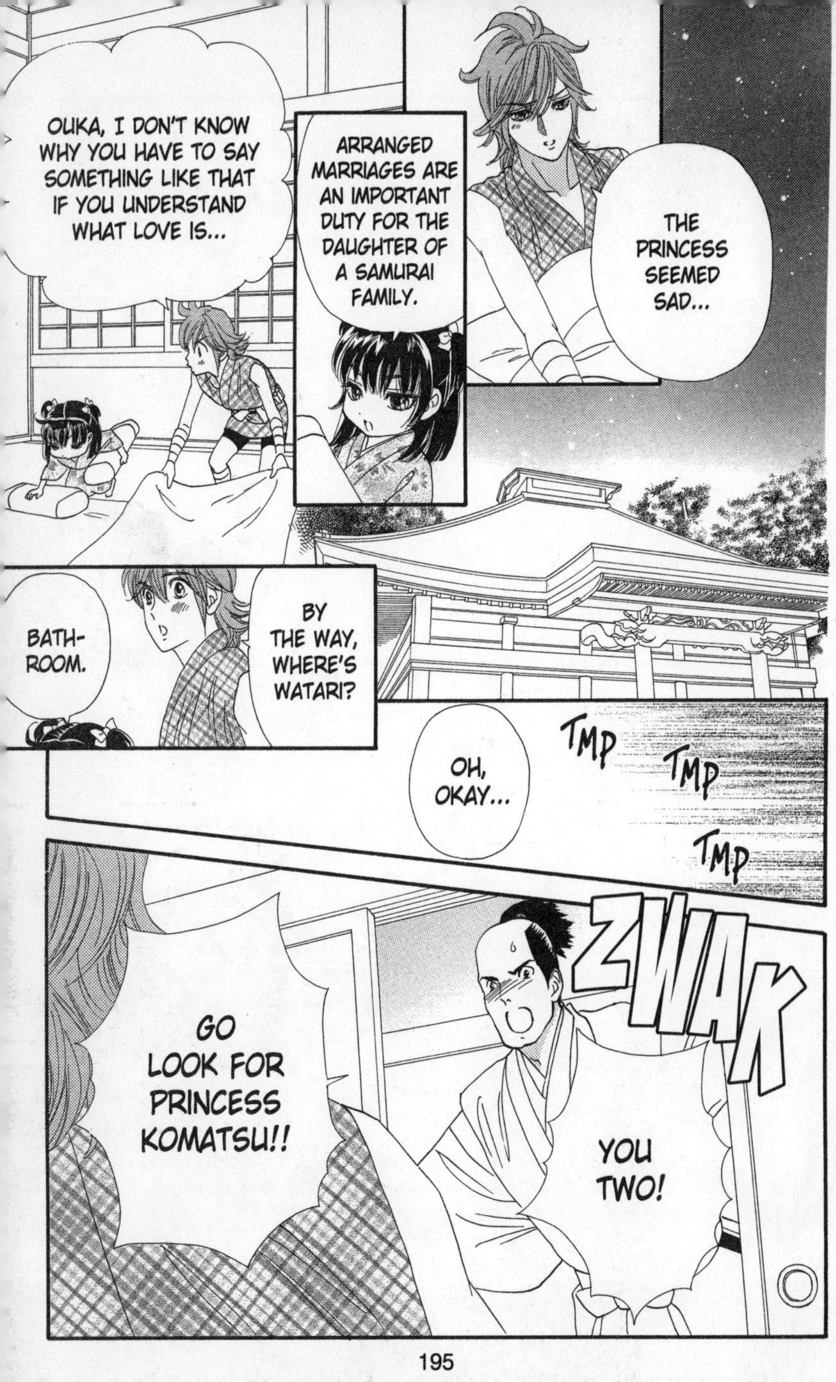
THE PRINCESS SEEMED SAD...
ARRANGED MARRIAGES ARE AN IMPORTANT DUTY FOR THE DAUGHTER OF A SAMURAI FAMILY.
OUKA, I DON'T KNOW WHY YOU HAVE TO SAY SOMETHING LIKE THAT IF YOU UNDERSTAND WHAT LOVE IS...
BY THE WAY, WHERE'S WATARI?
BATHROOM.
TMP
TMP
TMP
OH, OKAY...
ZWAK
YOU TWO!
GO LOOK FOR PRINCESS KOMATSU!!

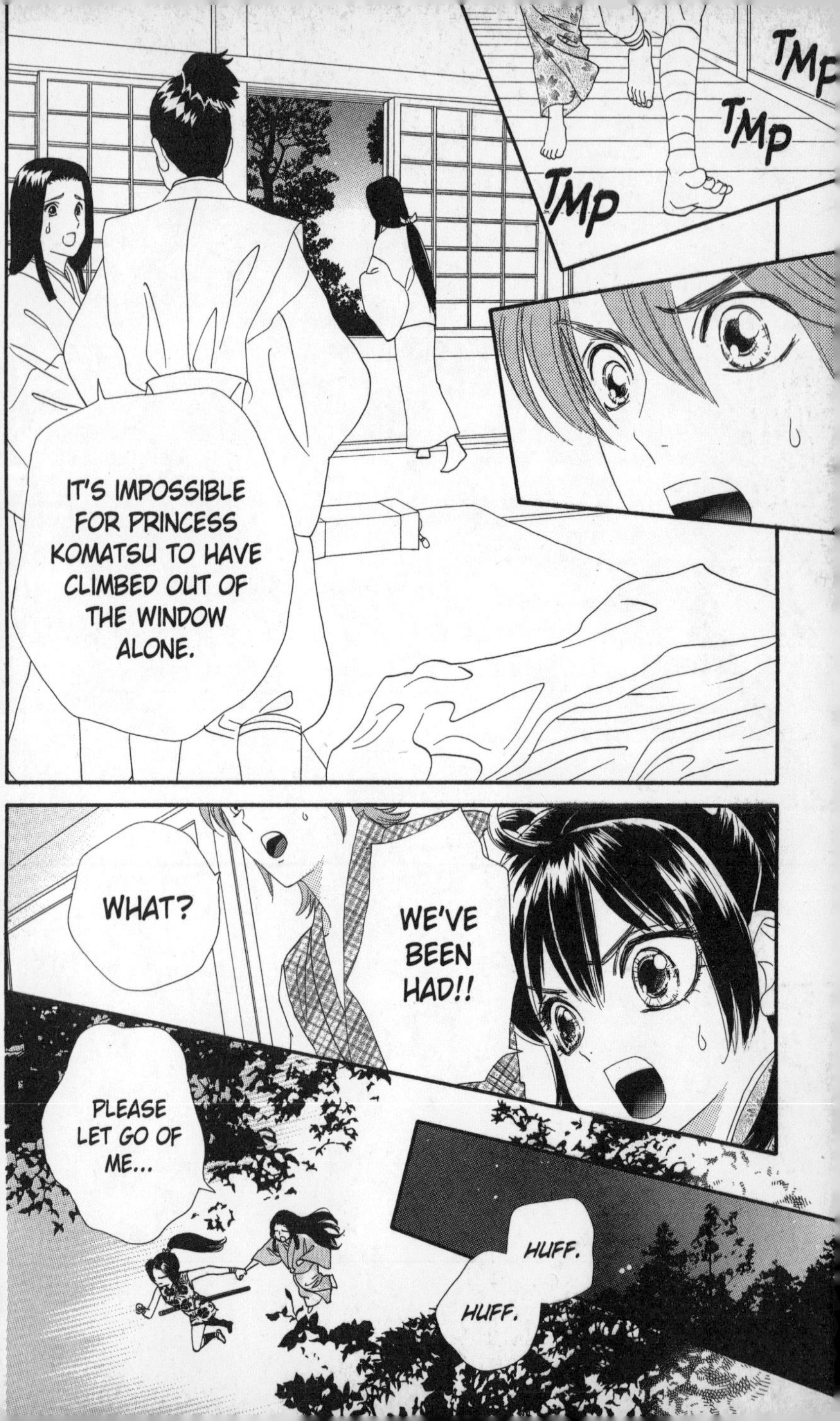
TMP
TMP
TMP
IT'S IMPOSSIBLE FOR PRINCESS KOMATSU TO HAVE CLIMBED OUT OF THE WINDOW ALONE.
WHAT?
WE'VE BEEN HAD!!
HUFF.
HUFF.
PLEASE LET GO OF ME...

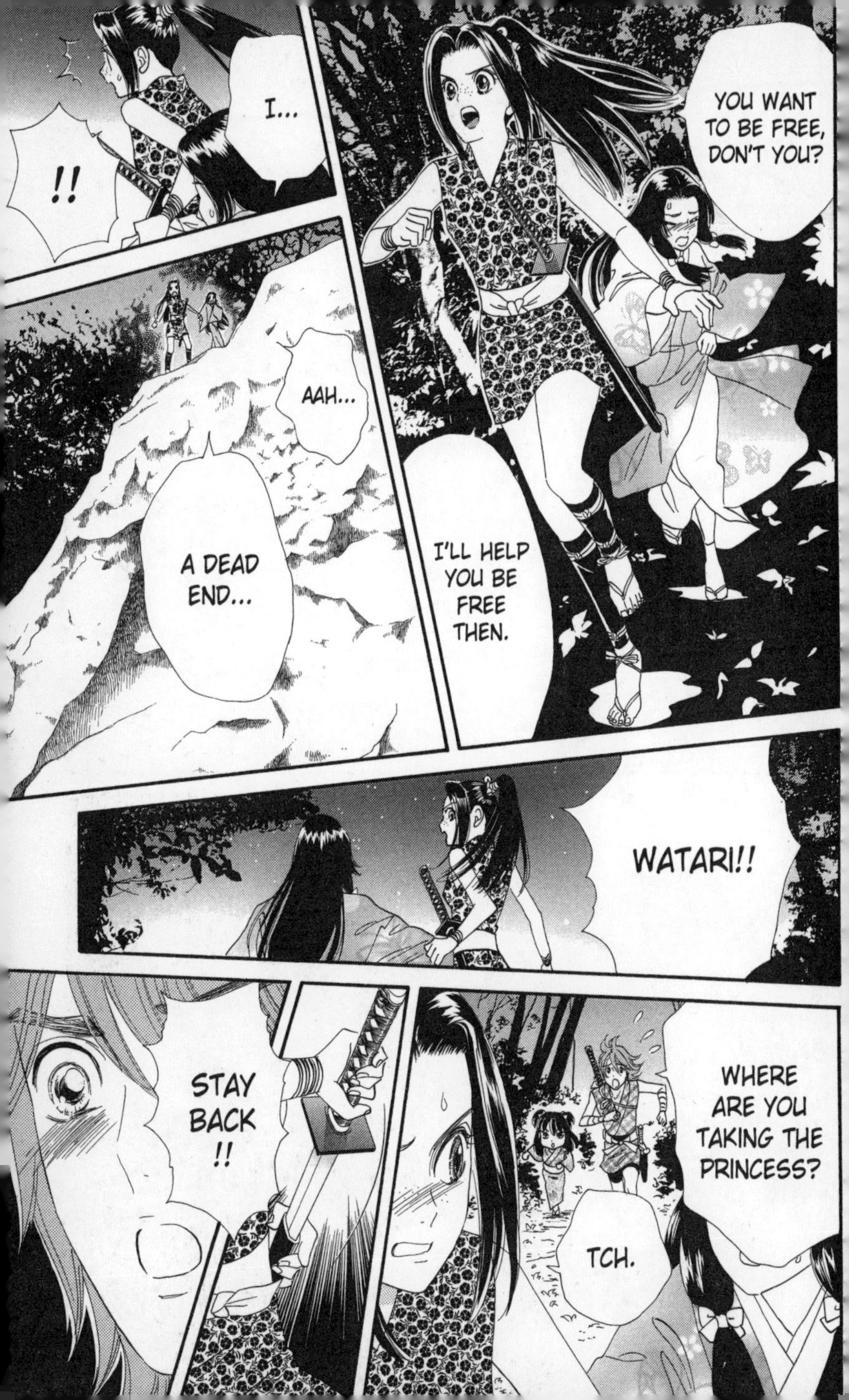
YOU WANT TO BE FREE, DON'T YOU?
I'LL HELP YOU BE FREE THEN.
I...
!!
AAH...
A DEAD END...
WATARI!!
WHERE ARE YOU TAKING THE PRINCESS?
TCH.
STAY BACK!!

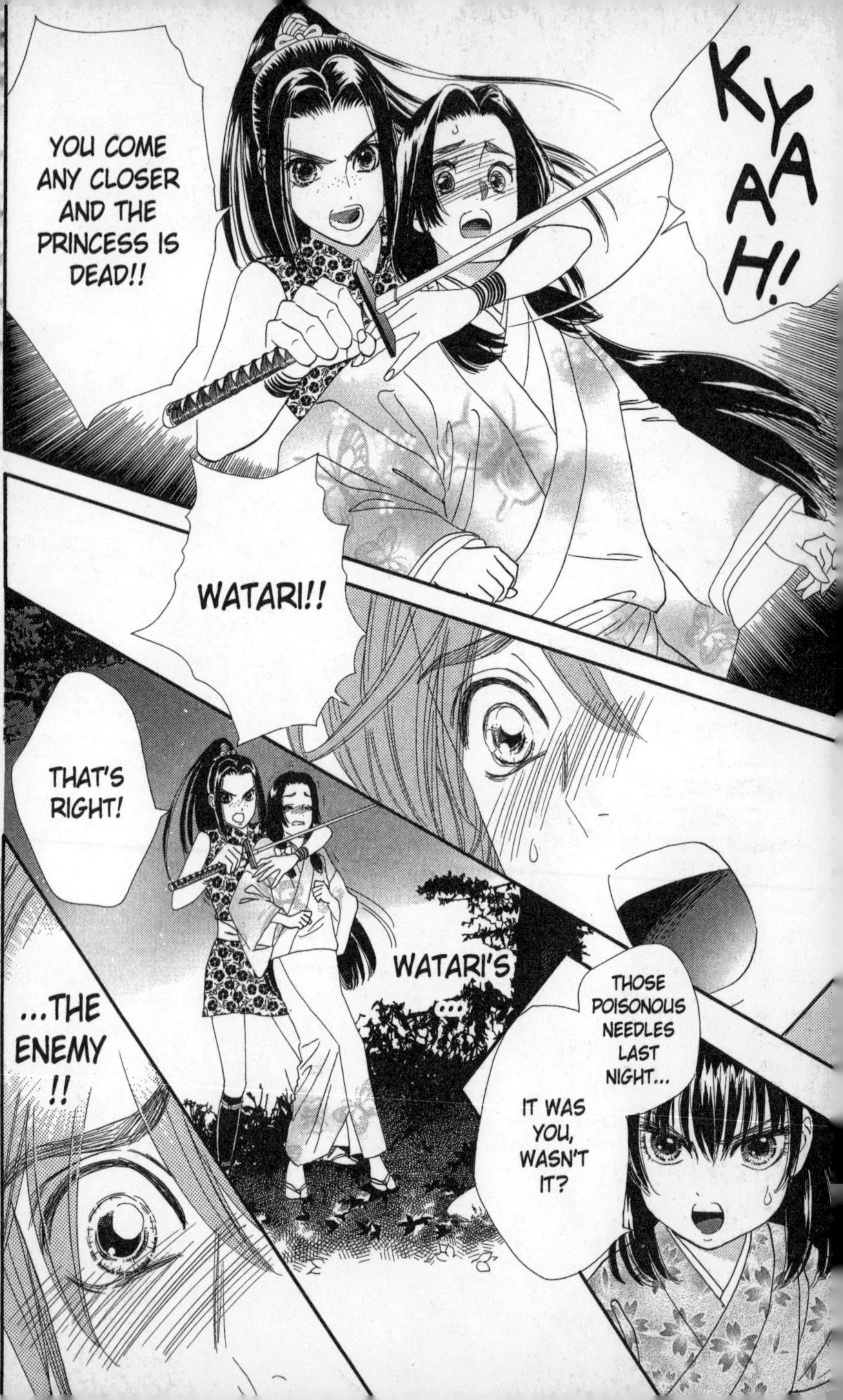
KYAAH!
YOU COME ANY CLOSER AND THE PRINCESS IS DEAD!!
WATARI!!
THOSE POISONOUS NEEDLES LAST NIGHT...
IT WAS YOU, WASN'T IT?
THAT'S RIGHT!
WATARI'S ...
...THE ENEMY!!

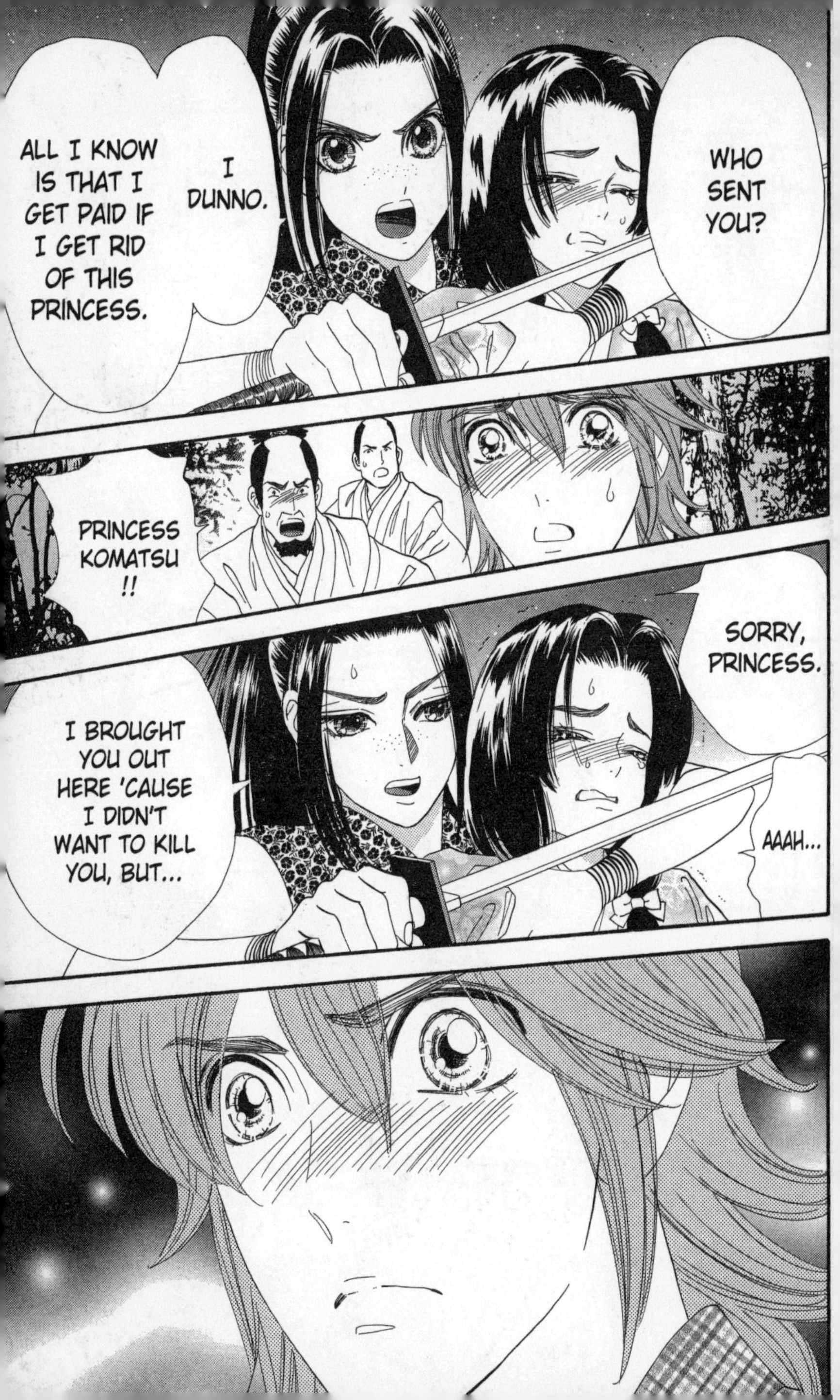
WHO SENT YOU?
I DUNNO.
ALL I KNOW IS THAT I GET PAID IF I GET RID OF THIS PRINCESS.
PRINCESS KOMATSU !!
SORRY, PRINCESS.
AAAH...
I BROUGHT YOU OUT HERE 'CAUSE I DIDN'T WANT TO KILL YOU, BUT...

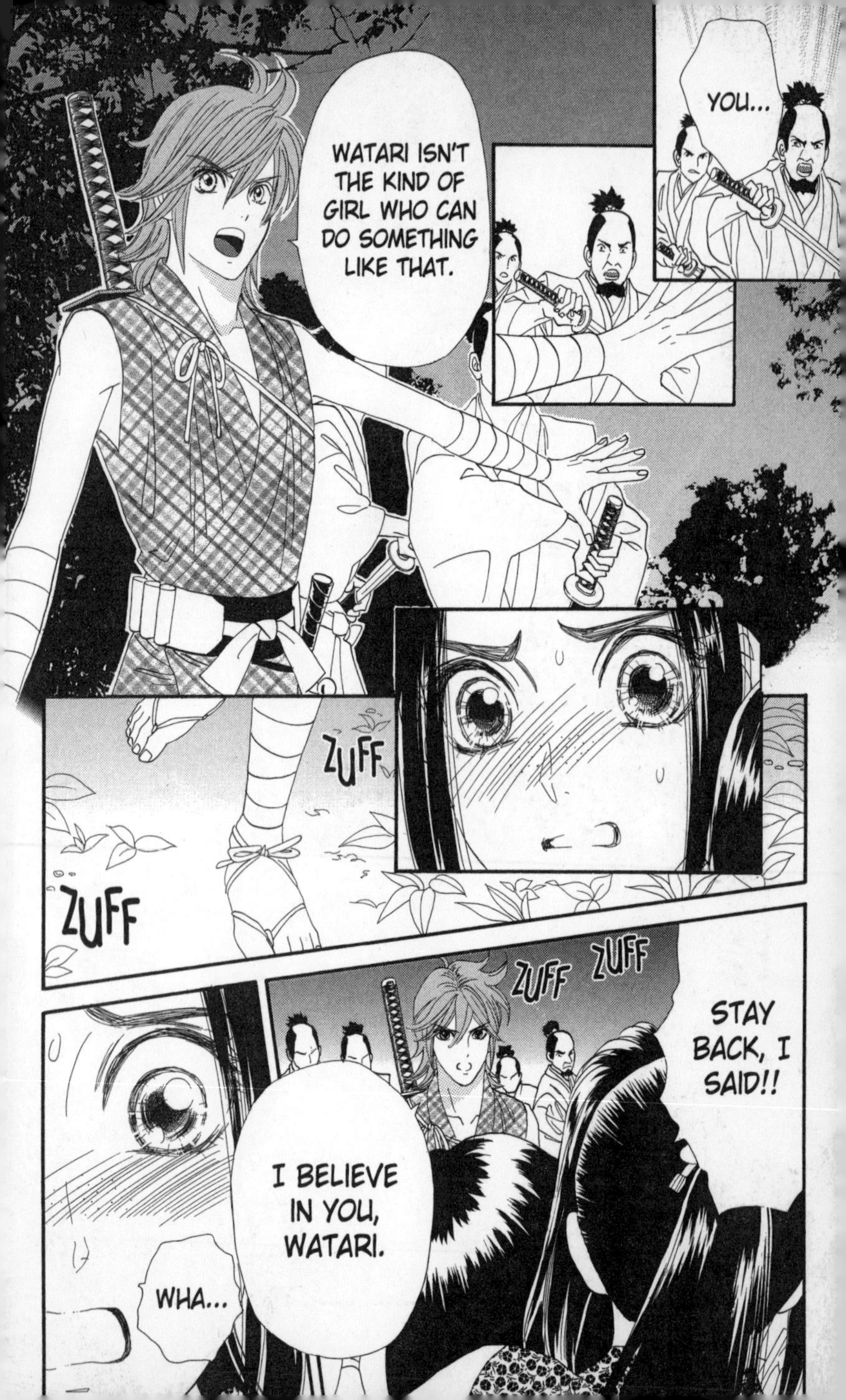
YOU...
WATARI ISN'T THE KIND OF GIRL WHO CAN DO SOMETHING LIKE THAT.
ZUFF
ZUFF
ZUFF ZUFF
STAY BACK, I SAID!!
I BELIEVE IN YOU, WATARI.
WHA...

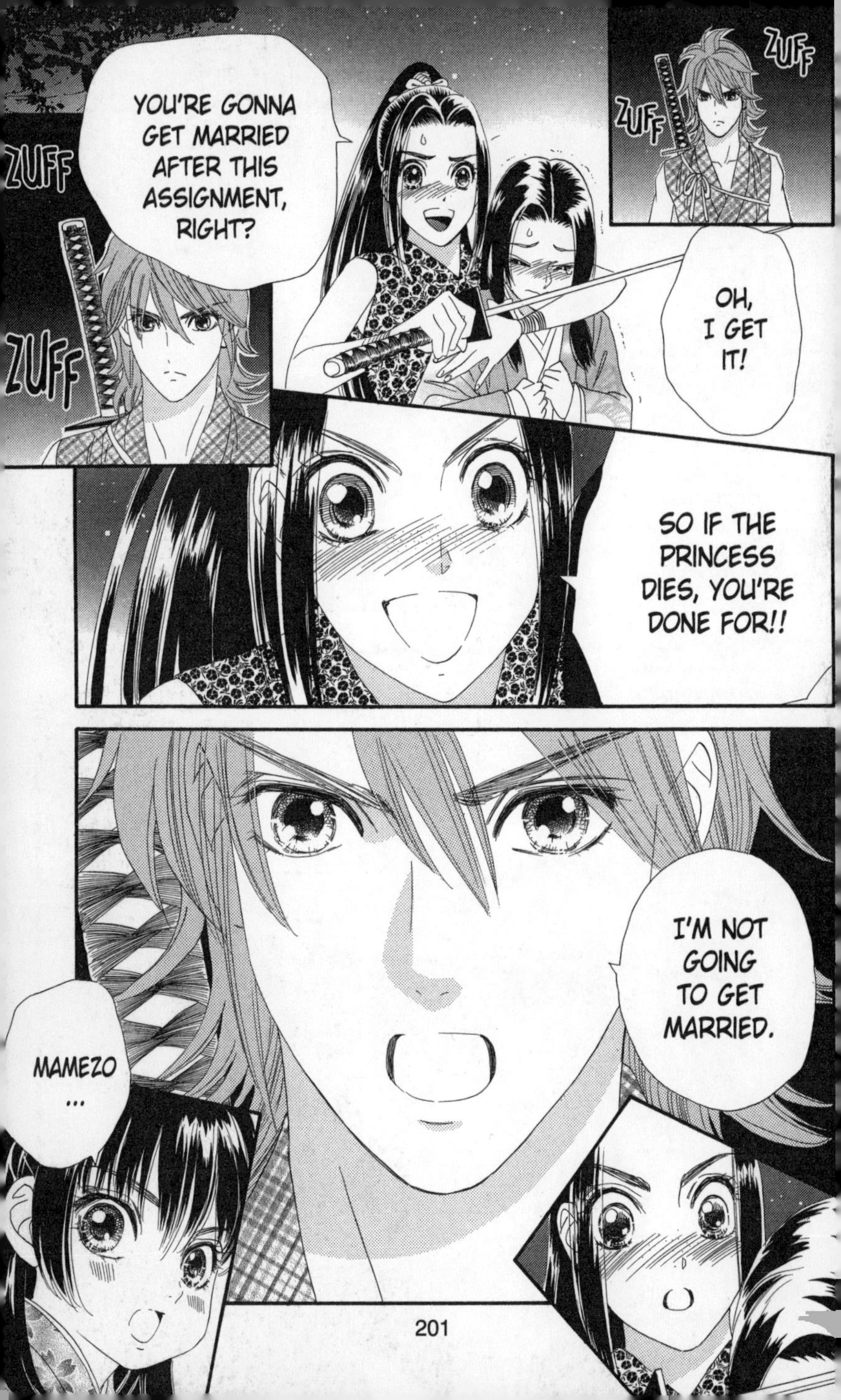
ZUFF
ZUFF
YOU'RE GONNA GET MARRIED AFTER THIS ASSIGNMENT, RIGHT?
ZUFF
ZUFF
OH, I GET IT!
SO IF THE PRINCESS DIES, YOU'RE DONE FOR!!
I'M NOT GOING TO GET MARRIED.
MAMEZO ...

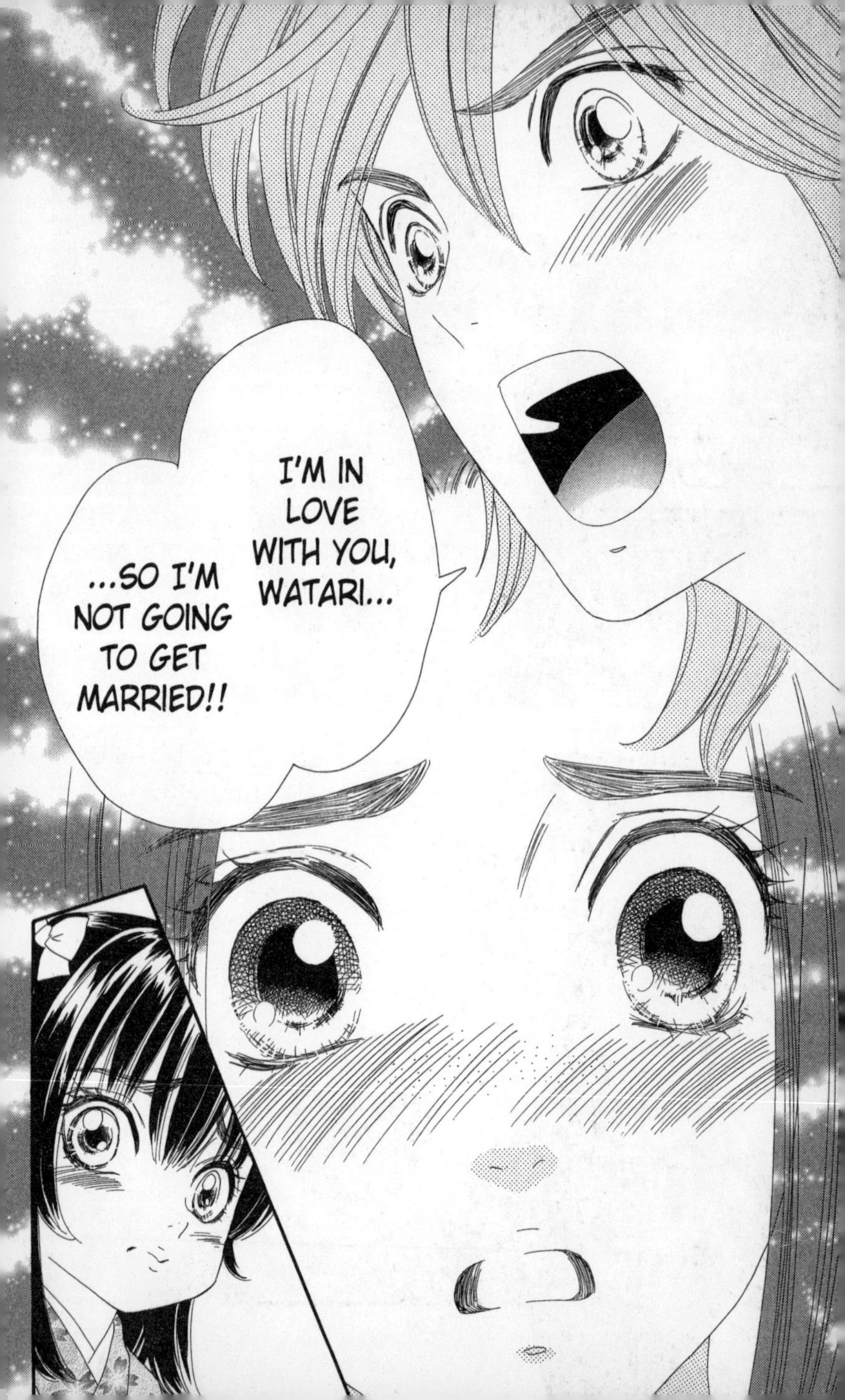
I'M IN LOVE WITH YOU, WATARI...
...SO I'M NOT GOING TO GET MARRIED!!

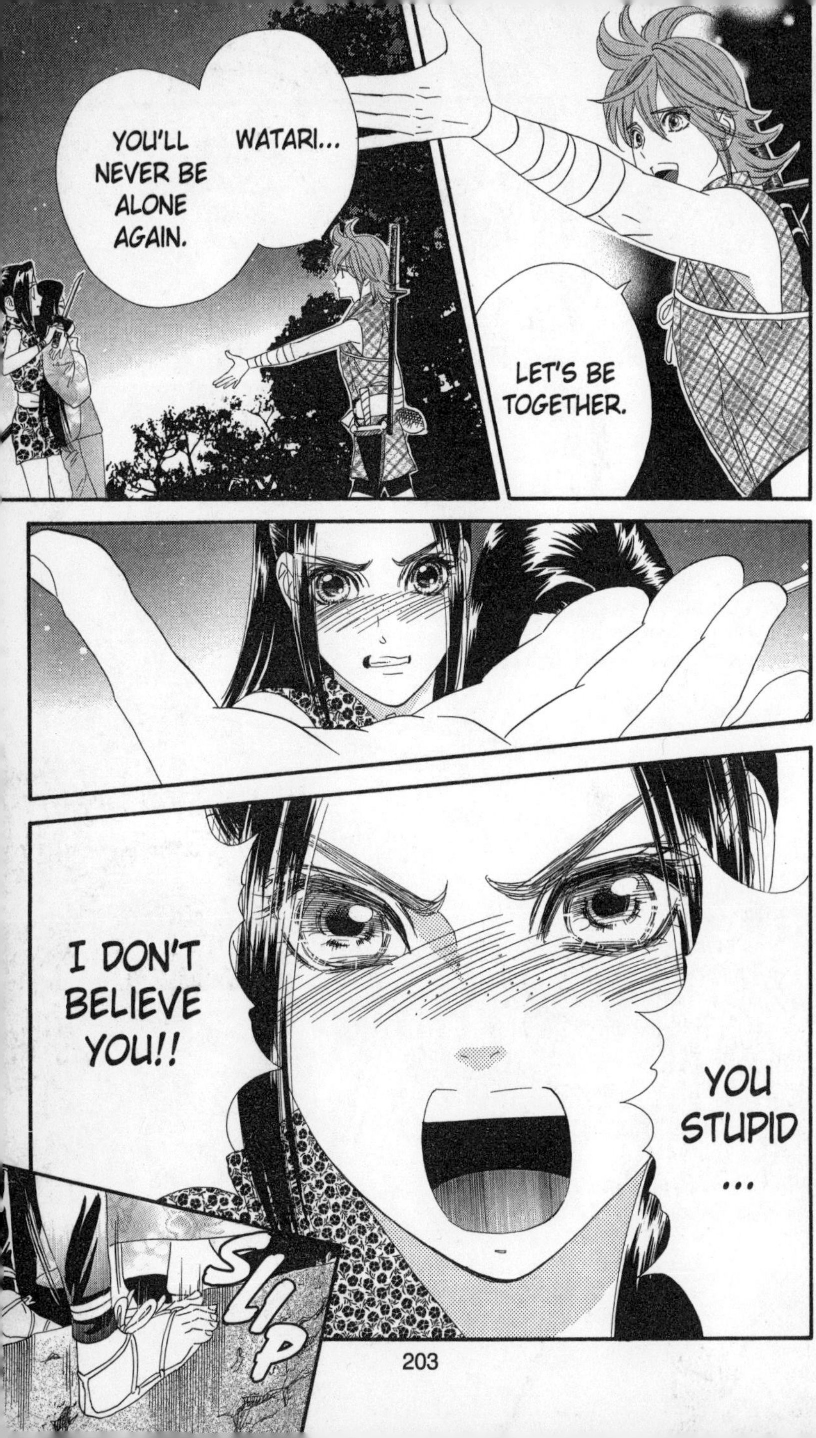
LET'S BE TOGETHER.
WATARI... YOU'LL NEVER BE ALONE AGAIN.
YOU STUPID ...
I DON'T BELIEVE YOU!!
SLIP

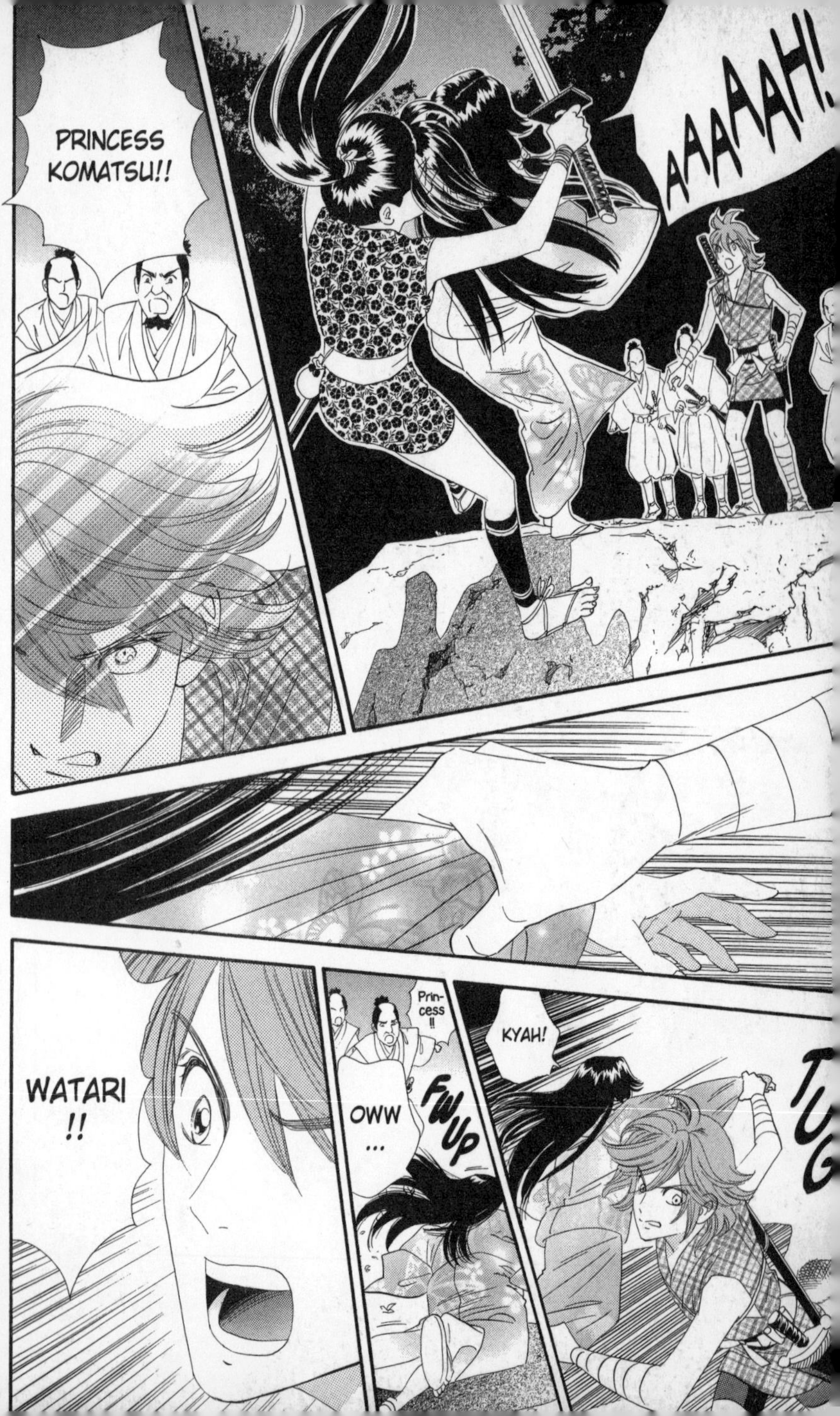
AAAAAH!
PRINCESS KOMATSU!!
KYAH!
TUG
Prin-cess !!
FWUP
OWW ...
WATARI !!

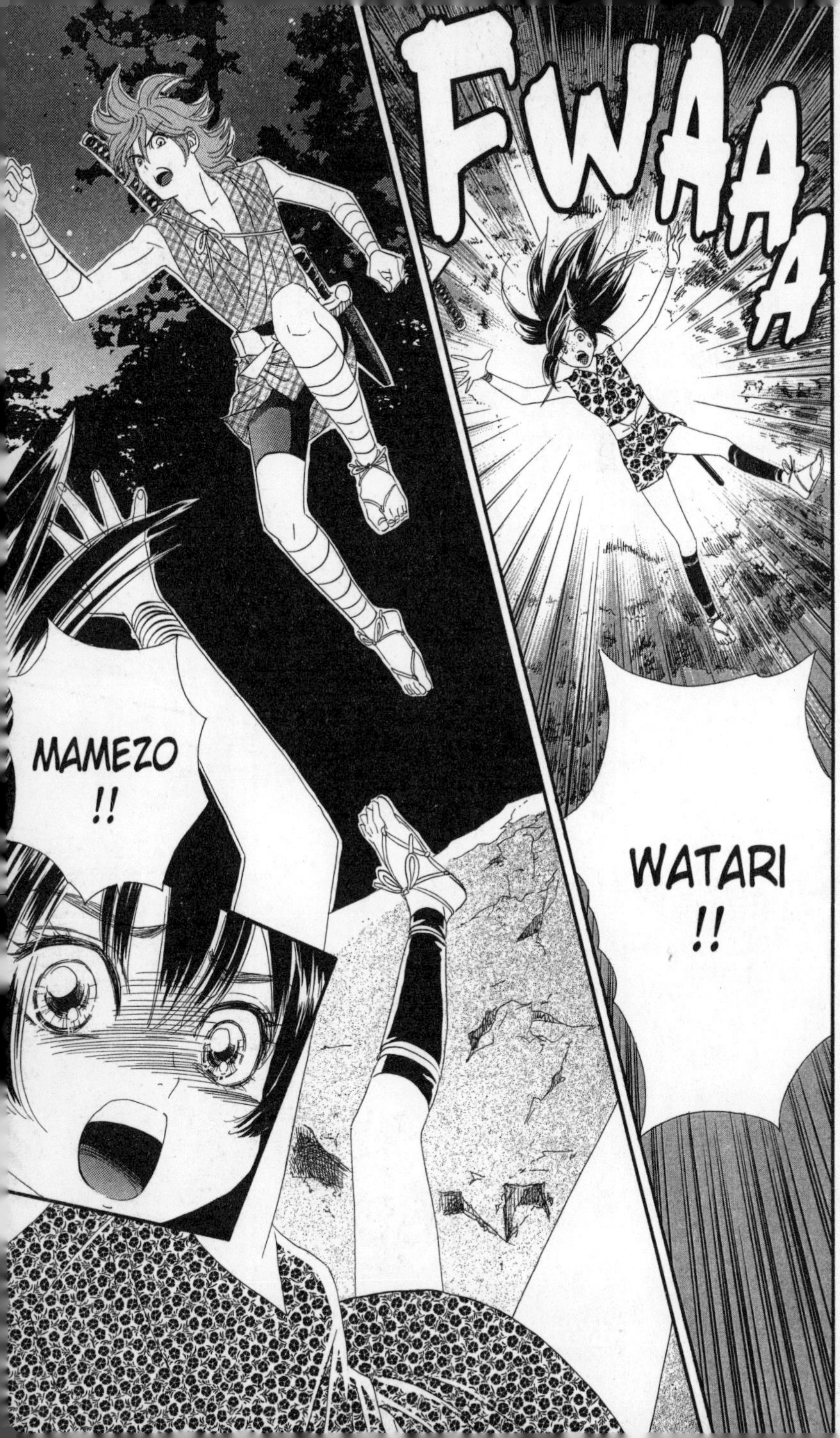
FWAAAA
WATARI !!
MAMEZO !!

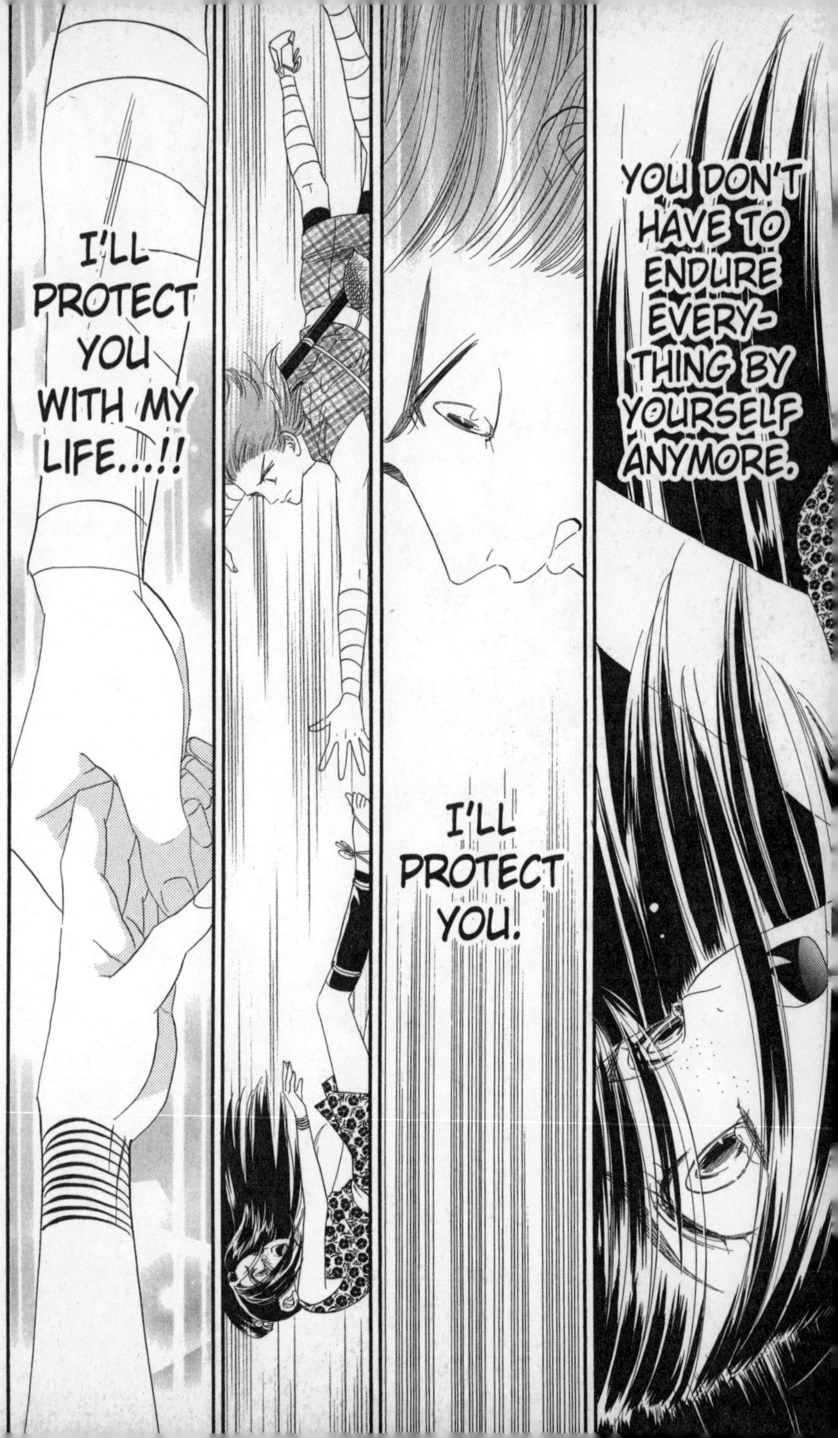
YOU DON'T HAVE TO ENDURE EVERY-THING BY YOURSELF ANYMORE.
I'LL PROTECT YOU.
I'LL PROTECT YOU WITH MY LIFE...!!

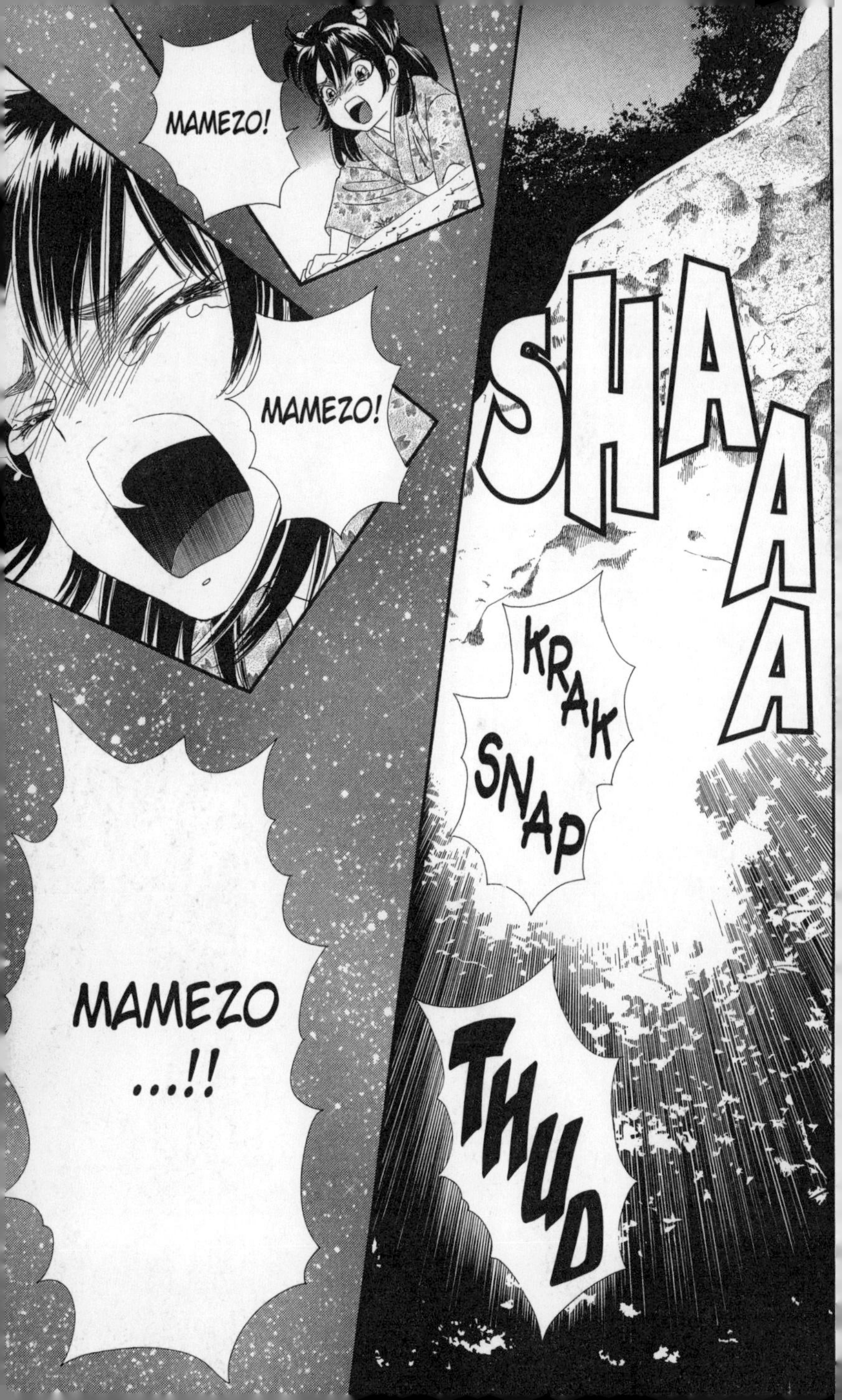

SHAAAA
KRAK
SNAP
THUD
MAMEZO!
MAMEZO!
MAMEZO
...!!

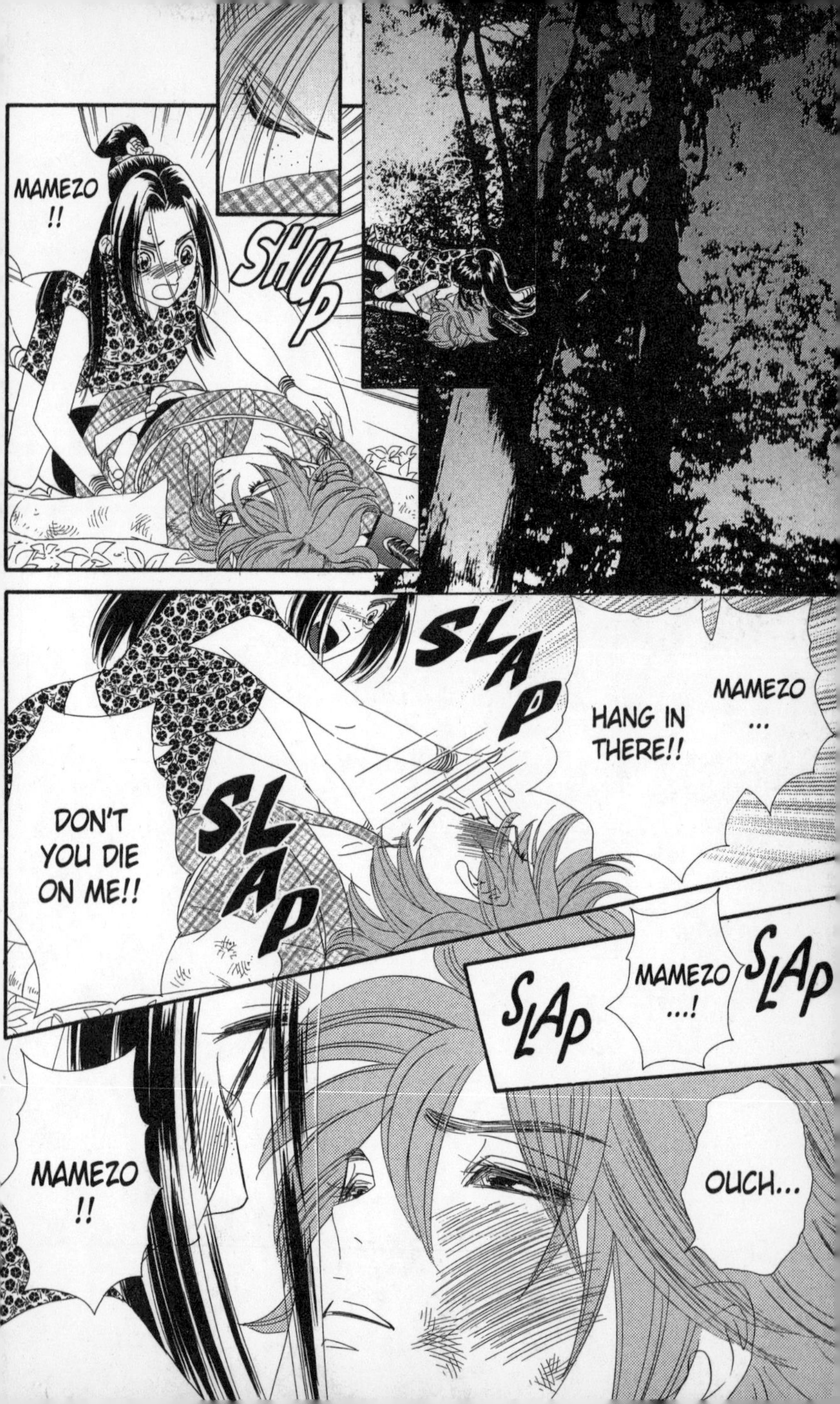
MAMEZO !!
SHUP
MAMEZO ...
HANG IN THERE!!
SLAP
SLAP
DON'T YOU DIE ON ME!!
SLAP
MAMEZO ...!
SLAP
OUCH...
MAMEZO !!

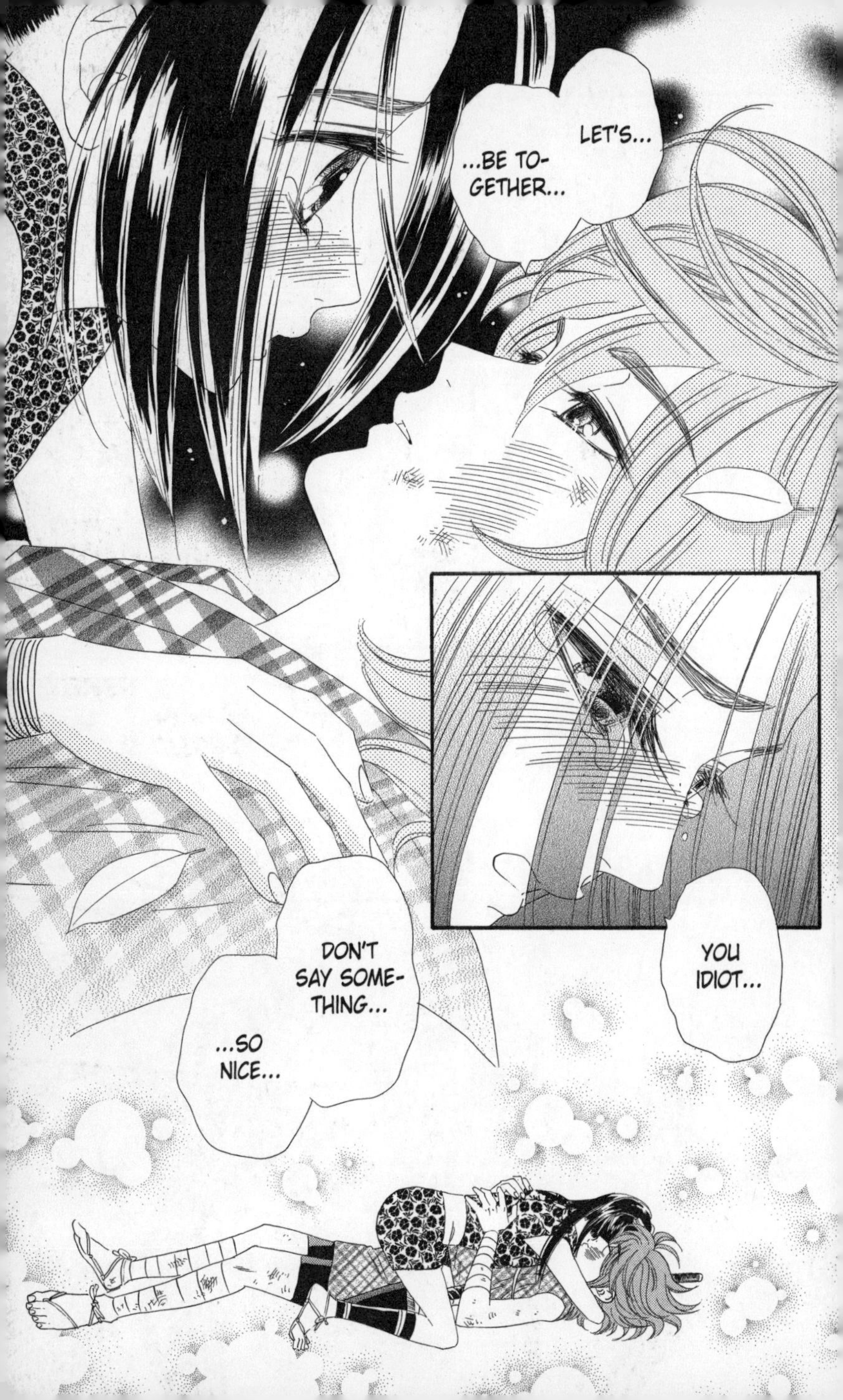
LET'S...
...BE TO-GETHER...
YOU IDIOT...
DON'T SAY SOME-THING...
...SO NICE...

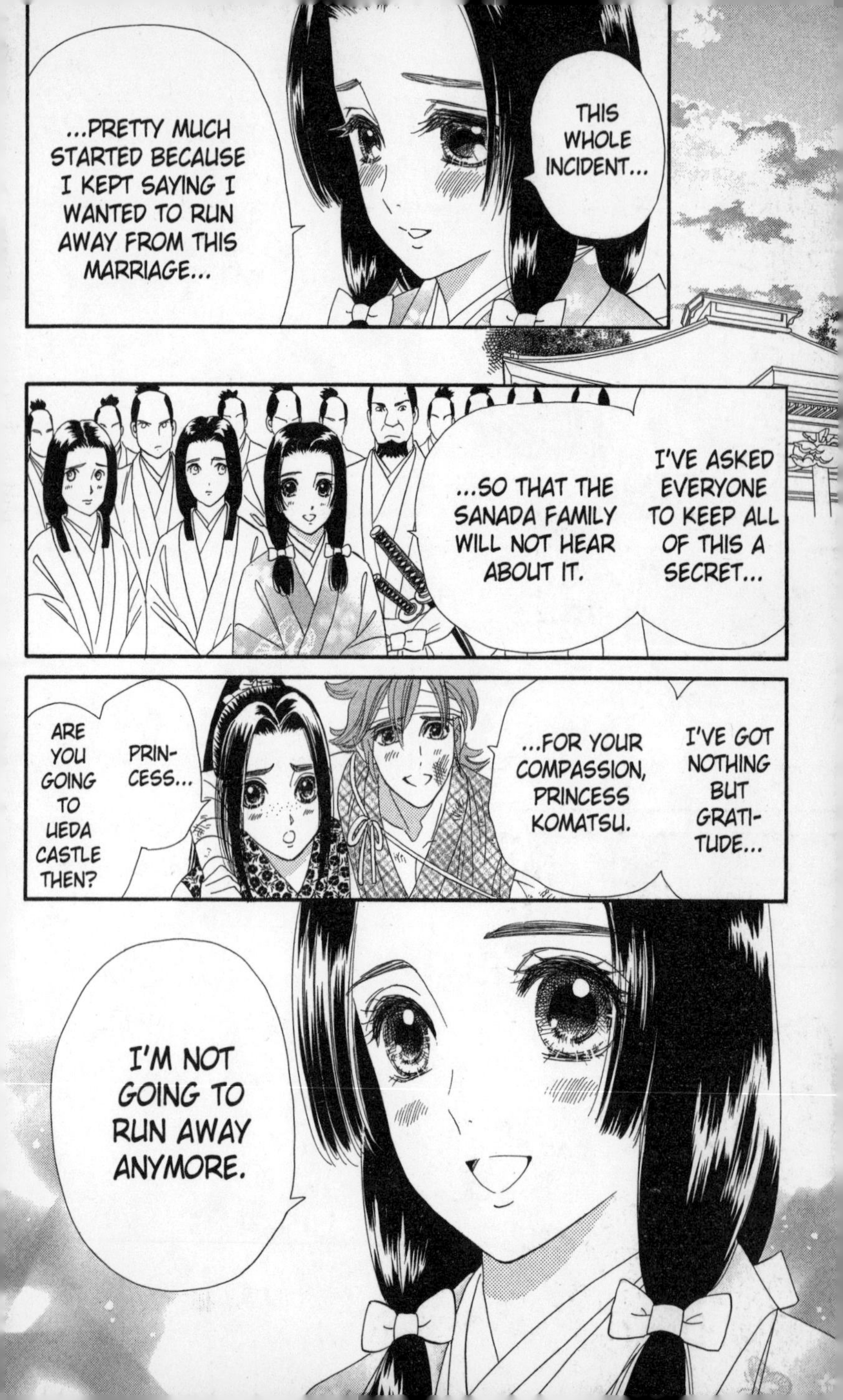
THIS WHOLE INCIDENT...
...PRETTY MUCH STARTED BECAUSE I KEPT SAYING I WANTED TO RUN AWAY FROM THIS MARRIAGE...
I'VE ASKED EVERYONE TO KEEP ALL OF THIS A SECRET...
...SO THAT THE SANADA FAMILY WILL NOT HEAR ABOUT IT.
I'VE GOT NOTHING BUT GRATITUDE...
...FOR YOUR COMPASSION, PRINCESS KOMATSU.
PRINCESS...
ARE YOU GOING TO UEDA CASTLE THEN?
I'M NOT GOING TO RUN AWAY ANYMORE.

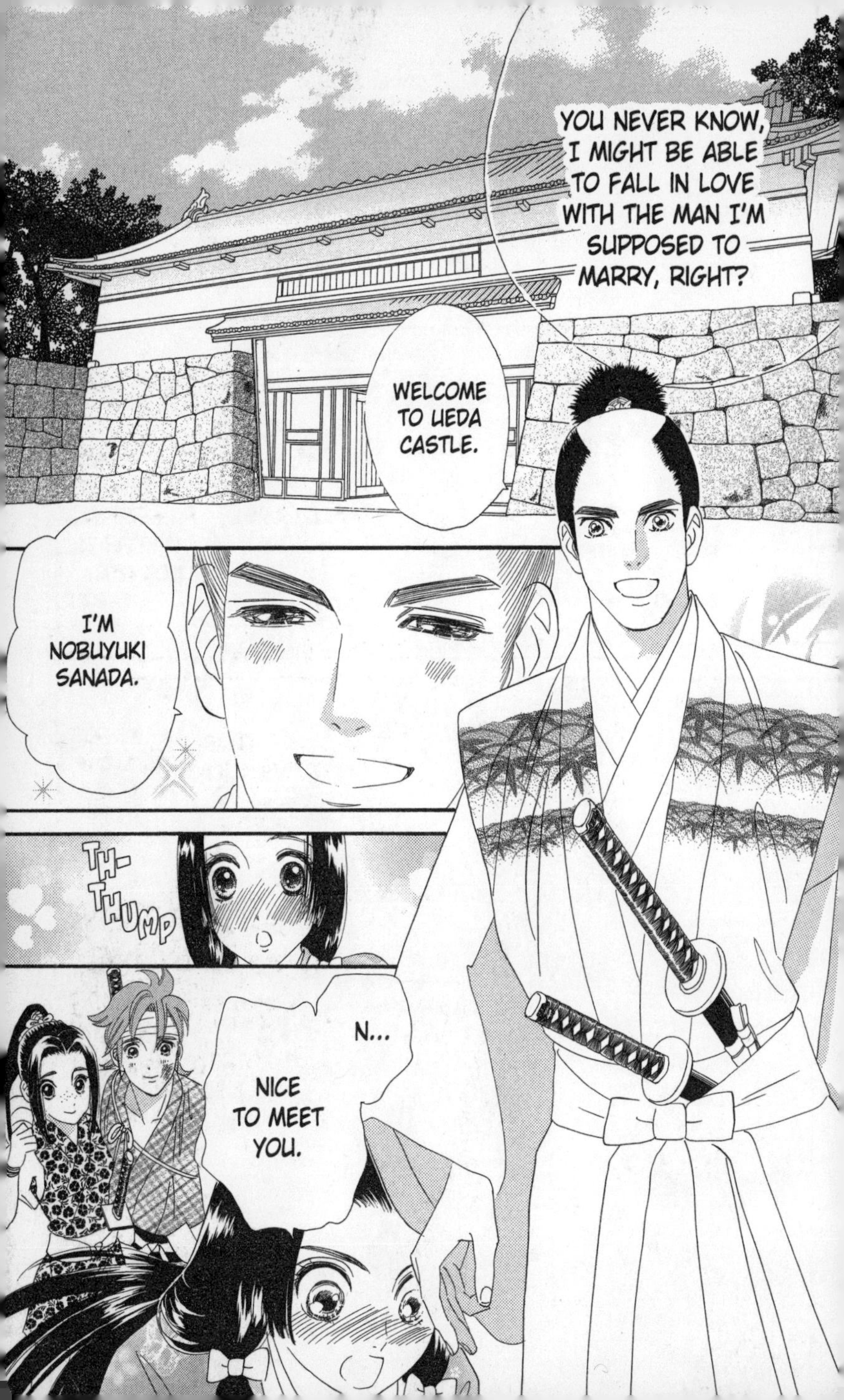
YOU NEVER KNOW, I MIGHT BE ABLE TO FALL IN LOVE WITH THE MAN I'M SUPPOSED TO MARRY, RIGHT?
WELCOME TO UEDA CASTLE.
I'M NOBUYUKI SANADA.
TH-THUMP
N...
NICE TO MEET YOU.

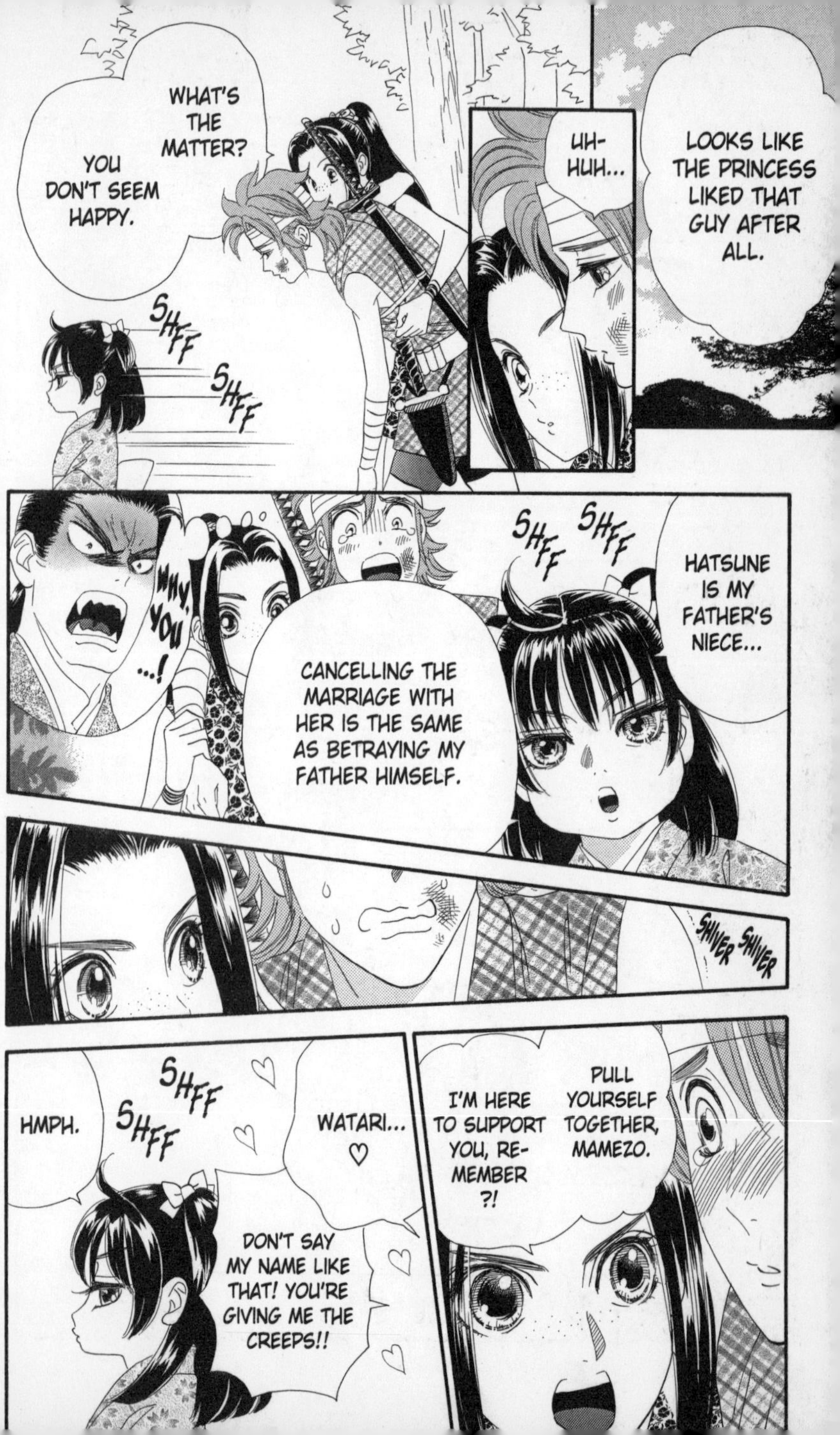
LOOKS LIKE THE PRINCESS LIKED THAT GUY AFTER ALL.
UH-HUH...
WHAT'S THE MATTER?
YOU DON'T SEEM HAPPY.
SHFF
SHFF
SHFF
SHFF
HATSUNE IS MY FATHER'S NIECE...
CANCELLING THE MARRIAGE WITH HER IS THE SAME AS BETRAYING MY FATHER HIMSELF.
WHY, YOU ...!
SHIVER SHIVER
PULL YOURSELF TOGETHER, MAMEZO.
I'M HERE TO SUPPORT YOU, RE-MEMBER ?!
WATARI... ♡
SHFF
SHFF
HMPH.
DON'T SAY MY NAME LIKE THAT! YOU'RE GIVING ME THE CREEPS!!

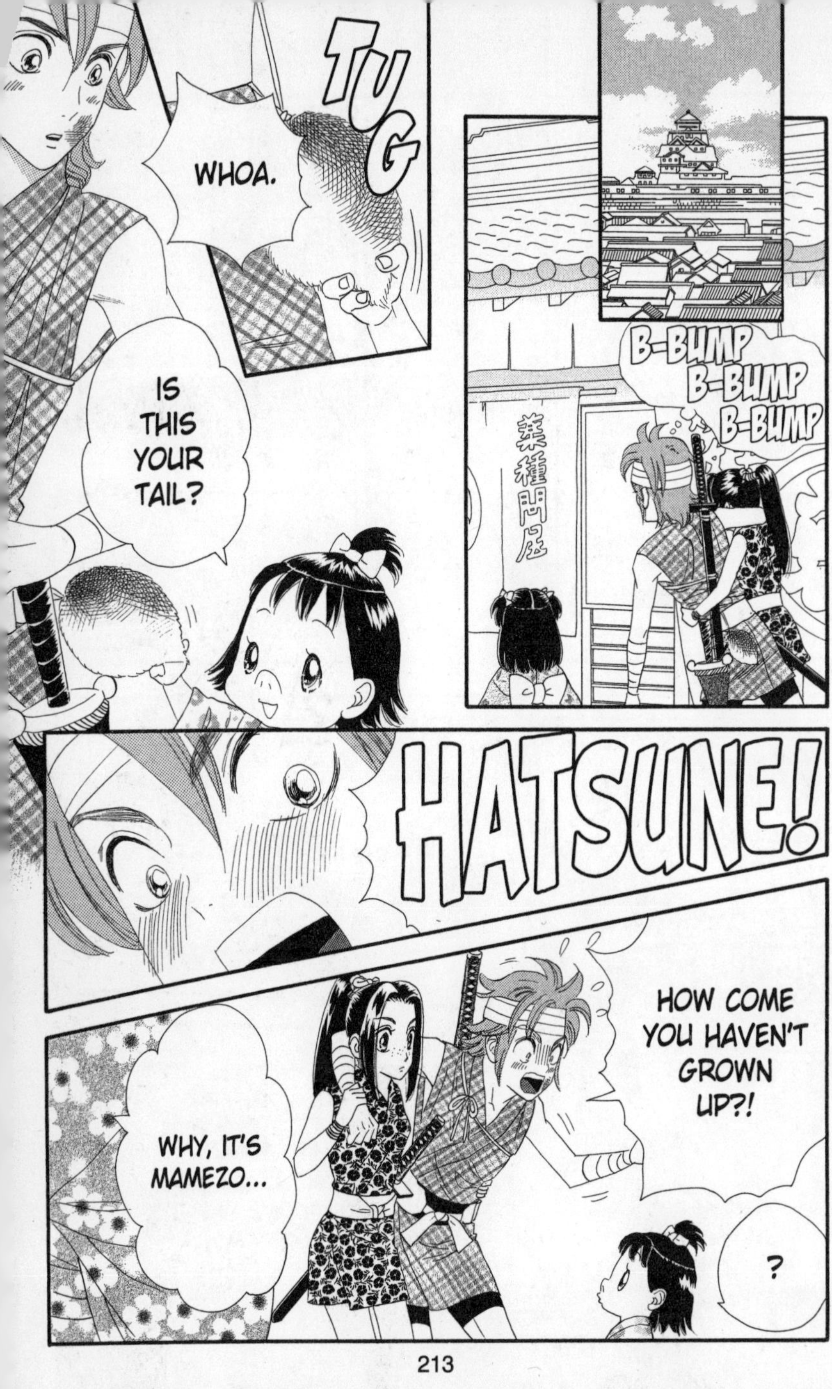
B-BUMP
B-BUMP
B-BUMP
薬種問屋
TUG
WHOA.
IS THIS YOUR TAIL?
HATSUNE!
HOW COME YOU HAVEN'T GROWN UP?!
WHY, IT'S MAMEZO...
?

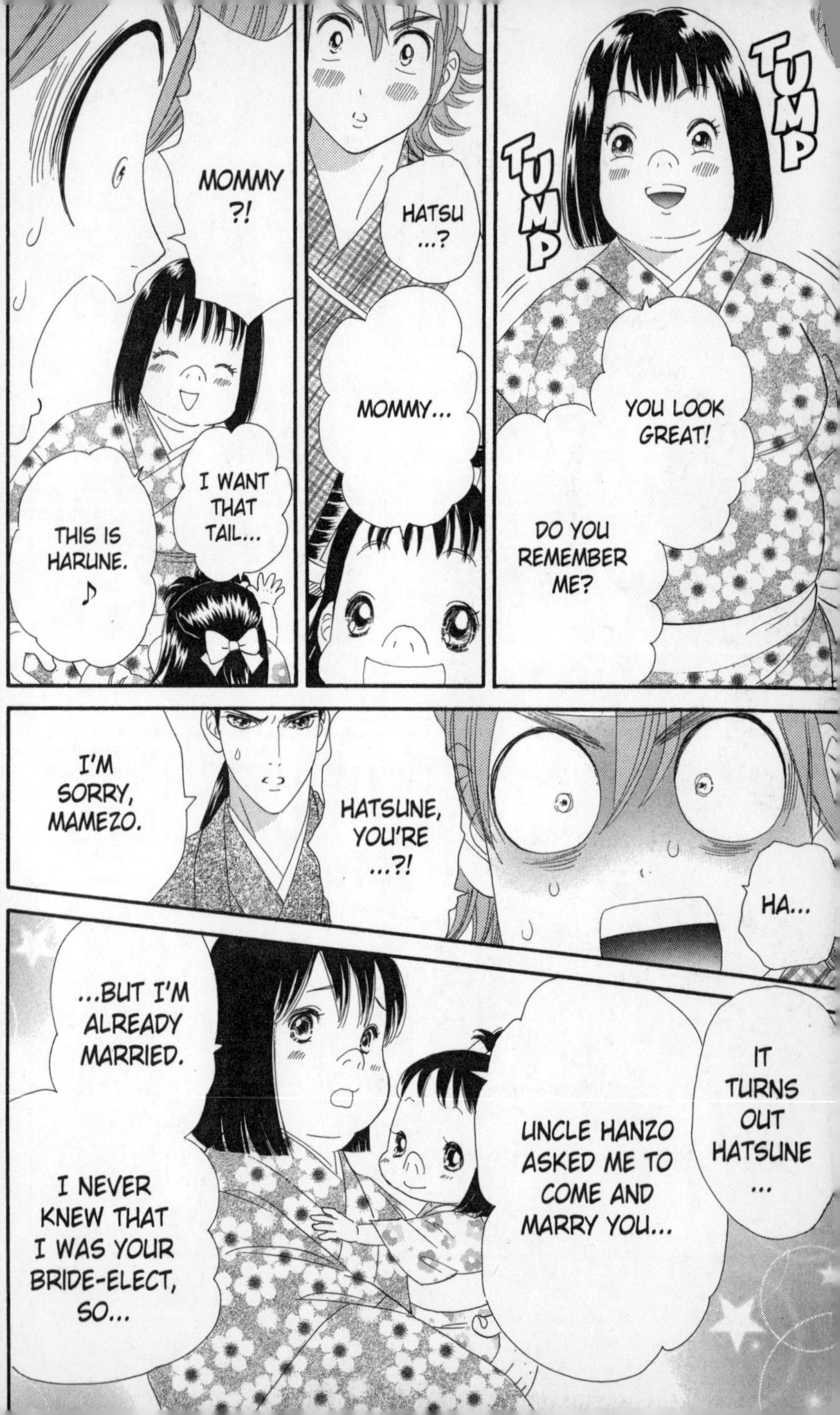
TUMP
TUMP
YOU LOOK GREAT!
DO YOU REMEMBER ME?
HATSU ...?
MOMMY...
MOMMY ?!
I WANT THAT TAIL...
THIS IS HARUNE. ♪
HA...
HATSUNE, YOU'RE ...?!
I'M SORRY, MAMEZO.
IT TURNS OUT HATSUNE ...
UNCLE HANZO ASKED ME TO COME AND MARRY YOU...
I NEVER KNEW THAT I WAS YOUR BRIDE-ELECT, SO...
...BUT I'M ALREADY MARRIED.

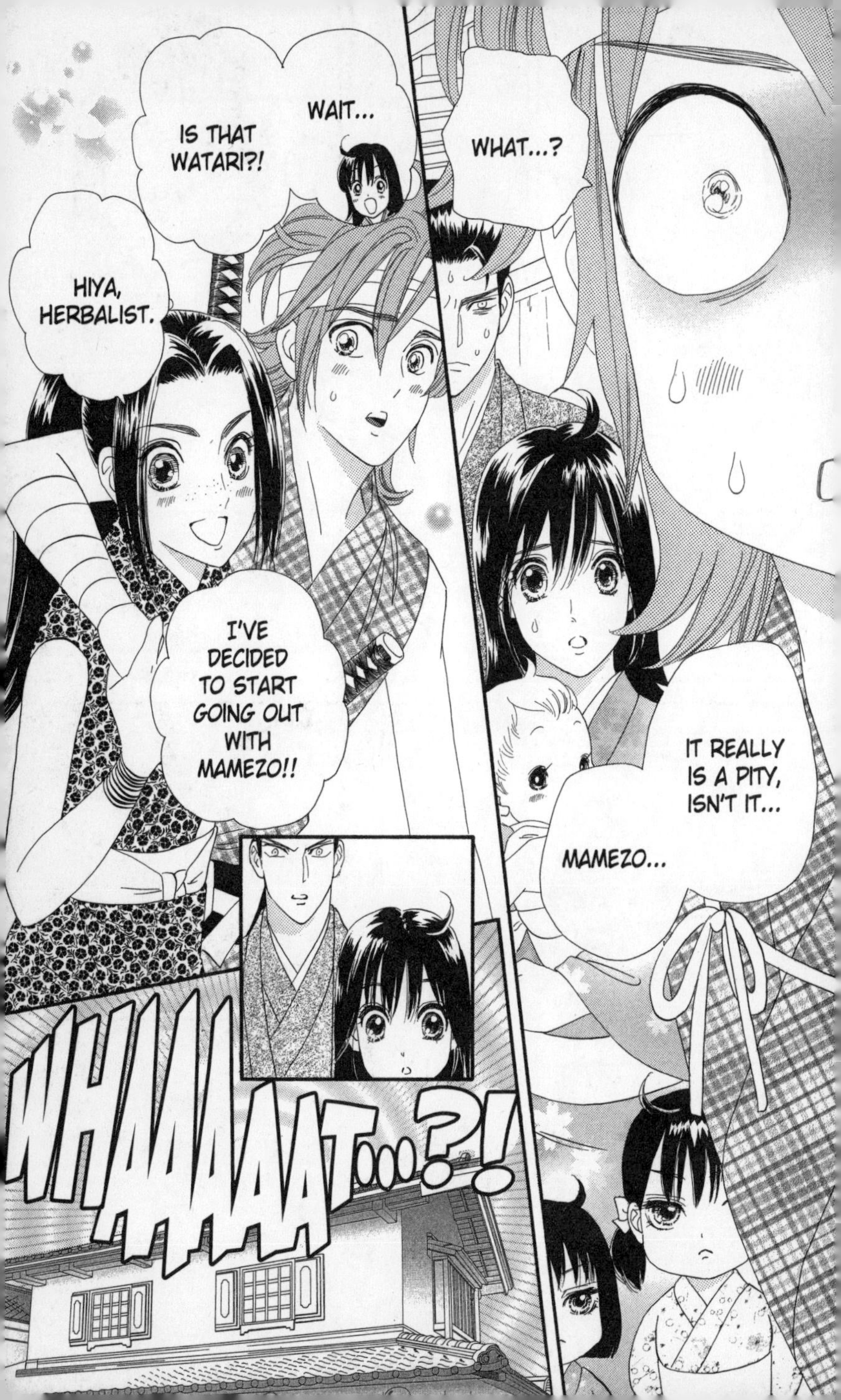
WHAT...?
IT REALLY IS A PITY, ISN'T IT...
MAMEZO...
WAIT...
IS THAT WATARI?!
HIYA, HERBALIST.
I'VE DECIDED TO START GOING OUT WITH MAMEZO!!
WHAAAAAT...?!

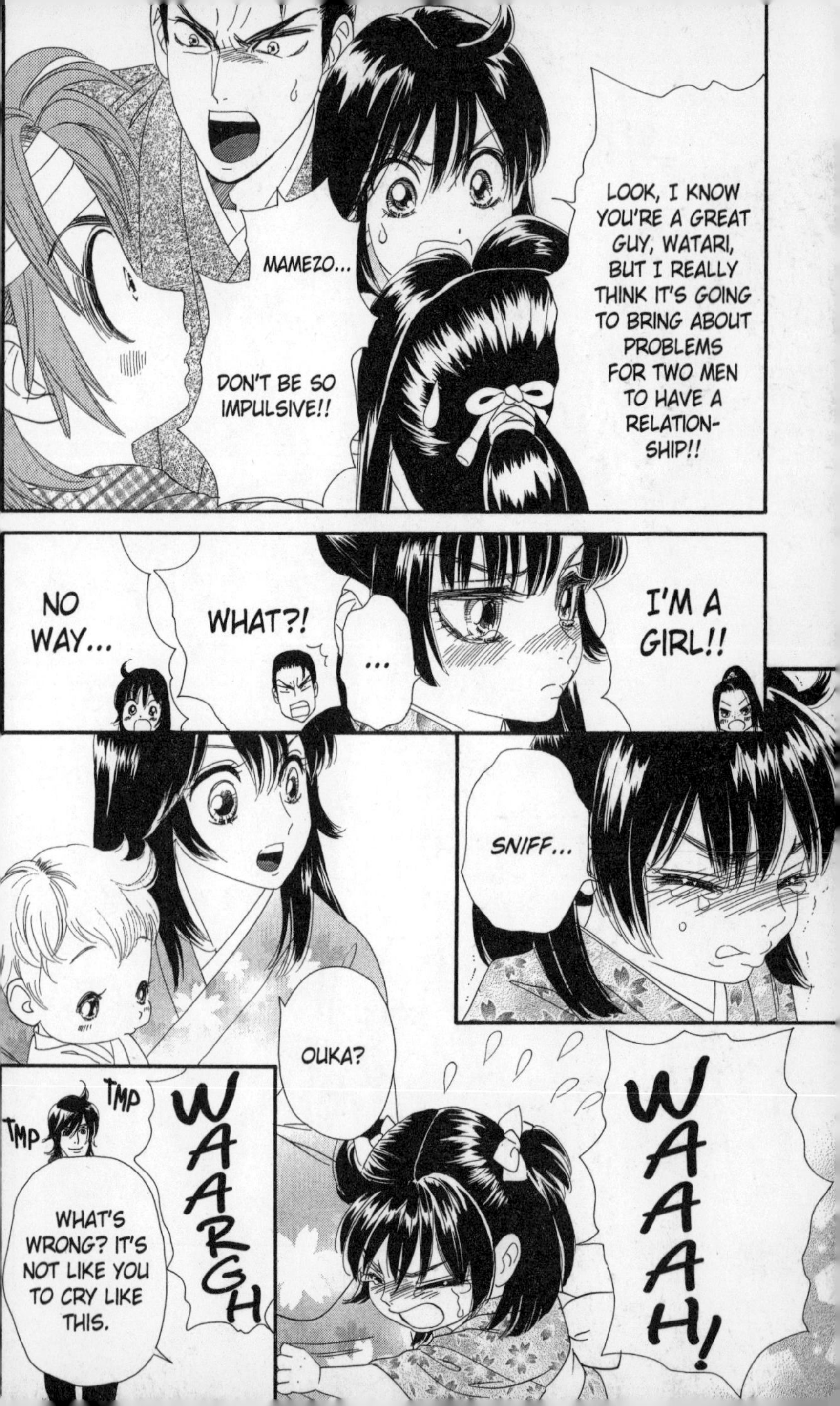
LOOK, I KNOW YOU'RE A GREAT GUY, WATARI, BUT I REALLY THINK IT'S GOING TO BRING ABOUT PROBLEMS FOR TWO MEN TO HAVE A RELATION-SHIP!!
MAMEZO...
DON'T BE SO IMPULSIVE!!
I'M A GIRL!!
...
WHAT?!
NO WAY...
SNIFF...
OUKA?
WAAAAH!
WAARGH
TMP
TMP
WHAT'S WRONG? IT'S NOT LIKE YOU TO CRY LIKE THIS.

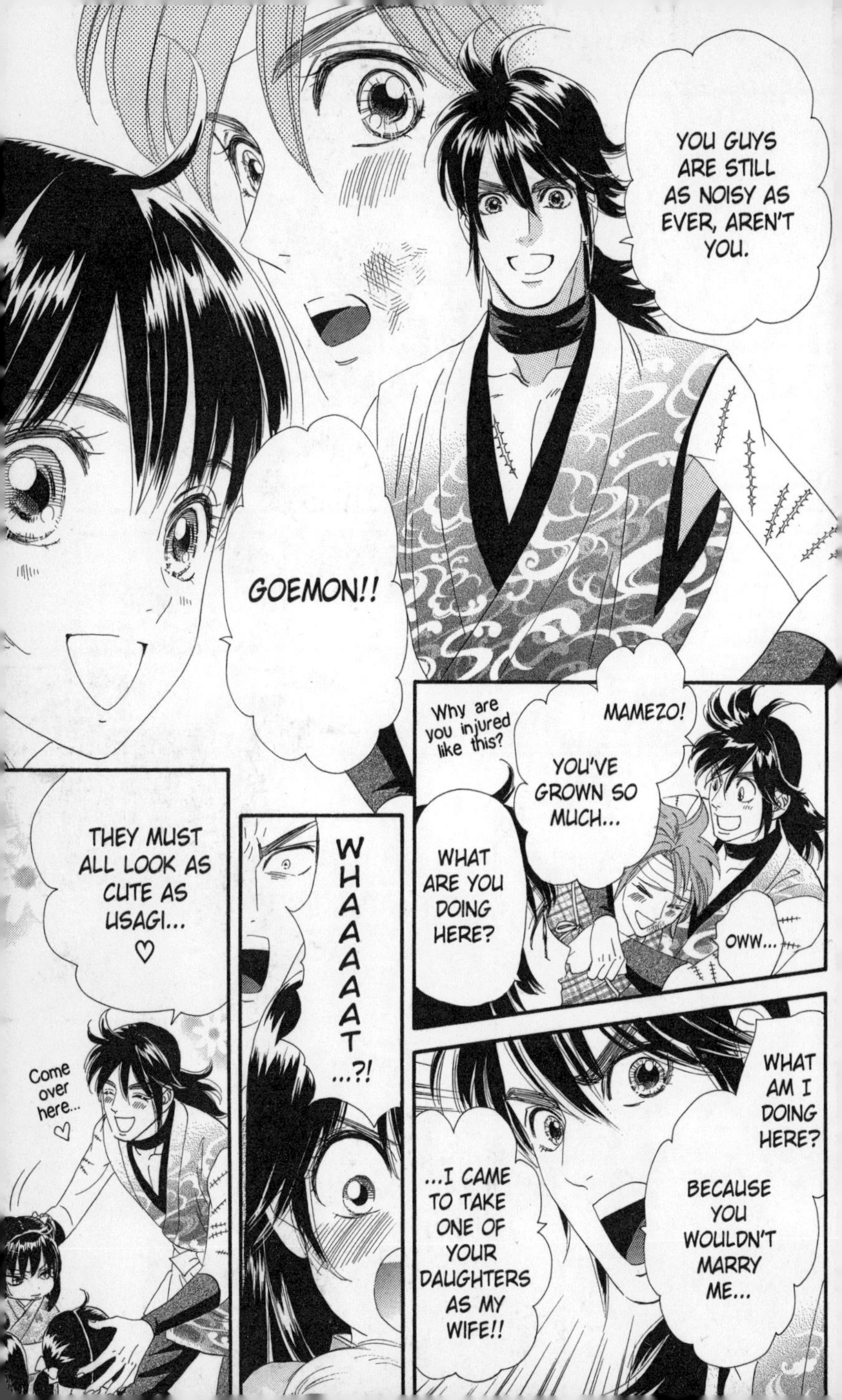
YOU GUYS ARE STILL AS NOISY AS EVER, AREN'T YOU.
GOEMON!!
MAMEZO!
YOU'VE GROWN SO MUCH...
Why are you injured like this?
OWW...
WHAT ARE YOU DOING HERE?
WHAT AM I DOING HERE?
BECAUSE YOU WOULDN'T MARRY ME...
...I CAME TO TAKE ONE OF YOUR DAUGHTERS AS MY WIFE!!
WHAAAAAT...?!
THEY MUST ALL LOOK AS CUTE AS USAGI... ♡
Come over here... ♡

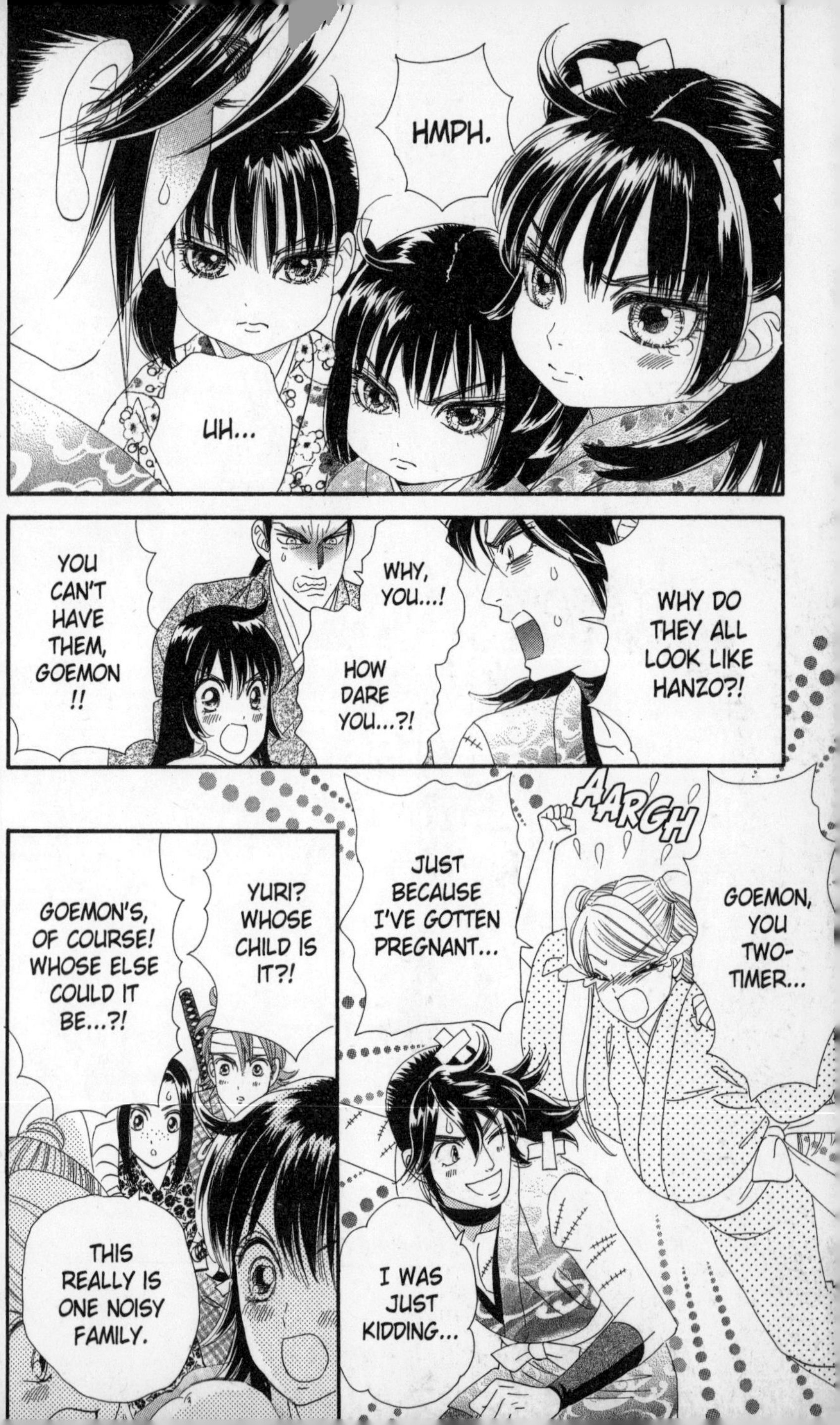
HMPH.
UH...
WHY DO THEY ALL LOOK LIKE HANZO?!
WHY, YOU...!
HOW DARE YOU...?!
YOU CAN'T HAVE THEM, GOEMON!!
AARGH
GOEMON, YOU TWO-TIMER...
JUST BECAUSE I'VE GOTTEN PREGNANT...
I WAS JUST KIDDING...
YURI? WHOSE CHILD IS IT?!
GOEMON'S, OF COURSE! WHOSE ELSE COULD IT BE...?!
THIS REALLY IS ONE NOISY FAMILY.

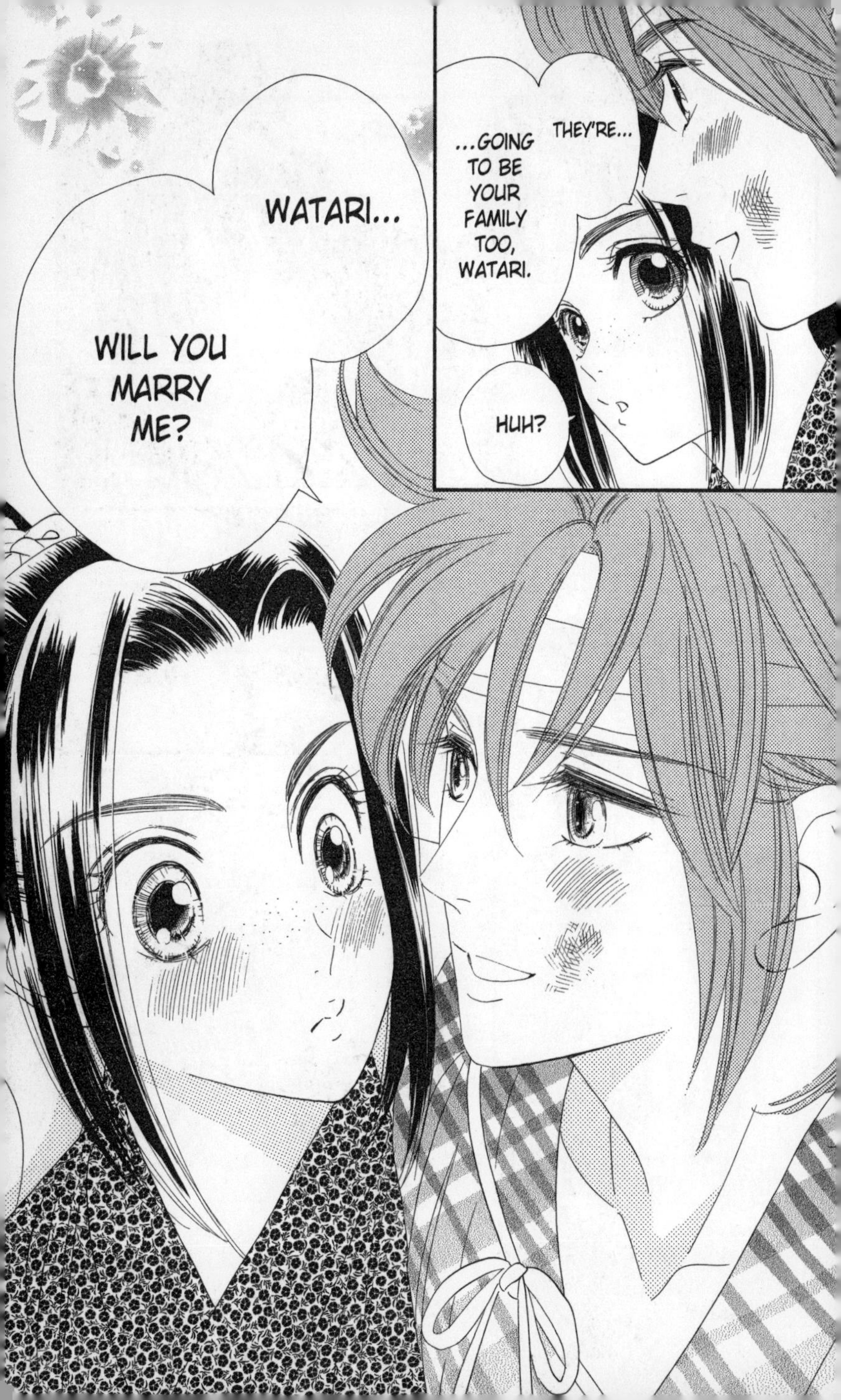
THEY'RE...
...GOING TO BE YOUR FAMILY TOO, WATARI.
HUH?
WATARI...
WILL YOU MARRY ME?

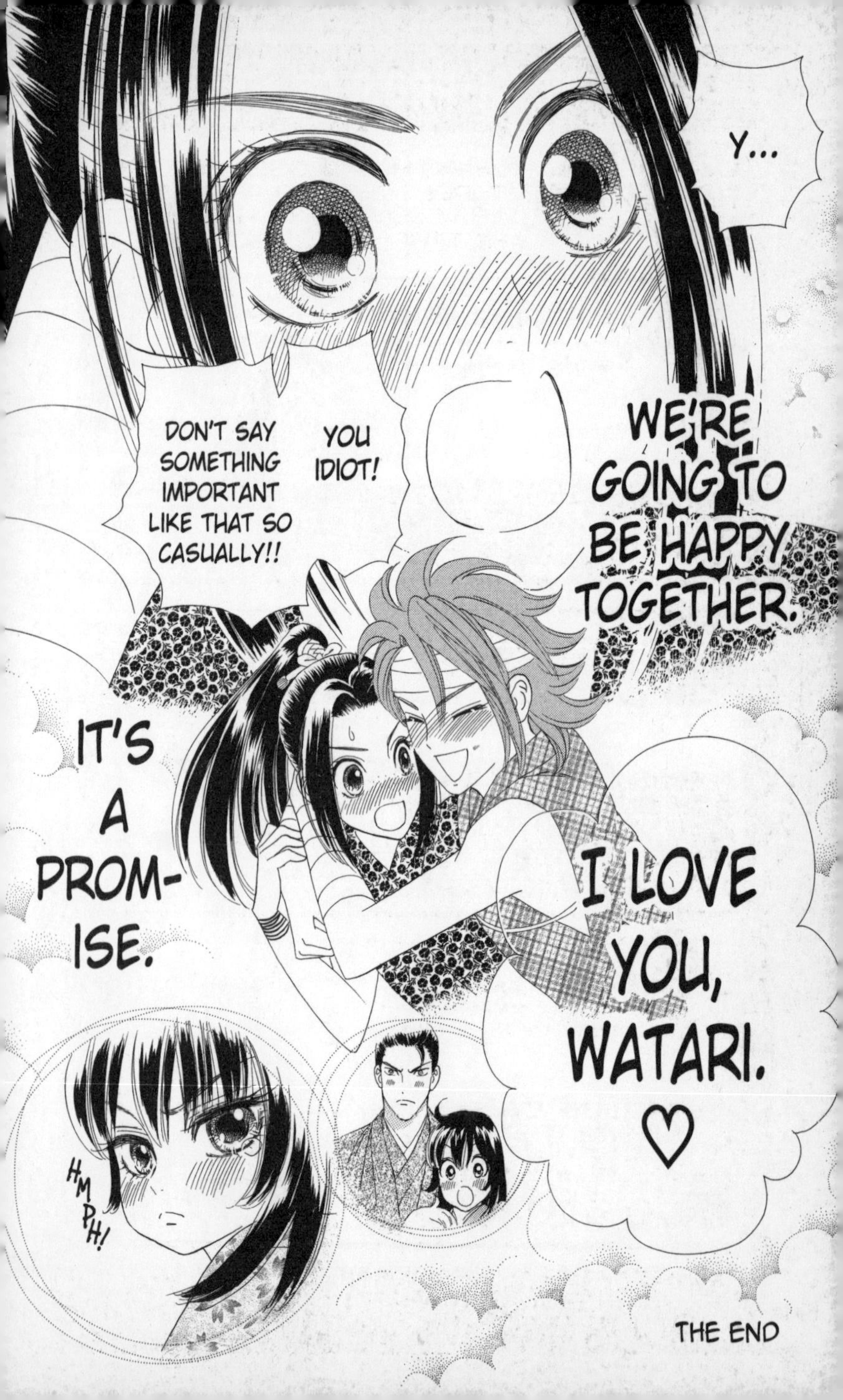
Y...
YOU IDIOT!
DON'T SAY SOMETHING IMPORTANT LIKE THAT SO CASUALLY!!
WE'RE GOING TO BE HAPPY TOGETHER.
I LOVE YOU, WATARI. ♥
IT'S A PROM-ISE.
HMPH!
THE END

SPECIAL PROJECT PART 2

UE-RIN'S FAVORITE SCENES

UE-RIN HAS CHOSEN HER TOP THREE SCENES OUT OF ALL 15 VOLUMES AND HAS ADDED HER THOUGHTS ABOUT THEM!!

FAVORITE SCENE 1 USAGI GAINS WEIGHT

(From Volume 4, Chapter 28)

YOU'VE GAINED TOO MUCH WEIGHT, USAGI.
SHOCK
GAINED WEIGHT ?!
YOU ARE 30% HEAVIER THAN WHEN WE PARTED IN HAMAMATSU.

I HAD GAINED A LOT OF WEIGHT WHEN I WAS DOING THIS SCENE, SO I FELT VERY SYMPATHETIC TO USAGI.

FAVORITE SCENE 2 POOR KAME

(From Volume 10, Chapter 65)

"IT WILL HELP YOU RUN AWAY QUICKLY FROM ANY DANGER YOU MIGHT ENCOUNTER."
THE LUCKY RABBIT'S FOOT...
...YOU GAVE ME...
YOU'VE...
...HAD IT WITH YOU ALL THIS TIME?

IT WAS AS IF USAGI WAS THE LIGHT AND KAME WAS THE DARK. I KEPT WEEPING, THINKING, "I FEEL SO SORRY FOR YOU, KAME..." WHILE I DREW THIS SCENE.

FAVORITE SCENE 3 SCARY RANMARU

(From Volume 13, Chapter 90)

RANMARU ...?!
I'VE NEVER BEEN ABLE TO FIND ANY OTHER WOMAN LIKE YOU.
I WANT YOU TO BE MINE.

I HAD A TOUGH TIME TRYING TO FIGURE OUT WHAT KIND OF CHARACTER RANMARU WAS. THIS WAS WHEN I WAS ABLE TO GET A CLEAR GRASP OF HIS CHARACTER.

The ways of the ninja are mysterious indeed, so here is a glossary of terms to help you navigate the intricacies of their world.

Page 2: Oda Nobunaga
Oda Nobunaga lived from 1534 to 1582, and came close to unifying Japan. He is probably one of the most famous Japanese warlords. He was the first warlord to successfully incorporate the gun in battle, and is notorious for his ruthlessness.

Page 2: Mitsuhide Akechi
Mitsuhide Akechi became one of Oda Nobunaga's retainers after Nobunaga's conquest of Mino province (now Gifu prefecture) in 1566. He is known to have been more of an intellectual and a pacifist than a warrior.

Page 7, panel 2: Sakamoto Castle
Located in Sakamoto, a small village in Shiga prefecture (once known as Omi province). In 1571, Mitsuhide Akechi was awarded the Sakamoto estate for serving Oda Nobunaga.

Page 17, panel 3: Sakai
Sakai is a city in Osaka prefecture that is one of the largest and most important seaports in Japan. Once known for samurai swords, Sakai is now famous for quality kitchen knives and other cutlery.

Page 19, panel 1: Honnoji
Honnoji is a temple in Kyoto. Oda Nobunaga often stayed here when he traveled to the capital.

Page 2: Tokugawa Ieyasu
Tokugawa Ieyasu (1543-1616) was the first Shogun of the Tokugawa Shogunate. He made a small fishing village named Edo the center of his activities. Edo thrived and became a huge town, and was later renamed Tokyo, the present capital.

Page 2: Okazaki Castle
Okazaki Castle is in the city of Okazaki in Aichi prefecture. This castle was home to various leaders throughout history, including Tokugawa Ieyasu. Though demolished in 1873, the castle was reconstructed in 1959.

Page 2: Iga
Iga is a region on the island of Honshu and also the name of the famous ninja clan that originated there. Another area famous for its ninja is Kouga, in the Shiga prefecture on Honshu. Many books claim that these two ninja clans were mortal enemies, but in reality inter-ninja relations were not as bad as stories might suggest.

Page 2: Azuchi Castle
Azuchi Castle was one of Oda Nobunaga's main castles. It is located on the shores of Lake Biwa in Shiga Prefecture. The castle's strategic location enabled Nobunaga to manage his foes more easily, namely the Uesugi clan to the north and the Mouri clan to the west.

Page 151, panel 1: Ueda Castle
Located in Nagano, Ueda Castle was built by daimyo Masayuki Sanada during the latter half of the 16th century and was the original home of the Sanada clan.

Page 155, panel 5: Kunoichi
A term often used for female ninja. The word is spelled くノー, and when combined, the letters form the kanji for woman, 女。

Page 211, panel 2: Nobuyuki Sanada
Nobuyuki Sanada (1566-1658) was the son of Masayuki Sanada. Tokugawa Ieyasu arranged to have him marry Komatsu-hime, his adopted daughter.

Page 40, panel 2: Ranmaru Mori
Ranmaru Mori is one of Oda Nobunaga's most famous vassals. He became Nobunaga's attendant at a young age and was recognized for his talent and loyalty.

Page 82, panel 3: Hagemu and Hageru
The words *hagemu* (strive hard) and *hageru* (go bald) are used in the original Japanese text to make a pun.

Page 85, panel 2: Oda Nobutada
Oda Nobutada (1557-1582) was the eldest son of Oda Nobunaga. He commanded armies under his father against the Takeda clan.

Page 102, panel 2: Okazaki
Okazaki is in Aichi Prefecture on the main island of Honshu, about 22 miles from Nagoya.

Page 124, panel 3: Tenkai
A Japanese Buddhist priest who worked for Tokugawa Ieyasu and advised the next two Tokugawa shoguns. Some people believe that he was actually Mitsuhide Akechi, but recent studies have found that he could have been somebody close to Mitsuhide (such as a cousin).

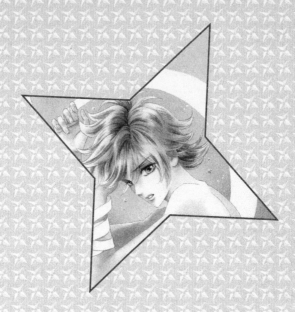

I've been creating this series with much doubt
and worry. The turnabouts in the story, when the
main characters made a move and all that…
I still don't know if the choices I made were right,
but I'm glad to have been able to end the series
with a happy, cheerful scene. I'm also glad I was
able to draw the after-stories about Mamezo and
the other characters.

–Rinko Ueda

Rinko Ueda is from Nara prefecture. She enjoys
listening to the radio, drama CDs, and Rakugo
comedy performances. Her works include *Ryo*, a
series based on the legend of Gojo Bridge; *Home*,
a story about love crossing national boundaries;
and *Tail of the Moon (Tsuki no Shippo)*, a romantic
ninja comedy.

TAIL OF THE MOON
Vol. 15
The Shojo Beat Manga Edition

STORY & ART BY
RINKO UEDA

Translation & Adaptation/Tetsuichiro Miyaki
Touch-up Art & Lettering/Mark McMurray
Design/Izumi Hirayama
Editor/Amy Yu

Editor in Chief, Books/Alvin Lu
Editor in Chief, Magazines/Marc Weidenbaum
VP, Publishing Licensing/Rika Inouye
VP, Sales & Product Marketing/Gonzalo Ferreyra
VP, Creative/Linda Espinosa
Publisher/Hyoe Narita

TSUKI-NO SHIPPO © 2002 by Rinko Ueda. All rights reserved.
First published in Japan in 2002 by SHUEISHA Inc., Tokyo. English
translation rights arranged by SHUEISHA Inc. The stories, characters
and incidents mentioned in this publication are entirely fictional.

No portion of this book may be reproduced or transmitted in
any form or by any means without written permission from the
copyright holders.

The rights of the author(s) of the work(s) in this publication to be
so identified have been asserted in accordance with the Copyright,
Designs and Patents Act 1988. A CIP catalogue record for this book
is available from the British Library.

Printed in Canada

Published by VIZ Media, LLC
P.O. Box 77064
San Francisco, CA 94107

Shojo Beat Manga Edition
10 9 8 7 6 5 4 3 2 1
First printing, February 2009

www.viz.com
store.viz.com

PARENTAL ADVISORY
TAIL OF THE MOON is rated T+ for Older Teen and is
recommended for ages 16 and up. This volume
contains brief nudity and ninja violence.
ratings.viz.com

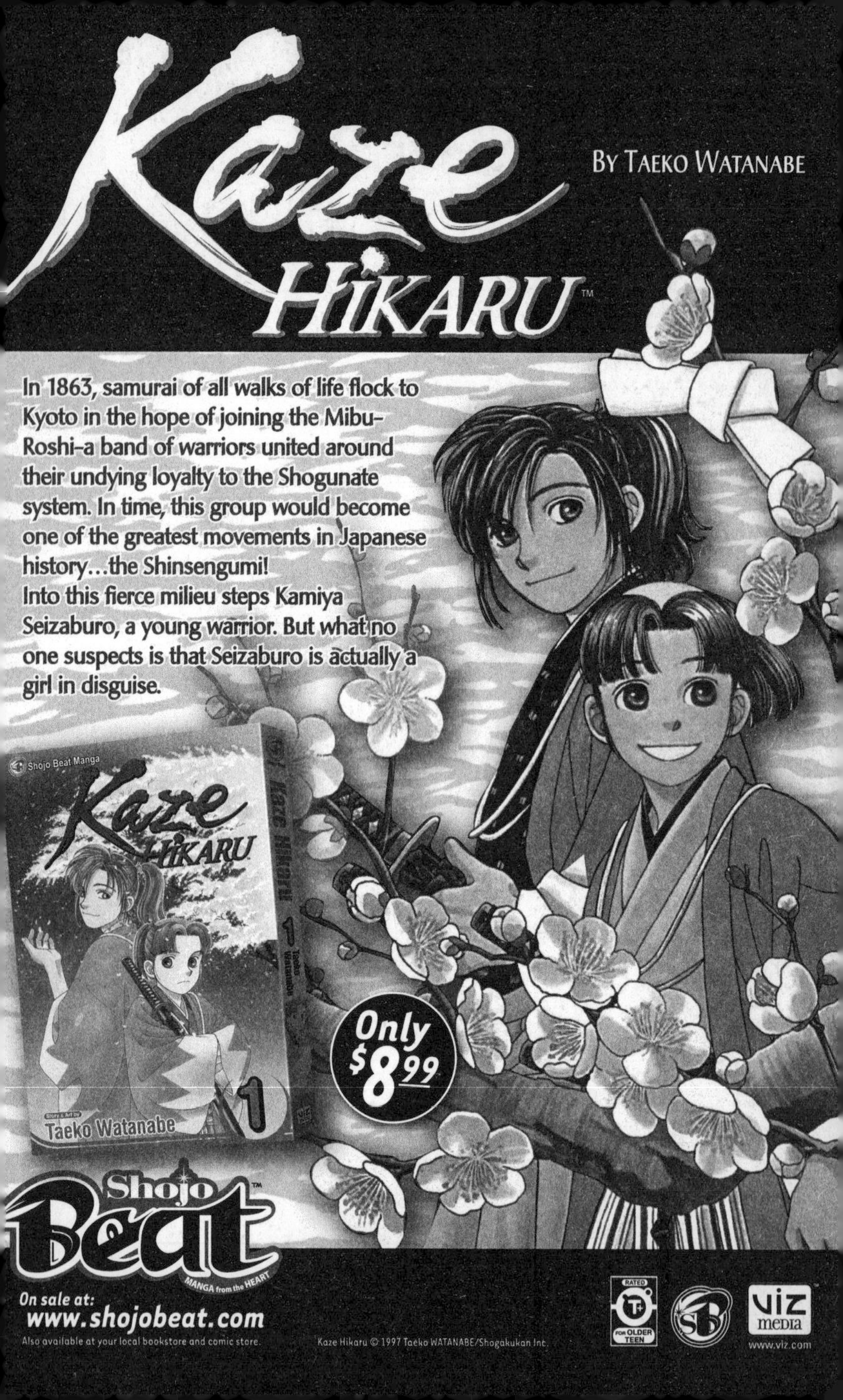
Kaze Hikaru™
By Taeko Watanabe
In 1863, samurai of all walks of life flock to Kyoto in the hope of joining the Mibu-Roshi–a band of warriors united around their undying loyalty to the Shogunate system. In time, this group would become one of the greatest movements in Japanese history…the Shinsengumi!
Into this fierce milieu steps Kamiya Seizaburo, a young warrior. But what no one suspects is that Seizaburo is actually a girl in disguise.
Shojo Beat Manga
Kaze Hikaru
1
Story & Art by
Taeko Watanabe
Only $8.99
Shojo Beat™
MANGA from the HEART
On sale at:
www.shojobeat.com
Also available at your local bookstore and comic store.
Kaze Hikaru © 1997 Taeko WATANABE/Shogakukan Inc.
RATED T+ FOR OLDER TEEN
viz media
www.viz.com

Short-Tempered Melancholic

and Other Stories

by Arina Tanemura

A Collection of Shorts by One of Shojo's Biggest Names

A one-volume manga featuring early short stories from the creator of *Full Moon*, *The Gentlemen's Alliance †*, *I•O•N* and *Time Stranger Kyoko*.

Find out what makes Arina Tanemura a fan favorite—buy *Short-Tempered Melancholic and Other Stories* today!

On sale at **www.shojobeat.com**
Also available at your local bookstore and comic store.

KANSHAKUDAMA NO YUUTSU © 1996 by Arina Tanemura/SHUEISHA Inc.

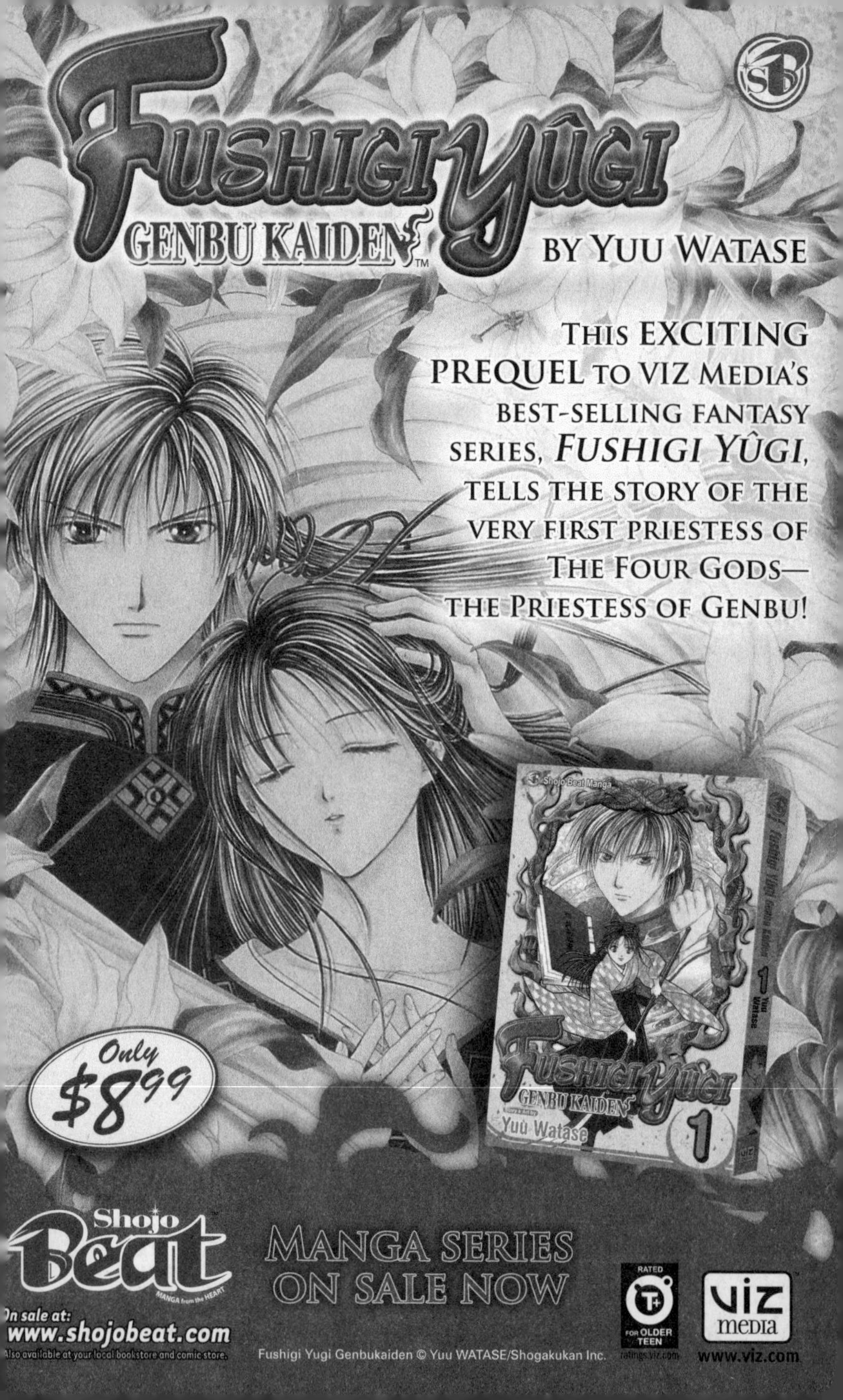

Fushigi Yûgi
Genbu Kaiden™
By Yuu Watase
This EXCITING PREQUEL to VIZ Media's best-selling fantasy series, Fushigi Yûgi, tells the story of the very first priestess of The Four Gods— the Priestess of Genbu!
Only $8.99
Shojo Beat Manga
Fushigi Yûgi Genbu Kaiden
Yuu Watase
1
Shojo Beat
MANGA from the HEART
Manga Series On Sale Now
On sale at:
www.shojobeat.com
Also available at your local bookstore and comic store.
Fushigi Yugi Genbukaiden © Yuu WATASE/Shogakukan Inc.
RATED
T+
FOR OLDER TEEN
ratings.viz.com
viz media
www.viz.com

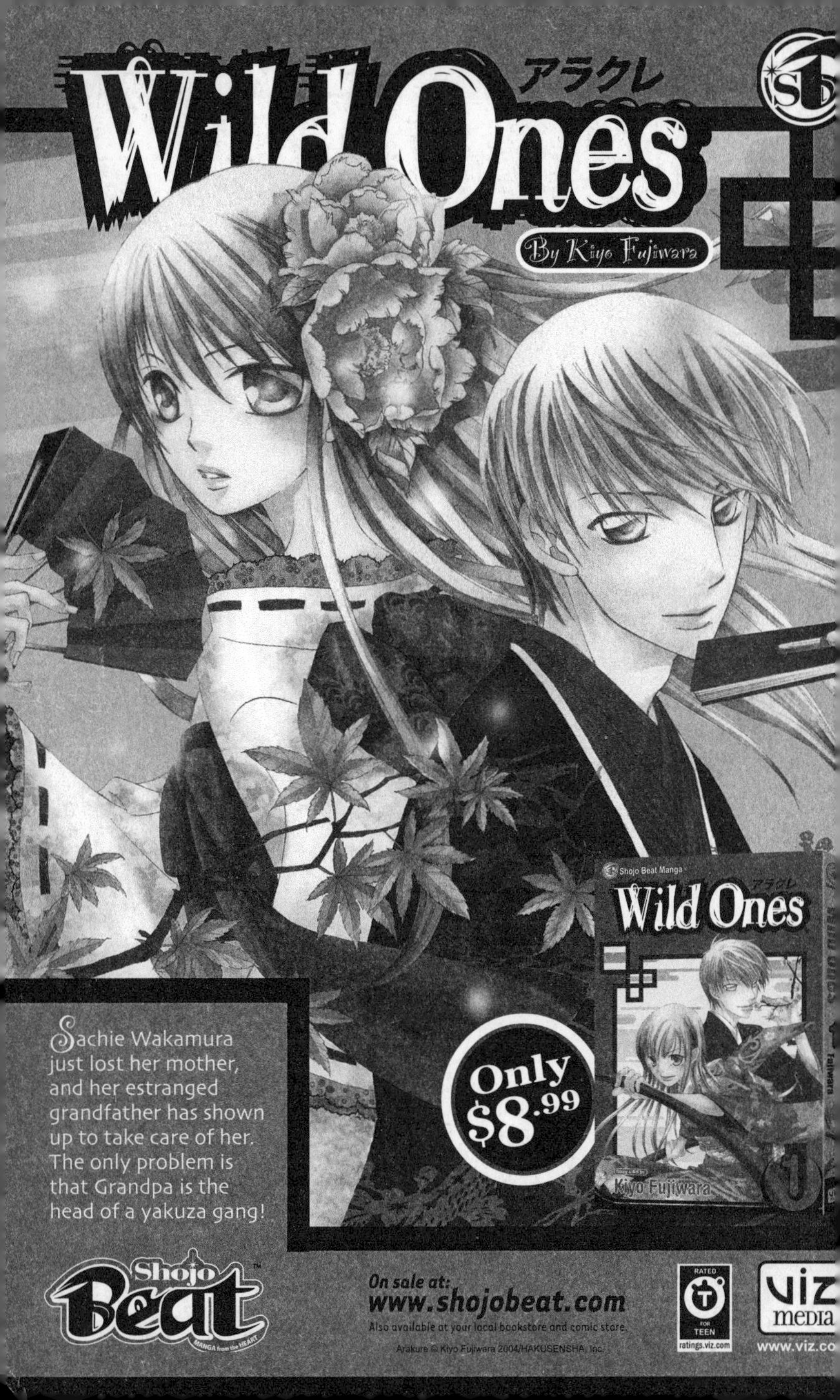
Wild Ones
アラクレ
By Kiyo Fujiwara
Shojo Beat Manga
Wild Ones
アラクレ
Kiyo Fujiwara
1
Only $8.99
Sachie Wakamura just lost her mother, and her estranged grandfather has shown up to take care of her. The only problem is that Grandpa is the head of a yakuza gang!
Shojo Beat
MANGA from the HEART
On sale at:
www.shojobeat.com
Also available at your local bookstore and comic store.
Arakure © Kiyo Fujiwara 2004/HAKUSENSHA, Inc.
RATED T FOR TEEN
ratings.viz.com
viz media
www.viz.co

Tell us what you think about Shojo Beat Manga!

Our survey is now available online. Go to:

shojobeat.com/mangasurvey

Help us make our product offerings better!

FULL MOON WO SAGASHITE © 2001 by Arina Tanemura/SHUEISHA Inc.
Fushigi Yûgi: Genbu Kaiden © 2004 Yuu WATASE/Shogakukan Inc.
Ouran Koko Host Club © Bisco Hatori 2002/HAKUSENSHA, Inc.

Shojo Beat™

MANGA from the HEART

The Shojo Manga Authority

12 GIANT issues for ONLY $34.99*

That's 51% OFF the cover price!

The most **ADDICTIVE** shojo manga stories from Japan **PLUS** unique editorial coverage on the arts, music, culture, fashion, and much more!

Subscribe **NOW** and become a member of the ① Sub Club!

- **SAVE** 51% OFF the cover price
- **ALWAYS** get every issue
- **ACCESS** exclusive areas of www.shojobeat.com
- **FREE** members-only gifts several times a year

Strictly VIP!

3 EASY WAYS TO SUBSCRIBE!

1) Send in the subscription order form from this book **OR**
2) Log on to: www.shojobeat.com **OR**
3) Call 1-800-541-7876

RATED T FOR OLDER TEEN
ratings.viz.com

Canada price for 12 issues: $46.99 USD, including GST, HST and QST. US/CAN orders only. Allow 6-8 weeks for delivery. Must be 16 or older to redeem offer. By redeeming this offer I represent that I am 16 or older.
Vampire Knight © Matsuri Hino 2004/HAKUSENSHA, Inc. Nana Kitade © Sony Music Entertainment (Japan), Inc.
SHOJO EVE ★ EVE'S APPLEWORK 24 HOURS © 2007 by Arina Tanemura/SHUEISHA Inc.
CRIMSON HERO © 2002 by Mitsuba Takanashi/SHUEISHA Inc.

VIZ MEDIA

www.viz.com

Save OVER 50% off the cover price!

Shojo Beat
MANGA from the HEART

The Shojo Manga Authority

This monthly magazine is injected with the most **ADDICTIVE** shojo manga stories from Japan. PLUS, unique editorial coverage on the arts, music, culture, fashion, and much more!

☑ **YES!** Please enter my one-year subscription (12 GIANT issues) to *Shojo Beat* at the LOW SUBSCRIPTION RATE of **$34.99**!

Over **300 pages** per issue!

NAME _____

ADDRESS _____

CITY _____ STATE _____ ZIP _____

E-MAIL ADDRESS _____ P7GNC1

☐ MY CHECK IS ENCLOSED (PAYABLE TO *Shojo Beat*) ☐ BILL ME LATER

CREDIT CARD: ☐ VISA ☐ MASTERCARD

ACCOUNT # _____ EXP. DATE _____

SIGNATURE _____

CLIP AND MAIL TO →

SHOJO BEAT
Subscriptions Service Dept.
P.O. Box 438
Mount Morris, IL 61054-0438

Canada price for 12 issues: $46.99 USD, including GST, HST and QST. US/CAN orders only. Allow 6-8 weeks for delivery. Must be 16 or older to redeem offer. By redeeming this offer I represent that I am 16 or older.

Vampire Knight © Matsuri Hino 2004/HAKUSENSHA, Inc. Nana Kitade © Sony Music Entertainment (Japan), Inc.
CRIMSON HERO © 2002 by Mitsuba Takanashi/SHUEISHA Inc.

CALGARY PUBLIC LIBRARY

JAN   2009

RATED
T+
FOR OLDER
TEEN
ratings.viz.com